Thomas Jefferson
TRAVELS

Thomas Jefferson

TRAVELS

Selected Writings
1784 – 1789

Edited by Anthony Brandt

 NATIONAL GEOGRAPHIC

WASHINGTON, D.C.

Published by the National Geographic Society

First printing, 2006
First paperback printing 2007, ISBN-10: 1-4262-0058-7, ISBN-13: 978-1-4262-0058-8

The Library of Congress has cataloged the hardcover edition as follows:

Jefferson, Thomas, 1743-1826.
Thomas Jefferson travels : selected writings 1784-1789 / edited by Anthony Brandt.
    p. cm.
    Includes bibliographical references and index.
    ISBN 0-7922-5486-4
    1. Jefferson, Thomas, 1743-1826—Correspondence. 2. Presidents—United States—Correspondence. 3. Diplomats—Europe—Correspondence. 4. Jefferson, Thomas, 1743-1826—Travel—Europe. 5. Europe—Description and travel. I. Brandt, Anthony. II. Title.
E322.86 2006
973.3'24092—dc22   2005036208

Title page photo credit: Bettmann/Corbis

Founded in 1888, the National Geographic Society is one of the largest nonprofit scientific and educational organizations in the world. It reaches more than 285 million people world-wide each month through its official journal, NATIONAL GEOGRAPHIC, and its four other magazines; the National Geographic Channel; television documentaries; radio programs; films; books; videos and DVDs; maps; and interactive media. National Geographic has funded more than 8,000 scientific research projects and supports an education program combating geographic illiteracy.

For more information, please call 1-800-NGS-LINE (647-5463) or write to the following address:
National Geographic Society
1145 17th Street N.W.
Washington, D.C. 20036-4688 U.S.A.

Log on to nationalgeographic.com; AOL Keyword: NatGeo.

Table of Contents

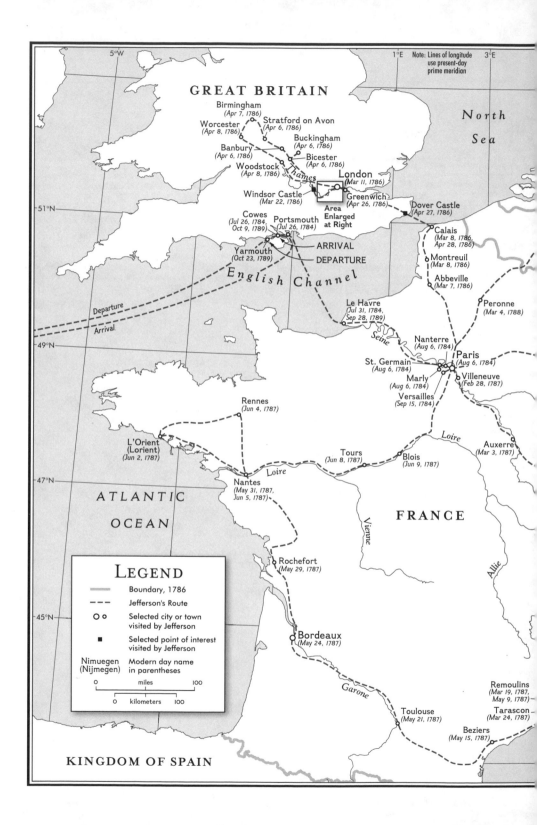

5°W

1°E   Note: Lines of longitude use present-day prime meridian

3°E

GREAT BRITAIN

North

Sea

Birmingham
(Apr 7, 1786)

Worcester
(Apr 8, 1786)

Stratford on Avon
(Apr 6, 1786)

Buckingham
(Apr 6, 1786)

Banbury
(Apr 6, 1786)

Bicester
(Apr 6, 1786)

Woodstock
(Apr 8, 1786)

Thames

London
(Mar 11, 1786)

Windsor Castle
(Mar 22, 1786)

Greenwich
(Apr 26, 1786)

Area
Enlarged
at Right

Dover Castle
(Apr 27, 1786)

51°N

Cowes
(Jul 26, 1784,
Oct 9, 1789)

Portsmouth
(Jul 26, 1784)

ARRIVAL

DEPARTURE

Calais
(Mar 8, 1786,
Apr 28, 1786)

Yarmouth
(Oct 23, 1789)

Montreuil
(Mar 8, 1786)

Abbeville
(Mar 7, 1786)

English Channel

Peronne
(Mar 4, 1788)

Departure

Arrival

Le Havre
(Jul 31, 1784,
Sep 28, 1789)

Seine

Nanterre
(Aug 6, 1784)

Paris
(Aug 6, 1784)

49°N

St. Germain
(Aug 6, 1784)

Marly
(Aug 6, 1784)

Villeneuve
(Feb 28, 1787)

Versailles
(Sep 15, 1784)

Rennes
(Jun 4, 1787)

Loire

Auxerre
(Mar 3, 1787)

L'Orient
(Lorient)
(Jun 2, 1787)

Loire

Tours
(Jun 8, 1787)

Blois
(Jun 9, 1787)

47°N

ATLANTIC

Nantes
(May 31, 1787,
Jun 5, 1787)

Vienne

FRANCE

OCEAN

Rochefort
(May 29, 1787)

Allie

LEGEND

Boundary, 1786

Jefferson's Route

Selected city or town
visited by Jefferson

Selected point of interest
visited by Jefferson

45°N

Nimuegen
(Nijmegen)

Modern day name
in parentheses

0   miles   100

0   kilometers   100

Bordeaux
(May 24, 1787)

Remoulins
(Mar 19, 1787,
May 9, 1787)

Garone

Toulouse
(May 21, 1787)

Tarascon
(Mar 24, 1787)

Beziers
(May 15, 1787)

KINGDOM OF SPAIN

THOMAS JEFFERSON'S TRAVELS IN EUROPE
JULY 1784 – OCTOBER 1789

LONDON AND ENVIRONS

Buckingham Palace
Chiswick
(Apr 2, 1786)
Kew
(Apr 14, 1786)
Richmond
(Apr 2, 1786)
London
(Mar 11, 1786,
Apr 3, 1786)
Twickenham
(Apr 2,3, 1786)
Weybridge
(Apr 2,3, 1786)
Hampton Court
(Apr 2, 1786)
Cobham
(Apr 2, 1786)
Thames

0   mi   8
0   km   8

NETHERLANDS

Haarlem
Mar 20, 1788) Amsterdam
(Mar 10, 1788)
Utrecht
(Mar 31, 1788)
Nimuegen
(Nijmegen)
(Mar 31, 1788)
The Hague
(Mar 9, 1788)
Cleves
(Kleve)
(Apr 1, 1788)
Rotterdam
(Mar 8, 1788) Cranenburg
(Kranenburg)
(Apr 1, 1788)
Dusseldorf
(Apr 2, 1788)
Bruxelles
(Mar 6, 1788)
Cologne
(Apr 3, 1788)
Rhine
Nassau
(Apr 5, 1788)
Hanau
(Apr 8, 1788)
Coblentz
(Koblenz)
(Apr 3, 1788)
Main
Chalons sur Marne
(Apr 21, 1788)
Worms
(Apr 12, 1788)
Mannheim
(Apr 12, 1788)
Nancy
(Apr 19, 1788)
Heidelberg
(Apr 14, 1788)
Strasbourg
(Apr 16, 1788)
Rhine

HOLY

ROMAN

EMPIRE

Danube

Dijon
(Mar 7, 1787)
Saone
Tournus
(Mar 8, 1787)
Macon
(Mar 9, 1787)
Lyons
(Lyon)
(Mar 11, 1787)
Loire
Vienne
(Mar 15, 1787)

SWITZERLAND

Milan
(Apr 20, 1787)
DUCHY OF MILAN
REPUBLIC OF VENICE
Pavia
(Apr 23, 1787)
Turin
(Apr 16, 1787)
Tortona
(Apr 24, 1787)
Po
45°N
Rhone
Orange
(Mar 18, 1787)
Durance
Bagnols
Mar 19, 1787)
St. Remy
(Mar 24, 1787)
Vaucluse
(May 8, 1787)
Orgon
(Mar 25, 1787)
Nice
(Apr 10, 1787)
Monaco
(May 1, 1787)
St. Cannat
(Mar 25, 1787)
Antibes
(Apr 9, 1787,
May 2, 1787)
Arles
Mar 24, 1787)
Aix
(Mar 25, 1787)
Pontroyal
(Mar 25, 1787)
Marseilles
(Mar 29, 1787,
May 4, 1787)
Toulon
(Apr 7, 1787)
KINGDOM OF SARDINIA
REPUBLIC OF GENOA
Genoa
(Apr 25, 1787)
DUCHY
OF
PARMA
DUCHY
OF
MODENA
PAPAL STATES
GRAND
DUCHY OF
TUSCANY
Mediterranean
Sea

5°E
7°E
9°E

Introduction

IT IS NO LONGER POSSIBLE TO IDOLIZE THOMAS JEFFERSON. ONE OF THE WORLD'S most eloquent defenders of the rights of man, the author of the words "all men are created equal," and one of the very first Virginians to try to bring the slave trade to an end, he nevertheless owned slaves himself and continued to own them, a large number of them in fact, until his death. The evidence that he fathered children by his slave Sally Hemings is fairly strong. He violated his own principles, and the United States Constitution, when he bought the territory of Louisiana from France without authorization from Congress. As governor of Virginia during the American Revolution he was something of a disaster. No one thinks of him anymore as one of our most effective Presidents. His first term was a success, but in his second term he tried to stop the depredations of the French and British on American shipping during the Napoleonic Wars by closing American ports to all but American ships. The policy was not just a mistake; it nearly bankrupted the country. He spent the last two years of his Presidency in virtual semiretirement.

Yet despite the contradictions between his beliefs and his behavior, despite his occasional duplicity, his naive idealism, and his failures as an administrator, he remains one of the great, dazzling, compelling figures in American history. He is a far more complicated, and far more interesting, person than the wooden, inaccessible George Washington; more charming and likable than the vain, touchy John Adams; much more engaging than the

Machiavellian Alexander Hamilton. His protégé James Madison was a match for the subtlety of his political thinking but did not share the enormous range of Jefferson's mind or the variety of his interests. Jefferson was brilliant not only as a political thinker but also as an architect and designer, and he was largely responsible for bringing the neoclassical style to the United States. While in Europe, he began to think about the invention of a new, more efficient moldboard for the common plow. Deeply interested in education, he thought long and hard about how a young man should prepare for life, as is evident in this anthology, and he founded (and designed) the University of Virginia. It was one of the three achievements among the many in his life that he wanted listed on his tombstone. The other two were his authorship of the Virginia Statute for Religious Freedom and the Declaration of Independence. The tombstone does not mention his Presidency.

We have by no means, furthermore, exhausted the catalog of his abilities and accomplishments in this brief list. He was for many years president of the American Philosophical Society, the country's first and most prominent scientific organization, and he kept up with new knowledge in natural history, aerostatics, steam engines, scientific instrumentation, weaponry, and a host of other fields. He was especially interested in paleontology. The giant ground sloth, an extinct American animal about which he wrote his only formal scientific paper, is named in his honor: Megalonyx jeffersonii. Agriculture was one of his passions, as were formal gardens. He tried to introduce the cultivation of olive trees to America. He understood the international politics and economics of whale fisheries as well as any man alive. He was America's first expert on fine wines. He did not speak foreign languages very well, although he was able to hold his own in the intellectual salons of Paris, but he read ancient Greek, Latin, French, Italian, and Spanish with ease.

And he might, arguably, have been as capable a foreign diplomat as this country has ever had if events had not conspired so thoroughly against him. He spent five years in France, arriving in August 1784 and leaving in October 1789, serving as the American minister plenipotentiary to the French court. He was sent to replace John Jay, who had helped negotiate the peace treaty with Great Britain , with a mandate to negotiate treaties formalizing trade relationships with the European powers. He served at a time when American military power was not just weak but practically nonexistent. The American government was an ineffective confederacy led by a Congress that could not levy taxes and often failed even to gather a quorum. Eighty percent of American trade with Europe was controlled by the British anyway, who would not negotiate. It was never even clear that the Continental Congress had the authority to regulate tariffs on a collective basis. During Jefferson's term abroad, in fact, more than one state set its own tariffs on certain goods without regard to Congress, thereby completely undercutting his role. The Constitutional Convention of 1787, which created the United States as we know it, grew in part out of frustration at the inability of the confederacy to get the states to act as one with respect to the conduct of international trade.

Despite these difficulties, Jefferson managed to persuade the French to lower the tariffs on American whale oil. He also negotiated the Consular Convention of 1788, which regulated the behavior of consuls in both France and America. This was a tough issue that had caused trouble on both sides of the Atlantic for a decade. Just before John Adams left his ministerial post in London in 1787, he and Jefferson met in Amsterdam and negotiated a new loan for the American government with Dutch bankers, thus saving the country's credit abroad. But Jefferson's overall success rate was not high.

He worked very hard, issuing report after report, explaining to the French all the advantages to opening their ports to American merchantmen, especially in the French West Indies. He believed in free trade, just as he believed in the free exchange of ideas. He spent five years trying to wrest control of the importation of American tobacco out of the hands of the Farmers-General—the enormous, intransigent French lobby that regulated the importation of all foreign agricultural products and collected duties on them for the crown. The Farmers-General set quotas for American tobacco imports, and they set the price. They gave the contract for this trade to one man, the Philadelphia merchant Robert Morris. Minister after French minister told Jefferson that he hated the system and saw the corruption inherent in it, but he could do nothing. The system fed the coffers of the crown, and the king depended on the income. Jefferson was wasting his time. (It is worth noting that the French government still sets unusually high tariffs on the importation of foreign agricultural products.)

But for all the futility of his efforts on so many fronts, Jefferson came to be one of the most respected diplomats in Paris. It was his habit to befriend

Americans who came to Paris, and one of these was Thomas Lee Shippen, son of a Philadelphia doctor and nephew of Arthur Lee, a planter prominent in Virginia affairs. In a letter to his father written in the late winter of 1788, Shippen described the day Jefferson took him to Versailles to introduce him to the court and diplomatic circle there. After affecting proper American scorn for the ritual and pomp of court, Shippen added this note: "I observed that although Mr. Jefferson was the plainest man in the room, and the most destitute of ribbands crosses and other insignia of rank that he was most courted and most attended to (even by the Courtiers themselves) of the whole Diplomatic corps." He was not as adored as Benjamin Franklin had been, but there was no question that the French, from the ministerial level on down, liked and respected him.

And for him, in many ways, these may have been his best years. He had few intellectual peers in America. Few shared his broad interests, the breadth and depth of his reading, his intense curiosity about the world. In Paris he could, and did, talk about natural history with the great Buffon, who had written the definitive work on the subject. He discussed political philosophy with Lafayette and Turgot and was a good friend of Condorcet, the philosopher who was even more radical than Jefferson himself; indeed, Jefferson became friendly with most of the more liberal thinkers and aristocrats in Paris, visited their country chateaus, went to their dinners, came to know their wives and children. Jefferson loved music and the theater, and in no other city in Europe was there more of each available than in Paris. His account book, where he recorded all his costs large and small, shows him buying tickets to all the best shows. While in London he ordered a harpsichord to be made for his daughter, Martha, known as Patsy—an instrument that would have been nearly impossible to obtain in America.

Even better perhaps from his point of view were the booksellers, scarce in America, abundant in Paris. Jefferson used the opportunity of residence there to build, quite systematically, one of the largest libraries in early America. Ultimately it became the core collection of the Library of Congress. He acquired volumes from London, providing sizable request lists to book dealers there as well. He sent books to American friends. One shipment to James Madison filled two trunks, mostly with books on political philosophy and ancient history, and it is said that Madison's reading of the Scottish philosopher David Hume, from books included in this shipment, formed the groundwork of his thinking during the 1787 Constitutional Convention.

Paris was the city of salons, identified with strong independent women who had real influence on political affairs, and Jefferson became friends with some of the best known of them: Madame d'Houdetot, Madame de Tott, Madame de Tesse, Madame de Corny. It was the city of wit and intellectual excitement. It was also the home of gastronomy. He took his household slave James Hemings with him to learn how to cook in the French style. He made friends with the city of Paris itself, taking long four- and five-mile walks through its streets and along the Seine. He explored the Bois de Boulogne on foot and horseback. He watched the construction of the Hotel de Salm across the Seine from the Tuileries, "violently smitten" by its design, as he told Mme. de Tesse, according to William Howard Adams's history of Jefferson's Paris years. Struck dumb, he stared in wonder at great paintings, stood in amazement before sculpture of a skill he could never have found in America. During his first year in Paris he arranged for Jean-Antoine Houdon, the best French sculptor of his time, to travel to America, meet Washington, and do the necessary preliminary work for the statue of Washington that now stands in the Virginia Capitol.

Jefferson lived as well through the beginnings of the French Revolution; he was even involved in it to a small degree. He saw the Bastille being torn down. He witnessed the riots, the skirmishes; he rode through huge crowds gathered in the great plazas; and he wrote vivid accounts to John Jay, James Madison, and other friends in America about what was happening. Some of the letters we print in the last section of this anthology make for very dramatic reading. One of the letters we print is a note from Lafayette begging Jefferson to put together that very day a dinner party to which he would invite some of the leading figures so they could try to reach compromises on the issues dividing them and put together a new constitution for the country.

Even though he was in Paris, Jefferson was also involved in the making of the U.S. Constitution. He had been sending not only books but also ideas to Madison and he helped persuade Madison that the Constitution as first written needed a Bill of Rights if it were to gain the full support of the American people. During the process of ratification Jefferson discussed the whole subject of a Bills of Rights and the concept behind it, the natural rights of mankind, with Lafayette and Thomas Paine. In the late winter of 1788, the three men spent evenings together after dinner at Jefferson's house, the Hotel de Langeac, just off the Champs-Elysées in the area where the Arc de Triomphe stands now. Lafayette was not only a hero of the American Revolution and Jefferson's intimate friend, but also one of the most liberal figures in French politics. We print the famous letter Paine wrote after one of these evenings, explaining his thoughts on what the basic rights of mankind were and what sources they derived from. We live by these thoughts today.

While resident in France, Jefferson traveled south to Provence and into Italy, then on another trip into Holland and Germany. He strolled with John Adams through some of the best gardens in England waiting for a response—which never came—to their overtures to the British government. He gazed, as he put it, like a lover at his mistress at the Maison Carrée in Nîmes, one of the great surviving examples of Roman architecture. It became the model for the Virginia Capitol in Richmond. His diplomatic efforts came to little or nothing, but he remained at the center of things. His correspondence with Madison is a rich source of news and political thought. He corresponded with Washington; James Monroe was another protégé; he kept John Jay up to speed on events in Europe and on his work. This was a man who wrote some 19,000 letters during his lifetime, and the Paris years fill nine volumes in the magisterial *Papers of Thomas Jefferson*, which Princeton University Press has been publishing since 1950 with no end in sight. I should say nine thick volumes. Jefferson wrote only one book—first published, incidentally, in Paris while he was there—but the sheer bulk of his correspondence, his reports, his notes on his travels, and all the other material that came from his pen is extraordinary.

That bulk has made it difficult to keep this selection of his writings from Paris under control. It seemed important to include as much of the back-and-forth nature of correspondence as possible. Correspondence loses much of its interest if the replies to letters are omitted. It would have made little sense, for example, to print his well-known letter to Anne Willing Bingham on the superiority of American society, much simpler than the rather dissolute society of France, without printing her equally interesting defense of French society and French women. The letters between Jefferson and Adams are wonderfully revealing of the personalities of each man and the way they interacted. You cannot read Jefferson's letters to

Madison, the American friend he trusted the most, without wanting to read Madison's responses.

Putting in the back-and-forth, however, meant excluding a fair number of correspondents from the selection entirely. And some subjects. While in Paris, Jefferson wrote quite a few letters on what was happening in scientific circles in Europe to scientifically-minded friends in America. I have included a very small sample of these letters, to David Rittenhouse, to his friend Francis Hopkinson, and one to Archibald Cary, asking him to arrange to have the skeleton, skin, and horns of an American elk sent to him, so that he could show Buffon that American animals were not undersized, as he had claimed, attributing it to the dampness of the climate. Buffon's disparaging remarks about North America, its climate, its animals, and its native peoples had become a major issue at the time, but except for the letter to Cary, I have chosen to skip it. Too much else was going on. Jefferson was able finally to persuade Buffon that perhaps he had made a mistake on this issue, but he extracted an admission from the French natural philosopher only in conversation. Buffon never went back on his claims in print.

I have downplayed the diplomatic work as well, not because it lacks interest but because so often Jefferson's efforts came to nothing. He saw being helpful and kind to traveling Americans as part of his job. He spent a great deal of his time grappling with the problems of American consuls in France and of American citizens in France, including some of his own friends. Particularly irritating to him were the affairs of John and Lucy Paradise, who separated while in Europe. Lucy Paradise wrote Jefferson constantly, asking for help. John, her husband, was hopelessly improvident. He contracted huge debts, and Jefferson was forced to find ways to settle them. He got letters from another friend Eliza House Trist, who followed her husband to New Orleans only to find out he had died there. I have left almost all of this material out.

He was a mentor to young male American travelers and often invited them to stay with him and be his guests. John Trumbull, the painter, became a good friend. He took with him to Paris William Short, a kinsman on his mother's side, as his personal secretary. Jefferson thought of him as a kind of son. He sponsored his grand tour to Italy and saw to it that Short was made American chargé d'affaires in Paris when he left. Short fell in love with the young wife of the duke de La Rouchefoucauld-Liancourt. Jefferson disapproved, but such affairs were common in France. Jefferson disapproved of that, too.

I have not, however, excluded Jefferson's own correspondence with Maria Cosway: the married woman with whom he himself fell in love. This anthology contains a substantial portion of their correspondence, because here we find Jefferson at his most common and his most human, overwhelmed with feelings he would normally suppress.

The anthology takes this tack. It tries to capture Thomas Jefferson the human being—complex, brilliant, patient, thoughtful, kind, astute, enthusiastic, sometimes wrongheaded, sometimes not entirely honest, and in love. At the same time I have tried to include as much about the most compelling events he dealt with, the making of the American Constitution and the revolution in France, as possible. I also concentrate on his travels in Europe, and, in the diplomatic field, his attempts to deal with the situation of American seamen enslaved by the Barbary states, a subject that occupied him well into his Presidency.

The arrangement is chronological, with significant exceptions. I have pursued certain themes I found particularly interesting in separate chapters that are chronological within themselves, but not within the overall frame of the book. One of these is Thomas Jefferson's attitudes toward the education of the young, which he addressed as the occasion arose in letters to his nephews, the sons of friends, and his oldest daughter. Another is his peculiar relationships with attractive women, two in particular: Maria Cosway and Angelica Schuyler Church. The two major trips he took in France during his stay also get separate attention.

One of the problems with publishing correspondence is that it often lacks context. Letters do not necessarily explain themselves. Accordingly I have written short introductions to each chapter in an attempt to provide context and give the collection as a whole some sense of the continuity of events and of the course of Jefferson's life during his five years in Paris. This book has no footnotes, but I have provided brief annotations from time to time in the letters themselves, wherever I thought they might be useful, using editorial interpolations printed in italics and placed in brackets.

The book ends with an epilogue. Jefferson left France slowly. His departure was delayed by contrary winds and by difficulties with his voluminous baggage. We are lucky to have a description of his last days there, at Le Havre and Cowes, off the coast of England, written by the brother of his friend, John Brown Cutting. It gives us an opportunity to tie up some loose ends.

It is no longer possible to idolize Thomas Jefferson, but if you work with his correspondence long enough, if you get to know him, it is impossible not to like him. The idea here is not to redeem his reputation but to deepen it, to let the public see him in action, to hear him speak for himself. He is consistently eloquent, nor is his eloquence a rhetorical screen for darker motives. It springs from the heart. To wish better of him is to wish for a perfection that does not exist in human beings. This is a man whose mind grew wings. He had a vision for America that was a step or two beyond the reach of human nature, but that vision remains an inspiration to the world, and the man himself stands as a silent reproach to the pettiness, arrogance, and folly of so many contemporary politicians.

Once there were giants on the Earth. Jefferson was one of them.

CHAPTER ONE

The First Year

J EFFERSON HAD WANTED TO TAKE THE TRADITIONAL GRAND TOUR OF EUROPE
as a young man, but circumstances had prevented it. He was 41 when he finally set
out, in July 1784, for Paris. His wife had died two years earlier, two of his five children
had died, and he would lose another child shortly after he left for Paris. With him he
took his oldest daughter, Martha, who was better known as Patsy, and he left his two
youngest behind in the care of his sister, Elizabeth Eppes.

His assignment was to join Benjamin Franklin and John Adams in Paris to help
negotiate favorable trade agreements with the European powers, most particularly
with France but with others as well. He was replacing John Jay, who returned home
to take charge of foreign affairs for the newborn American republic. Within a little over
a year Adams and Franklin would both depart, too, Adams for London, Franklin for
Philadelphia, leaving Jefferson alone in Paris.

Before Jefferson left America he toured the New England states to ground himself in the issues that affected New England trade with Europe and the West Indies,
making one of those detailed, thorough studies of the situation he became known for.
We know little about this tour except that he stopped in New Haven and visited with
Ezra Stiles, then President of Yale University, who wrote in his diary that Jefferson
was "a most ingenuous Naturalist and Philosopher, a truly scientific and learned Man,
and every way excellent," and added that "Govr. Jefferson has seen many of the great
Bones dug up on the Ohio. He has a thighbone Three Feet long and a tooth
weighing sixteen pounds." Shortly after this visit Jefferson wrote Stiles and asked him

to forward any information he might come across about paleontology. Stiles later sent Jefferson an honorary Yale degree.

As Patsy describes in the first letter in this chapter, the voyage to Europe was a remarkably pleasant one, which was no doubt a relief to Jefferson, who suffered badly from seasickness. The voyage took only 19 days, which was unusually quick, and the weather was calm. Jefferson spent the time reading Don Quixote in Spanish in an attempt to master the language. They saw whales and watched the seamen catch cod. Patsy got sick when they approached the English Channel and the two travelers spent a few days in England while a doctor treated her. They reached Le Havre early in August and made their way to Paris. Jefferson had brought his own coach.

Jefferson's writings do not describe in any detail his acclimatization to Paris. Franklin was living in the village of Passy, just west of what was then the Paris city limits, and Adams settled into the nearby village of Auteuil. Because of Franklin's age—he suffered from kidney stones and any jarring in a carriage was painful—the three men gathered at Franklin's house to conduct business. Jefferson chose to live in Paris, the first month or two in hotels, then in a house in the Cul-de-sac Taitbout, which he rented for about a year. He placed Patsy in a convent school almost immediately, the Abbaye Royale de Panthemont, which was regarded as the best school in Paris for foreign children. Patsy learned French rapidly; Jefferson struggled with it for quite some time and claimed that he was never fluent, but he was fluent enough to make his way in Parisian salons and among the philosophes he talked to. It took a while to enter this world, however. During his first year he spent a good deal of time with John Adams and his wife, Abigail, and their daughter Abby, all of whom became Jefferson's close friends. Later he became friendly as well with Col. William Stephens Smith, a veteran of the Revolution, who served as Adams' secretary when Adams was transferred to London, where he married Abby Adams.

Jefferson arrived in August; William Short did not arrive until November, personal business having kept him in America. In the meantime Jefferson, who was alone in his house, befriended Col. David Humphreys, another Revolutionary War veteran who had served as an aide to George Washington and was now secretary to the three-man commission. Jefferson invited Humphreys to live with him and became fond of him, but Humphreys, who was by all reports stiff and self-important, does not figure largely in this history, and he decamped for London early on. It was Short who was Jefferson's real protégé. In his 20s and evidently dazzled by Parisian life, to which he was introduced at its highest levels, he emerges slowly as a likable young man, but perhaps not entirely up to his role. We shall have more to say of him later. He was an integral part of Jefferson's household in any case. His duties were largely confined to copying out the voluminous correspondence Jefferson maintained. Jefferson made and kept copies of almost everything. He was meticulous to a fault, well organized, and highly attentive to detail.

Part of this was no doubt a response to the difficulties involved in maintaining a correspondence at all. For one thing, it took a letter anywhere from three months to a year, occasionally longer, to cross the ocean and reach its destination. Some mail never got there at all. The odds for packages were even more chancy; they often wound up in a warehouse in some port, forwarded to the proper address only after repeated inquiries.

For another, the French and British authorities felt no compunction whatsoever about opening mail from or to American diplomats, and reading it. Jefferson put the significant parts of his official mail into code, and so did those who wrote to him. On both sides of the Atlantic, correspondents tried to avoid using the official mails at all, sending letters by private individuals they could trust who were crossing the ocean. Not infrequently, therefore, one finds him listing in a letter to Madison, say, the letters he has written to him previously and the letters he has received from him, all by date, so that each man knows what the other is referring to. As one reads these letters one must keep these circumstances in mind. Jefferson was often writing in response to old news. This only made him long all the more for news from home, any sort of news, and he engaged people in New York, Philadelphia, and Richmond to send him newspapers, pamphlets, anything at all that they thought would interest him. It was not uncommon for someone to knock on his door, announce his recent arrival from Boston or New York or Norfolk, and hand over a hefty package full of printed material and private letters.

Similarly, Jefferson saw it as part of his job to keep his friends in the United States as well informed as he could about what was going on in Europe. Some of his letters, indeed, were meant to be printed, at least in part, and they were. To some extent one can think of Jefferson as a journalist, a source of news, the Edward R. Murrow of his time, reporting not on the blitz from London but on the revolution from Paris. In fact that's the main interest of his letters in his final year in Paris. He was there for the beginnings of the French Revolution. He saw a great deal of what was going on and he knew most of the major participants.

During his first year he was getting acquainted, looking and learning, being introduced at court, becoming friends with Adams and Franklin, both of whom liked him. Many of his letters from this period are preoccupied with conflicts, real or potential, between the European powers, in particular the possibility of war over the navigation of the Schelde, Antwerp's access to the sea, which was a perennial source of conflict between the Hapsburg emperor and the Dutch Republic. This was a war that never happened, but one must remember how minor a power the United States was in the late 18th century, and how vulnerable to attack. The sentiment in England was that, war or no war, the fledgling country would fall apart and beg to return, state by state, to the protection of the British Empire. France and England were always at odds, and any war between them was bound to involve United States interests in one way or another, as indeed happened during the Napoleonic Wars. And any European conflict that drew in either of these great powers threatened to draw America in as well. Most of the conflicts Jefferson reported came to nothing, but one never knew what might happen. Conflict and shifting alliances were endemic to European politics. He was always worried about them.

Other preoccupations that quickly emerge in his correspondence are with the Barbary pirates, a subject Jefferson was still dealing with 20 years later during his presidency, and with his own personal funds. When they appointed him, Congress made no allowance for what he called his "outfit"—all the things he needed to carry on the business of diplomacy. They also cut his salary. Adams and Franklin were being paid 25 percent more than he was. Jefferson had to buy furniture, curtains, pots and pans; he had to buy proper clothes; he had to entertain; he needed servants besides his cook, James Hemings; he needed horses and people to care for them. The costs ran to a year's salary at least, and Jefferson paid for it out of his own pocket. The subject comes up in his first letter to James Monroe, who was a member of the Continental Congress. Could he discreetly raise the issue? It appears again and again thereafter, right to the end of his years in Paris. Not until 1792, when a new government under a new Constitution had been formed, did Jefferson finally receive compensation for these expenses. It was an important issue for him because he had large debts, many of them inherited from his father-in-law's estate, and his income never quite matched his style of living. He was not an extravagant man, but he had exceptionally good taste and he indulged it. He moralized frequently against the splurging on luxuries and the running up of debt that followed the end of the American Revolution, but he himself was one of the offenders.

Jefferson, it is worth noting, was sick much of his first winter in Paris. Paris is known for its winter bleakness—cold, windy, rainy—and Jefferson was a creature of the sun. At one point he was confined to his house for six weeks. During this time, in late January, he learned of the death of his youngest daughter, Lucy, and decided to bring his only other surviving child, Mary, known as Polly, to France to join him and Patsy. In May the Adams family left for London, depriving Jefferson of his chief source of friendly American companionship, but Adams's departure is the beginning of their correspondence, which is delightful. Franklin left in July. We close this section with Jefferson's August letter to Eliza House Trist on the character of the French, whom by now he had come to love.

∽

[Though written a year after their arrival, this remains the most vivid account of the Jeffersons' trip across the Atlantic.]

Martha Jefferson to Eliza House Trist
de l'abbey royale de Panthemont a Paris
MY DEAREST FRIEND   [after 24 Aug. 1785]

Your letter put an end to the inquietude that your silence had caused us. Be assured that I will remember you as long as I live. I am very happy in the convent and it is with reason for there wants nothing but the presence of my friends of America to render my situation worthy to be envied by the happiest. I do not say kings, for far from it. They are often more unfortu-nate than the lowest of their subjects. I have seen the king and the queen but at too great a distance to judge if they are like their pictures in Philadelphia. We had a lovely passage in a beautiful new ship that had only made one voyage before. There were only six passengers, all of whom papa knew, and a fine sun shine all the way, with the sea which was as calm as a river. I should have no objections at making an other voyage if I could be sure it would be as agreeable as the first. We landed in England where we made a very short stay. The day we left it we set off at six a clock the evening, and arived in France at 7 the next morning. I can not say that this voyage was as agreable as the first, tho it was much shorter. It rained violently and the sea was exceedingly rough all the time, and I was allmost as sick as the first time, when I was sick two days. The cabane was not more than three feet wide and about four long. There was no other furniture than an old bench which was fast to the wall. The door by which we came in at was so little that one was obliged to enter on all four. There were two little doors at the side of the cabane was the way to our beds, which were composed of two boxxes and a couplle of blankets with out eather bed or matras, so that I was obliged to sleep in my cloathes. There being no winder in the cabane, we were obliged to stay in the dark for fear of the rains coming in if we opended the door. I fear we should have fared as badly at our arrival for papa spoke very little french and me not a word, if an Irish gentleman, an entire stranger to us, who seeing our embarrassment, had not been so good as to conduct us to a house and was of great service to us. It is amazing to see how they cheat the strangers. It cost papa as much to have the bagadge brought from the shore to the house, which was about a half a square apart, as the bringing it from Philadelphia to Boston. From there we should have had a very agreable voyage to Paris, for havre de grace is built at the mouth of the seine, and we follow the river all the way thro the most beautiful country I ever saw in my life, it is a perfect garden if the singulairty of our cariage had not atracted us the attention of all we met, and when ever we stopped we were surrounded by the beggars. One day I counted no less than nine while we stopped to change horses. We saw a great number of chalk hills near Rouen, where we saw allso a church built by William the conqueror, and another at Ment which had as many steps to go to the top as there are days in the year. There are many pretty statues in it. The architectures is beautiful. All the winders are died glass of the most beautiful colours that form all kinds of figures. I wish you could have been with us when we arrived. I am sure you would have laughfed, for we were obliged to send imediately for the stay maker, the mantumaker, the milliner and even a shoe maker, before I could go out. I have never had the friseur but once, but I soon got rid of him and turned down my hair in spite of all they could say, and I differ it now as much as possible, for I think it allways too soon to suffer. I have seen two nuns take the veil. I'll tell you about that when I come to see you. I was placed in a convent at my arival and I leave you to judge of my situation. I did not speak a word of french, and no one here knew english but a little girl of 2 years old that could hardly speak french. There are about fifty or sixty pensioners in the house, so that speaking as much as I could with them I learnt the language very soon. At present I am charmed with my situation. I am afraid that you will be very much disapointed if you expect to see me perfect, for I have made very little progress. Give my love to Mrs. House, Brouse and Polly and when you will see hetty Rittenhouse scold her for me. She has never answered any of my letters. Send my compliments to Mrs. Tamage and Mrs. Thomson, in short evry body that I know. I do not doubt but that you were very much astonished at hearing that colonel floyed was maried. So was I, but as every one has a different mind we must leave the world to itself and follow what we think wrighte. Tho you have a great deal of patience I am afraid that this scrawl will tire it. But if you knew the pleasure I take in writing to you and receiving letters from you, you would pardon me. Pray write me very long letters by evry occassion. I should be very glad to write for papa, but I am sure that he could not have an occupation which gives him more pleasure than that. How ever when he cant leave his business I will do it with pleasure. I do not know when we shall come. Pardon this letter, being so badly written for I have not the time at present. There comes in some new pensionars evry day. The classe is four rooms exceedingly large for the pensionars to sleep in, and there is a fith and sixth one for them to stay in in the day and the other in which they take their lessens. We were the uniform which is crimson made like a frock laced behind with the tail like a robe de cour hoocked on muslin cufs and tuckers. The masters are all very good except that for the drawing. I end here for I am sure my letter must tire you. Papa sends his most affectionate compliments to you and Mrs. House and begs you not to forget that you are indebted a letter to him particularly on the subject of Brouses relations. Adieu my dear freind, be assured that I am and ever will be yours affectionately,

—MARTHA JEFFERSON

Be so good as to let Mrs. Hopkinson know that I remember her with great gratitude and affection as well as Mrs. Rittenhouse.

From St. John de Crèvecoeur
SIR   Boston 1st. Septm. 1784

Dining the other day with H.E. Govr. Hancock. I was shew'd a Virginia
Gazette wherein I saw with the most Sincere pleasure a Vote of Your
House, ordering a white marble Statue of General Washington to be
Executed in Paris under your Care. I observed also an order from Gov.
Harrisson to Mr. Peale forthwith to draw a whole-length Picture of the great
Man, to be forwarded to you; this Last Circomstance is the Reason I have
for troubling you this day. The most-perfectly painted resemblance, in my
opinion, is Insufficient to Enable a Statuary, however skillfull, to represent
perfectly the desired object; if this is really the Case, some other Means must
be Look'd for, in order to procure the True features and the most perfect
resemblance of that General. So Great is my veneration for him that I most
Earnestly wish that the French artists may give us an Exact Copy if I dare
use that word, and a striking representation of that Head to the Internal
organization of which we were all so highly Indebted. There are but Two
Means of obtaining this End: 1st. the Presence of the General—but he is
too Great to visit Europe. 2ly: a Mould En Creux of his Face, without it the
Statuary never will make General Washington breathe in Marble. For that
purpose few Pounds of Ready baked Plaister shou'd be sent to Mr. Peal with
proper directions how to pulverise it, and how to Make the Impression of
that General's Face; by obtaining his consent to this operation (a Little Novel
for an American I acknowledge). It may be done Two Ways—1st. a certain
Quantity of this Pulverised Plaister must be mixed with a proportionate
one of water in a Large Bowl; and Instant before it hardens Itself, the
General having previously annointed his face with oyl, must condescend
To Stoop and Impress it on the Plastick surface. Few seconds are sufficient
for this operation. This Mould once obtained must be very Carefully
Packed up and sent back to you, and with it you Easily conceive with what
Ease the Statuary can obtain the True Lineaments of the face by casting into
it Liquid Plaister. The Second Method wou'd be Still more disagreable,
because it wou'd require the partial application of some plaister on the face,
which when dried and reunited wou'd Equally, tho' not so precisely, procure the desired Mould. This Statue is to go down to posterity, thousand

of Busts will be made from it at Paris either in Terre Cuite, Plaister or Bronze; it cannot therefore resemble to nearly to the original. Such are the hints which I have thought myself obliged. To Communicate you, being Equally anxiuos with the rest of the Americans to contribute my mite towards the Completion of this Great Monument of Publick Gratitude and Respect. I believe that from the mode of your Embarkation here Col. Humphreys will be at Paris before you. I hope the Sea Voyage, the change of Climate &c. has been usefull to your health as well as to that of Miss Jefferson, who has at last accomplish'd her desire of Seeing 9 States out of 13. [This refers to the tour Jefferson took through New England to sound out merchants there on the problems they faced before he sailed for France. Martha was with him.] I dread the reflections which so many new and Singular Political and Relligious objects will unavoidably raise in Your Mind. The Marquis de Chatelux has no doubt Introduced you to the Prince de Beauveau as well as to the Family of La Rochefoucauld for which Good Personages I Intended, had You returned to New York to have given You Letters. I Earnestly beg you'd Inquire for Mr. Target avocat au Parlement Rue Ste. Croix de la Bretonnerie Marais Paris. [Charles Bernini, an Italian then living in America who had lived in France, had given Jefferson a list of people he should get to know.] You'll find in him a most Enlighten'd head united with a most Excellent heart. He will be to you the most usefull, agreable, and Interesting acquaintance you possibly can make, and in a Little while I am Sure you'll Love and Esteem him as much as I do. I write him concerning Govr. Jefferson. I hope you have not forgot the Magnolia Seeds. I have duely a note of the Marchand at Richemond who is to Send me a Box for you, which I shall not fail to forward as expeditiously as possible. I shall address it to the directeurs des Messageries a Lorient, which is I am told the most Eligible way of sending any thing to France. Wou'd you be so good as to present my best respects to the Mis. de Chatelux. The days after he proceeded to Virginia; every body here have been Glad to see him again. I wish you Very Sincerely health and Good acquaintance as well as an happy Completion of the Treaty of commerce you are about Settling and am with unfeigned Respect & Esteem sir Your Very Humble Servant,

—ST. JOHN

To James Monroe
DEAR SIR   Paris Nov. 11. 1784

Your journey to the Westward having prevented my writing to you till now that a letter may probably find you at Congress, I shall resume the correspondence discontinued since I left Boston. My passage was remarkeably short, being only 19 days from land to land, and I suffered little by sickness. Having very thick weather when we approached the coast of Europe, we fell in with no vessel which could take me and put me on the French coast as I had intended. I therefore went ashore at Portsmouth where I was detained three or four days by a fever which had seized my daughter two days before we landed. As soon as she was clear of it I hired a vessel to carry me over to Havre, from whence I came on this place, thro' a country than which nothing can be more fertile, better cultivated or more elegantly improved. It was at the time when harvest was beginning, and it is principally a farming country.

I informed you from Boston that before I had received your letters of May 25. and June 1. I had packed up our cypher and therefore could not there make out the passages which were put into cypher. I have tried it here and find that by some unfortunate mistake, probably in the young gentleman who wrote the cypher, it will not explain a single syllable. He has arranged all the numbers in their regular order, and then placed against each the words, syllables &c. in alphabetical order. You can judge whether this was the plan of it. The want of the cypher would have restrained me from mentioning some things were I not assured of the fidelity of the bearer hereof Colo. Le Maire.

I am to acknolege the receipt of your letter of Aug. 9. from New-york, but not of the previous one therein mentioned to be sent by Mr. Short, he being not yet come, nor any tidings of him.

The die is thrown here and has turned up war. Doubts whether an accomodation may not yet take place are still entertained by some, but I hold it impossible. [An accommodation did take place. The Hapsburg emperor gained access to the Schelde, which bordered his Belgian possessions, but there was always talk of war in Europe. In a couple of years it would break out to the east, against the Turks, Russia and the Hapsburgs fighting them on the Black Sea. John Paul Jones would serve on the Russian side, essentially as a mercenary.] Probably the Emperor will encourage negotiations during the winter, while no warlike operations may go on, in order to amuse his adversary and lessen their preparations. It is believed the campaign will open on the Scheld. How the other nations of Europe will conduct themselves seems very doubtful. The probability is that France, Prussia, and the Porte will take an active part with the Dutch, and Russia with the Germans. It is to be presumed that England will endeavor to keep out of the scrape 1. because she cannot borrow money to take part in it, 2. because Ireland is likely to give her disturbance, 3. because her disputes with us are not settled by a full execution of the articles of the treaty, and the hatred of her people towards us has arisen to such a height as to prepare their minds for a recommencement of hostilities should their government find this desireable. Supposing we are not involved in a new contest with Great Britain, this war may possibly renew that disposition in the powers of Europe to treat with us on liberal principles, a disposition which blazed out with enthusiasm on the conclusion of peace, but which had subsided as far below the just level in consequence of the anarchy, and depravation of principle which the British papers have constantly held forth as having taken place among us. I think when it shall become certain that war is to take place, that those nations at least who are engaged in it will be glad to ensure our neutrality and friendly dispositions by a just treaty. Such a one, or none is our business. With England nothing will produce a treaty but an enforcement of the resolutions of Congress proposing that there should be no trade where there is no treaty. The infatuation of that nation seems really preternatural. If any thing will open their eyes it will be an application to the avarice of their merchants who are the very people who have opposed the treaty first mediated, and who have excited the spirit of hostility at present prevailing against us. Deaf to every principle of common sense, insensible of the feelings of man, they firmly beleive they shall be permitted by us to keep all the carrying trade and that we shall attempt no act of retaliation because they are pleased to think it our interest not to do so. A gentleman immediately from England dined the other day at the same house with an American. They happened to sit next to each other at table, and spoke on the subject of our commerce. He had the air of a man of credibility. He said that just before his departure from England he had a conversation with Mr. Pitt, in which Mr. Pitt assured him the proclamation of which we complain would be passed into an act at the next session of parliament.—In the despatches we send to Congress you will see a great interval between the Spanish Ambassador's answer to us and our reply to him. The reason of our keeping back was the hope that in the mean time he would get an answer from his court which would save us the difficulty of answering him. I have had a hint that they may agree to make New Orleans a free port for our vessels coming down the Missisipi, but without permission to us to export our produce thence. [*American navigation of the Mississippi remained a contentious issue until the Louisiana Purchase solved the problem in 1804.*] All the inadequacies of this to our purpose strike me strongly. Yet I would wish you to sound your acquaintances on the subject and let me know what they think of it; and whether if nothing more can be obtained, this or no treaty, that is to say, this or war would be preferred.—Can nothing be done for young Franklin. He is sensible, discreet, polite, and good humoured, and fully qualified as a Secretaire d'Ambassade. His grandfather has none annexed to his legation at this court. He is most sensibly wounded at his grandson's being superseded. Should this war take place it would certainly be acceptable to Congress to receive regular, early, and authentic intelligence of it's operations. In this view would it not be worth while to continue the agency of Dumas. [*C. F. W. Dumas, although his position was largely informal, was dedicated to American interests. He lived in a house owned by the United States in The Hague and served as a source of intelligence on Dutch affairs. He was frequently in correspondence with Jefferson and continued in his role for many years.*] His intelligence has all these qualities. He is undoubtedly in the confidence of some one who has a part in the Dutch government, and who seems to allow him to communicate to us.—Before my arrival here, Mr. Barclay, in consequence of the powers given him by his commission, had made an appointment or two of Consuls for some of the ports of this country; particularly of Franks for Marseilles. He is very anxious to be continued in it, and is now there in the exercise of his office. If I have been rightly informed, his services and sacrifices during the war have had their merit, and I should suppose Congress would not supersede him but on good grounds. I promised him that I would communicate his wishes to some of my friends, that his pretensions might not be set aside for want of being known.—There is an idea here of removing the packets from L'Orient to Havre. This latter may be considered as the port of Paris itself, because the transportation between them is down the Seine in boats and makes scarcely a greater addition to the price than a transportation from a warehouse to the waterside. Paris is the only place at which all the productions and manufactures of France are brought to a point. Mr. Tracy, who is here from Boston, has carefully examined into all their manufactures, and finds them of almost every kind, as good as in England, and cheaper generally. This truth once known, and our ships coming hither for those articles which England thinks she alone can furnish us, will advantage us first in opening to double markets, and secondly in the shock it will communicate across the channel. L'Orient is convenient in war, and therefore should be left as it is, a free port. But conveyances from hence thither are by land, long, precarious and expensive. I think our merchants will turn their views on Havre.—There is here some person, a Frenchman from Philadelphia (perhaps Perée) who has drawn up a visionary scheme of a settlement of French emigrants, 500 in number on the Ohio. He supposes Congress, flattered by the prospect of such an addition to our numbers, will give them 400,000 acres of land, and permit them to continue French subjects. My opinion has been asked, and I have given it, that Congress will make bargains with nobody, that they will lay down general rules, to which all applicants must conform themselves by applying the proper offices and not perplexing Congress with their visions: that they are sufficiently assured that the land office will absorb all their certificates of public debt, beyond which they have no object but to provide that the new governments shall admit an easy and firm union with the old; and that therefore I did not think they would encourage a settlement in so large a body of strangers whose language, manners and principles were so heterogeneous to ours.—I shall subscribe for you to the Encyclopedie methodique. It will be in about 60 vols. and will cost 751 livres equal to 30 English guineas. If you should not chuse to take it, it will be only a sacrifice of the subscription money, which is a guinea and half. The subscription is daily expected to be closed. There is about two fifths of the work now ready to be delivered amounting to about 300 livres.—We have taken some pains to find out the sums which the nations of Europe give to the Barbary states to purchase their peace. They will not tell this; yet from some glimmerings it appears to be very considerable; and I do expect that they would tax us at one, two, or perhaps three hundred thousand dollars a year. Surely our people will not give this. Would it not be better to offer them an equal treaty. If they refuse, why not go to war with them? Spain, Portugal, Naples and Venice are now at war with them. Every part of the Mediterranean therefore would offer us friendly ports. We ought to begin a naval power, if we mean to carry on our own commerce. Can we begin it on a more honourable occasion or with a weaker foe? I am of opinion Paul Jones with half a dozen frigates would totally destroy their commerce: not by attempting bombardments as the Mediterranean states do wherein they act against the whole Barbary force brought to a point, but by constant cruising and cutting them to peices by peicemeal.—I must say a word on my own affairs, because they are likely to be distressed. All the ministers who came to Europe before me, came at a time when all expences were paid, and a sum allowed in addition for their time. Of course they all had their outfit. Afterwards they were put on fixed salaries, but still these were liberal. Congress in the moment of my appointment, struck off 500 guineas of the salary, and made no other provision for the outfit but allowing me to call for two quarter's salary in advance. The outfit has cost me near a thousand guineas; for which I am in debt and which, were I to stay here seven years, I could never make good by savings out of my salary: for be assured we are the lowest and most obscure of the whole diplomatic tribe. When I was in Congress I chose never to intermeddle on the subject of salary, first because I was told the eyes of some were turned on me for this office; and secondly because I was really ignorant what might be it's expences. The latter reason ceases; the former which presents me as an interested person shall still keep me silent with all the world but your-self, to whose secrecy and delicacy I can trust. I live here about as well as we did at Annapolis. I keep a hired carriage and two horses. A riding horse I cannot afford to keep. This stile is far below the level, yet it absorbs the whole allowance, and return when I will to America, I shall be the out-fit in debt to Congress. I think I am the first instance in the world where it has not been given. I mention these circumstances to you that if you should think the allowance reasonable and any opportunity should occur while you are in Congress wherein it can be decently obtained, you would be so good as to think of it. I would wish it could be done on some general occasion. The article of houserent in Mr. Adam's account in Holland, and in Dr. Franklin's here may perhaps afford an occasion of touching on this article as to myself. Mr. A. has lived at the Hague in a house belonging to the U.S. The question is whether you will charge him rent. Dr. F. has lived in a house the rent of which (6000. livres per. ann.) has been always charged to the U.S. The question on that is whether you will reject that and make him pay eight or nine years rent. If these articles pass it will of course add houserent to the salaries, which will be some aid but not an adequate one for the ministers in general. When this matter shall be considered, the difference which has taken place between them and me as to the article of outfit may perhaps be mentioned and redressed. Otherwise, as I before mentioned, I shall return that much in debt, and be obliged to sell to pay it: a circumstance which I shall think hard. I ask nothing for my time, but I think my expenses should be paid in a stile equal to that of those with whom I am classed.—I must ask the favor of you on behalf of Mr. Adams as well as myself to explain the following transaction to our Commissioners of the Treasury. Congress you know directed the financier to advance me two quarters salary. He gave me a letter of credit to Mr. Grand. Relying on the effect of this I had ordered furniture for a small hotel which I rent: and had entered into engagements for paying part of the rent in advance. A little before the parties were to call on me for the money I applied to Mr. Grand [the Paris banker who handled U. S. funds in France], but our funds were out and I found he was not disposed to advance the money. Nothing could equal my distress. In this situation Mr. Adams thought himself justifiable in drawing in my favor on the fund in Holland for 6000 florins, knowing of the order of Congress in my favor, of the failure of the funds here and that it could not be important to Congress from what part the money came. It was unlucky I did not know of the failure here before I had contracted the debt because I could have hired furniture for one third or one half of it's worth annually. But this was such miserable oeconomy, amounting to from $33^{1}/3$ to 50 percent per ann. for the use of money, as induced me to buy. I wish this to be explained to the Commissioners to save Mr. Adams from censure. I am with sincere esteem Dr. Sir Your affectionate friend & servt,

—TH: JEFFERSON

∽

To George Washington
DEAR SIR   Paris Dec. 10. 1784

Every thing on this side the water seems to indicate a certainty of war. The Emperor seems decided in not receding from the right to navigate the Scheld; and the Dutch as determined not to yeild it. I suppose that this court and that of Berlin will take part with the Dutch. The Turks of course become parties in a war against the Emperor; and it seems as probable that the Empress of Russia will join him. There are many who beleive he will yet retract; but every public appearance is against this supposition. I own myself astonished he should have gone so far; but I should be more so were he now to retire. He is indeed in a perillous predicament. If he recedes, his character, which his public acts have placed on very high ground, dwindles to that of a petty bully, and is marked, as his enemies denote it, with eccentricity and inconsistence; if he persists, the probable combination against him seems to threaten his ruin. When the season arrives for opening a campaign we shall know decidedly and probably not before.

The disposition of Gr. Britain does not seem very favourable to us. All information from thence represents the people and still more the merchants as extremely hostile. I think it probable we shall take a trip to that court in order to bring their intentions to a decisive issue. It seems probable also that Spain will refuse to treat at this place, and oblige us to visit Madrid. I had lately a letter from Mr. Carmichael [the American chargé d'affaires to the Spanish court] at Madrid. He informs me that a Mr. Harrison of Cadiz had on your behalf applied to him to procure permission to send you a Jack of the best race; and that on his making the application of the king had ordered two of the very best to be procured and sent you as a mark of his respect. Besides the pleasure I receive from every testimonial of this kind, I view this present as likely to be of great public utility. I had before intended to endeavor to procure a male of that race; but shall now change my object to the procuring one or more females, that we may be enabled to propagate and preserve the breed. Should I go to Spain, I shall surely be able to effect this.

The executive of our state have remitted to Dr. Franklin and myself the care of having the statue made which the assembly directed as a mark of their gratitude to you. I was unwell when I received the letter and have not yet been able to see and confer with Doctr. Franklin on the subject. I find that a Monsr. Houdon of this place possesses the reputation of being the first statuary in the world. I sent for him and had some conversation with him on the subject. He thinks it cannot be perfectly done from a picture; and is so enthusiastically fond of being the executor of this work that he offers to go himself to America for the purpose of forming your bust from the life, leaving all his business here in the mean time. He thinks that being three weeks with you would suffice to make his model of plaister with which he will return here, and the work will employ him three years. If Dr. Franklin concurs with me, we shall send him over, not having time to ask your permission and await your answer. I trust having given to your country so much of your time heretofore, you will add the short space which this operation will require to enable them to transmit to posterity the form of the person whose actions will be delivered to them by History. Monsr. Houdon is at present engaged in making a statue of the king of France. A bust of Voltaire executed by him is said to be one of the first in the world.

I beg leave to present my respectful compliment to Mrs. Washington and to assure yourself of the high esteem and veneration with which I have the honour to be Dr. Sir Your most obedient and most humble servt.,

—TH: JEFFERSON

ॐ

To Francis Hopkinson
DEAR SIR   Paris Jan. 13. 1785

I wrote you the 11th of November. Since that I have received no proposition on the subject of the quill of the harpsichord. The artisans here will not readily beleive that any thing good can be invented but in London or Paris: and to shew them the invention would be to give it up. However I shall still endeavor to find some one who will do justice to it.

War and peace hang in doubtful balance. The people here in general beleive there will be no war; while not a circumstance can be produced, not a symptom mentioned in the conduct of the emperor which does not breathe a determination for war. The season for arms alone will ultimately inform us. Mr. Blanchard of this country and Dr. Jefferies of Massachuests arrived here the day before yesterday from Dover, having crossed the channel on the 7th. in a Balloon. [*Balloon ascensions were then very much the fashion, and Jefferson, like everyone else, went to see them from time to time.*] They were two hours from land to land. It was filled with inflammable air. We are told here of a method of extricating this from pit coal, cheaply and speedily, but it is not yet reduced to experience. M. Pigott, who had discovered the periodical variations of light in the star Algol, has discovered the like in the (Eta) of Antinous. The period of variation is 7D-4H-30'. The increase of light continues 63 hours, and it's decrease 36 hours. The number of double stars discovered by Herschel amounts now to upwards of 900, being twice the number which he gave in the Philosophical Transactions. Be so good as to communicate these articles to Mr. Rittenhouse. The madness of animal magnetism [*also known to us as mesmerism, after its inventor, or hypnotism*] is absolutely ceased. It is who now can clear their hands of it. It has been brought on the stage, ridiculed in the public papers, and is an imputation of so grave a nature as would bear an action at law in America.

Nothing can equal the dearth of American intelligence in which we live here. I had formed no conception of it. We might as well be in the moon. Congress were to meet the 3d. of November. We are now at the 13th. of Jan. and no American, public or private, here, is informed whether they have met, where they are sitting, who presides, nor any thing else about them. Our friends think that facts known to every body there, cannot be unknown here. And all thinking so, no one writes them. To remedy this I have by this packet written to the different states to have newspapers sent to me monthly by the French packet. I take the liberty of imposing this office on you in Philadelphia, and of praying you by every French packet to send me the papers intervening between that and the preceding packet. The first parcel may have retrospect to Nov. 1. if to be had. As you have two parties there, I would wish a paper from a press of each, and that which is best for American intelligence, as the European articles will be of little value here. The expence of this I will take care to remit you in any form you please. Direct the paper to the care of Mr. Neill Jamieson in New York, who is my postmaster general there. My daughter is well and joins me in affectionate respects to Mrs. Hopkinson the elder and younger. I am with great esteem Dr. Sir Your... [A corner with his closing is torn.]

—TH: JEFFERSON

P.S. Can you inform me from Mr. Wright whether I am yet at liberty to permit a copy to be taken of Gl. Washington's picture?

&

[Hearing of the death of his youngest daughter—this brought his losses to four: his wife and three children—Jefferson determined to bring his second youngest, Mary, known as Polly, to France to be with him.]

From Elizabeth Wayles Eppes
DEAR SIR   Eppington October. 13. 1784

It's impossible to paint the anguish of my heart on this melancholy occasion. A most unfortunate Hooping cough has deprived you, and us of two sweet Lucys, within a week. Ours was the first that fell a sacrifice. She was thrown into violent convulsions linger'd out a week and then expired. Your dear angel was confined a week to her bed, her sufferings were great though nothing like a fit. She retain'd her senses perfectly, calld me a few moments before she died, and asked distinctly for water. Dear Polly has had it most violently, though always kept about, and is now quite recovered. My heart shudders for my poor Bolling, who is reduced to a skeleton, and the cough still very obstinate. Life is scarcely supportable under such severe afflictions.

Be so good as to remember me most affectionately to my dear Patsy, and beg she will excuse my not writing until the gloomy scene is a little forgotten. I sincerely hope you are both partaking of every thing that can in the smallest degree entertain, and make you happy. Our warmest affections attend you both. Your sincere friend,

—E. EPPES

&

[I am omitting the first portions of this letter, which deal with the code in which portions of it were written. Those portions were decoded by the editors of the Princeton edition of Jefferson's papers and are here represented by italics in the text.]

To James Monroe
DEAR SIR   [6 Feb. 1785]

... Our business goes on very slowly. No answers from Spain or Britain. The backwardness of the latter is not new. Perhaps Mr. Jay or Mr. Lawrence [Laurens] who have been at that court since the present ministry have been in place may have been able to account for this on better grounds than we can. The English parliament Irish parliament and Irish convention sitting together will surely bring their disputes to a crisis. Scotland too seems to be stepping in as a third party with her difficulties. And their affairs in the East Indies are in a wretched situation. The opposition have opened their campaign on the East Indian regulations, the proceedings with Ireland, and the late taxes. The minister having declared he will propose a plan of parliamentary reform, they have taken the contrary side of course on that question. I am anxious to see whether the parliament will take any and what steps as to our commerce. The effecting treaties with the powers holding possessions in the West Indies I consider as the important part of our business. It is not of great consequence whether others treat or not. Perhaps trade may go on with them well enough without. But Britain, Spain, Portugal [and] France are consequent, and Holland, Denmark [and] Sweden may be of service too. We have hitherto waited for favorable circumstances to press matters with France. We are now about to do it tho I cannot say the prospect is good. The merchants of this country are very clamorous against our admission into the West Indies and ministers are afraid for their places. The pamphlet which I send you is approved by the sensible people here, and I am in hopes has been of some service. There are warm ones writ against it. [Jefferson here begins to talk at length about the Barbary states and their depredations on shipping in the Mediterranean and just outside Gibraltar. From the beginning he was in favor of war, not ransom.] Our affairs with the pyratical states are distressing. It is impossible I fear to find out what is given by other countries. Either shame or jealousy makes them wish to keep it secret. Several of their ministers to whom we have applied have promised to procure information. These pyrates are contemptibly weak. Morocco who has first dared to commit an outrage on us owns only four or five frigates, of 18 or 20 guns. There is not a port in their country which has more than 13. feet water. Tunis is not quite so strong (having 3. or 4. frigates only, small and worthless), is more mercantile than predatory, and would easily be led to treat, either by money or fear. Tripoli has one frigate only. Algiers alone possesses any power, and they are brave. As far as I have been able to discover she possesses about 16. vessels from 22 up to 52 guns. But the vessels of all these powers are wretched in the last degree, being mostly built of the discordant peices of other vessels which they take and pull asunder. Their cordage and sails are of the same kind, taken from vessels of different sizes and forms, seldom any two guns of the same bore, and all of them light. These states too are divided, and jealous of each other, and especially of Algiers the most powerful. The others would willingly see her reduced. We have two plans to pursue. The one to carry nothing for ourselves, and thereby render ourselves invulnerable to the European states; the other (which our country will be for) is to carry as much as possible. But this will require a protecting force on the sea. Otherwise the smallest powers in Europe, every one which possesses a single ship of the line may dictate to us, and enforce their demands by captures on our commerce. Some naval force then is necessary if we mean to be commercial. Can we have a better occasion of beginning one? Or find a foe more certainly within our dimensions? The motives pleading for war rather than tribute are numerous and honourable, those opposing them are mean and shortsighted: however if it be decided that their peace shall be bought it shall engage my most earnest endeavours. It is as incertain as ever whether we are to have war or peace.—The ministers of this country intimate peace and Monsr. de Maillebois who is to command the Dutch army is not set out. I should consider his departure as an indication of war.

I must pray you to send your letters by the French packet. They come by that conveyance with certainty, having first undergone the ceremony of being opened and read in the post office which I am told is done in every country in Europe. Letters by the way of England are sometimes months getting from London here. Give me fully always the Congressional news, and by every letter if you please the journals of Congress.

I would make an additional observation or two as to the pyratical states. If we enter into treaty there, a consul must be kept with each to recover our vessels taken in breach of their treaty. For these violations they practise constantly against the strongest nations, and the vessels so taken are recovered with trouble and always some loss and considerable delay. The attempts heretofore made to suppress these powers have been to exterminate them at one blow. They are too numerous and powerful by land for that. A small effort, but long continued, seems to be the only method. By suppressing their marine and trade totally and continuing this till the present race of seamen should be pretty well out of the way and the younger people betaken to husbandry for which their soil and climate is well fitted, these nests of banditti might be reformed. I am not well enough acquainted with the present dispositions of the European courts to say whether a general confederacy might be formed for suppressing these pyracies. Such as should refuse would give us a just right to turn pyrates also on their West India trade, and to require an annual tribute which might reimburse what we may be obliged to pay to obtain a safe navigation in their seas. Were we possessed even of a small naval force what a bridle would it be in the mouths of the West India powers and how respectfully would they demean themselves toward us. Be assured that the present disrespect of the nations of Europe for us will inevitably bring on insults which must involve us in war. A coward is much more exposed to quarrels than a man of spirit.

Be so good as to present one of the pamphlets with my esteem to Mr. Gherry and let him know he is a letter in my debt. I am Dr. Sir Yours affectionately,

—TH: JEFFERSON

ᴇᴚᴏ

[This letter from Virginia begins the correspondence on the Virginia Capitol, whose design Jefferson will choose and hire the French architect Charles Louis Clerriseau to execute.]

From James Buchanan and William Hay

SIR   Richmond March 20th. 1785

The active part which you took before your departure from Virginia, as a director of the public buildings, leads us to believe, that it will not be now unacceptable to you, to cooperate with us as far as your engagements will permit.

We foresee, that in the execution of our commission, the Commonwealth must sustain a heavy expence, and that we can provide no shield so effectual against the censures which await large disbursements of public money, as the propriety of making them. For this purpose we must intreat you to Consult an able Architect on a plan fit for a Capitol, and to assist him with the information of which you are possessed.

You will recollect, Sir, that the first act directed separate houses for the accommodation of the different departments of government. But fearing that the Assembly would not countenance us in giving sufficient magnificence to distinct buildings, we obtained leave to consolidate the whole under one roof, if it should seem adviseable. The inclosed draught will show that we wish to avail ourselves of this license. But, altho it contains many particulars it is not intended to confine the architect except as to the number and area of the rooms.

We have not laid down the ground, it being fully in your power to describe it, when we inform You that the Hill on which Gunns yellow house stands and which you favoured as the best situation, continues to be preferd by us and that we have allocated 29 half acre lots, including Marsdon's tenement, and Minzie's lots in front of Gunns. The Legislature have not limited us to any sum; nor can we, as yet at least, resolve to limit ourselves to a precise amount. But we wish to unite oeconomy with elegance and dignity. At present the only funds submitted to our order are nearly about £10,000 Virga. Currency.

We have already contract'd with Edward Voss of Culpepper, for the laying of 1500 thousand Bricks. He is a workman of the first reputation here, but skillful in plain and rubbed work alone. We suppose he may commence his undertaking by the beginning of August, and have therefore stipulated with him to be in readiness by that time. This circumstance renders us anxious for expedition in fixing the plans, especially too as the foundation of the Capitol will silence the enimies of Richmond in the next October Session.

Should an assistant be thought necessary whose employment will be either independent of Voss or subordinate to him, we will pay him.

We shall send to Europe for any Stone which may be wanted.

The roof will be covered with lead, as we conceive that to be better than Copper or tiles.

In the remarks, which accompany the plan, we have requested a draught for the Governor's house and prison. But we hope that the Capitol will be first drawn and forwarded to us, as there is no hurry for the other buildings.

We trust, Sir, you will excuse the trouble which we now impose on you, and will ascribe to it our belief of your alacrity to serve your Country on this occasion. We have the honour to be very respectfully Sir Your most obt. hble. Servts.,

—JAMES BUCHANAN

❧

To William Short
TH: J TO W.S.   Apr. 2. 1785

I inclose you a letter from l'Orient. When are we to see you? [*Short was living with a French family in a Paris suburb, learning French.*] Your letters leave us in doubt whether you mean to protract this odious term of the 4th. of April, or to return to your quarters then and be content to go on with your French at leisure. I am in hopes this will be your choice. You lost much by not attending the Te-deum at Notre dame yesterday. It bids defiance to description. I will only observe to you in general that there were more judges, ecclesiastics and Grands seigneurs present, than Genl. Washington had of simple souldiers in his army, when he took the Hessians at Trenton, beat the British at Princeton, and hemmed up the British army at Brunswick a whole winter. Come home like a good boy and you will always be in the way of these wonders. Adieu. [*Abby, Abigail Adams' daughter, had this to say about the above occasion in her diary: "I believe I may say with truth there were millions of people. Mr. Jefferson, who rode from the Marquis' with us, supposed there were as many people in the streets as there were in the State of Massachusetts, or any other of the States. Every house was full—every window and door, from the bottom to the top." All this was to pay homage to the birth of the Duke of Normandy. The marquis she mentions was no doubt the Marquis de la Fayette.*]

❧

To James Monroe
DEAR SIR   Paris Apr. 15. 1785

We wrote a public letter to Mr. Jay the day before yesterday. We were induced to hasten it, because young Mr. Chaumont was to set out yesterday for l'Orient to go to N. York in the packet, and a private conveyance is alone to be depended on for secrecy. I have put off writing any letters as long as I could, expecting the arrival of the packet. She is arrived, as the packet of the last month did without bringing a scrip of a pen public or private to any American here. This perplexes us extremely. From your letter of Dec. 14. and from one written at the same time by Mr. Jay to Dr. Franklin we have reason to beleive Congress have done something in the affairs with England and Spain. We also thought something would be said to us on the subject of the Barnaby States. We therefore deferred moving lest we should have to change our move which is always dishonourable. We particularly expected instructions as to the posts still held by the English. We shall do the best we can under our old instructions. The letter from the Duke of Dorset will I dare say surprise you all. It is a folly above the highest that could have been expected. I know from one who saw his instructions that he softened them much in the letter to us. The following paragraph is from a letter I received from Doctor Price about ten days ago. 'There is, I fancy, no probability that Britain can be brought to consent to that reciprocity in trade which the United States expect. This is sad policy for Britain but it may turn out to be best for America and should the issue be our exclusion from the American ports we may be ruined but I do not see that America would suffer in it's true interest. The fixed conviction however is that we are able to supply America on so much better terms than any other country that do what we will we must have its trade.' It is dated March twenty first. He is said to be in great intimacy with Mr. Pitt and I verily beleive this paragraph contains the genuine creed of the nation and ministry. You will observe that the 4th. article of our original draught of a treaty transmitted to the several courts was contrary to a right reserved by the states in the confederation. We shall correct it in every instance. War and peace still doubtful. It rather seems that the peace may continue a while yet. But not very long. The Emperor has a head too combustible to be quiet. He is an eccentric character. All enterprize, without calculation, without principle, without feelings. Ambitious in the extreme, but too unsteady to surmount difficulties. He has had in view at one time to open the Scheld, to get Maestricht from the Dutch, to take a large district from the Turks, to exchange some of his Austrian dominions for Bavaria, to create a ninth electorate, to make his nephew king of the Romans, and to change totally the constitution of Hungary. Any one of these was as much as a wise prince would have undertaken at any one time. Quod vult, valde vult, sed non diu vult.

I send you Voltaire's legacy to the K. of Prussia, a libel which will do much more injury to Voltaire than to the king. Many of the traits in the character of the latter to which the former give a turn satyrical and malicious, are real virtues. I should remind you that two packets have now come without bringing me a letter from you, and should scold you soundly, but that I consider it as certain evidence of your being sick. If this be so, you know you have my sincere prayers for better health. But why has no body else written to me? Is it that one is forgotten as soon as their back is turned? I have a better opinion of men. It must be either that they think that the details known to themselves are known to every body and so come to us thro' a thousand channels, or that we should set no value on them. Nothing can be more erroneous than both those opinions. We value those details, little and great, public and private, in proportion to our distance from our own country: and so far are they from getting to us through a thousand channels, that we hear no more of them or of our country here than if we were among the dead. I have never received a title from any [mem]ber of Congress but yourself and one letter from Dr. Williamson. The D. de Rochefoucault is kind enough to communicate to us the intelligence which he receives from Mr. St. John, and the M. de la F. what he gets from his correspondents. These have been our only sources of intelligence since the middle of December....

Since the warm weather has set in I am almost perfectly reestablished. I am able now to walk six or eight miles a day which I do very regularly. This must supply the place of the journey I had meditated into the South of France. Tho' our business does not afford constant occupation, it is of such a nature one does not know when our presence may be wanted. I need add no signature but wishing you ever happiness bid you Adieu.

∾

From John Adams
MY DEAR SIR   Montreuil sur mer May 22. 1785

We left Auteuil the 20th. afternoon and have made easy Journeys. Indeed We could not have done otherwise, because the Post-horses were enraged, by the unusual Number of Travellers, in such Numbers that We have been sometimes obliged to wait. The Country is an heap of Ashes. Grass is scarcely to be seen and all sorts of Grain is short, thin, pale and feeble while the Flax is quite dead. You see indeed more green Things than in some of our sharp Drouths in America, but as the Heat of this Clymate is not sufficient to destroy vegetation so effectually as with us, it is not enough neither to produce so rapid a Revivication of the Universe, upon the Return of Rains, so that their Prospects are more melancholly than ours upon such Occasions. I pity this People from my soul. There is at this Moment as little appearance of a change of Weather as ever.

Tomorrow we shall reach Calais, but I cannot calculate how long it will take us to cross the Channel. I allow two days from Dover to London as I am determined to be in a hurry about nothing from the Beginning to the End of this Adventure. It is best to give myself as well as others time to think.

The Ladies join in respects to you and Mr. Humphreys and Mr. Williams, the Marquis and his Lady and all other Friends. Be so good as to inform me, if you learn any Thing of the sailing of the Packet, and of the Health of my Boy. I thank you kindly for your Book [Notes on the State of Virginia, just published.] It is our Meditation all the Day long. I cannot now say much about it, but I think it will do its Author and his Country great Honour. The Passages upon Slavery, are worth Diamonds. They will have more effect than Volumes written by mere Philosophers. The Ladies say you should have mentioned West and Copely at least among your American Genius's, because they think them the greatest Painters of the Age. Madam[e says] I have not expressed her sentiments politely enough. It should run thus: The Ladies desire that in the next Edition you would insert West and Copeley &c.

The melancholly Face of Nature, added to the dull political Prospect before us, on the other side of the Channell, coming upon the Black of our natural Regretts at parting with our Son and our fine Summer Situation at Auteuil, and all our Friends in and about Paris, make the Journey rather triste, but we have passed through scenes bien plus triste encore. Adieu.

—J. ADAMS

From John Adams
DEAR SIR   Dessin's Calais May 23. 1785. Monday.

We are just arrived, covered with Dust, and we have hired our Boat, to go over tomorrow at ten. No green Peas, no Sallad, no Vegetables to be had upon the Road, and the Sky is still as clear dry and cold as ever. The Flocks of Sheep and herds of Cattle, through the Country, stalk about the Fields like Droves of Walking Skeletons. The Sheep are pastured chiefly. I think in the plowed grounds, upon the Fibres as I suppose of the Roots of Grass turn'd up by the Plow.

From a motive of Humanity I wish that our Country may have plentifull Rains, and our Husbandmen Industry, that they may supply the Wants of their Suffering Fellow Creatures in Europe. You see I have nothing so mean as a selfish or even a patriotic wish in all this. But from the same regard to Europe and her worthy Colonists in the West Indies, I hope that these rainless, heatless Heavens will convince them that it is abundantly for their good that we should bring and carry freely, our Flour, Wheat, Corn, Rice, Flesh, and Fish for their Soulagement. Yours affectionately,

—J. ADAMS

The Ladies Compliments of course.
RC (DLC); endorsed.

❧

[The Adams family's departure from Paris, as John Adams took up ministerial duties in London, was a blow to Jefferson; he had become very close to them. It was in Paris that they had established their deep friendship, which ultimately survived the bitter political campaign of 1800 and Jefferson's intense dislike of the Alien and Sedition Acts, which were Adams's attempt to suppress free speech.]

To John Adams
DEAR SIR   Paris May 25. 1785

Your letter of the 22d. from Montreuil sur mer is put into my hands this moment, and having received information of your son, and two American gentlemen being to set out for London tomorrow morning, I seize a moment to inform you that he had arrived well at l'Orient and was well on the 20th. when the packet was still detained by contrary winds. Mr. Barclay, who is arrived, had also seen him. Be so good as to inform the ladies the Mrs. Hayes is arrived. I have not yet seen her, but am this moment going to perform that duty. I fear the ladies have had a more triste journey than we had calculated on. The poverty of the country and distress of the drought would of course produce this effect. I am the more convinced of this as you say they have found the amusement in my notes. They presented themselves to their notice under fortunate circumstances. I am happy if you find any thing in them worthy your approbation. But my country will probably estimate them differently. A foreknowlege of this has retarded my communicating them to my friends two years. But enough of them. The departure of your family has left me in the dumps. My afternoons hang heavily on me. I go sometimes to Passy and Mont Parnasse. When they are gone too I shall be ready for the dark and narrow house of Ossian. We attended the Queen's entrance yesterday, but lost the sight of her. You can calculate, and without many figures, the extent of this mortification to me. To render it more complete I had placed myself and my daughter in my carriage very finely before the Palais Bourbon to see the illuminations of the Garde meubles which are to cost the king of Spain two or three thousand guineas. But they sent a parcel of souldiers to drive us all away. We submitted without making battle; I carried my daughter to the Abbaye and came home to bed myself. I have now given you all the news of Paris as far as I know it and after recommending myself to the friendly recollection of the ladies I conclude with assurances of the esteem with which I have the honour to be dear Sir Your affectionate friend & servt.,

—TH: JEFFERSON

P.S. Send me your address au plutot.

∾

From Abigail Adams, with Enclosure
London Bath Hotel Westminster
DEAR SIR   June 6. 1785

Mr. Adams has already written you that we arrived in London upon the 27 of May. We joureny'd slowly and sometimes silently. I think I have somewhere met with the observation that nobody ever leaves paris but with a degree of tristeness. I own I was loth to leave my garden because I did not expect to find its place supplied. I was still more loth of account of the increasing pleasure, and intimacy which a longer acquaintance with a respected Friend promised, to leave behind me the only person with whom my Companion could associate with perfect freedom, and unreserve: and whose place he had no reason to expect supplied in the Land to which he is destined. [*She means Jefferson, of course.*]

At leaving Auteuil our domisticks surrounded our Carriage and in tears took leave of us, which gave us that painfull kind of pleasure, which arises from a consciousness, that the good will of our dependants is not misplaced.

My little Bird I was obliged, after taking it into the Carriage to resign to my parisian chamber maid, or the poor thing would have fluttered itself to Death. I mourned its loss, but its place was happily supplied by a present of two others which were given me on board the Dover pacquet, by a young Gentleman whom we had received on Board with us, and who being excessively sick I admitted into the cabin, in gratitude for which he insisted upon my accepting a pair of his Birds. As they had been used to travelling I brought them here in safety, for which they hourly repay me by their melodious notes. When we arrived we went to our old Lodgings at the Adelphia, but could not be received as it was full, and almost every other hotel in the city. From thence we came to the Bath Hotel where we at present are, and where Mr. Storer had partly engaged Lodgings for us, tho he thought we should have objections on account of the Noise, and the constant assemblage of carriages round it, but it was no time for choice, as the sitting of parliament, the Birth Day of the King, and the celebration of Handles Musick had drawn together such a Number of people as allready to increase the price of Lodgings near double. We did not however hesitate at keeping them, tho the four rooms which we occupy costs a third more than our House and Garden Stables &c. did at Auteuil. I had lived so quietly in that calm retreat, that the Noise and bustle of this proud city almost turnd my Brain for the first two or three Days. The figure which this city makes in respect to Equipages is vastly superiour to Paris, and gives one the Idea of superiour wealth and grandeur. I have seen few carriages in paris and no horses superiour to what are used here for Hackneys. My time has been much taken up since my arrival in looking out for a House. I could find many which would suit in all respects but the price, but none realy fit to occupy under

240 £. 250. besides the taxes, which are serious matters here. At last I found one in Grovenor Square which we have engaged.

Mr. Adams has written you an account of his reception at Court, which has been as gracious and as agreeable as the reception given to the Ministers of any other foreign powers. Tomorrow he is to be presented to the Queen. Mr. Smith appears to be a modest worthy man, if I may judge from so short an acquaintance. I think we shall have much pleasure in our connection with him. All the Foreign Ministers and the Secretaries of Embassies have made their visits here, as well as some English Earls and Lords. Nothing as yet has discovered any acrimony. Whilst the Coals are cover'd the blaize will not burst, but the first wind which blows them into action will I expect envelop all in flames. If the actors pass the ordeal without being burnt they may be considered in future of the Asbestos kind. Whilst I am writing the papers of this day are handed me. From the publick Advertiser I extract the following. "Yesterday morning a messenger was sent from Mr. Pitt to Mr. Adams the American plenipotentiary with notice to suspend for the present their intended interview" (absolutely false). From the same paper:

"An Ambassador from America! Good heavens what a sound! The Gazette surely never announced any thing so extraordinary before, nor once on a day so little expected. This will be such a phoenomenon in the Corps Diplomatique that tis hard to say which can excite indignation most, the insolence of those who appoint the Character, or the meanness of those who receive it. Such a thing could never have happened in any former Administration, not even that of Lord North. It was reserved like some other Humiliating circumstances to take place

Sub Jove, sed Jove nondum
Barbato _____."

From the morning post and daily advertiser it is said that "Mr. Adams the Minister plenipotenitary from America is extremly desirious of visiting Lord North whom he Regards as one of the best Friends the Americans ever had." Thus you see sir the beginning squibs.

I went last week to hear the musick in Westminster Abbey. The Messiah was performd. It was sublime beyond description. I most sincerely wisht for your presence as your favorite passion would have received the highest gratification. I should have sometimes fancied myself amongst a higher order of Beings; if it had not been for a very troublesome female, who was unfortunately seated behind me; and whose volubility not all the powers of Musick could still.

I thank you sir for the information respecting my son from whom we received Letters. He desires to be remembered to you, to Col. Humphries and to Mr. Williamos. My Daughter also joins in the same request. We present our Love to Miss Jefferson and compliments to Mr. Short. I suppose Madam de la Fayette is gone from paris. If she is not, be so good sir as to present my respects to her. I design writing her very soon. I have to apoligize for thus freely scribling to you. I will not deny that there may be a little vanity in the hope of being honourd with a line from you. Having heard you upon some occasions express a desire to hear from your Friends, even the Minutia respecting their Situation, I have ventured to class myself in that number and to subscribe myself, Sir, your Friend and Humble Servant,

—A. ADAMS

ENCLOSURE
The publick Advertiser—

"Yesterday Lord George Gordon had the Honour of a long conference with his Excellency John Adams (honest John Adams), the Ambassador of America, at the hotel of Mons. de Lynden Envoye extrordinaire de Leur Hautes puissances." This is true, and I suppose inserted by his Lordship who is as wild and as enthusiastic as when he headed the mob. His Lordship came here but not finding Mr. Adams at home was determined to see him, and accordingly followed him to the Dutch Ministers. The conversation was curious, and pretty much in the Stile of Mrs. Wright with whom his Lordship has frequent conferences.

An other paragraph from the same paper—"Amongst the various personages who drew the attention of the drawing-room on Saturday last, Mr. Adams, plenipotentiary from the States of America was not the least noticed. From this gentleman the Eye of Majesty and the Court glanced on Lord _____; to whose united Labours this Country stands indebted for the loss of a large territory and divided and interrupted Commerce."

From John Adams
DEAR SIR   Bath Hotel Westminster June 7. 1785

I have received yours of 25. May, and thank you for the News of my Son, and
for the News of Paris. I wished to have seen the Queens Entrance into Paris,
but I saw the Queen of England on Saturday, the Kings Birth day, in all her Glory.
It is paying very dear to be a King or Queen to pass One such a day in a year.
To be obliged to enter into Conversation with four or five hundred, or four or
five Thousand People of both Sexes, in one day and to find Small Talk enough
for that Purpose, adapted to the Taste and Character of every one, is a Task which
would be out all Proportion to my Forces of Mind or Body. The K and Q. speak
to every Body. I stood next to the Spanish Minister, with whom his Majesty conversed in good French, for half or Quarter of an Hour, and I did not loose any
Part of the discourse, and he said several, clever Things enough. One was Je
suis convaincu que le plus grand Ennemy du Bien, est le mieux. You would have
applied it as I did, to the Croud of Gentlemen present who had advised his
Majesty, to renounce the Bien for the Mieux in America, and I believe he too
had that Instance in his mind. Thursday I must be presented to the Queen, who
I hope will say as many pretty Things to me, as the K. did.

You would die of ennui here, for these Ceremonies are more numerous and
continue much longer here than at Versailles.

I find I shall be accablé with Business and Ceremony together, and I miss
my fine walks and pure Air at Auteuil. The Smoke and Damp of this City is
ominous to me. London boasts of its Trottoir, but there is a space between
it and the Houses through which all the Air from Kitchens, Cellars, Stables
and Servants Appartements ascends into the Street and pours directly on the
Passenger on Foot. Such Whiffs and puffs assault you every few Steps as are
enough to breed the Plague if they do not Suffocate you on the Spot.

For Mercy Sake stop all my Wine but the Bourdeaux and Madeira, and
Frontenac. And stop my order to Rouen for 500 Additional Bottles. I shall be
ruined, for each Minister is not permitted to import more than 5 or 600 Bottles
which will not more than cover what I have at the Hague which is very rich wine
and my Madeira Frontenac and Bourdeaux at Auteuil. Petit will do the Business.

Regards to Coll. Humphreys and Mr. Williams. Adieu.

—JOHN ADAMS

✑

[Chastellux was a French major-general, one of three serving under Rochambeau, who fought in the American Revolution. Jefferson knew him well from meetings between them at Monticello.]

To Chastellux
DEAR SIR   Paris June 7, 1785

I have been honoured with the receipt of your letter of the 2d. instant, and am to thank you, as I do sincerely for the partiality with which you receive the copy of the Notes on my country. As I can answer for the facts therein reported on my own observation, and have admitted none on the report of others which were not supported by evidence sufficient to command my own assent, for I am not afraid that you should make any extracts you please for the Journal de physique which come within their plan of publication. The strictures on slavery and on the constitution of Virginia are not of that kind, and they are the parts which I do not wish to have made public, at least till I know whether their publication would do most harm or good. It is possible that in my own country these strictures might produce an irritation which would indispose the people towards the two great objects I have in view, that is the emancipation of their slaves, and the settlement of their constitution on a firmer and more permanent basis. If I learn from thence, that they will not produce that effect, I have printed and reserved just copies enough to be able to give one to every young man at the College. It is to them I look, to the rising generation, and not to the one now in power for these great reformations. The other copy delivered at your hotel was for Monsr. de Buffon. I meant to ask the favour of you to have it sent to him, as I was ignorant how to do it. I have one also for Monrs. Daubenton: but being utterly unknown to him I cannot take the liberty of presenting it till I can do it through some common acquaintance.

I will beg leave to say here a few words on the general question of the degeneracy of animals in America. 1. As to the degeneracy of the man of Europe transplanted to America, it is no part of Monsr. de Buffon's system. He goes indeed within one step of it, but he stops there. The Abbé Raynal alone has taken that step. Your knowledge of America enables you to judge this question, to say whether the lower class of people in America, are less informed and less susceptible of information than the lower class in Europe: and whether those in America who have received such an education as that country can give, are less improved by it than Europeans of the same degree of education. 2. As to the Aboriginal man of America, I know of no respectable evidence on which the opinion of his inferiority of genius has been founded but that of Don Ulloa. As to Robertson, he never was in America, he relates nothing on his own knowledge, he is a compiler only of the relations of others, and a mere translator of the opinions of Monsr. de Buffon. I should as soon therefore add the translators of Robertson to the witnesses of this fact, as himself. Paw, the beginner of this charge, was a compiler from the works of others; and of the most unlucky description; for he seems to have read the writings of travellers only to collect and republish their lies. It is really remarkeable that in three volumes 12mo. of small print it is scarcely possible to find one truth, and yet that the author should be able to produce authority for every fact he states, as he says he can. Don Ulloa's testimony is of the most respectable. He wrote of what he saw. But he saw the Indian of South America only, and that after he had passed through ten generations of slavery. It is very unfair, from this sample, to judge of the natural genius of this race of men: and after supposing that Don Ulloa had not sufficiently calculated the allowance which should be made for this circumstance, we do him no injury in considering the picture he draws of the present Indians of S. America as no picture of what their ancestors were 300 years ago. It is in N. America that we are to seek their original character: and I am safe in affirming that the proofs of genius given by the Indians of N. America, place them on a level with Whites in the same uncultivated state. The North of Europe furnishes subjects enough for comparison with them, and for a proof of their equality. I have seen some thousands myself, and conversed much with them, and have found in them a male, sound understanding. I have had much information from men who had lived among them, and whose veracity and good sense were so far known to me as to establish a reliance on their information. They have all agreed in bearing witness in favour of the genius of this people. As to their bodily strength, their manners rendering it disgraceful to labour, those muscles employed in labour will be weaker with them than with the European labourer: but those which are exerted in the chase and those faculties which are employed in the tracing an enemy or a wild beast, in contriving ambuscades for him, and in carrying them through their execution, are much stronger than with us, because they are more exercised. I beleive the Indian then to be in body and mind equal to the whiteman. I have supposed the blackman, in his present state, might not be so. But it would be hazardous to affirm that, equally cultivated for a few generations, he would not become so. 3. As to the inferiority of the other animals of America, without more facts I can add nothing to what I have said in my Notes. As to the theory of Monsr. de Buffon that heat is friendly and moisture adverse to the production of large animals, I am lately furnished with a fact by Doctr. Franklin which proves the air of London and of Paris to be more humid than that of Philadelphia, and so creates a suspicion that the opinion of the superior humidity of America may perhaps have been too hastily adopted. And supposing that fact admitted, I think he physical reasoning urged to shew that in a moist country animals must be small, and that in a hot one they must be large, are not built on the basis of experiment. These questions however cannot be decided ultimately at this day. More facts must be collected, and more time flow off, before the world will be ripe for decision. In the mean time doubt is wisdom.

I have been fully sensible of the anxieties of your situation, and that your attentions were wholly consecrated, where alone they were wholly due, to the succour of friendship and worth. However much I prize your society I wait with patience the moment when I can have it without taking what is due to another. In the mean time I am solaced with the hope of possessing your friendship, and that it is not ungrateful to you to receive assurances of that with which I have the honour to be Dear Sir Your most obedient and most humble servt.,

—TH: JEFFERSON

∽

To James Monroe
DEAR SIR   Paris, June 17. 1785

[The first part of this letter repeats much from earlier letters about possible war over the navigation of the Schelde, problems with Congress, and the cost of his outfit. We pick it up here.]

... I will take the liberty of hazarding to you some thoughts on the policy of entering into treaties with the European nations, and the nature of them. I am not
wedded to these ideas, and therefore shall relinquish them chearfully when
Congress shall adopt others, and zealously endeavour to carry theirs into effect.
First as to the policy of making treaties. Congress, by the Confederation have
no original and inherent power over the commerce of the states. But by the
9th. article they are authorised to enter into treaties of commerce. The moment
these treaties are concluded the jurisdiction of Congress over the commerce of
the states springs into existence, and that of the particular states is superseded
so far as the articles of the treaty may have taken up the subject. There are two
restrictions only on the exercise of the powers of treaty by Congress. 1st. That
they shall not by such treaty retrain the legislatures of the state from imposing
such duties on foreigners as their own people are subjected to: 2dly. nor from
prohibiting the exportation or importation of any particular species of goods.
Leaving these two points free, Congress may by treaty establish any system of commerce they please. But, as I before observed, it is by treaty alone they can do it.
Tho' they may exercise their other powers by resolution or ordinance, those
over commerce can only be exercised by forming a treaty and this probably by
an accidental wording of our confederation. If therefore it is better for the
states that Congress should regulate their commerce, it is proper that they
should form treaties with all nations with whom we may possibly trade. You see
that my primary object in the formation of treaties is to take the commerce of
the states out of the hands of the states, and to place it under the superintendance
of Congress, so far as the imperfect provisions of our constitution will admit,
and until the states shall by new compact make them more perfect. I would say
then to every nation on earth, by treaty, your people shall trade freely with us, and
ours with you, paying no more than the most favoured nation, in order to put
an end to the right of individual states acting by fits and starts to interrupt our
commerce or to embroil us with any nation. As to the terms of these treaties, the
question becomes more difficult. I will mention three different plans. 1. That no
duties shall be laid by either party on the productions of the other. 2. That each
may be permitted to equalize their duties to those laid by the other. 3. That most
favoured nations pay. 1. Were the nations of Europe as free and unembarrassed
of established system as we are, I do verily beleive they would concur with us in
the first plan. But it is impossible. These establishments are fixed upon them,

they are interwoven with the body of their laws and the organisation of their government, and they make a great part of their revenue; they cannot get rid of them. 2. The plan of equal imposts presents difficulties insurmountable. For how are the equal imposts to be effected? Is it by laying in the ports of A an equal percent on the goods of B. with that which B has laid in his ports on the goods of A? But how are we to find what is that percent? For this is not the usual form of imposts. They generally pay by the ton, by the measure, by the weight, and not by the value. Besides if A. sends a million's worth of goods to B. and takes back but the half of that, and each pays the same percent, it is evident that A. pays the double of what he recovers in the same way with B. This would be our case with Spain. Shall we endeavour to effect equality then by saying A may levy so much of the sum of B's importations into his ports, as B does on the sum of A's importations into the ports of B? But how find out that sum? Will either party lay open their customhouse books candidly to evince this sum? Does either keep their books so exactly as to trouble to do it? This proposition was started in Congress when our instructions were formed, as you may remember, and the impossibility of executing it occasioned it to be disapproved. Besides who should have a right of deciding when the imposts were equal. A. would say to B. my imposts do not raise so much as yours; I raise them therefore. B. would then say you have made them greater than mine, I will raise mine, and thus a kind of auction would be carried on between them, and a mutual irritation, which would end in any thing sooner than equality, and right. 3. I confess then to you that I see no alternative left but that which Congress adopted, of each party placing the other on the footing of the most favoured nation. If the nations of Europe from their actual establishments are not at liberty to say to America that she shall trade in their ports duty free, they may say she may trade there paying no higher duties than the most favoured nation and this is valuable in many of these countries where a very great difference is made between different nations. There is no difficulty to the execution of this contract, because there is not a merchant who does not know, or may not know, the duty paid at liberty to regulate their own commerce by general rules; while it secures the other from partial and oppressive discriminations. The difficulty which arises in our case is, with the nations having American territory. Access to the West Indies is indispensably necessary to us. Yet how to gain it when it is the established system of these nations to exclude all foreigners from their colonies. The only chance seems to be this.

Our commerce to the mother countries is valuable to them. We must endeav-our then to make this the price of an admission into their West Indies, and to those who refuse the admission we must refuse our commerce or load theirs by odious discrimination in our ports. We have this circumstance in our favor too that what one grants us in their islands the others will not find it worth their while to refuse. The misfortune is that with this country we gave this price for their aid in the war, and we have now nothing more to offer. She being withdrawn from the competition leaves Gr. Britain much more at liberty to hold out against us. This is the difficult part of the business of treaty, and I own it does not hold out the most flattering prospect.—I wish you would consider this subject and write me your thoughts on it. Mr. Gherry wrote me on the same subject. Will you give me leave to impose on you the trouble of communicating this to him? It is long, and will save me much labour in copying. I hope he will be so indulgent as to consider it as an answer to that part of his letter, and will give me his further thoughts on it.

Shall I send you so much of the Encyclopedie as is already published or reserve it here till you come? It is about 40. vols., which probably is about half the work. Give yourself no uneasiness about the money. Perhaps I may find it convenient to ask you to pay trifles occasionally for me in America. I sin-cerely wish you may find it convenient to come here. The pleasure of the trip will be less than you expect but the utility greater. It will make you adore your own country, it's soil, it's climate, it's equality, liberty, laws, people and man-ners. My god! How little do my countrymen know what precious blessings they are in possession of, and which no other people on earth enjoy. I con-fess I had no idea of it myself. While we shall see multiplied instances of Europeans going to live in America, I will venture to say no man now living will ever see an instance of an American removing to settle in Europe and continuing there. Come then and see the proofs of this, and on your return add your testimony to that of every thinking American, in order to satisfy our countrymen how much it is their interest to preserve uninfected by conta-gion those peculiarities in their government and manners to which they are indebted for these blessings. Adieu my dear friend. Present me affectionately to your collegues. If any of them think me worth writing to, they may be assured that in the epistolary account I will keep the debit side against them. Once more Adieu.

June 19.

Since writing the above we receive the following account. Monsr. Pilatre de Rosieres, who has been waiting some months at Boulogne for a fair wind to cross the channel, at length took his ascent with a companion. The wind changed after a while and brought him back on the French coast. Being at a height of about 6000 feet, some accident happened to his baloon or inflammable air, it burst, they fell from that height, and were crushed into atoms. There was a Montgolfier combined with the balloon of inflammable air. It is suspected the heat of the Montgolfier rarified too much the inflammable air of the other and occasioned it to burst. The Mongolfier came down in good order.

&

To Abigail Adams
DEAR MADAM   Paris June 21. 1785

I have received duly the honor of your letter, and am now to return your thanks for your condescension in having taken the first step for settling a correspondence which I so much desired; for I now consider it as settled and proceed accordingly. I have always found it best to remove obstacles first. I will do so therefore in the present case by telling you that I consider your boasts of the splendour of your city and of it's superb hackney coaches as a flout, and declaring that I would not give the polite, self-denying, feeling, hospitable, goodhumoured people of this country and their amability in every point of view, (tho' it must be confessed our streets are somewhat dirty, and our fiacres rather indifferent) for ten such races of rich, proud, hectoring, swearing, squibbing, carnivorous animals as those among whom you are; and that I do love this people with all my heart, and think that with a better religion and a better form of government and their present governors their condition and country would be most enviable. I pray you to observe that I have used the term people and that this is a noun of the masculine as well as feminine gender. I must add too that we are about reforming our fiacres, and that I expect soon an Ordonance that all their drivers shall wear breeches unless any difficulty should arise whether this is a subject for the

THE FIRST YEAR   41

police or for the general legislation of the country, to take care of. We have lately had an incident of some consequence, as it shews a spirit of treason, and audaciousness which was hardly thought to exist in this country. Some eight or ten years ago a Chevalier — was sent on a message of state to the princess of — of — of (before I proceed an inch further I must confess my profound stupidity; for tho' I have heard this story told fifty times in all it's circumstances, I declare I am unable to recollect the name of the ambassador, the name of the princess, and the nation he was sent to; I must therefore proceed to tell you the naked story, shorn of all those precious circumstances) some chevalier or other was sent on some business or other to some princess or other. Not succeeding in his negociation, he wrote on his return the following song.

[The song, in effect, offers half a kingdom (presumably the French) for half of the Princess's bed. Jefferson—and all Paris—knew perfectly well who the principals were: The Princess, Christine of Saxony, was the sister of the Hapsburg Emperor, Joseph II; the ambassador sent to her, one Chevalier de Boufflers.]

Ennivré de brillant poste
Que j'occupe récemment,
Dans une chaise de poste
Je me campe fierement:
Et je vais en ambassade
Au nom de mon souverain
Dire que je suis malade,
Et que lui se porte bien.

Avec une jou enflée
Je debarque tout honteux:
La princesse boursoufflée,
Au lieu d'une, en avoit deux;
Et son altesse sauvage
Sans doute a trouvé mauvais
Que j'eusse sur mon visage
La moitié de ses attraits.

Princesse, le roi mon maitre
M'a pris pour Ambassadeur;
Je viens vous faire connotrie
Quelle est pour vous son ardeur.
Quand vous seriez sous le chaume,
Il donneroit, m'a-il dit,
La moitié de son royaume
Pour celle de votre lit.

La princesse à son pupitre
Compose un remerciment:
Elle me donne une epitre
Que j'emporte lestement,
Et je m'en vais dans la rue
Fort satisfait d'ajouter
A l'honneur de l'avoir vue
Le plaisir de la quitter.

This song run through all companies and was known to every body. A book was afterwards printed, with a regular license, called 'Les quatres saisons litteraires' which being a collection of little things, contained this also, and all the world bought it or might buy it if they would, the government taking no notice of it. It being the office of the Journal de Paris to give an account and criticism of new publications, this book came in turn to be criticised by the redacteur, and he happened to select and print in his journal this song as a specimen of what the collection contained. He was seised in his bed that night and has been never since heard of. Our excellent journal de Paris then is suppressed and this bold traitor has been in jail now three weeks, and for ought any body knows will end his days there. Thus you see, madam, the value of energy in government; our feeble republic would in such a case have probably been wrapt in the flames of war and desolation for want of a power lodged in a single hand to punish summarily those who write songs. The fate of poor Pilatre de Rosiere will have reached you before this does, and with more certainty than we yet know it. This will damp for a while the ardor of the Phaetons of our race who are endeavoring to learn us the way to heaven on wings of our own. I took a trip yesterday to Sannois and commenced an acquaintance with the old Countess d'Hocquetout. I received much pleasure from it and hope it has opened a door of admission for me to the circle of literati with which she is environed. I heard there the Nightingale in all it's perfection: and I do not hesitate to pronounce that in America it would be deemed a bird of the third rank only, our mockingbird, and fox-coloured thrush being unquestionably superior to it. The squibs against Mr. Adams are such as I expected from the polished, mild tempered truth speaking people he is sent to. It would be ill policy to attempt to answer or refute them. But counter-squibs I think would be good policy. Be pleased to tell him that as I had before ordered his Madeira and Frontignac to be forwarded, and had asked his orders to Mr. Garvey as to the residue, which I doubt not he has given, I was afraid to send another order about the Bourdeaux lest it should produce confusion. In stating my accounts with the United States, I am at a loss whether to charge house rent or not. It has always been allowed to Dr. Franklin. Does Mr. Adams mean to charge this for Auteuil and London? Because if he does, I certainly will, being convinced by experience that my expences here will otherwise exceed my allowance. I ask this information of you, Madam, because I think you know better than Mr. Adams what may be necessary and right for him to do in occasions of this class. I will beg the favor of you to present my respects to Miss Adams. I have no secrets to communicate to her in cypher at this moment, what I write to Mr. Adams being mere commonplace stuff, not meriting a communication to the Secretary. I have the honour to be with the most perfect esteem Dr. Madam Your most obedient & most humble servt.,

—TH: JEFFERSON

To James Buchanan and William Hay
GENTLEMEN   Paris Aug. 13. 1785

Your favor of March 20. came to hand the 14th. of June, and the next day I wrote to you acknowleging the receipt, and apprising you that between the date and the 1st. of August it would be impossible to procure and get to your hands the draughts you desired. I did hope indeed to have had them prepared before this, but it will yet be some time before they will be in readiness. I flatter myself however they will give you satisfaction when you receive them and that you will think the object will not have been lost by the delay. I was a considerable time before I could find an architect whose taste had been formed on a study of the antient models of this art: the style of architecture in this capital being far from chaste. I at length heard of one, to whom I immediately addressed myself, and who perfectly fulfills my wishes. He has studied 20 years in Rome, and has given proofs of his skill and taste by a publication of some antiquities of this country. You intimate that you should be willing to have a workman sent to you to superintend the execution of this work. Were I to send one on this errand from hence, he would consider himself as the Superintendant of the Directors themselves and probably of the Government of the state also. I will give you my ideas of this subject. The columns of the building and the external architraves of the doors and windows should be of stone. Whether these are made here, or there, you will need one good stone-cutter, and one will be enough because, under his direction, negroes who never saw a tool, will be able to prepare the work for him to finish. I will therefore send you such a one, in time to begin work in the spring. All the internal cornices and other ornaments not exposed to the weather will be much handsomer, cheaper and more durable in plaister than in wood. I will therefore employ a good workman in this way and send him to you. But he will have no employment till the house is covered, of course he need not be sent till next summer. I will take him on wages so long beforehand as that he may draw all the ornaments in detail, under the eye of the architect, which he will have to execute when he comes to you. It will be the cheapest way of getting them drawn and the most certain of putting him in possession of his precise duty. Plaister will not answer for your external cornice, and stone will be too dear. You will probably find yourselves obliged to be contented with wood. For this therefore, and for your windowsashes, doors, forms, wainscoating &c. you will need a capital housejoiner, and a capital one he ought to be, capable of directing all the circumstances in the construction of the walls which the execution of the plans will require. Such a workman cannot be got here. Nothing can be worse done than the house-journey of Paris. Besides that his speaking the language perfectly would be essential. I think this character must be got from England. There are no workmen in wood in Europe comparable to those of England. I submit to you therefore the following proposition: to wit,

I will get a correspondent in England to engage a workman of this kind. I will direct him to come here, which will cost five guineas. We will make proof of his execution. He shall also make himself, under the eye of the architect, all the drawings for the building which he is to execute himself: and if we find him sober and capable, he shall be forwarded to you. I expect that in the article of the drawings and the cheapness of passage from France you will save the expence of his coming here. But as to this workman I shall do nothing unless I receive your commands. With respect to your stone work, it may be got much cheaper here than in England. The stone of Paris is very white and beautiful, but it always remains soft, and suffers from the weather. The cliffs of the Seine from hence to Havre are all of stone. I am not yet informed whether it is all liable to the same objections. At Lyons and all along the Rhone is a stone as beautiful as that of Paris, soft when it comes out of the quarry, but very soon becoming hard in the open air, and very durable. I doubt however whether the commerce between Virginia and Marseilles would afford opportunities of conveiance sufficient. It remains to be enquired what addition to the original cost would be made by the short land carriage from Lyons to the Loire and the water transportation down that to Bourdeaux, and also whether a stone of the same quality may not be found on the Loire. In this and all other matters relative to your charge you may command my services freely.

—TH: JEFFERSON

To Eliza House Trist
DEAR MADAM   Paris Aug. 18. 1785

Your favor of Dec. 25. came to hand on the 22d. of July, and on the next day I had the pleasure of receiving that of May. 4. I was happy to find that you had taken the first step for a return to your own country, tho' I was sensible many difficult ones still remained. I hope however these are surmounted, and that this letter will find you in the bosom of your friends. Your last letter is an evidence of the excellence of your own dispositions which can be so much excited by so small a circumstance as the one noticed in it. Tho' I esteem you too much to wish you may ever need services from me or any other person, yet I wish you to be assured that in such an event no one would be more disposed to render them, nor more desirous of receiving such a proof of your good opinion as would be your applying for them. By this time I hope your mind has felt the good effects of time and occupation. They are slow physicians indeed, but they are the only ones. Their opiate influence lessens our sensibility tho their power does not extend to dry up the sources of sorrow. I thought there was a prospect the last winter of my taking a trip to England. Tho' I did not know who and where were Browse's relations in that country, yet I knew he had some so nearly connected as to claim their attention. I should have endeavored to have seen them, and disposed them to feel an interest both in you and him. Tho' the probability of my going there is very much lessened, yet it is not among impossible events. Will you be so good as to let me know what relations he has there and where they live, and if I should at any time go there I will certainly see them. Patsy is well, and is happily situated in the Convent of Panthemont the institutions of which leave me nothing to wish on that head. It is attended by the best masters. The most disagreeable circumstance is that I have too little of her company. I am endeavoring by some arrangements to alter this. My present anxiety is to get my other daughter over to me: for tho' my return is placed at a period not very distant, yet I cannot determine to leave her so long without me. But indeed the circumstances of such a passage, to such an infant, under any other care than that of a parent, are very distressing. My wishes are fixed, but my resolution is wavering.

I am much pleased with the people of this country. The roughnesses of the human mind are so thoroughly rubbed off with them that it seems as if one might glide thro' a whole life among them without a justle. Perhaps too their manners may be the best calculated for happiness to a people in their situation. But I am convinced they fall far short of effecting a happiness so temperate, so uniform and so lasting as is generally enjoyed with us. The domestic bonds here are absolutely done away. And where can their compensation be found? Perhaps they may catch some moments of transport above the level of the ordinary tranquil joy we experience, but they are separated by long intervals during which all the passions are at sea without rudder or compass. Yet fallacious as these pursuits of happiness are, they seem on the whole to furnish the most effectual abstraction from a contemplation of the hardness of their government. Indeed it is difficult to conceive how so good a people, with so good a king, so well disposed rulers in general, so genial a climate, so fertile a soil, should be rendered so ineffectual for producing human happiness by one single curse, that of a bad form of government. But it is a fact. In spite of the mildness of their governors the people are ground to powder by the vices of the form of government. Of twenty millions of people supposed to be in France I am of opinion there are nineteen millions more wretched, more accursed in every circumstance of human existence, than the most conspicuously wretched individual of the whole United states.—I beg your pardon for getting into politics. I will add only one sentiment more of that character. That is, nourish peace with their persons, but war against their manners. Every step we take towards the adoption of their manners is a step towards perfect misery.—I pray you to write to me often. Do not you turn politician too; but write me all the small news; the news about persons and not about states. Tell me who die, that I may meet these disagreeable events in detail, and not all at once when I return: who marry, who hang themselves because they cannot marry &c. &c. Present me in the most friendly terms to Mrs. House, and Browse, and be assured of the sincerity with which I am Dear Madam your affectionate friend & servant,

—TH: JEFFERSON

CHAPTER TWO

Jefferson the Mentor

THE EDUCATION OF THE YOUNG IS ONE OF THE PRINCIPAL THEMES IN JEFFERSON'S work and thought, something he returned to again and again during his life. He himself was as well-educated as any man in America, certainly as well-read. He could not live without books, he once told John Adams. The love of knowledge comes for him just after the love of country. In fact the two are related. He believed that education was indispensable to liberty. As he put it in 1816, in a letter to Col. Charles Yancey, "If a nation expects to be ignorant and free, in a state of civilization, it expects what never was and never will be." When he drafted his "Bill for the More General Diffusion of Knowledge" for the Virginia legislature in 1779, he wrote in its preamble that even under the most liberal forms of government "those entrusted with power have, in time, and by slow operations, perverted it into tyranny," and that the best way to prevent this was "to illuminate, as far as practicable, the minds of the people at large." He fought for a free press as a means of such illumination, but he also knew that a free press was meaningless if people could not read. The bill in question was a proposal to establish what we would now call primary schools all over the state, to make sure that people could read and write. He wanted to use these schools, furthermore, not only to make the population at large fully literate, but also to find and nurture talent, selecting the top scholars from each school for higher education at the state's expense. Education was for him schooling for liberty, at all levels, for the people and for those talented souls who would become its leaders. His role in founding the University of Virginia late in his life was of a piece with this goal.

He did not stop thinking about the education of the young in France. Seeing what happened to young men in French society, in fact, deepened his views on the subject. At the time it was not unusual for upper-class Americans to send their sons to Europe for education and seasoning. He came to feel this was a mistake, and he argues forcefully against it in these letters. He had the example of William Short before him in his own household. Short was in his early 20s when he arrived in Paris. He was apparently a genial, charming young man and Jefferson became very fond of him. But he clearly did not approve of Short's love affair with Rosalie, the pretty young wife of his friend the Duke de Rochefoucauld-Liancourt. He does not name Short when he lists the dangers of a Continental education for young American men, but he must have had him in mind. Even before this affair developed, Short had become involved with the daughter of a family with whom he boarded in Saint-Germain-en-Laye, a suburb of Paris, to improve his French.

But Jefferson is nothing if not contradictory. He found the life led by his aristocratic friends extremely attractive. He very much liked them, he was comfortable in their company, and while he had trouble with the casualness with which they regarded marital fidelity, he himself had his own "affair" with a married woman while in France. When young Americans did come to France, he introduced them to the most illustrious of his friends, sent them enthusiastically on tours of the country, gave them entrée to the salons, even to the court. Jefferson the idealist lived inside Jefferson the lover of talk and wit, the genial host, the wine lover, the art lover—all attributes he enlarged and developed in France. His warnings to the young did not apply to himself: Thomas Jefferson returned to America completely versed in European culture and society.

The letters largely speak for themselves. Most of them are well-known. One written to Patsy, his oldest daughter, when he was away from Paris on his trip to the south of France outlines as well as any he ever wrote his views on the role in life a young American woman should prepare for: a traditional role. He was no revolutionary when it came to the position of women in society. Like most of the founding fathers, he believed that, as William Howard Adams put it, "women carried the entire burden of the family and, by extension, social harmony." Women should learn to sew, therefore, because they ought to have something to do with their hands while sitting through tea, say, with dull people. He was liberal enough with his own daughter, to be sure, to insist that Patsy stick to her Livy, which she found hard to read. (Later she confessed to her father that she never did get through that particular Roman historian.) But he is much more interested that Patsy learn to play the harpsichord, to sew, to draw—in short, to please. It would never have occurred to him to envision a political role for her.

The other well-known letters were written to one of his nephews Peter Carr, whose education he regarded as his personal responsibility; to the younger Thomas Mann Randolph, then in Edinburgh, who would later marry Patsy and become his son-in-law; and to John Banister, Jr., the son of Ann Blair, an old friend from Williamsburg. Banister was in France for his health, living in Avignon at the time. Jefferson did what he could for him. Another example he might have used of the dangers of Europe for young American men, Banister ran up serious debts in Paris—very easy to do, living the high life. His health did not improve. He died soon after he returned to America.

It would be interesting to know what effect Jefferson's advice had on the young people who received it. The reading he recommends to them is truly formidable. An education in the classics was common among the American elite of the time, but Jefferson goes well beyond the standard curriculum. It's clear, furthermore, that Jefferson himself had read everything he recommends: all the classics, all the political philosophy, the law, the history, both ancient and modern. Then he goes on to recommend that these young people walk two hours a day, every day, no matter what the weather. These letters are not just about education; they're about how to live as well. But who, without being Jefferson, could follow in his footsteps? Who has that much self-discipline? It must have been intimidating to have Thomas Jefferson as a mentor.

⁂

To Peter Carr
DEAR PETER   Paris Aug. 19. 1785

I received by Mr. Mazzei your letter of April 20. I am much mortified to hear that you have lost so much time, and that when you arrived in Williamsburgh you were not at all advanced from what you were when you left Monticello. Time now begins to be precious to you. Every day you lose, will retard a day your entrance on that public stage whereon you may begin to be useful to yourself. However the way to repair the loss is to improve the future time. I trust that with your dispositions even the acquisition of science is a pleasing employment. I can assure you that the possession of it is what (next to an honest heart) will above all things render you dear to your friends, and give you fame and promotion in your own country. When your mind shall be well improved with science, nothing will be necessary to place you in the highest points of view but to pursue the interests of your country, the interests of your friends, and your own interests also with the purest integrity, the most chaste honour. The defect of these virtues can never be made up by all the other acquirements of body and mind. Make these then your first object. Give up money, give up fame, give up science, give the earth itself and all it contains rather than do an immoral act. And never suppose that in any possible situation or under any circumstances that it is best for you to do a dishonourable thing however slightly so it may appear to you. Whenever you are to do a thing tho' it can never be known but to yourself, ask yourself how you would act were all the world looking at you, and act accordingly. Encourage all your virtuous dispositions, and exercise them whenever an opportunity arises, being assured that they will gain strength by exercise as a limb of the body does, and that exercise will make them habitual. From the practice of the purest virtue you may be assured you will derive the most sublime comforts in every moment of life and in the moment of death. If ever you find yourself environed with difficulties and perplexing circumstances, out of which you are at a loss how to extricate yourself, do what is right, and be assured that that will extricate you the best out of the worst situations. Tho' you cannot see when you fetch one step, what will be the next, yet follow truth, justice, and plain-dealing, and never fear their leading you out of the labyrinth in the easiest manner possible. The knot which you thought a Gordian one will untie itself before you. Nothing is so mistaken as the supposition that a person is to extricate himself from a difficulty, by intrigue, by chicanery, by dissimulation, by trimming, by an untruth, by an injustice. This increases the difficulties ten-fold, and those who pursue these methods, get themselves so involved at length that they can turn no way but their infamy becomes more exposed. It is of great importance to set a resolution, not to be shaken, never to tell an untruth. There is no vice so mean, so pitiful, so contemptible and he who permits himself to tell a lie once, finds it much easier to do it a second and third time, till at length it becomes habitual, he tells lies without attending to it, and truths without the world's beleiving him. This falsehood of the tongue leads to that of the heart, and in time depraves all it's good dispositions.

An honest heart being the first blessing, a knowing head is the second. It is time for you now to begin to be choice in your reading, to begin to pursue a regular course in it and not to suffer yourself to be turned to the right or left by reading any thing out of that course. I have long ago digested a plan for you, suited to the circumstances in which you will be placed. This I will detail to you from time to time as you advance. For the present I advise you to begin a course of antient history, reading every thing in the original and not in translations. First read Goldsmith's history of Greece. This will give you a digest view of the feild. Then take up antient history in the detail, reading the following books in the following order. Herodotus. Thucydides. Xenophontis helenica. Xenophontis Anabasis. Quintus Curtius. Justin. This shall form the first stage of your historical reading, and is all I need mention to you now. The next will be of Roman history. From that we will come down to Modern history. In Greek and Latin poetry, you have read or will read at school Virgil, Terence, Horace, Anaceron, Theocritus, Homer. Read also Milton's paradise lost, Ossian, Pope's works, Swift's works in order to form your style in your own language. In morality read Epictetus, Xenophontis memorabilia, Plato's Socratic dialogues, Cicero's philosophies. In order to assure a certain progress in this reading, consider what hours you have free from the school and the exercise; for health must not be sacrificed to learning. A strong body makes the mind strong. As to the species of exercise, I advise the gun. While this gives a moderate exercise to the body, it gives boldness, enterprize, and independance to the mind. Games played with the ball and others of that nature, are too violent for the body and stamp no character on the mind. Let your gun therefore be the constant companion of your walks. Never think of taking a book with you. The object of walking is to relax the mind. You should therefore not permit yourself even to think while you walk. But divert your attention by the objects surrounding you. Walking is the best possible exercise. Habituate yourself to walk very far. The Europeans value themselves on having subdued the horse to the uses of man. But I doubt whether we have not lost more than we have gained by the use of this animal. No one has occasioned so much the degeneracy of the human body. An Indian goes on foot nearly as far in a day, for a long journey, as an enfeebled white does on his horse, and he will tire the best horses. There is no habit you will value so much as that of walking far without fatigue. I would advise you to take your exercise in the afternoon. Not because it is the best time for exercise for certainly it is not: but because it is the best time to spare from your studies; and habit will soon reconcile it to health, and render it nearly as useful as if you gave to that the more precious hours of the day. A little walk of half an hour in the morning when you first rise is adviseable also. It shakes off sleep, and produces other good effects in the animal oeconomy. Rise at a fixed and an early hour, and go to bed at a fixed and an early hour also. Sitting up late at night is injurious to the health, and not useful to the mind.—Having ascribed proper hours to exercise, divide what remain (I mean of your vacant hours) into three portions. Give the principal to history, the other two, which should be shorter, to Philosophy and Poetry. Write me once every month or two and let me know the progress you make. Tell me in what manner you employ every hour in the day. The plan I have proposed for you is adapted to your present situation only. When that is changed, I shall propose a corresponding change of plan. I have ordered the following books to be sent to you from London to the care of Mr. Madison. [Not James Madison, but the Rev. James Madison, who taught at Williamsburg.] Herodotus. Thucydides. Xenophon's Hellenics, Anabasis, and Memorabilia. Cicero's works. Baretti's Spanish and English dictionary. Martin's philosophical grammar and Martin's philosophia Britannica. I will send you the following from hence. Bezout's mathematics. De la Lande's astronomy. Muschenbroek's physics. Quintus Curtius. Justin, a Spanish grammar, and some Spanish books. You will observe that Martin, Bezout, De la Lande and Muschenbroek are not in the preceding plan. They are not to be opened till you go to the University. You are now I expect learning French. You must push this: because the books which will be put into your hands when you advance into Mathematics, Natural philosophy, Natural history, &c. will be mostly French, these sciences being better treated by the French than the English writers. Our future connection with Spain renders that the most necessary of the modern languages, after the French. When you become a public man you may have occasion for it, and the circumstance of your possessing that language may give you a preference over other candidates. I have nothing further to add for the present, than to husband well your time, cherish your instructors, strive to make every body your friend, & be assured that nothing will be so pleasing, as your success, to Dear Peter yours affectionately,

—TH: JEFFERSON

✑

To Walker Maury, with a List of Books
DEAR SIR   Paris Aug. 19. 1785

I received your favor on April 20. by Mr. Mazzei on the 22d. of July. I am much
obliged to you for your kind attention to my nephew. His education is one of
the things about which I am most anxious. I think he posseses that kind of genius
which will be solid and useful to himself and his country. When I came here I
was not certain whether I might not find it better to send for him hither. But
I am thoroughly cured of that Idea. Of all the errors which can possibly be committed in the education of youth, that of sending them to Europe is the most
fatal. I see [clearly] that no American should come to Europe under 30 years of
age: and [he who] does, will lose in science, in virtue, in health and in happiness,
for which manners are a poor compensation, were we even to admit the hollow,
unmeaning manners of Europe to be preferable to the simplicity and sincerity
of our own country. I am well pleased with your having taken my nephew
among your private pupils. I would have him lose no advantage on account of
any difference in expence. His time begins now to be precious, and every
moment [may] be valued in money, as it will retard or hasten the period when
he may enter on the stage whereon he may begin to reap the benefit of his
talents and acquirements. My intention had been that he should learn French
and Italian, of the modern languages. But the latter must be given up (for the
present at least) and Spanish substituted in it's place. I have ordered some books
to be [sent] him from London. Among these is a Spanish Dictionary. I shall
send him [so]me others from hence, among which shall be a Spanish grammar
and other b[ooks] for his reading in that language. I will point out to him from
time to time [the] course of reading I would wish him to pursue and take care
to send him the [nece]ssary books, so far as he happens not to possess them.
According to yo[ur des]ire I note hereon such French writers as I suppose might
possibly come within [the pla]n you mention. I have inserted several books of
American travels th[inking] they will be a useful species of reading for an
American youth. In ge[neral] you may estimate 12mos. at $2^1/2$. livres, 8vos. at 5.
or 6 livres, 4tos. at [10? or] 15 livres, folios at 25 or 30 livres, remembering that we
call a [half] crown is 6. livres. Where these prices are departed from, I have note[d]

cost as I have found in my own purchases. Books cost here bu[t] two thirds or three fourths of what they do in England. I must except Greek, Latin, and English books. The latter of course are much dearer here [because they] are first bought in England. If I can be useful to you in pr[ocuring any] thing in this way I shall do it with pleasure. After running [thro the stocks] of many booksellers, and suffering, numberless cheats, I have at length [found] one who serves me very honestly, and finds whatever I want at the [best] prices. I need not repeat to you Sir how much you will oblige me [by your] friendly counsels to my nephew, for the preservation of his morals and improvement of his mind. I am with much esteem Dear Sir Your most obedt. humble servt.,

—TH: JEFFERSON

❧

To John Banister, Jr.
DEAR SIR   Paris Oct. 15, 1785

I should sooner have answered the paragraph in your favor of Sep. 19 respecting the best seminary for the education of youth in Europe, but that it was necessary for me to make enquiries on the subject. The result of these has been to consider the competition as resting between Geneva and Rome. They are equally cheap, and probably are equal in the course of education pursued. The advantage of Geneva is that students acquire there the habits of speaking French. The advantages of Rome are the acquiring a local knowlege of a spot so classical and so celebrated; the acquiring the true pronuntiation of the Latin language; the acquiring a just taste in the fine arts, more particularly those of painting, sculpture, Architecture, and Music; a familiarity with those objects and processes of agriculture which experience has shewn best adapted to a climate like ours; and lastly the advantage of a fine climate for health. It is probable too that by being boarded in a French family the habit of speaking that language may be obtained. I do not count on any advantage to be derived in Geneva from a familiar acquaintance with the principles of it's government. The late revolution has rendered it a tyrannical aristocracy more likely to give ill than good ideas to an American. I think the balance in favor of Rome. Pisa is sometimes spoken of as a place of education. But it does not offer the 1st. and 3d. of the advantages of Rome. But why send an American youth to Europe for education? What are the objects of an useful American education? Classical knowlege, modern languages and chiefly French, Spanish, and Italian; Mathematics; Natural philosophy; Natural History; Civil History; Ethics. In Natural philosophy I mean to include Chemistry and Agriculture, and in Natural history to include Botany as well as the other branches of those departments. It is true that the habit of speaking the modern languages cannot be so well acquired in America, but every other article can be as well acquired at William and Mary College as at any place in Europe. When College education is done with and a young man is to prepare himself for public life, he must cast his eyes (for America) either on Law or Physic. For the former where can he apply so advantageously as to Mr. Wythe? [*George Wythe had been Jefferson's mentor in the law at William and Mary, and the two were longstanding friends.*] For the latter he must come to Europe; the medical class of students therefore is the only one which need come to Europe. Let us view the disadvantages of sending a youth to Europe. To enumerate them all would require a volume. I will select a few. If he goes to England he learns drinking, horse-racing and boxing. These are the peculiarities of English education. The following circumstances are common to education in that and the other countries of Europe. He acquires a fondness for European luxury and dissipation and a contempt for the simplicity of his own country; he is fascinated with the privileges of the European aristocrats, and sees with abhorrence the lovely equality which the poor enjoys with the rich in his own country: he contracts a partiality for aristocracy or monarchy; he forms foreign friendships which will never be useful to him, and loses the season of life for forming in his own country those friendships which of all others are the most faithful and permanent: he is led by the strongest of all the human passions into a spirit for female intrigue destructive of his own and others happiness, or a passion for whores destructive of his health, and in both cases learns to consider fidelity to the marriage bed as an ungentlemanly practice and inconsistent with happiness: he recollects the voluptuary dress and arts of the European women and pities and despises the chaste affections and simplicity of those of his own country; he retains thro' life a fond recollection and a hankering after those places which were the scenes of his first pleasures and of his first connections; he returns to his own country, a foreigner, unacquainted with the practices of domestic economy necessary to preserve him from ruin; speaking and writing his native tongue as a foreigner, and therefore unqualified to obtain those distinctions which eloquence of the pen and tongue ensures in a free country; for I would observe to you that what is called style in writing or speaking is formed very early in life while the imagination is warm, and impressions are permanent. I am of the opinion that there never was an instance of a man's writing or speaking his native tongue with elegance who passed from 15. to 20. years of age out of the country where it was spoken. Thus no instance exists of a person writing two languages perfectly. That will always appear to be his native language which was most familiar to him in his youth. It appears to me then that an American coming to Europe for education loses in his knowledge, in his morals, in his health, in his habits, and in his happiness. I had entertained only doubts on this head before I came to Europe: what I see and hear since I come here proves more than I had even suspected. Cast your eye over America: who are the men of most learning, of most eloquence, most beloved by their country and most trusted and promoted by them? They are those who have been educated among them, and whose manners, morals and habits are perfectly homogeneous with those of the country.— Did you expect by so short a question to draw such a sermon on yourself? I dare say you did not. But the consequences of foreign education are alarming to me as an American. I sin therefore through zeal whenever I enter on the subject. You are sufficiently American to pardon me for it. Let me hear of your health and be assured of the esteem with which I am Dear Sir Your friend & servant,

—TH: JEFFERSON

❧

To Thomas Mann Randolph, Jr.
[Randolph, who would become his son-in-law, was then studying in Edinburgh.]
DEAR SIR   Paris Aug. 27. 1786

I am honoured with your favour of the 16th. instant, and desirous, without delay, of manifesting my wishes to be useful to you, I shall venture to you some thoughts on the course of your studies which must be submitted to the better advice with which you are surrounded. A longer race through life may have enabled me to seise some truths which have not yet been presented to your observation. A more intimate knowledge of the country in which you are to live and of the circumstances in which you will be placed, may enable me to point your attention to the branches of science which will administer the most to your happiness there. The foundation which you have laid in languages and mathematics are proper for every superstructure. The former exercises our memory while that and no other faculty is yet matured, and prevents our acquiring habits of idleness; the latter gives exercise to our reason, as soon as that has acquired a certain degree of strength, and stores the mind with truths which are useful in other branches of science. At this moment then a second order of preparation is to commence. I shall propose to you that it be extensive, comprehending Astronomy, Natural history, Anatomy, Botany and Chemistry. No inquisitive mind will be content to be ignorant of any one of these branches. But I would advise you to be contented with a course of lectures in most of them, without attempting to make yourself completely master of the whole. This is more than any genius, joined to any length of life is equal to. You will find among them some one study to which your mind will more particularly attach itself. This then I would pursue and propose to attain eminence in. Your own country furnishes the most aliment for Natural history, Botany and Physics, and as you express a fondness for the former you might make it your principal object, endeavouring however to make myself more acquainted with the two latter than with other branches likely to be less useful. In fact you will find botany offering it's charms to you at every step, during summer, and Physics in every season. All these branches of science will be better attained by attending courses of lectures in them; you are now in a place where the best courses upon earth are within your reach, and being delivered in your native language, you lose no part of their benefit. Such an opportunity you will never again have. I would therefore strongly press on you to fix no other limitation to your stay in Edinburgh, than your having got thro this whole circle. The omission of any one part of it will be an affliction and a loss to you as long as you live. Besides the comfort of knowledge, every science is auxiliary to every other. While you are attending these courses you can proceed by yourself in a regular series of historical reading. It would be a waste of time to attend a professor of this. It is to be acquired from books, and if you pursue it by yourself, you can accommodate it to your other reading so as to fill up those chasms of time not otherwise appropriated. There are portions of the day too when the mind should be eased. Particularly after dinner it should be applied to lighter occupations. History is of this kind. It exercises principally the memory. Reflection also indeed is necessary, but not generally in a laborious degree. To conduct yourself in this branch of science you have only to consider what areas of it merit a general and what a particular attention, and in each aera also to distinguish between the countries the knowlege of whose history will be useful, and those where it suffices only to be not altogether ignorant. Having laid down your plan as to the branches of history you would pursue, the order of time will be your sufficient guide. After what you have read in Antient history, I should suppose Millot's digest would be useful and sufficient. The histories of Greece and Rome are worthy a good degree of attention. They should be read in the original authors. The transition from Antient to modern history will be best effected by reading Gibbons, then a general history of the principal states of Europe, but particular ones of England. Here too the original writers are to be preferred. Kennet published a considerable collection of these in 3. vols. folio but there are some others, not in his collection, well worth being read. After the history of England, that of America will claim your attention. Here too original authors, and not compilers, are best. An author who writes of his own times, or of times near his own, presents in his own ideas and manner the best picture of the moment of which he writes. History need not be hurried, but may give way to the other sciences; because history can be pursued after you shall have left your present situation, as well as while you remain in it.

When you shall have got thro' this second order of preparation, the study of the law is to be begun. This, like history, is to be acquired from books. All the aid you will want will be a catalogue of the books to be read, and the order in which they are to be read. It being absolutely indifferent in what place you carry on this reading, I should propose your doing it in France. The advantages of this will be that you will at the same time acquire the habit of speaking French which is the object of a year or two, you may be giving attention to such of the fine arts as your taste may lead you to, and you will be forming an acquaintance with the individuals and character of a nation with whom we must long remain in the closest intimacy, and to whom we are bound by the strong ties of gratitude and policy; a nation in short of the most amiable dispositions on earth, the whole mass of which is penetrated with an affection for us. You might, before your return to your own country, make a visit to Italy also.

I should have performed the office of but half a friend were I to confine myself to the improvement of the mind only. Knowlege indeed is a desireable, a lovely possession, but I do not scruple to say that health is more so. It is of little consequence to store the mind with science if the body be permitted to become debilitated. If the body be feeble, the mind will not be strong. The sovereign invigorator of the body is exercise, and of all the exercises walking is best. A horse gives but a kind of half exercise, and a carriage is no better than a cradle. No one knows, till he tries, how easily a habit of walking is acquired. A person who never walked three miles will in the course of a month become able to walk 15. or 20. without fatigue. I have known some great walkers and had particular accounts of many more; and I never knew or heard of one who was not healthy and long lived. This species of exercise therefore is much to be advised. Should you be disposed to try it, as your health has been feeble, it will be necessary for you to begin with a little, and to increase it by degrees. For the same reason you must probably at first ascribe to it hours the most precious for study, I mean those about the middle of the day. But when you shall find yourself strong, you may venture to take your walks in the evening after the digestion of the dinner is pretty well over. This is making a composition between health and study. The latter would be too much interrupted were you to take from it the early hours of the day, and habit will soon render the evening's exercise as salutary as that of the morning. I speak this from my own experience, having, from an attachment to study, very early in life, made this arrangement of my time, having ever observed it, and still observing it, and always with perfect success. Not less than two hours a day should be devoted to exercise, and the weather should be little regarded. A person not sick will not be injured by getting wet. It is but taking a cold bath, which never gives a cold to any one. Brute animals are the most healthy, and they are exposed to all weather, and of men, those are healthiest who are the most exposed. The recipe of those two descriptions of beings is simple diet, exercise and the open air, be it's state what it will; and we may venture to say that this recipe will give health and vigor to every other description. —By this time I am sure you will think I have sermonized enough. I have given you indeed a lengthy lecture. I have been led through it by my zeal to serve you; if in the whole you find one useful counsel, that will be my reward and a sufficient one. Few persons in your own country have started from as advantageous ground as that whereon you will be placed. Nature and fortune have been liberal to you. Every thing honourable or profitable there is placed within your own reach, and will depend on your own efforts. If these are exerted with assiduity, and guided by unswerving honesty, your success is infallible: and that it may be as great as you wish is the sincere desire of, Dear Sir, your most affectionate humble servant,

—TH: JEFFERSON

P.S. Be so good as to present me affectionately to your brother and cousin.

❧

To Martha Jefferson   Aix en Provence March. 28. 1787

I was happy, my dear Patsy, to receive, on my arrival here, your letter informing me of your health and occupations. I have not written to you sooner because I have been almost constantly on the road. My journey hitherto has been a very pleasing one. It was undertaken with the hope that the mineral waters of this place might restore strength to my wrist. [Jefferson had injured his right wrist badly the previous fall.] Other considerations also concurred. Instruction, amusement, and abstraction from business, of which I had too much at Paris. I am glad to learn that you are employed in things new and good in your music and drawing. You know what have been my fears for some time past; that you do not employ yourself so closely as I could wish. You have promised me a more assiduous attention, and I have great confidence in what you promise. It is your future happiness which interests me, and nothing can contribute more to it (moral rectitude always excepted) than the contracting a habit of industry and activity. Of all the cankers of human happiness, none corrodes it with so silent, yet so baneful a tooth, as indolence. Body and mind both unemployed, our being becomes a burthen, and every object about us loathsome, even the dearest. Idleness begets ennui, ennui the hyphochondria, and that a diseased body. No laborious person was ever yet hysterical. Exercise and application produce order in our affairs, health of body, chearfulness of mind, and these make us precious to our friends. It is while we are young that the habit of industry is formed. If not then, it never is afterwards. The fortune of our lives therefore depends on employing well the short period of youth. If at any moment, my dear, you catch yourself in idleness, start from it as you would from the precipice of a gulph. You are not however to consider yourself as unemployed while taking exercise. That is necessary for your health, and health is the first of all objects. For this reason if you leave your dancing master for the summer, you must increase your other exercise. I do not like your saying that you are unable to read the antient print of your Livy, but with the aid of your master. We are always equal to what we undertake with resolution. A little degree of this will enable you to decypher your Livy. If you always lean on your master, you will never be able to proceed without him. It is a part of the American character to consider nothing as desperate; to surmount every difficulty by resolution and contrivance. In Europe there are shops for every want. It's inhabitants therefore have no idea that their wants can be furnished otherwise. Remote from all other aid, we are obliged to invent and execute; to find means within ourselves, and not to lean on others. Consider therefore the conquering your Livy as an exercise in the habit of surmounting difficulties, a habit which will be necessary to you in the country where you are to live, and without which you will be thought a very helpless animal, and less esteemed. Music, drawing, books, invention and exercise will be so many resources to you against ennui. But there are others which to this object add that of utility. These are the needle, and domestic economy. The latter you cannot learn here, but the former you may. In the country life of America there are many moments when a woman can have recourse to nothing but her needle for employment. In a dull company and in dull weather for instance. It is ill manners to read; it is ill manners to leave them; no card playing there among genteel people; that is abandoned to blackguards. The needle then is a valuable resource. Besides without knowing to use it herself, how can the mistress of a family direct the works of her servant? You ask me to write you long letters. I will do it my dear, on condition you will read them from time to time, and practice what they will inculcate. Their precepts will be dictated by experience, by a perfect knowledge of the situation in which you will be placed, and by the fondest love for you. This it is which makes me wish to see you more qualified than common. My expectations from you are high: yet not higher than you may attain. Industry and resolution are all that are wanting. No body in this world can make me so happy, or so miserable as you. Retirement from public life will ere long become necessary for me. To your sister and yourself I look to render the evening of my life serene and contented. It's morning has been clouded by loss after loss till I have nothing left but you. I do not doubt either your affection or dispositions. But great exertions are necessary, and you have little time left to make them. Be industrious then, my dear child. Think nothing insurmountable by resolution and application, and you will be all that I wish you to be. You ask me if it is my desire you should dine at the abess's table? It is. Propose it as such to Madame de Traubenheim with my respectful compliments and thanks for her care of you. Continue to love me with all the warmth with which you are beloved by, my dear Patsy, yours affectionately,

—TH: JEFFERSON

From Martha Jefferson
MY DEAR PAPA   Panthemont, April 9th, 1787

I am very glad that the beginning of your voyage has been so pleasing, and I hope that the rest will not be less so, as it is a great consolation for me, being deprived of the pleasure of seeing you, to know at least that you are happy. I hope your resolution of returning in the end of April is always the same. I do not doubt but what Mr. Short has written you word that my sister sets off with Fulwar Skipwith in the month of May, and she will be here in July. Then, indeed, shall I be the happiest of mortals; united to what I have the dearest in the world, nothing more will be requisite to render my happiness complete. I am not so industrious as you or I would wish, but I hope that in taking pains I very soon shall be. I have already begun to study more. I have not heard any news of my harpsichord; it will be really very disagreeable if it is not here before your arrival. [Jefferson had ordered a harpsichord made for his daughter in London; it took a long time to arrive.] I am learning a very pretty thing now, but it is very hard. I have drawn several little flowers, all alone, that the master even has not seen; indeed, he advised me to draw as much alone as possible, for that is of more use than all I could do with him. I shall take up my Livy, as you desire it. I shall begin it again, as I have lost the thread of the history. As for the hysterics, you may be quiet on that head, as I am not lazy enough to fear them. Mrs. Barett has wanted me out, but Mr. Short told her that you had forgotten to tell Madame L'Abbesse to let me go out with her. There was a gentleman, a few days ago, that killed himself because he thought that his wife did not love him. They had been married ten years. I believe that if every husband in Paris was to do as much, there would be nothing but widows left. I shall speak to Madame Thaubeneu about dining at the Abbess's table. As for needlework, the only kind that I could learn here would be embroidery, indeed netting also; but I could not do much of those in America, because of the impossibility of having proper silks; however, they will not be totally useless. You say your expectations for me are high, yet not higher than I can attain. Then be assured, my dear papa, that you shall be satisfied in that, as well as in any thing else that lies in my power; for what I hold most precious is your satisfaction, indeed I should be miserable without it. You wrote me a long letter, as I asked you; however it would have been much more so without so wide a margin. Adieu, my dear papa. Be assured of the tenderest affection of your loving daughter,

—M JEFFERSON

Pray answer me very soon—a long letter, without a margin. I will try to follow the advise they contain with the most scrupulous exactitude.

✑

To Peter Carr, with Enclosure
DEAR PETER   Paris Aug. 10. 1787

I have received your two letters of Decemb. 30. and April 18. and am very happy to find by them, as well as by letters from Mr. Wythe, that you have been so fortunate as to attract his notice and good will: I am sure you will find this to have been one of the most fortunate events of your life, as I have ever been sensible it was of mine. I inclose you a sketch of the sciences to which I would wish you to apply in such order as Mr. Wythe shall advise: I mention also the books in them worth your reading, which submit to his correction. Many of these are among your father's books, which you should have brought to you. As I do not recollect those of them not in his library, you must write to me for them, making out a catalogue of such as you think you shall have occasion for in 18 months from the date of your letter, and consulting Mr. Wythe on the subject. To this sketch I will add a few particular observations.

    1. Italian. I fear the learning this language will confound your French and Spanish. Being all of them degenerated dialects of the Latin, they are apt to

mix in conversation. I have never seen a person speaking the three languages who did not mix them. It is a delightful language, but late events having rendered the Spanish more useful, lay it aside to prosecute that.

2. Spanish. Bestow great attention on this, and endeavor to acquire an accurate knowlege of it. Our future connections with Spain and Spanish America will render that language a valuable acquisition. The antient history of a great part of America too is written in that language. I send you a dictionary.

3. Moral philosophy. I think it lost time to attend lectures in this branch. He who made us would have been a pitiful bungler if he had made the rules of our moral conduct a matter of science. For one man of science, there are thousands who are not. What would have become of them? Man was destined for society. His morality therefore was to be formed to this object. He was endowed with a sense of right and wrong merely relative to this. This sense is as much a part of his nature as the sense of hearing, seeing, feeling; it is the true foundation of morality, and not the truth [Jefferson spells it in Greek here, too], &c., as fanciful writers have imagined. The moral sense, or conscience, is as much a part of man as his leg or arm. It is given to all human beings in a stronger or weaker degree, as force of members is given them in a greater or less degree. It may be strengthened by exercise, as may any particular limb of the body. This sense is submitted indeed in some degree to the guidance of reason; but it is a small stock which is required for this: even a less one than what we call Common sense. State a moral case to a ploughman and a professor. The former will decide it as well, and often better than the latter, because he has not been led astray by artificial rules. In this branch therefore read good books because they will encourage as well as direct your feelings. The writings of Sterne particularly form the best course of morality that ever was written. [Jefferson was a great fan of Laurence Sterne's writings and knew them well.] Besides these read the books mentioned in the inclosed paper; and above all things lose no occasion of exercising your dispositions to be grateful, to be generous, to be charitable, to be humane, to be true, just, firm, orderly, couragious &c. Consider every act of this kind as an exercise which will strengthen your moral faculties, and increase your worth.

4. Religion. Your reason is now mature enough to receive this object. In the first place divest yourself of all bias in favour of novelty and singularity of opinion. Indulge them in any other subject rather than that of religion. It is

too important, and the consequences of error may be too serious. On the other hand shake off all the fears and servile prejudices under which weak minds are servilely crouched. Fix reason firmly in her seat, and call to her tribunal every fact, every opinion. Question with boldness even the existence of a god; because, if there be one, he must more approve the homage of reason, than that of blindfolded fear. You will naturally examine first the religion of your own country. Read the bible then, as you would read Livy or Tacitus. The facts which are within the ordinary course of nature you will believe on the authority of the writer, as you do those of the same kind in Livy and Tacitus. The testimony of the writer weighs in their favor in one scale, and their not being against the laws of nature does not weigh against them. But those facts in the bible which contradict the laws of nature, must be examined with more care, and under a variety of faces. Here you must recur to the pretensions of the writer to inspiration from god. Examine upon what evidence his pretensions are founded, and whether that evidence is so strong as that it's falshood would be more improbable than a change of the laws of nature in the case he relates. For example in the book of Joshua we are told the sun stood still several hours. Were we to read that fact in Livy or Tacitus we should class it with their showers of blood, speaking of statues, beasts &c., but it is said that the writer of that book was inspired. Examine therefore candidly what evidence there is of his having been inspired. The pretension is entitled to your enquiry, because millions believe it. On the other hand you are Astronomer enough to know how contrary it is to the law of nature that a body revolving on it's axis, as the earth does, should have stopped, should not by that sudden stoppage have prostrated animals, trees, buildings, and should after a certain time have resumed it's revolution, and that without a second general prostration. Is this arrest of the earth's motion, or the evidence which affirms it, most within the law of probabilities? You will next read the new testament. It is the history of a personage called Jesus. Keep in your eye the opposite pretensions. 1. Of those who say he was begotten by god, born of a virgin, suspended and reversed the laws of nature at will, and ascended bodily into heaven: and 2. of those who say he was a man, of illegitimate birth, of a benevolent heart, enthusiastic mind, who set out without pretensions to divinity, ended in believing them, and was punished capitally for sedition by being gibbeted according to the Roman law which punished the first commission of that offence by whipping, and the second by exile or death in furcâ. See this law in the Digest Lib. 48. tit. 19 § 28. 3. and Lipsius Lib. 2. de cruce. cap. 2. These questions are examined in the books I have mentioned under the head of religion, and several others. They will assist you in your enquiries, but keep your reason firmly on the watch in reading them all. Do not be frightened from this enquiry by any fear of it's consequences. If it ends in a belief that there is no god, you will find incitements to virtue in the comfort and pleasantness you feel in it's exercise, and the love of others which it will procure you. If you find reason to believe there is a god, a consciousness that you are acting under his eye, and that he approves you, will be a vast additional incitement. If that there be a future state, the hope of a happy existence in that increases the appetite to deserve it; if that Jesus was also a god, you will be comforted by a belief of his aid and love. In fine, I repeat that you must lay aside all prejudice on both sides, and neither believe nor reject any thing because any other person, or description of persons have rejected or believed it. Your own reason is the only oracle given you by heaven, and you are answerable not for the rightness but uprightness of the decision. —I forgot to observe when speaking of the New testament that you should read all the histories of Christ, as well of those whom a council of ecclesiastics have decided for us to be Pseudo-evangelists, as those they named Evangelists, because these Pseudo-evangelists pretended to inspiration as much as the others, and you are to judge their pretensions by your own reason, and not by the reason of those ecclesiastics. Most of these are lost. There are some however still extant, collected by Fabricius which I will endeavor to get and send you.

5. Travelling. This makes men wiser, but less happy. When men of sober age travel, they gather knowlege which they may apply usefully for their country, but they are subject ever after to recollections mixed with regret, their affections are weakened by being extended over more objects, and they learn new habits which cannot be gratified when they return home. Young men who travel are exposed to all these inconveniences in a higher degree, to others still more serious, and do not acquire that wisdom for which a previous foundation is requisite by repeated and just observations at home. The glare of pomp and pleasure is analogous to the motion of their blood, it absorbs all their affection and attention, they are torn from it as from the only good in this world, and return to their home as to a place of exile and condemnation. Their

eyes are for ever turned back to the object they have lost, and it's recollection poisons the residue of their lives. Their first and most delicate passions are hackneyed on unworthy objects here, and they carry home only the dregs, insufficient to make themselves or any body else happy. Add to this that a habit of idleness, an inability to apply themselves to business is acquired and renders them useless to themselves and their country. These observations are founded in experience. There is no place where your pursuit of knowlege will be so little obstructed by foreign objects as in your own country, nor any wherein the virtues of the heart will be less exposed to be weakened. Be good, be learned, and be industrious, and you will not want the aid of travelling to render you precious to your country, dear to your friends, happy within yourself. I repeat my advice to take a great deal of exercise, and on foot. Health is the first requisite after morality. Write to me often and be assured of the interest I take in your success, as well as of the warmth of those sentiments of attachment with which I am, dear Peter, your affectionate friend,

—TH: JEFFERSON

P.S. Let me know your age in your next letter. Your cousins here are well and desire to be remembered to you.

CHAPTER THREE

The Labyrinth of Diplomacy

A YEAR OR SO AFTER HIS ARRIVAL IN PARIS, JEFFERSON MOVED FROM HIS PREVIOUS address to a house known as the Hôtel de Langeac, just off the Champs-Elysées, close to what were then the Paris city limits. The house, neoclassical in design, was larger than his previous house without being grand. Behind it was what Jefferson called a "clever" garden in the English style, then fashionable in France. A minister to the previous king Louis XV had built it for a mistress. Always the architect, Jefferson had the interior altered somewhat to suit his needs. The man who complained of the costs of his "outfit" seldom hesitated to spend money when it suited him. He spent the next four years in this house, however, and one can hardly blame him for wanting to be comfortable.

Jefferson had settled in by now. Lafayette, in Paris, was a friend from Revolutionary days and introduced Jefferson to his own circle of friends. He was a passionate admirer of America and Americans, and he worked all through Jefferson's stay in France on behalf of American interests. Lafayette introduced Jefferson to his aunt, Madame de Tesse—who became a good friend and whose salon he frequented—and also to the Duc de la Rouchefoucauld-Liancourt. The latter introduced Jefferson to Condorcet and invited him and Short to his mother's chateau La Roche-Guyon from time to time. Others introduced Jefferson to the salon of Madame Helvetius, who had been Benjamin Franklin's favorite hostess. (Indeed, he had wanted to marry her.)

Dumas Malone, one of Jefferson's biographers, makes the point that Jefferson did not became as beloved among the French as Franklin had been. Jefferson was always more serious, busier, not nearly as sly as the elder statesman. But over his five years there he made a great many friends, among them some of the most interesting and distinguished men and women in French society. He also took a great deal of delight in the pleasures of Paris—plays, comedies, music, food, and wine—and in French manners, which he wished he could import to the United States.

Jefferson printed his Notes on the State of Virginia during his first year in Paris. He had written it four years earlier in response to a series of questions sent to people in all 13 states by the secretary of the French legation to the United States, the Marquis de Barbe-Marbois. Jefferson was the only person to write a book-length reply. He was in no hurry to get it published. The printing—200 copies—was private and not for sale; he distributed it to a few influential people in France, sent a copy to Adams in England, and shipped more to trustworthy friends in America. The book contains animadversions on American slavery, and he was worried it would make him enemies throughout the South—as to some extent it did. Receiving his copy, Charles Thomson, then presiding over Congress, wrote presciently to Jefferson that "This is a cancer that we must get rid of. It is a blot in our character that must be wiped out. If it cannot be done by religion, reason and philosophy, confident I am that it will one day be by blood."

Jefferson never wanted his book published any more widely, but he was forced into it. A copy got into the hands of a French printer, and he became alarmed that a bad translation would appear, which the English would at once translate back even worse. He thereupon arranged for a friend, the Abbé Morrelet, to translate the book into French. Unhappy with the Abbé's treatment of the text, Jefferson enlarged it a bit, ordered a map made to accompany the edition, and had it printed in England.

It would not have occurred to Jefferson that he might make money on the book. His idea was that he would send some of these copies to his alma mater William and Mary College in Williamsburg for the use of students. For all his eloquence, Jefferson had little interest in making a mark as an author. One might even argue that he found that kind of ambition distasteful. When he first went to France it was not generally known that he was the author of the Declaration of Independence; indeed this fact was not widely known even in America.

His concern about the fate of his book crops up from time to time in the following letters, but I have not made it a major theme in this collection. In the first half of 1786 he also went to a great deal of trouble to correct the mistakes made by a young man named Jean Nicolas Demeunier in his contribution, not to Diderot's great Encyclopedie, but to the Encyclopedie Méthodique, its successor. Demeunier had written a long section on the United States, basing his observations on those of Buffon and the Abbé

Raynal, whose works denigrated the New World at large and America in particular. The animals in America, for example, were supposed to be smaller than those of Europe, the Indians less charged with sexual energy than the people of Europe, the climate more humid, the number of species fewer, and the whole thing—the discovery of America, that is—a kind of mistake. Jefferson's corrections, covering mostly the political aspects of Demeunier's manuscript, run to the size of a large pamphlet and are not reprinted here. We do reprint, however, several letters relaying his concerns about Buffon's denigration of American animals. Jefferson went to a great deal of trouble and spent his own money to get examples of American elk, deer, and moose bones and skins to Europe so he could personally show Buffon that it simply wasn't true: that there was nothing inferior, in size or any other feature, about American wildlife. At the time, no American had ever seen a grizzly bear, or Jefferson might well have sent an example of that animal, too. Here also, to complete that thread, is more of his correspondence about the Virginia Capitol. He had to write Madison frantically to stop the Virginians from building a Capitol much inferior to the copy of the Maison Carrée in Nimes that he had chosen. This chapter also includes a few of the letters on shopping that he exchanged with Abigail Adams and her daughter Abby in London, a letter to David Rittenhouse that speculates on the location of fossil seashells, and one or two others.

But the bulk of this section of the book deals with Jefferson's strenuous, fruitless efforts to negotiate, in company with John Adams, a trade agreement with Portugal, to improve trade agreements with the French, and to ransom the 21 men from two American ships taken by one of the Barbary states, Algiers, about a year after he arrived in France. This kind of work was what Jefferson was in Europe to do in the first place, and for all its futility it occupied a great deal of his time. It is fascinating to read about the difficulties involved in diplomatic work, the slow pace at which it proceeds, and the numerous contending interests that have to be satisfied.

Jefferson's diplomatic efforts were germane to more than just the prosperity of American merchants. At this infantile stage in its history, the United States was the weakest of powers, hardly a nation at all. It had no effective executive power, no navy, no army. In their trade relationships, the various states did not act in concert. They opened or closed their ports in competition with each other, and they raised or lowered duties for the same reason, thereby discouraging their European trading partners from making deals of any kind. The country had no money to pay its debts to the Dutch bankers who had financed its future. It could not even make interest payments on the debts owed to the French officers who had served in America during the Revolution and who had been promised pay for those services. In one of the letters, Jefferson has to explain to Madison why European investors would have no interest in investing in American canal projects. The French government, he points out, was also in somewhat dire straits financially at the time. They made quarterly interest payments with what he calls "religious punctuality," sweetening their borrowings with "douceurs," or gifts. The debt lay in Europe, not 3,000 miles away, in a country that allowed its debts to languish unpaid for years. Faced with such a choice, who would want to invest in America?

And why would a European government want to make a trade agreement with the United States? Indeed, with whom would they be making it? New Hampshire but not Massachusetts? Virginia but not New York? Adams and Jefferson thought they had accomplished one success by negotiating an agreement with the Portuguese in London— but in the end, the Portuguese government refused to sign it. The Barbary states wanted to treat with the United States, but that meant they expected the country to do what all the European powers did: Give them large sums of money annually to keep them from seizing their merchant ships. The British simply refused to treat with the United States at all. After a year or so of frustration and insults in London, John Adams just wanted to go home. The French were of course friendly and the count de Vergennes, the principal minister, was an intelligent, capable man who understood that trade with America could be advantageous to both countries. But even after years of work, during which Vergennes unfortunately died, Jefferson was only able to obtain small concessions for American merchants—and he never broke the tobacco monopoly.

The fate of American trade was tied up, in fact, with the fate of the new American government. We see this in the correspondence, especially the letters between Jefferson and Madison and Jefferson and John Jay. America was waking up to the fact that without a unified trade policy, the confederacy itself could not survive. In 1786 Madison tried to assemble a "commerce convention" in Annapolis to rewrite the Articles of Confederation and unify the country's trade policies. This convention, like Congress itself on so many occasions, failed to gather a quorum. But it led to the Constitutional Convention of 1787, and we catch a glimpse of the beginnings of this process in Madison's letters to Jefferson in this chapter. No one would argue that the Constitution as we have it was simply the product of an attempt to fix the country's trade problems. Many people had come to recognize that the Articles of Confederation were unworkable for a lot of reasons. But it sheds new light on this period to watch Jefferson struggle with the situation created by his own government's lack of effectiveness, and lack of respect, in the courts and salons of Europe. He must have felt like a minnow among whales.

The most interesting problem he had, and perhaps the most illustrative of his own powerlessness, was the problem with the Barbary states. The first capture of an American ship took place when the so-called Sallee Rovers of Morocco took a ship named the Betsey in 1784. The Emperor of Morocco returned the ship and its crew as a gesture of good-will. But a year later, in the summer of 1785, two Algerine ships captured two more American ships, the Dauphin and the Maria, and demanded ransom. Jefferson spent four years trying to find a way to get the 21 crew members of the two ships home. The problem, once again, was the weakness of the American government and its lack of funds. Congress could pay only a very small amount to ransom these captives. The Algerines expected a great deal more. The result was a stalemate. American sailors became slaves. American ship captains, thanks to their rank, languished in Algerine castles, half guests, half prisoners. For the Americans, both war and ransom were too expensive. During George Washington's Presidency, the United States finally started paying tribute to the Barbary states in an amount equivalent to 15 percent of the nation's annual budget. During his Presidency, Jefferson fought an indecisive war with these states. Not until 1815 did the United States finally bring the Algerines to their knees. A year later, a joint Dutch-British bombardment of Algiers ended the problem for good.

The important correspondence about the Barbary states situation presented here includes the affecting letters from Richard O'Brien, one of the American captains kept prisoner by the Algerines. In March 1786, Adams asked Jefferson to London to help negotiate the trade agreement with Portugal, as well as an agreement—i.e., an annual tribute—with the roving ambassador from Tripoli. The agreement with Portugal was concluded while Jefferson was in London, but the talks with the ambassador from Tripoli went nowhere and the English court was barely civil to Jefferson. Adams had had some slight indication that the English at last might be willing to talk trade, but it proved illusory, as seen in correspondence here. Not included here are the notes Jefferson made on a trip he took with Adams to some of the most notable gardens in England. They had nothing to do while they waited for a response to their overtures from the English government, and the trip lasted about two weeks. Jefferson took with him a copy of Thomas Whately's Observations on Modern Gardening, which describes many of the gardens Jefferson visited. Jefferson's notes are brief, cryptic, and constitute in effect nothing more than footnotes to Whately's book. Adams reports in his diary that they also visited Stratford-on-Avon, Shakespeare's birthplace. At the house where Shakespeare was supposed to have been born, he writes, "They showed us an old wooden chair in the chimney corner where he sat. We cut off a chip according to custom …. The curse upon him who should remove his bones, which is written on his gravestone, alludes to a pile of some thousands of human bones which lie exposed in that church .... His name is not even on his gravestone." You have to wonder how many visitors cut off a chip from the chair before the owners of the house replaced it with another.

⧏

To James Monroe
DEAR SIR   Paris Aug. 28. 1785

I wrote you on the 5th. of July by Mr. Franklin and on the 12th. of the same month by Monsr. Houdon. Since that date yours of June 16. by Mr. Mazzei is received. Every thing looks like peace here. The settlement between the Emperor and the Dutch is not yet published, but it is believed to be agreed. Nothing is done as yet between him and the Porte. He is much wounded by the Confederation of several of the Germanic body at the head of which is the king of Prussia, and to which the king of England as elector of Hanover is believed to accede. The object is to preserve the constitution of that empire. It shews that these princes entertain serious jealousies of the ambition of the emperor, and this will very much endanger the election of his nephew as king of the Romans. A late arret of this court against the admission of British manufactures produces a great sensation in England. I wish it may produce a disposition there to receive our commerce in all their dominions on advantageous terms. This is the only balm which can heal the wounds that has recieved. It is but too true that that country furnished markets for three fourths of the exports of the eight northernmost states, a truth not proper to be spoken of, but which should influence our proceedings with them. How that negociation advances you are probably better informed than I am. The infidelity of the post offices rendering the communication between Mr. Adams and myself difficult, the improvement of our commerce with France will be advanced more by negociations at Saint James's than at Versailles.

The July French packet being arrived without bringing any news of Mr. Lambe [the American sent by Congress to negotiate the release of the Algerine captives], if the English one of the same month be also arrived without news of him, I expect Mr. Adams will concur with me in sending some other person to treat with the Barbary states. Mr. Barclay is willing to go, and I have proposed him to Mr. Adams but have not yet received his answer. The peace expected between Spain and Algiers will probably not take place. It is said the former was to have given a million of dollars. Would it not be prudent to send a minister to Portugal? Our commerce with that country is very important, perhaps more so than with any other country in Europe. It is possible too that they might permit our whaling vessels to refresh in Brazil or give some other indulgencies in America. The lethargic character of their ambassador here gives a very unhopeful aspect to a treaty on this ground. I lately spoke with him on the subject and he has promised to interest himself in obtaining an answer from his court.

I have waited to see what was the pleasure of Congress as to the secretary-ship of my office here; that is, to see whether they proposed to appoint a secretary of legation, or leave me to appoint a private secretary. Colo. Humphrey's occupation in the dispatches and records of the matters which relate to the general commissions does not afford him leisure to aid me in my office, were I entitled to ask that, and, in the mean time the lengthy papers which often accompany the communications between the ministers here and myself, and the other business of the office absolutely require a scribe. I shall therefore on Mr. Short's return from the Hague appoint him my private secretary till Congress shall think proper to signify their pleasure. The salary allowed Mr. Franklin in the same office was 1000 Dollars a year. I shall presume that Mr. Short may draw the same allowance from the funds of the U.S. here. As soon as I shall have made this appointment I shall give official notice of it to Mr. Jay, that Congress may, if they disapprove of it, say so.

I am much pleased with your land ordinance, and think it improved from the first in the most material circumstances. I had mistaken the object of the division of the lands among the states. I am sanguine in my expectations of lessening our debts by this fund, and have expressed my expectations to the minister and others here. I see by the public papers you have adopted the dollar as your money unit. In the arrangement of coins I had proposed, I ought to have inserted a gold coin of 5. dollars, which being within $2/3$ of the value of a guinea will be very convenient. The English papers so incessantly repeating their lies about the tumults, the anarchy, the bankruptcies and distresses of America, these ideas prevail very generally in Europe. At a large table where I dined the other day, a gentleman from

Switzerland expressed his apprehensions for the fate of Doctr. Franklin as he said he had been informed he would be received with stones by the people who were generally dissatisfied with the revolution and incensed against all those who had assisted in bringing it about. I told him his apprehensions were just, and that the people of America would probably salute Dr. Franklin with the same stones as they had thrown at the Marquis Fayette. The reception of the Doctor is an object of very general attention, and will weigh in Europe as an evidence of the satisfaction or dissatisfaction of America with their revolution. As you are to be in Williamsburgh early in November, this is the last letter I shall write you till about that time; I am with very sincere esteem Dr. Sir Your friend & servt.,

—TH: JEFFERSON

℘

To Chastellux
[Chastellux was one of the major-generals who fought under Rochambeau during the American Revolution. He was a friend of Jefferson's, having spent some time at Monticello on his travels around America. His book Travels in North America in the Years 1780, 1781 and 1782 is very complimentary to Jefferson.]
DEAR SIR   Paris Sep. 2. 1785

You were so kind as to allow me a fortnight to read your journey through Virginia. But you should have thought of this indulgence while you were writing it, and have rendered it less interesting if you meant that your readers should have been longer engaged with it. In fact I devoured it at a single meal, and a second reading scarce allowed me sang froid enough to mark a few errors in the names of persons and places which I note on a paper herein inclosed, with an inconsiderable error or two in facts which I have also noted because I supposed you wished to state them correctly. From this general approbation however you must allow me to except about a dozen pages in the earlier part of the book which I read with a continued blush from beginning to end, as it presented me a lively picture of what I wish to be, but am not. No, my dear Sir, the thousand millionth part of what you there say, is more than I deserve. It might perhaps have passed in Europe at the time you wrote it, and the exaggeration might not have been detected. But consider that the animal is now brought there, and that every one will take his dimensions for himself. The friendly complexion of your mind has betrayed you into a partiality of which the European spectator will be divested. Respect to yourself therefore will require indispensably that you expunge the whole of those pages except your own judicious observations interspersed among them on Animal and physical subjects. With respect to my countrymen there is surely nothing which can render them uneasy, in the observations made on them. They know that they are not perfect, and will be sensible that you have viewed them with a philanthropic eye. You say much good of them, and less ill than they are conscious may be said with truth. I have studied their character with attention. I have thought them, as you found them, aristocratical, pompous, clannish, indolent, hospitable, and I should have added, disinterested, but you say attached to their interest. This is the only trait in their character wherein our observations differ. I have always thought them so careless of their interests, so thoughtless in their expences and in all their transactions of business that I had placed it among the vices of their character, as indeed most virtues when carried beyond certain bounds degenerate into vices. I had even ascribed this to it's cause, to that warmth of their climate which unnerves and unmans both body and mind. While on this subject I will give you my idea of the characters of the several states.

In the North they are
cool
sober
laborious
persevering
independent
jealous of their own liberties, and just to
those of others
interested
chicaning
superstitious and hypocritical in their

religion.
In the South they are
fiery
Voluptuary
indolent
unsteady
independent
zealous for their own liberties, but trampling on those of others
generous
candid.
without attachment or pretentions to any
religion but that of the heart.

These characteristics grow weaker and weaker by gradation from North to South and South to North, insomuch that an observing traveller, without the aid of the quadrant may always know his latitude by the character of the people among whom he finds himself. It is in Pennsylvania that the two characters seem to meet and blend and to form a people free from the extremes both of vice and virtue. Peculiar circumstances have given to New York the character which climate would have given had she been placed on the South instead of the North side of Pennsylvania. Perhaps too other circumstances may have occasioned in Virginia a transplantation of a particular vice foreign to it's climate. You could judge of this with more impartiality than I could, and the probability is that your estimate of them is the most just. I think it for their good that the vices of their character should be pointed out to them that they may amend them; for a malady of either body or mind once known is half cured.

I wish you would add to this piece of your letter to Mr. Madison on the expediency of introducing the arts into America. I found in that a great deal of matter, very many observations, which would be useful to the legislators of America, and to the general mass of citizens. I read it with great pleasure and analysed it's contents that I might fix them in my own mind. I have the honor to be with very sincere esteem Dear Sir Your most obedient & most humble servt.,

—TH: JEFFERSON

ℋ

To Abigail Adams
DEAR MADAM   Paris Sep. 4. 1785

I was honoured with your letter of Aug. 21. by Mr. Smith who arrived here on
the 29th. I am sorry you did not repeat the commission you had favoured me with
by Mr. Short as the present would have been an excellent opportunity of sending
the articles you wished for. As Mr. Short's return may yet be delayed, will you be
so good as to write me by post what articles you desired, lest I should not otherwise know in time to send them by either of the Mr. Smiths. The French packet
brought me letters from Mr. Jay and Dr. Ramsay only. They were dated July 13. They
do not mention the arrival of your son. Dr. Ramsay's letter was on a particular
subject, and Mr. Jay's letter was official. He may have arrived therefore, tho these
letters do not mention it. However as he did not sail till June, and Westernly
winds prevail in the summer I think the 13th. of July was too early to expect him
to have arrived. I will certainly transmit you information of his arrival the moment
I know it.

    We have little new and interesting here. The Queen has determined to wear
none but French gauzes hereafter. How many English looms will this put down?
You will have seen the affair of the Cardinal de Rohan so well detailed in the Leyden
gazette that I add nothing on that head. [This was the "Affair of the Diamond
Necklace," in which the cardinal was duped by an impecunious adventuress into trying to
sell the queen a necklace. She had not ordered it, but he was told she had. Even though the
queen was a victim in this case, the story highlighted her endless appetite for "luxure" and
was a factor in the decline of the French monarchy before the Revolution.] The Cardinal
is still in the Bastille. It is certain that the Queen has been compromitted without the smallest authority from her: and the probability is that the Cardinal has
been duped into it by his mistress Madme. de la Motte. There results from this
two consequences not to his honour, that he is a debauchee, and a booby. The Abbés
are well. They have been kept in town this summer by the affairs of the Abbé Mably.
I have at length procured a house in a situation much more pleasing to me than
my present. It is at the grille des champs Elysees, but within the city. It suits me
in every circumstance but the price, being dearer than the one I am now in. It has
a clever garden to it. I will pray you to present my best respects to Miss Adams

and to be assured of the respect & esteem with which I have the honour to be Dear Madam Your most obedient & most humble servt.,

—TH: JEFFERSON

∽

To Charles Bellini
DEAR SIR   Paris Sep. 30. 1785

Your estimable favour covering a letter to Mr. Mazzei came to hand on the 26th. inst. The letter to Mr. Mazzei was put into his hands in the same moment, as he happened to be present. I leave to him to convey to you all his complaints, as it will be more agreeable to me to express to you the satisfaction I received on being informed of your perfect health. Tho' I could not receive the same pleasing news of Mrs. Bellini, yet the philosophy with which I am told she bears the loss of health is a testimony the more how much she deserved the esteem I bear her.—Behold me at length on the vaunted scene of Europe! It is not necessary for your information that I should enter into details concerning it. But you are perhaps curious to know how this new scene has struck a savage of the mountains of America. Not advantageously I assure you. I find the general fate of humanity here most deplorable. The truth of Voltaire's observation offers itself perpetually, that every man here must be either the hammer or the anvil. It is a true picture of that country to which they say we shall pass hereafter, and where we are to see god and his angels in splendor, and crouds of the damned trampled under their feet. While the great mass of the people are thus suffering under physical and moral oppression, I have endeavored to examine more nearly the condition of the great, to appreciate the true value of the circumstances in their situation which dazzle the bulk of the spectators, and especially to compare it with that degree of happiness which is enjoyed in America by every class of people. Intrigues of love occupy the younger, and those of ambition the more elderly part of the great. Conjugal love having no existence among them, domestic happiness, of which that is the basis, is utterly unknown. In lieu of this are substituted pursuits which nourish and invigorate all our bad passions, and which offer only moments of extasy amidst days and months of restlessness and torment. Much, very much inferior this to the tranquil permanent felicity with which domestic society in America blesses most of it's inhabitants, leaving them to follow steadily those pursuits which health and reason approve, and rendering truly delicious the intervals of these pursuits. In science, the mass of people is two centuries behind ours, their literati half a dozen years before us. Books, really good, acquire just reputation in that time, and so become known to us and communicate to us all their advances in knowlege. Is not this delay compensated by our being placed out of the reach of that swarm of nonsense which issues daily from a thousand presses and perishes almost in issuing? With respect to what are termed polite manners, without sacrificing too much the sincerity of language, I would wish my countrymen to adopt just so much of European politeness as to be ready to make all those little sacrifices of self which really render European manners amiable, and relieve society from the disagreeable scenes to which rudeness often exposes it. Here it seems that a man might pass a life without encountering a single rudeness. In the pleasures of the table they are far before us, because with good taste they unite temperance. They do not terminate the most sociable meals by transforming themselves into brutes. I have never yet seen a man drunk in France, even among the lowest of the people. Were I to proceed to tell you how much I enjoy their architecture, sculpture, painting, music, I should want words. It is in these arts they shine. The last of them particularly is an enjoiment, the deprivation of which with us cannot be calculated. [*Jefferson was immensely fond of music.*] I am almost ready to say it is the only thing which from my heart I envy them, and which in spight of all the authority of the decalogue I do covet.—But I am running on in an estimate of things infinitely better known to you than to me, and which will only serve to convince you that I have brought with me all the prejudices of country, habit and age ....

—TH: JEFFERSON

∽

To James Madison
DEAR SIR   Fontainebleau Oct. 28. 1785

Seven o'clock, and retired to my fireside, I have determined to enter into conversation with you; this is a village of about 5,000 inhabitants when the court is not here and 20,000 when they are, occupying a valley thro' which runs a brook, and on each side of it a ridge of small mountains most of which are naked rock. The king comes here in the fall always, to hunt. His court attend him, as do also the foreign diplomatic corps. But as this is not indispensably required, and my finances do not admit the expence of a continued residence here, I propose to come occasionally to attend the king's levees, returning again to Paris, distant 40 miles. This being the first trip, I set out yesterday morning to take a view of the place. For this purpose I shaped my course towards the highest of the mountains in sight, to the top of which was about a league. As soon as I had got clear of the town I fell in with a poor woman walking at the same rate with myself and going the same course. Wishing to know the condition of the laboring poor I entered into conversation with her, which I began by enquiries for the path which would lead me into the mountain: and thence proceeded to enquiries into her vocation, condition and circumstance. She told me she was a day labourer, at 8. sous or 4 d. sterling the day; that she had two children to maintain, and to pay a rent of 30 livres for her house (which would consume the hire of 75 days), that often she could get no emploiment, and of course was without bread. As we had walked together near a mile and she had so far served me as a guide, I gave her, on parting 24 sous. She burst into tears of a gratitude which I could perceive was unfeigned, because she was unable to utter a word. She had probably never before received so great an aid. This little attendrissement, with the solitude of my walk led me into a train of reflections on that unequal division of property which occasions the numberless instances of wretchedness which I had observed in this country and is to be observed all over Europe. The property of this country is absolutely concentered in a very few hands, having revenues of from half a million of guineas a year downwards. These employ the flower of the country as servants, some of them having as many as 200 domestics, not labouring. They employ also a great number of manufacturers, and tradesmen, and lastly the class of labouring husbandmen. But after all these comes the most numerous of all the classes, that is, the poor who cannot find work. I asked myself what could be the reason that so many should be permitted to beg who are willing to work, in a country where there is a very considerable proportion of uncultivated lands? These lands are kept idle mostly for the sake of game. It should seem then that it must be because of the enormous wealth of the proprietors which places them above attention to the increase of their revenues by permitting these lands to be laboured. I am conscious that an equal division of property is impracticable. But the consequences of this enormous inequality producing so much misery to the bulk of mankind, legislators cannot invent too many devices for subdividing property, only taking care to let their subdivisions go hand in hand with the natural affections of the human mind. The descent of property of every kind therefore to all the children, or to all the brothers and sisters, or other relations in equal degree is a politic measure, and a practicable one. [In Virginia, years before, Jefferson had been the sponsor of a bill to ban primogeniture, the system by which the oldest son was the only person able to inherit an estate.] Another means of silently lessening the inequality of property is to exempt all from taxation below a certain point, and to tax the higher portions of property in geometrical progression as they rise. Whenever there is in any country, uncultivated lands and unemployed poor, it is clear that the laws of property have been so far extended as to violate natural right. The earth is given as a common stock for man to labour and live on. If, for the encouragement of industry we allow it to be appropriated, we must take care that other employment be furnished to those excluded from the appropriation. If we do not the fundamental right to labour the earth returns to the unemployed. It is too soon yet in our country to say that every man who cannot find employment but who can find uncultivated land, shall be at liberty to cultivate it, paying a moderate rent. But it is not too soon to provide by every possible means that as few as possible shall be without a little portion of land. The small landholders are the most precious part of a state .... [Jefferson concludes this letter by passing on to the subject of fruits and the difference between those he finds in France and those in America.]

—TH: JEFFERSON

☙

To John Jay, with Report on Conversations with Vergennes
SIR   Paris January 2. 1786

Several Conferences and Letters having passed between the Count de Vergennes and myself on the Subject of the Commerce of this Country with the U.S. I think them sufficiently interesting to be communicated to Congress. They are stated in the Form of a Report and are herein inclosed. [This letter, with its accompanying report, illustrates as well as anything the difficulties Jefferson faced in negotiating trade agreements in Europe, particularly the fact that the separate American states tended to act on their own, regardless of the provisions of the Articles of Confederation, so that it became impossible to write a treaty with the United States that would apply in all states.] The Length of this Despatch perhaps needs Apology. Yet I have not been able to abridge it without omitting Circumstances which I thought Congress would rather chuse to know. Some of the Objects of these Conferences present but small Hopes for the present, but they seem to admit a Possibility of Success at some future Moment.

The inclosed Letter from the Baron Thulemeyer will inform you of the Ratification by the King of Prussia, of the Treaty concluded with him. My Answer accompanies it. I have no Doubt but you have long ago recieved Notice of this from Mr. Adams whose Opportunities of conveying Letters are so much more frequent than mine, especially since the French Packets have been nearly discontinued. Mr. Crevecoeur is labouring to re-establish them, and under some Hopes of Success.

From Mr. Adams you have doubtless been also notified of the Overtures from Portugal to trade with us at London. We are probably indebted for this new Spur towards us to the commercial Arrangements which are on the Tapis between France and England, and I think it fortunate that they have chosen to commit the Negociation to their Minister in London rather than to their Ambassador here, whose torpid Character would probably have spun it to a great Length.

I communicated to the Count de Vergennes according to your Commands the Report of Capt. Shaw's Voiage to China, making at the same time those Acknolegements which were due for these new Proofs of the Friendship of the French Nation towards us. I inclose you my Letter and his Answer, whereby you will see that he thought it a proper Occasion to express the Dissatisfaction of this Court with the Acts of some of the American Legislatures on the Subject of foreign Commerce, and to hint that their Continuance would render Measures necessary here to countervail the Inequalities they supposed us to be establishing. I also inclose my Reply, and have now the Honor to submit those Transactions to the Consideration of Congress, who are best able to calculate the Result of such a commercial Contest, should it arise, and who will be so good as to instruct me as to their Pleasure herein, as an Answer will be expected by this Court, within such Time as they think reasonable. I have been long in conveying this Correspondence to you. But I have never since it was closed, had a confidential Opportunity of transmitting it, and am now obliged to trust it with the other Despatches enclosed, to a Gentleman going to London who promises to seek a safe Conveiance from thence to New York. I send you at the same Time the Arrets of Aug. 30. 1784. Sept. 18. and 25. 1785. which were spoken of in my Letter.

Having observed by the Journals of Congress that the Establishment of a Mint has been under their Consideration, I send a late Declaration of the King by which will be seen the Proportion between the Value of Gold and Silver as newly established here.

My former Letters will have notified to you Mr. Lambe's Departure for Algiers. I have recieved no Letter from him since he left this Place. We know only that he was at Madrid on the 10th. of December.

When Mr. Barclay was on the point of setting out for Morocco, Mr. Beaumarchais (who had hitherto declined settling with him) tendered him a Settlement of his Accounts. The immense Amount of these Accounts, with the Hope that they would not occupy much Time, and a Persuasion that no Man on Earth could so well settle them as Mr. Barclay, who is intimately acquainted with many of the Transactions on which they are founded, induced me to think the Interests of the U.S. would not suffer so much by a short Delay of the Journey to Morocco, from whence nothing disagreeable was to be immediately apprehended, as they would suffer by leaving such Accounts as these to be settled by Persons less competent; I advised Mr. Barclay to proceed to the Settlement. I wrote to Mr. Adams asking his Opinion thereon, and to Mr. Carmichael praying him to find Means of making known to the Emperor of Morocco that a Negociator was actually commissioned and would soon proceed to his Court. Mr. Adams concurred with me in Opinion, and those Accounts are now in such Forwardness that Mr. Barclay assures me he shall be able to set out the ensuing Week. I inclose two Letters from Capt. Stevens one of our Captives at Algiers to Mr. Harrison of Cadiz, which were forwarded to me by Mr. Carmichael.

I have taken Opportunities of speaking with the Chevr. de la Luzerne on the Subject of his Return to America, and to press it by all those Inducements which Assurances of the Esteem entertained for him there were likely to excite. He told me there was no Place he would prefer to America for the Exercise of his Functions, but he said with great Candor, that as in the diplomatic Line there are different Grades of Emploiment, and that an Advancement from one to the other of these was usual, he wished if possible to avail himself of present Circumstances to obtain a Promotion. I suppose in Fact that if he can be sent to London in the Room of the Count d'Adhemar, or to Holland in the Room of the Marquis de Verac, who wishes to be translated to London, as these are Embassies, he will not in either of those Cases return to America. In the mean Time the Emoluments of his Office are, as I suspect, rendered necessary to him by the Expences he incurred in America.

From your Favor of Nov. 2. by Mr. Houdon, which I recieved three Days ago, it would seem that an Estimate is expected from him of the Cost of the equestrian Statue of Genl. Washington. But as this would depend altogether on the Dimensions of the Statue, he will be unable to make an Estimate till these Dimensions be decided.

The Gazettes of France and Leyden from the 25th. of October to this Date are forwarded herewith.

I had the Honour of writing to you by the Way of London on the 24th. of the last Month, and have now that of assuring you of those Sentiments of Esteem & Respect with which I am Sir, your most obedient & most humble Servant.

—TH: JEFFERSON

ENCLOSURE

Jefferson's Report on Conversations with Vergennes   [Dec. 1785]

Hearing frequent Complaints in this Country that little of our Commerce came to it, that while our Flag covered the Thames it was rarely to be seen in a Port of France, and that this proceeded from national Prejudices, and observing that this Complaint was often repeated and particularly relied on by those who had opposed our Admission into the French Islands, I thought it necessary on every possible Occasion to shew how much the Cause was mistaken, while the Fact was admitted to be true. In every Conversation therefore with the Count de Vergennes I had endeavoured to convince him that were national Prejudice alone listened to, our Trade would quit England and come to France, but that the Impossibility of making Paiments here prevented our making Purchases. On a particular Occasion in the Month of August, I enumerated to him our Exports and shewed him that for some of them there was no Demand here, and that others were recieved under such Circumstances as discouraged their being brought. When, in going through this Enumeration, I came to the Article of Tobacco, he observed that the King recieved such a Revenue on that as could not be renounced. I told him we did not wish it to be renounced or even lessened, but only that the Monopoly should be put down. That this might be effected in the simplest Manner by obliging the Importer to pay on Entrance a Duty, equal to what the King now recieved, or to deposit his Tobacco in the King's Warehouses till it was paid, and then permitting him a free Sale of it. 'Ma foi, (said the Count) c'est une bonne Idée: il faut y penser,' or, 'y travailler' I do not recollect which. This Answer was encouraging, and another Circumstance rendered it necessary to press this Article at this particular Moment. Tho' the general Farm of the Revenues had still more than a twelve-month to run, the Treaty for the Renewal of it was actually begun between the Controller general and the Farmers general, and it was expected to be concluded during the Voiage of Fontainbleau which was now approaching. Tobacco making an Article of that Farm, it seemed to be the Moment when it might be withdrawn from that Contract. I had therefore intended to make a Representation on the Subject which should bring under the View of the King's Council the ill Consequences of that Monopoly, and induce them to discontinue it. The Manner in which the Count de Vergennes appeared to be struck with the Idea suggested in the Conversation beforementioned, determined me to make this Representation immediately. As soon as I returned to Paris therefore, I wrote him the following Letter wherein I digested and added to, what I had said to him under the Head of Tobacco.

To this Letter I recieved no other Answer but that he had transmitted it to the Comptroller-general. The general Farm was not renewed at Fontainbleau.

In the Beginning of November a Mr. Boylston of Massachusets brought a Cargo of Whale oil to Havre, with Letters to the Marquis de la Fayette and myself, recommending him to our Assistance in the Disposal of it. He wished us to endeavour to obtain for his Cargo the Exemption from Duty which the Marquis had obtained the preceding Year for a particular Company. I observed to the Marquis that this was doing Business by Piece-meal and making many Favors of one. That it would be better to take up the Subject generally, to get it placed on equal Ground for all our Citizens, and to try what Government would do in a general Way to encourage the Importation of this Article. He came into these Ideas. As my Applications could only be to the Count de Vergennes, and the Delays which follow official Propositions which are to be handed from one Department to another, backwards and forwards, were likely to be too long to answer Boylston's Purpose, the Marquis with that Zeal and Activity with which he seizes every Opportunity of serving our Country, applied immediately to M. de Calonnes the Comptroller general, making Boylston's Case the Occasion of the Application, but proposing a general Regulation. He pressed the Proposition so efficaciously that he obtained in a few Days from Monsieur de Calonnes an Agreement to recieve our Oils on the footing on which they recieve those of the Hanseatic Towns, by which Means the Duties, which had been at 36. Livres 15. Sols the Barrel of 500. lb. French Weight, as may be seen by a statement given me by Monsr. Sangrain, were now reduced to 11. Livres 5. sols, being about 2. Livres on the English hundred, or a Guinea and a half the Ton, as the Ton is estimated in England. But this Indulgence was limited to one Year's Continuance. For the Particulars of this I refer to the Letter of M. de Calonnes to the Marquis de la Fayette dated Nov. 17. 1785, and to that of the Count de Vergennes to me dated Nov. 30. 1785.

The next Levée Day at Versailles I meant to bring again under the View of the Count de Vergennes the whole Subject of our Commerce with France; but the Number of Audiences of Ambassadors and other Ministers which take Place of Course before mine, and which seldom indeed leave me an Opportunity of Audience at all, prevented me that Day. I was only able to ask of the Count de Vergennes, as a particular Favor, that he would permit me to wait on him some Day that Week. He did so, and I went to Versailles the Friday following, 9th. of December. M. de Rayneval was with the Count. Our Conversation began with the usual Topic that the Trade of the U.S. had not yet learnt the Way to France, but continued to center in England tho no longer obliged by Law to go there. I observed that the real Cause of this was to be found in the Difference of the commercial Arrangements in the two Countries. That Merchants would not and could not trade but where there was to be some Gain; that the Commerce between two Countries could not be kept up but by an Exchange of Commodities; that if an American Merchant was forced to carry his Produce to London, it could not be expected he would make a Voiage from thence to France with the Money to lay it out here; and in like Manner that if he could bring his Commodities with Advantage to this Country, he would not make another Voiage to England with the Money to lay it out there, but would take in Exchange the Merchandize of this Country. The Count de Vergennes agreed to this, and particularly that where there was no Exchange of Merchandize, there could be no durable Commerce, and that it was natural for Merchants to take their Returns in the Port where they sold their Cargo. I desired his Permission then to take a summary View of the Productions of the U.S. that we might see which of them could be brought here to Advantage. 1. Rice. France gets from the Mediterranean a Rice not so good indeed, but cheaper than ours. He said that they bought of our Rice, but that they got from Egypt also Rice of a very fine Quality. I observed that such was the actual State of their Commerce in that Article that they take little from us. 2. Indico. They make a Plenty in their own Colonies. He observed that they did and that they thought it better than ours. 3. Flour, Fish, and Provisions of all Sorts they produce for themselves. That these Articles might therefore be considered as not existing for Commerce between the U.S. and the Kingdom of France. I proceeded to those capable of becoming Objects of Exchange between the two Nations. 1. Peltry and Furs. Our Posts being in the Hands of the English, we are cut off from that Article. I am not sure even whether we are not obliged to buy of them for our own Use. When these Posts are given up, if ever they are, we shall be able to furnish France with Skins and Furs to the Amount of 2. Millions of Livres in Exchange for her Merchandize: but at present these Articles are to be counted as nothing. 2. Pot-ash. An Experiment is making whether this can be brought here. We hope it may, but at present it stands for nothing. He observed that it was much wanted in France and he thought it would succeed. 3. Naval Stores. Trials are also making on these as Subjects of Commerce with France. They are heavy and the Voiage long. The Result therefore is doubtful. At present they are as nothing in our Commerce with this Country. 4. Whale-oil. I told him I had great Hopes the late Diminution of Duty would enable us to bring this Article with Advantage to France: that a Merchant was just arrived (Mr. Barrett) who proposed to settle at L'Orient for the Purpose of selling the Cargoes of this Article and chusing the Returns. That he had informed me that in the first Year, it would be necessary to take one third in Money, and the Remainder only in Merchandize; because the Fishermen require indispensably some Money. But he thought that after the first Year, the Merchandize of the preceding Year would always produce Money for the ensuing one, and that the whole Amount would continue to be taken annually afterwards in Merchandize. I added that tho' the Diminution of Duty was expressed to be but for one Year, yet I hoped they would find their Advantage in renewing and continuing it: for that if they intended really to admit it for one Year only, the Fishermen would not find it worth while to rebuild their Vessels and to prepare themselves for the Business. The Count expressed Satisfaction on the View of commercial Exchange held up by this Article. He made no Answer as to the Continuance of it. And I did not chuse to tell him at that Time that we should claim its Continuance under their Treaty with the Hanseatic Towns which fixes this Duty for them, and our own Treaty, which gives us the Rights of the most favored Nation. 5. Tobacco. I recalled to the Memory of the Count de Vergennes, the Letter I had written to him on this Article, and the Object of the present Conversation being how to facilitate the Exchange of commerciable Articles between the two Countries, I pressed that of Tobacco in this Point of View, observed that France at present paid us ten Millions of Livres for this Article, that for such Portions of it as were bought in London, they sent the Money directly there, and for what they bought in the United States, the Money was still remitted to London on Bills of Exchange. Whereas, if they would permit our Merchants to sell this Article freely they would bring it here and take the Returns on the Spot in Merchandize, not Money. The Count observed that my Proposition contained what was doubtless useful, but that the King recieved on this Article at present a Revenue of 28. millions, which was so considerable as to render them fearful of tampering with it; that the Collection of this Revenue by Way of Farm, was of very antient Date, and that it was always hazardous to alter Arrangements of long standing and of such infinite Combinations with the fiscal System. I answered that the Simplicity of the Mode of Collection proposed for this Article withdrew it from all Fear of deranging other Parts of their System, that I supposed they would confine the Importation to some of their principal Ports, probably not more than five or six, that a single Collector in each of these, was the only new Officer requisite, that he could get rich himself on six Livres a hogshead, and would recieve the whole Revenue and pay it into the Treasury, at short hand. M. de Rayneval entered particularly into this Part of the Conversation, and explained to the Count, more in Detail the Advantages and the Simplicity of it, and concluded by observing to me that it sometimes happened that useful

Propositions, tho' not practicable at one Time, might become so at another. I told him that that Consideration had induced me to press the Matter when I did, because I had understood the Renewal of the Farm was then on the Carpet, and that it was the precise Moment when I supposed that this Portion might be detached from the Mass of the Farms. I asked the Count de Vergennes whether, if the Renewal of the Farm was pressing, this Article might not be separated, merely in Suspence, till Government should have Time to satisfy themselves on the Expediency of renewing it. He said no Promises could be made.

In the Course of this Conversation he had mentioned the Liberty we enjoyed of carrying our Fish to the French Islands. I repeated to him what I had hinted in my Letter of Nov. 20. 1785. that I considered as a Prohibition the laying such Duties on our Fish and giving such Premiums on theirs as made a Difference between their and our Fisher-men of fifteen Livres the Quintal in an Article which sold but for fifteen Livres. He said it would not have that Effect for two Reasons.

1. That their Fishermen could not furnish Supplies sufficient for their Islands, and of Course the Inhabitants must of Necessity buy our Fish.

2. That from the Constancy of our Fishery and the short Season during which theirs continued, also the Economy and Management of ours compared with the Expence of theirs, we had always been able to sell our Fish in the Islands at 25. Livres the Quintal, while they were obliged to ask 36. Livres. (I suppose he meant the Livre of the French Islands.) That thus the Duty and Premium had been a necessary Operation on their Side to place the Sale of their Fish on a Level with ours, and that without this, theirs could not bear the Competition.

I have here brought together the Substance of what was said on the preceding Subjects, not pretending to give it verbatim, which my Memory does not enable me to do. I have probably omitted many Things which were spoken, but have mentioned nothing which was not. It was interrupted at Times with collateral Matters. One of these was important; the Count de Vergennes complained and with a good Deal of Stress, that they did not find a sufficient Dependence on Arrangements taken with us. This was the third Time too he had done it; first in a Conversation at Fontainbleau when he first complained to me of the Navigation acts of Massachusets and New-hampshire: secondly in his Letter of Oct. 30. 1785. on the same Subject; and now in the present Conversation, wherein he added as another Instance, the Case of the Chevalier de Mezieres, Heir of General Oglethorpe, who, notwithstanding that the 11th. Article of the Treaty provides that the Subjects or Citizens of either Party shall succeed ab intesta, to the Lands of their Ancestors within the Dominions of the other, had been informed from Mr. Adams, and by me also, that his Right of Succession to the General's Estate in Georgia was doubtful. He observed too that the Administration of Justice with us was tardy, insomuch that their Merchants, when they had Money due to them within our States, considered it as desperate; and that our commercial Regulations in general were disgusting to them. These Ideas were new, serious, and delicate. I decided therefore not to enter into them in that Moment, and the rather as we were speaking in French, in which Language I did not chuse to hazard myself, I withdrew from the Objections of the Tardiness of Justice with us, and the Disagreeableness of our commercial Regulations, by a general Observation that I was not sensible they were well founded. With Respect to the Case of the Chevr. de Mezieres, I was obliged to enter into some Explanations. They related chiefly to the legal Operation of our Declaration of Independance, to the undecided Question whether our Citizens and British Subjects were thereby made Aliens to one another, to the general Laws as to Conveiances of Land to Aliens, and the Doubt whether an Act of the Assembly of Georgia might not have been passed to confiscate General Oglethorpe's Property, which would of Course prevent its Devolution on any Heir. Mr. Rayneval observed that in this Case it became a mere Question of Fact, whether a Confiscation of these Lands had taken Place before the Death of General Oglethorpe, which Fact might be easily known by Enquiries in Georgia where the Possessions lay. I thought it very material that the Opinion of this Court should be set to Rights on these Points. On my Return therefore I wrote the following Observations on them, which, the next Time I went to Versailles, (not having an Opportunity of speaking to the Count de Vergennes) I put into the Hands of M. Reyneval, praying him to read them and to ask the Favor of the Count to do the same.

Having put this Paper into the Hands of Monsr. Rayneval, we entered into Conversation again on the Subject of the Farms, which were now understood to be approaching to a Conclusion. He told me that himself was decidedly of Opinion that the Interest of the State required the Farm of Tobacco to be discontinued, that he had accordingly given every Aid to my Proposition which laid within his Sphere: that Count de Vergennes was very clearly of the same

Opinion and had supported it strongly with Reasons of his own when he transmitted it to the Comptroller general; but that the Comptroller, in the Discussions of this Subject which had taken Place, besides the Objections which the Count de Vergennes had repeated to me, and which are before-mentioned, had added that the Contract with the Farmers general was now so far advanced that the Article of Tobacco could not be withdrawn from it without unravelling the whole Transaction. Having understood that in this Contract there was always reserved to the Crown a Right to discontinue it at any Moment, making just Re-imbursements to the Farmers, I asked Mr. Rayneval, if the Contract should be concluded in its present Form, whether it might still be practicable to have it discontinued as to the Article of Tobacco at some future Moment. He said it might be possible.

Upon the whole, the true Obstacle to this Proposition has penetrated in various Ways through the Veil which covers it. The Influence of the Farmers general has heretofore been found sufficient to shake a Minister in his Office. Monsieur de Calonne's Continuance or Dismission has been thought for some Time to be on a Poise. Were he to shift this great Weight therefore out of his own Scale into that of his Adversaries, it would decide their Preponderance. The joint Interests of France and America would be an insufficient Counterpoise in his Favor.

It will be observed that these Efforts to improve the Commerce of the U.S. have been confined to that Branch only which respects France itself, and that nothing passed on the Subject of our Commerce with the West Indies, except an incidental Conversation as to our fish. The Reason of this was no Want of a due Sense of its importance. Of that I am thoroughly sensible. But Efforts in Favour of this branch would at present be desperate. To Nations with which we have not yet treated, and who have Possessions in America, we may offer a free Vent of their Manufactures in the U.S. for a full or a modified Admittance into those Possessions. But to France we were obliged to give that Freedom for a different Compensation, to wit, for her Aid to effect our Independence. It is difficult therefore to say what we have now to offer her for an Admission into her West Indies. Doubtless it has its Price. But the Question is what this would be, and whether worth our while to give it. Were we to propose to give to each other's Citizens all the Rights of Natives, they would of Course count what they should gain by this Enlargement of Right, and examine whether it would be worth to them as much as their Monopoly of their West Indian Commerce. If not, that commercial Freedom which we wish to preserve, and which indeed is so valuable, leaves us little else to offer. An Expression in my Letter to the Count de Vergennes of Nov. 20. wherein I hinted that both Nations might perhaps come into the Opinion that the Condition of Natives might be a better Ground of Intercourse for their Citizens than that of the most favored Nation, was intended to furnish an Opportunity to the Minister of parleying on that Subject, if he was so disposed, and to myself of seeing whereabouts they would begin, that I might communicate it to Congress, and leave them to judge of the Expediency of pursuing the Subject. But no Overtures have followed; for I have no Right to consider as coming from the Minister, certain Questions which were very soon after proposed to me by an Individual. It sufficiently accounts for these Questions that that Individual had written a Memorial on the Subject for the Consideration of the Minister, and might wish to know what we would be willing to do. The Idea that I should answer such Questions to him, is equally unaccountable, whether we suppose them originating with himself, or coming from the Minister. In Fact I must suppose them to be his own; and I transmit them only that Congress may see what one Frenchman at least thinks on the Subject. If we can obtain from Gr. Britain reasonable Conditions of Commerce (which in my Idea must forever include an Admission into her Islands) the freest Ground between these two Nations would seem to be the best. But if we can obtain no equal Terms from her, perhaps Congress might think it prudent as Holland has done, to connect us unequivocally with France. Holland has purchased the Protection of France. The Price she pays is Aid in Time of War. It is interesting for us to purchase a free Commerce with the French Islands. But whether it is best to pay for it by Aids in War, or by Privileges in Commerce, or not to purchase it at all; is the Question.

༆

[Jefferson went to a great deal of trouble to refute the imprecations on the size of American animals made by Buffon, whose lengthy work on natural history was taken to be definitive at the time. Later he tried to obtain the skin and horns of a moose. Buffon, like other of his time, believed that climate controlled these things and that the dampness of American climate vitiated the robustness of fauna in America.]

To Archibald Cary
DEAR SIR   Paris Jan. 7. 1786

It will be a misfortune to the few of my countrymen (and very very few they are indeed) who happen to be punctual. Of this I shall give you a proof by the present application, which I should not make to you if I did not know you to be superior to the torpidity of our climate. In my conversations I find him Count de Buff on the subjects of Natural history, unacquainted with our Elk and our deer. He has hitherto beleived that our deer never had horns more than a foot long; and has therefore classed them with the roe-buck, which I am sure you know them to be different from. I have examined some of the red deer of this country at the distance of about 60. yards and I find no other difference between them and ours, but a shade or two in the colour. Will you take the trouble to procure for me the largest pair of bucks horns you can, and a large skin of each colour, that is to say a red and a blue? If it were possible to take these from a buck just killed, to leave all the bones of the head in the skin, with the horns on, to leave the bones and hoofs of the legs and feet in the skin, so that having only made an incision all along the belly and neck, to take the animal out at, we could by sewing up that incision and stuffing the skin, present the true size and form of the animal, it would be a most precious present. Our deer have been often sent to England and Scotland. Do you know (with certainty) whether they have ever bred with the red deer of those countries? With respect to the Elk, I despair of your being able to get for me any thing but the horns of it. David Ross I know has a pair; perhaps he would give them to us. It is useless to ask for the skin and skeleton, because I think it not in your power to get them, otherwise they would be most desirable. A gentleman, fellow passenger with me from Boston to England, promised to send to you in my name some hares, rabbets, pheasants and partridges, by the return of the ship which was to go to Virginia, and the captain promised great care of them. My friend procured the animals, and, the ship changing her destination, he kept them in hopes of finding some other conveyance, till they all perished. I do not despair however of finding some opportunity still of sending a colony of useful animals. I am making a collection of vines for wine and for the table, some trees also, such as the Cork oak, &c. &c.

Every thing is absolutely quiet in Europe. There is not therefore a word of news to communicate. I pray you to present me affectionately to your family and that of Tuckahoe. Whatever expence is necessary for procuring me the articles abovementioned I will instantly replace either in cash or in any thing you may wish from hence. I am with very sincere esteem Dear Sir your most obedient humble servant,

—TH: JEFFERSON

✑

[The question of how fossil seashells found their way to the tops of mountains was a lively one in the natural history of the day. Jefferson examines the options here, and more or less rejects them all. The final option mentioned here is the correct one. The floors of oceans have indeed been thrust up over time into mountains, by the action of continental drift.]

To David Rittenhouse
DEAR SIR   Paris Jan. 25. 1786

Your favor of Sep. 28. came to hand a few days ago. I thank you for the details on the Southern and Western lines. There remains thereon one article however which I will still beg you to inform me of, viz. how far is the Western boundary beyond the Meridian of Pittsburgh? This is necessary to enable me to trace that boundary in my map. I shall be much gratified also with a communication of your observations on the curiosities of the Western country. It will not be diffi-cult to induce me to give up the theory of the growth of shells without their being the nidus of animals. It's only an idea, and not an opinion with me. In the Notes with which I trouble you I had observed that there were three opinions as to the origin of these shells. 1. That they have been deposited even in the highest mountains by a universal deluge. 2. That they with all the calcareous stones and earths are animal remains. 3. That they grow or shoot as chrystals do. I find that I could swallow the last opinion sooner than either of the others; but I have not yet swallowed it. Another opinion might have been added, that some throw of nature has forced up parts which had been the bed of the ocean. But have we any better proof of such an effort of nature than of her shooting a lapidific juice into the form of a shell? No such convulsion has taken place in our time, nor within the annals of history; nor is the distance greater between the shooting of the lapidific juice into the form of a chrystal or a diamond which we see, and into the form of a shell which we do not see, than between the forcing Volcanic matter a little above the surface where it is in fusion, which we see, and the forcing the bed of the sea fifteen thousand feet above the ordinary surface of the earth, which we do not see. It is not possible to believe any of these hypotheses; and if we lean towards any of them it should be only till some other is produced more analogous to the known operations of nature. In a letter to Mr. Hopkinson I mentioned to him that the Abbe Rochon, who discovered the double refracting power in some of the natural chrystals, had lately made a telescope with the metal called Platina, which while it is susceptible of as perfect a polish as the metal heretofore used for the specula of telescopes, is inattackable by rust as gold and silver are. There is a person here who has hit on a new method of engraving. He gives you an ink of his composition. Write on copper plates any thing which you would wish to take several copies; and in an hour the plate will be ready to strike them off. So of plans, engravings &c. This art will be amusing to individuals if he should make it known. I send you herewith the Nautical almanacs for 1786. 1787. 1788. 1789. 1790. which are as late as they are published. You ask how you may reimburse the expence of these trifles? I answer, by accepting of them, as the procuring you a gratification is a higher one to me than money. We have had nothing curious published lately. I do not know whether you are fond of chemical reading. There are some things in this science worth reading. I will send them to you if you wish it. My daughter is well and joins me in respects to Mrs. Rittenhouse and the young ladies. After asking when we are to have the lunarium? I will close with assurances of the sincere ... [The surviving manuscript copy of this letter stops here.]

৵

From John Adams

DEAR SIR   Grosvenor Square Feb. 17. 1786

I was sometime in doubt, whether any Notice Should be taken of the Tripoline Ambassador; but receiving Information that he made Enquiries about me, and expressed a Surprise that when the other foreign Ministers had visited him, the American had not; and finding that He was a universal and perpetual Ambassador, it was thought best to call upon him. Last Evening, in making a Tour of other Visits, I Stopped at his Door, intending only to leave a Card, but the Ambassador was announced at Home and ready to receive me. I was received in State. Two great Chairs before the Fire, one of which was destined for me, the other for his Excellency. Two Secretaries of Legation, men of no Small Consequence Standing Upright in the middle of the Room, without daring to Sitt, during the whole time I was there, and whether they are not yet upright upon their Legs I know not. Now commenced the Difficulty. His Excellency Speaks Scarcely a Word of any European Language, except Italian and Lingua Franca, in which you know I have Small Pretensions. He began soon to ask me Questions about America and her Tobacco, and I was Surprized to find that with a pittance of Italian and a few French Words which he understands, We could so well understand each other. "We make Tobacco in Tripoli," said his Excellency "but it is too Strong. Your American Tobacco is better." By this Time, one of his secretaries or *upper servants* brought two Pipes ready filled and lighted. The longest was offered me; the other to his Excellency. It is long since I took a Pipe but as it would be unpardonable to be wanting in Politeness in so ceremonious an Interview, I took the Pipe with great Complacency, placed the Bowl upon the Carpet, for the Stem was fit for a Walking Cane, and I believe more than two Yards in length, and Smoked in aweful Pomp, reciprocating Whiff for Whiff, with his Excellency, untill Coffee was brought in. His Excellency took a Cup, after I had taken one, and alternately Sipped at his Coffee and whiffed at his Tobacco, and I wished he would take a Pinch in turn from his Snuff box for Variety; and I followed the Example with Such Exactness and Solemnity that the two secretaries, appeared in Raptures and the superiour of them who speaks a few Words of French cryed out in Extacy, Monsieur votes etes un Turk.—The necessary Civilities being thus compleated, His Excellency began upon Business; asked many Questions about America: the soil Climate Heat and Cold, &c. and said it was a very great Country. But "Tripoli is at War with it." I was "Sorry to hear that." "Had not heard of any War with Tripoli." "America had done no Injury to Tripoli, committed no Hostility; nor had Tripoli done America any Injury or committed any Hostility against her, that I had heard of." True said His Excellency "but there must be a Treaty of Peace. There could be no Peace without a Treaty. The Turks and Affricans were the souvereigns of the Mediterranean, and there could be no navigation there nor Peace without Treaties of Peace. America must treat as France and England did, and all other Powers. America must treat with Tripoli and then with Constantinople and then with Algiers and Morocco." Here a Secretary brought him some Papers, one of which a Full Power in French from the Pacha, Dey and Regency of Tripoli, as Ambassador, to treat with all the Powers of Europe, and to make what Treaties he pleased and to manage in short all the foreign Affairs of his Country, he delivered me to read. He was ready to treat and make Peace. If I would come tomorrow or next day, or any other day and bring an Interpreter, He would hear and propose Terms, and write to Tripoli and I might write to America, and each Party might accept or refuse them as they should think fit. How long would it be before one could write to Congress and have an Answer? Three months. This was rather too long but he should stay here sometime. When I had read his French Translation of his Full Power He Shewed me the original in his own Language. You perceive that his Excellency was more ready and eager to treat than I was as he probably expected to gain more by the Treaty. I could not see him Tomorrow nor next day but would think of it.

I must now my dear sir beg of you to send me a Copy of the Project of a Treaty sent by Mr. Barclay and Mr. Lamb, as I had not time to take one, when it was here. You will please to write me your Thoughts and Advice upon this Occasion. This is a Sensible Man, well known to many of the foreign Ministers who have seen him before, in Sweeden, at Vienna, in Denmark &c. He has been so much in Europe that he knows as much of America, as anybody; so that nothing new will be suggested to him or his Constituents by our having Conferences with him. It seems best then to know his Demands. They will be higher I fear, than we can venture.

The King told one of the foreign Ministers in my hearing at the Levee, that the Tripoline Ambassador refused to treat with his Ministers and insisted upon an Audience. But that all he had to say was that Tripoli was at Peace with England and desired to continue so. The King added all he wants is, a Present, and his Expences born to Vienna or Denmark.

The Relation of my Visit is to be sure very inconsistent with the Dignity of your Character and mine, but the Ridicule of it was real and the Drollery inevitable. How can We preserve our Dignity-in negotiating with Such Nations? And who but a Petit Maitre would think of Gravity upon such an occasion. With great Esteem your most obedient

—JOHN ADAMS

❧

[Four days later Adams wrote Jefferson urgently to come from Paris to deal with the ambassador from Tripoli, which occasioned Jefferson's trip in March to London.]

To John Jay

SIR   London Mar. 12. 1786

The date of a letter from London will doubtless be as unexpected to you as it was unforeseen by myself a few days ago. On the 27th. of the last month Colo. Smith arrived in Paris with a letter from Mr. Adams informing me that there was at this place a minister from Tripoli, having general powers to enter into treaties on behalf of his state, and with whom it was possible we might do something in our commission to that power; and that he gave reason to believe he could also take arrangements with us for Tunis. He further added that the minister of Portugal here had received ultimate instructions from his court, and that probably that treaty might be concluded in the space of three weeks, were we all on the spot together. [The treaty was negotiated and signed by Adams, Jefferson, and the Portuguese ambassador, but the King of Portugal refused to endorse it.] He therefore pressed me to come over immediately. The first of these objects had some weight on my mind because as we had sent no person to Tripoli or Tunis, I thought, if we could meet a minister from them on this ground, our arrangements would be settled much sooner and at less expence. But what principally decided with me was the desire of bringing matters to a conclusion with Portugal before the term of our commission should expire, or any new turn in the negociations of France and England should abate their willingness to fix a connection with us. A third motive had also it's weight. I hoped that my attendance here, and the necessity of shortening it, might be made use of to force a decisive answer from this court. I therefore concluded to comply with Mr. Adams's request. I went immediately to Versailles, and apprised the count de Vergennes that circumstances of public duty called me hither for three or four weeks, arranged with him some matters, and set out with Colo. Smith for this place, where we arrived last night, which was as early as the excessive rigour of the weather admitted. I saw Mr. Adams immediately, and again to-day. He informs me that the minister of Portugal was taken ill five or six days ago, has been very much so, but is now somewhat better. It would be very mortifying indeed should this accident, with the shortness of the term to which I limit my stay here, defeat what was the principal object of my journey, and that without which I should hardly have undertaken it. With respect to this country, I had no doubt but that every consideration had been urged by Mr. Adams which was proper to be urged. Nothing remains undone in this way. But we shall avail ourselves of my journey here as if made on purpose, just before the expiration of our commission, to form our report to Congress on the execution of that commission, which report, they may be given to know, cannot be formed without decisive information of the ultimate determination of their court. There is no doubt what that determination will be; but it will be useful to have it, as it may put an end to all further expectations on our side the water, and shew that the time is come for doing whatever is to be done by us for counteracting the unjust and greedy designs of this country. ["This country" is England. Jefferson hated the English so much he seems to have had trouble here naming them.] We shall have the honour, before I leave this place, to inform you of the result of the several matters which have brought me to it.

A day or two before my departure from Paris, I received your letter of January [19.] The question therein proposed How far France considers herself as bound to insist on the delivery of the posts, would infallibly produce another, How far we consider our-selves as guarantees of their American possessions, and bound to enter into any future war in which these may be attacked? [The posts Jefferson is referring to are the border posts in the Northwest Territory that, by the treaty that ended the American Revolution, the English had agreed to vacate. They had yet to comply.] The words of the treaty of alliance seem to be without ambiguity on either head. Yet I should be afraid to commit Congress by answering without authority. I will endeavour on my return to sound the opinion of the minister if possible, without exposing myself to the other question. Should any thing forcible be meditated on these posts, it would possibly be thought prudent previously to ask the good offices of France to obtain their delivery. In this case they would probably say we must first execute the treaty on our part by repealing all acts which have contravened it. Now this measure if there be any candour in the court of London, would suffice to obtain a delivery of the posts from them, without the mediation of any third power. However if this mediation should be finally needed, I see no reason to doubt our obtaining it, and still less to question it's omnipotent influence on the British court.

I have the honour to be with sentiments of the highest respect & esteem Sir Your most obedient & most humble servt.,

—TH: JEFFERSON

❧

American Commissioners to John Jay

SIR   Grosr. Square March 28th. 1786

Soon after the arrival of Mr. J. in London, we had a conference with the Ambassador of Tripoli, at his House.

The amount of all the information we can obtain from him was that a perpetual peace was in all respects the most advisable, because a temporary treaty would leave room for increasing demands upon every renewal of it, and a stipulation for annual payments would be liable to failures of performance which would renew the war, repeat the negotiations and continually augment the claims of his nation and the difference of expence would by no means be adequate to the inconvenience, since 12,500 Guineas to his Constituents with 10 pr. Cent upon that sum for himself, must be paid if the treaty was made for only one year.

That 30,000 Guineas for his Employers and £3,000 for himself were the lowest terms upon which a perpetual peace could be made and that this must be paid in Cash on the delivery of the treaty signed by his sovereign, that no kind of Merchandizes could be accepted.

That Tunis would treat upon the same terms, but he could not answer for Algiers or Morocco.

We took the liberty to make some inquiries concerning the Grounds of their pretentions to make war upon Nations who had done them no Injury, and observed that we considered all mankind as our friends who had done us no wrong, nor had given us any provocation.

The Ambassador answered us that it was founded on the Laws of their

Prophet, that it was written in their Koran, that all nations who should not have acknowledged their authority were sinners, that it was their right and duty to make war upon them wherever they could be found, and to make slaves of all they could take as Prisoners, and that every Musselman who should be slain in battle was sure to go to Paradise.

That it was a law that the first who boarded an Enemy's Vessell should have one slave, more than his share with the rest, which operated as an incentive to the most desperate Valour and Enterprise, that it was the Practice of their Corsairs to bear down upon a ship, for each sailor to take a dagger in each hand and another in his mouth, and leap on board, which so terrified their Enemies that very few ever stood against them, that he verily believed the Devil assisted his Countrymen, for they were almost always successful. We took time to consider and promised an answer, but we can give him no other, than that the demands exceed our Expectations, and that of Congress, so much that we can proceed no further without fresh instructions.

There is but one possible way that we know of to procure the money, if Congress should authorize us to go to the necessary expence, and that is to borrow it in Holland. We are not certain it can be had there. But if Congress should order us to make the best terms we can with Tunis, Tripoli, Algiers and Morocco, and to procure this money wherever we can find it, upon terms like those of the last loan in Holland, our best endeavours shall be used to remove this formidable obstacle out of the way of the prosperity of the United States.

Inclosed is a Copy of a Letter from P. R. Randall Esqr. at Barcelona, the last from Mr. Barclay was dated Bayonne. It is hoped we shall soon have news from Algiers and Morocco, and we wish it may not be made more disagreable than this from Tunis and Tripoli. We are &c.

—J.A.
—T.J.

ॐ

To John Jay
SIR   London April 23. 1786

In my letter of Mar. 12. I had the honour of explaining to you the motives which had brought me to this place. A joint letter from Mr. Adams and myself, sent by the last packet, informed you of the result of our conferences with the Tripoline minister. The conferences with the minister of Portugal have been drawn to a greater length than I expected. However, every thing is now agreed and the treaty will be ready for signature the day after tomorrow. I shall set out for Paris the same day. With this country nothing is done; and that nothing is intended to be done on their part admits not the smallest doubt. The nation is against any change of measures; the ministers are against it, some from principle, others from subserviency; and the king more than all men is against it. If we take a retrospect to the beginning of the present reign we observe that amidst all the changes of ministry no change of measures with respect to America ever took place: excepting only at the moment of the peace, and the minister of that moment was immediately removed. Judging of the future by the past, I do not expect a change of disposition during the present reign, which bids fair to be a long one as the king is healthy and temperate. That he is persevering we know. If he ever changes his plan it will be in consequence of events which neither himself nor his ministers at present place among those which are probable. Even the opposition dares not open their lips in favor of a connection with us, so unpopular would be the topic. It is not that they think our commerce unimportant to them. I find that the merchants here set sufficient value on it. But they are sure of keeping it on their own terms. No better proof can be shewn of the security in which the ministers think themselves on this head, than that they have not thought it worth while to give us a conference on the subject, tho' on my arrival we exhibited to them our commission, observed to them that it would expire on the 12th. of the next month, and that I had come over on purpose to see if any arrangements could be made before that time. Of the two months which then remained, 6 weeks have elapsed without one scrip of a pen, or one word from a minister except a vague proposition at an accidental meeting. We availed of ourselves even of that to make another essay to extort some sort of declaration from the court. But their silence is invincible. But of all this, as well as of the proceedings in the negociation with Portugal, Information will be given you by a joint letter from Mr. Adams and myself. The moment is certainly arrived when, the plan of this court being out of all doubt, Congress and the states may decide what their own measures should be.

The Marquis of Lansdowne spoke of you in very friendly terms and desired me to present his respects to you in the first letter I should write. He is thoroughly sensible of the folly of the present measures of this country, as are a few other characters about him. Dr. Price is among these, and is particularly disturbed at the present prospect. He acknowleges however that all change is desperate; which weighs the more as he is intimate with Mr. Pitt. This small band of friends, favorable as it is, does not pretend to say one word in public on our subject.

I have the honor to be with sentiments of the highest esteem and respect Sir your most obedient & most humble servt.,

—TH: JEFFERSON

✍

To John Jay, with Enclosure
SIR   Paris May 27. 1786

In my letter of January 2. I had the honour of stating to you what had passed here on the subject of the commerciable articles between this country and the United States. I beg leave now to resume that subject. I therein informed you that this government had agreed to receive our fish oils on the footing on which they receive those of the Hanseatic towns, which gave us a reduction of duty from 36^{tt} 15s on the barrique to 11^{tt} 5s amounting to about 42^{tt} on the English ton, according to a statetment by Monsr. Sangrain inclosed in that letter. This was true; but there was another truth which neither that statement nor any other evidence I then had, enabled me to discover, and which it is but lately I could be ascertained of; which is that there is another duty called the Droit des huiles et savons, to which the Hans towns are subject as we are also, of consequence. This is of 6. deniers on the nett pound, and 10. sous per livre on that, amounting to 3^{tt} 5s on the nett hundred, French weight, or to 60^{tt} 13s. 6d the English ton. This with the reduced duty makes about 102^{tt} 13s. 6d., or very nearly four guineas according to the present exchange, on the English ton. Tho this be still advantageous when compared with the English duty of 18. guineas, yet it is less so than we had expected, and it will remain, when we apply for a renewal of the indulgence, to see whether we can obtain further reduction.

The fur trade is an object of desire in this country. London is at present their market for furs. They pay for them there in ready money. Could they draw their furs into their own ports from the U.S. they would pay us for them in productions. Nor should we lose by the change of market, since, tho the French pay the London merchants in cash, those merchants pay us with manufactures. A very wealthy and well connected company is proposing here to associate themselves with an American company, each to possess half the interest and to carry on the fur trade between the two countries. The company here expect to make the principal part of the advances; they also are solliciting considerable indulgencies from this government from which the part of the company on our side the water will reap half the advantage. As no exclusive idea enters into this scheme, it appears to me worthy of encouragement. It is hoped the government here will interest themselves for it's success. If they do, one of two things may happen: either the English will be afraid to stop the vessels of a company consisting partly of French subjects and patronized by the court; in which case the commerce will be laid open generally; or if they stop the vessels, the French company, which is strongly connected with men in power, will complain in form to their government, who may thus be interested as principals in the rectification of this abuse. As yet however, the proposition has not taken such a form, as to assure us that it will be prosecuted to this length.

As to the article of tobacco, which had become an important branch of remittance to almost all the states, I had the honour of communicating to you my proposition to the Court to abolish the monopoly of it in their farm; that the Ct. de Vergennes was, I thought, thoroughly sensible of the expediency of this proposition, and disposed to befriend it, that the renewal of the lease of the farms had been consequently suspended six months and was still in suspence; but that so powerful were the Farmers general, and so tottering the tenure of the Minister of finance in his office, that I despaired of preventing the renewal of the farm at that time. Things were in this state when the M. de la Fayette returned from Berlin. On communicating to him what was on the carpet, he proposed to me a conference with some persons well acquainted with the commercial system of this country. We met. They proposed the endeavoring to have a committee appointed to enquire into the subject. The proposition was made to the Ct. de Vergennes, who befriended it, and had the M. de la Fayette named a member of the committee. He became of course the active and truly zealous member for the liberty of commerce, others tho' well disposed, not chusing to oppose the farm openly. This committee has met from time to time. It shewed an early and decisive conviction that the measure taken by the farm to put the purchase of their tobaccoes into monopoly on that side the water, as the sale of them was on this, tended to the annihilation of commerce between the two countries. Various palliatives were proposed from time to time. I confess that I met them all with indifference, my object being a radical cure of the evil by discontinuing the farm, and not a mere assuagement of it for the present moment which, rendering it more bearable, might lessen the necessity of removing it totally, and perhaps prevent that removal. [Jefferson, it is worth noting, never cracked the Farmers-General. It took the French people to do that during the Revolution.] In the mean time the other branches of the farm rendered the renewal of the lease necessary; and it being said to be too far advanced to have the article of tobacco separated from it and suspended, it was signed in the month of March, while I was in England, with a clause, which is usual, that the king may discontinue when he pleases on certain conditions. When I returned, I found here a Memorial from the merchants of l'Orient complaining of their having 6000 hhds. of tobacco on hand, and of the distresses they were under from the loss of this medium of remittance. I inclosed it to the Count de Vergennes and asked his interference. I saw him on the 23d. inst. and spoke to him on the subject. He told me there was to be a committee held the next day at Berni, the seat of the Comptroller general, and that he would attend it himself to have something done. I asked him if I was to consider the expunging that article from the farm as desperate. He said that the difficulty of changing so antient an institution was immense, that the king draws from it a revenue of 29. millions of livres, that an interruption of this revenue, at least, if not a diminution, would attend a change, that their finances were not in a condition to bear even an interruption, and in short that no minister could venture to take upon himself so hazardous an operation. This was only saying explicitly, what I had long been sensible of, that the Comptroller general's continuance in office was too much on a poise to permit him to shift this weight out of his own scale into that of his adversaries; and that we must be contented to await the completion of the public expectation that there will be a change in this office, which change may give us another chance for effecting this desireable reformation. Incidents enough will arise to keep this object in our view, and to direct the attention to it as the only point on which the interests and harmony of the two countries (so far as this article of their commerce may influence) will ultimately find repose. The Committee met the next day. The only question agitated was how best to relieve the trade under it's double monopoly. The committee found themselves supported by the presence and sentiments of the Count de Vergennes. They therefore resolved that the contract with Mr. Morris, if executed on his part, ought not to be annulled here, but that no similar one should ever be made hereafter; that, so long as it continued, the farmers should be obliged to purchase from twelve to 15,000. hhds. of tobacco a year, over and above what they should receive from Mr. Morris, from such merchants as should bring it in French or American vessels, on the same conditions contracted with Mr. Morris; providing however that where the cargo shall not be assorted, the prices shall be 38^{tt} 36^{tt} and 34^{tt} for the 1st. 2d and 3d qualities of whichsoever the cargo may consist. In case of dispute about the quality, specimens are to be sent to the council, who will appoint persons to examine and decide on it.

This is indeed the least bad of all the palliatives which have been proposed; but it contains the seeds of perpetual trouble. It is easy to foresee that the farmers will multiply difficulties and vexations on those who shall propose to sell to them by force, and that these will be making perpetual complaints, so that both parties will be kept on the fret. If, without fatiguing the friendly dispositions of the ministry, this should give them just so much trouble as may induce them to look to the demolition of the monopoly as a desire-able point of rest, it may produce a permanent as well as temporary good. This determination of the committee needs the king's order to be carried into effect. I have been in hourly expectation of receiving official information that it is ultimately confirmed by him. But as yet it is not come, and the post will set out to-day. Should it arrive in time, I will inclose it. Should it not arrive, as I do not apprehend any danger of it's being rejected, or even altered materially (seeing that M. de Vergennes approved of it, and M. de Calonnes acquiesced) I have supposed you would wish to be apprized of it's substance, for a communication of which I am indebted to the M. de la Fayette. Tho' you cannot publish it formally till you know it is confirmed by the king yet an unauthoritative kind of notice may be given to the merchants to put them on their guard. Otherwise the merchants here, having first knowlege of it, may by their agents purchase up all the tobaccoes they have on hand, at a low price, and thus engross to themselves all the benefit.

In the same letter of January 2. I mentioned that the Rice of Carolina compared with that of the Mediterranean was better and dearer. This was on my own observation, having examined both in the shops here where they are retailed. Further enquiries give me reason to beleive that the rice of Carolina, on it's arrival, is fouler and cheaper; and that it is obliged to be cleaned here before it is saleable; that this advances the price, but at the same time the quality also, beyond that of the mediterranean. Whether the trouble of this operation discourages the merchant, or the price the consumer, or whether the merchants of Carolina have not yet learnt the way to this market, I cannot tell. I find in fact that but a small proportion of the rice consumed here is from the American market. But the consumption of this article here is immense. If the makers of American rice would endeavor to adapt their preparation of it to the taste of this country, so as to give it over the Mediterranean rice the advantage of which it seems susceptible, it would very much increase the quantity for which they may find sale. As far as I have been able to find it is received here on a favourable footing.

I shall reserve my letter open to the last moment in hopes of being able to put into it the order of the king to the farmers general. [I have the honour of inclosing a copy of their contract with Mr. Morris] to which the resolution of the Committee refers, and to be with sentiments of the most perfect esteem & respect, Sir, your most obedient & most humble servant,

—TH: JEFFERSON

❧

[The following letter from Adams responds to one of Jefferson's in which he floated the idea of waging war against the Barbary states, rather than paying tribute to them, as all the European states did.]

From John Adams
DEAR SIR   Grosvenor Square June 6. 1786

Yesterday I received your Favour of 30. May with its Inclosures. You have Since that day no doubt received my answer to yours of the 11th., in which I agreed perfectly with you in the Propriety of Sending Mr. Lamb to Congress without Loss of time. I am content to send Mr. Randal with him but had rather he Should come to you first and then to me, and embark in London after we shall have had opportunity from his Conversation to learn as much as we can.

The Comte de Vergennes is undoubtedly right in his Judgment that Avarice and Fear are the only Agents at Algiers, and that we shall not have Peace with them the cheaper, for having a Treaty with the Sublime Porte. But is he certain we can ever at any Price have Peace, with Algiers, unless we have it previously with Constantinople? And do not the Turks from Constantinople, send Rovers into the Mediterranean? And would not even Treaties of Peace with Tunis, Tripoli, Algiers and Morocco be ineffectual for the Security of our Mediterranean Trade, without a Peace with the Porte? The Porte is at present the Theater of the Politicks of Europe, and commercial Information might be obtained there.

The first Question is, what will it cost us to make Peace with all five of them? Set it if you will at five hundred Thousand Pounds Sterling, tho I doubt not it might be done for Three or perhaps for two.

The Second Question is, what Damage shall we suffer, if we do not treat.

Compute Six or Eight Per Cent Insurance upon all your Exports, and Imports. Compute the total Loss of all the Mediterranean and Levant Trade.

Compute the Loss of half your Trade to Portugal and Spain. These computations will amount to more than half a Million sterling a year.

The third Question is what will it cost to fight them? I answer, at least half a Million sterling a year without protecting your Trade, and when you leave off fighting you must pay as much Money as it would cost you now for Peace.

The Interest of half a Million Sterling is, even at Six Per Cent, Thirty Thousand Guineas a year. For an Annual Interest of 30,000£ st. then and perhaps of 15,000 or 10,000, we can have Peace, when a War would sink us annually ten times as much.

But for Gods Sake dont let us amuse our Countrymen with any further Projects of Sounding. We know all about it, as much ever we can know, untill we have the Money to offer. We know if we Send an Ambassador to Constantinople, he must give Presents. How much, the Comte de Vergennes can tell you better than any Man in Europe.

We are fundamentally wrong. The first Thing to be done is for Congress to have a Revenue. Taxes [and] Duties must be laid on by Congress or the

Assemblies and appropriated to the Payment of Interest. The Moment this is done we may borrow a Sum adequate to all our Necessities. If it is not done in my Opinion you and I as well as every other Servant of the United States in Europe ought to go home, give up all Points, and let all our Exports and Imports be done in European Bottoms. My Indignation is roused beyond all Patience to see the People in all the United States in a Torpor, and see them a Prey to every Robber, Pirate and Cheat in Europe. Jews and Judaizing Christians are now Scheeming to buy up all our Continental Notes at two or three shillings in a Pound, in order to oblige us to pay them at twenty shillings a Pound. This will be richer Plunder than that of Algerines or Loyds Coffee House. My dear friend Adieu,

—JOHN ADAMS

∾

[The following long but fascinating letter from Richard O'Brien describes in detail the situation along the Barbary coast, as well as the disastrous behavior of John Lamb, the man Congress had sent to buy back the American captives from their captivity.]

From Richard O'Bryen and Others
HONOURED SIR   Algiers June 8th. 1786

I take the Liberty of addressing these letters to you hoping you will excuse the freedom of an American &c. and unfortunate captive at present. No doubt but Mr. Lamb has given you and Mr. Adams every particular information respecting the state of affairs in Algiers. I am much surprized when I look at the date of your letter to us being the 4th. of November and with orders to Mr. Lamb to redeem us Americans. I am surprized that from the 4th. of November until the 20th. of March that Mr. Lamb did not get our redemption ascertained by some person in Algiers. But he retarding the time until he could make it convenient to come himself and not informing himself of the method generally used towards the redemption of captives, but on the contrary comes to Algiers and gives out that he came to redeem the Americans.

It was immediately signified to the Dey that Mr. Lamb had brought money for that purport, it became such a town talk that the Dey hardly knew what sum to ask. After a few days the Dey asks what sum Mr. Lamb would give. Mr. Lamb signified he would give ten thousand dollars. The Dey then said 50,000. I think the demand was very apropos to the offer of Mr. Lamb. Mr. Lamb tried to get the Dey to lower his price, but the Dey was determined not to lower his price any thing worth mentioning.

We are much surprized that Mr. Lamb should bring so trifling a sum as five or six thousand dollars to redeem 21. Even if the Dey had let us go agreeable to your calculation he could not have redeemed us. But Mr. Lamb when he first arrived told us he would get us along in a few days, which much disappointed us, for he afterwards told us he had no money to redeem us. What he had was for presents if he succeeded in a cessation of hostilities with this Regency. One time he would say his funds were in Holland, then in Spain, and then that you and Mr. Adams had given no power only to draw for £3300 strg. and that Mr. Randal must write the order. So that in his own language his hands were tyed by the ministers. I believe the Dey of Algiers was well convinced that Americans would give the sum he asked. I have reason to suspect that the Dey had a hint conveyed to him by the British Consul, who you may be assured is an inveterate enemy to the Americans. About 5 months ago I wrote Mr. Carmichael that the British Consul had put himself to great trouble in sending expresses to his court. About that time was the first time that he knew that it was the intention of the Americans to sue for a peace with the Barbary States. It is not the interest of any commercial nation that the Americans should obtain a peace with the Barbary States, whilst they reap such benefits in being the carriers of our commerce, particularly the English, French and Spanish being jealous of us. Consider Sir what great insurance we pay in getting our vessels insured. In a short time the great insurance we pay would obtain us a peace, or our ships obliged to be sold or with the greatest difficulty in procuring English registers and passes. If not soon remedied our trade must fall into some other chanel, and with the greatest difficulty we shall retrieve it again, our seamen having no longer employment in the United states but must through necessity seek a living in some other country. The British Consul I think informs his court respecting the time when the Algerine cruisers generally go out; by that means the people of England take the greatest advantage on insuring American property. And [it] is their policy and benefit to spread the alarm much greater than it really is. There is no danger of our commerce being prevented by the Algerines if we keep clear of the streights, coasts of Spain &c. Portugal and the Madeiras. We may trade to France, England, Holland, Sweden and any where to the N. of 44°. N. Latitude.

The Algerine cruisers generally go out in April but uncommon they went out the 25th. of May this year. They generally make three cruises a year, finish about the 20th. November and then unrig and ly by until the next year. The Algerines have no merchant ships or vessels for trade excepting a few coasting craft which go along shore with wheat &c. the French being their carriers in commerce and nothing great. Their marine strength is nine sail of xebecs, one of 32 guns, one of 30. three of 24 and three of 18. and one of 12. guns. The vessels are small to the metal they carry. $^{1}/8$ of the crews are Turks the remainder Algerine Moors.

A war with the Algerines would be a very expensive war. They having no merchant men it would be attended with a very great expence. On our side the expence of building a force adequate to the Algerines, to get men to keep that force in commission, and still it would be a great risque to trade. You are fully sensible the sum it would take to redeem a few and then it would alter the insurance but trifling.

The United States should use every means to obtain a peace with the Barbary States, although it would cost vast sums, for until all obstacles are removed that prevent commerce we cannot expect to be a commercial nation. It is bad policy to use any threats or make any parade with cruisers if we intend suing for a peace, but on the contrary let these people see that we are inclinable for a peace. No doubt but it was great policy in the Dey to refuse Mr. Lamb at first on the terms of peace. Consider Sir the policy of this Regency in all their transactions with the Christian nations. But I believe they are inclinable to a peace with the Americans but should for political views be negociated very private, particularly by the Americans. I believe they gave Mr. Lamb sufficient reason to believe so. They seem well inclined to a peace with us, and I believe would take some naval stores as masts, yards, planks, scantling, tar and turpentine. The English, French, Dutch, Danes and Swedes and I may say all nations are tributary to them, making them valuable presents and supplying them. The Algerines would never redeem or make an exchange with any nation they should be at war with. The Dey of Algiers cares not about his people particularly the Moors. The Turks he sets a little store by. Those nations that he has been at war with for ages have experienced it. It is the policy of Christian nations to keep those nations of Turks and Moors at war with other Christian Nations. And the people in general here wish for a war with those nations in the streights, for I am sure that nothing but so great a sum as the Spaniards are to give would reconcile those people to the Spaniards, they having such an inveteracy against them for persecuting the Mahometan religion. But money is the God of Algiers and Mahomet their prophet. They like those nations that they are afraid of and that give them most. But should the Algerines be influenced by the commercial Christian nations not to make a peace with the United States, then we should exert ourselves and fit out ships mounting about 24. guns, nine of that force and two brigs, a schooner, also fast sailing vessels and have them coppered, for the sooner we would harrass those people the better for we should if so lucky as to take two or three of them they would be inclinable to a peace and on easier terms for us. To rendezvous at Mahon and Gibraltar, and often to come in sight of Algiers, and I make no doubt when they found as spirited nation against them they would alter their opinion, not to be afraid of them like unto those dastardly nations, that have given them such reason to boast of a superiority in courage to Christians. The Algerines have 55. gun boats in case of an invasion or attack on the city which is very strong, being well fortified, and I think they are a tolerable smart active people, spirited in an attack, but with anything of a warm reception easily repulsed. They put great confidence in boarding therefore ought to be well barracked. If they can avoid an action it is their choice to be off.

The Algerines do not expect to derive any great advantage by being at war with the Americans. Our country being so far situated from them, they will not attempt to approach our coasts. They have very little Idea of America and I believe the British Consuls used their influence in signifying to the Algerines the unjustness of our cause, but since we arrived here we used our influence to convince them of the justness of our quarrel which they say that if they were in our situation they would do the same. There is a great difference between negociating with these people and a Christian nation. The foundation of all treaties should be laid by some person or Consul in Algiers that knows how to treat with them for there are certain times and seasons for those affairs. The

Dey's sentiments always ought to be well sounded and the sentiments of his ministers and head men for it is by them all business is transacted with him, for they have the Dey's ear at command, particularly the Causennage who is head minister. The Micklassha is the next. He is son in law to the Causennage and is Generalissimo of all the Fortifications, entire direction of the Marine, a particular favorite of the Dey, and I think no man fills his office better. A valuable present to the Micklassha and Causennage chosen by some man that is well acquainted with what suits those men best, I am sure it would be very requisite and not hove away. The Dey is well advanced in years, and I am sure when he goes to his long home that there will be a very great change in the state of affairs in this Regency. The Causennage will be his successor and the Micklassha will be the prime minister. If anyone knows those peoples policy I should think the Count D'Expilly does; being a year here negociating the Spanish peace and has had so many conferences with the Dey and his ministers. He has got the great men in office on his side. Give a Turk money with one hand and you may take his Eyes out with the other.

Since the Brig arrived from Tunis which is the brig which Mr. Lamb came to Algiers in, the brig was overhawled and the Captain examined by the Micklassha respecting the property. I am credibly informed by a Gentleman by the name of Capt. Bassline, who is a great favorite of the Micklassha's, that the Micklassha was well convinced by the information he had that the brig was an American property, which I heard the evening the brig arrived in Algiers. But the Micklassha despised any such mean action but signified to the Dey that the report was false. I hope this particular favor shewn the Americans by the Micklassha will not escape your notice but by every prudent step cultivate the friendship of so great and so good a man. The information by all I can learn and I have every reason to believe was given by the British Consul, Mr. Lamb's bosom friend. It is said and I have been credibly informed that Mr. Logie had the information from a Mr. Gregory British Consul in Barcelona, and I should think it a very dangerous affair for the brig to come to Algiers again particularly with money for or [our] redemption as there is no knowing the policy and political views of these people in Algiers. Permit me to mention to you that if it was not conven-ient to redeem us when the time is advanced which Mr. Lamb signified to the Dey that it would be good policy to get us on the Spanish list as the

Spaniards have not yet agreed on the price for their people; and inasmuch as the Count D'Expilly may get us for less than what the Dey asks, and as we were taken on the time when the Spaniards were about settling a truce unknown to the Americans. Delays breed danger and opportunity once lost is not easily recovered, and our captivity will become an old affair and here we shall remain. The American peace hangs on a thread but I make no doubt if well planned but the United states will obtain it.

The Neapolitan and Portuguese Ambassadors are shortly expected here, it is uncertain that they will obtain a peace, but if they do I will engage. The Portuguese particularly will pay well for it. The Spaniards have not surmounted all their difficulties yet with those people, but I believe it will take some time yet. A few days ago arrived a Venitian and a French Vessel with shot &c. for the Dey. The Venitian brought their tribute which was about 10,000 Algerine sequins and about 5,000 dollars worth of presents, but they accepted the tribute and I believe would not accept the presents so that it is supposed when the Algerines settle with the Spaniards that they will be apt to commit hostilities on the Venitians. Such tricks are very common to them.

It is believed Mr. John Wolfe will not get to be Spanish Consul in Algiers, but I am very sure he is a very good man; no one in Algiers better acquainted with the ways and policy of this Regency and would be a very fit man to trans-act any business for any nation. I refer you to Mr. Carmichael and Mr. Randall for his character and must observe that there is no doing any thing among those people without money. All the crowned heads in Europe to write to the Dey of Algiers would avail but very little. To negotiate a peace with the Algerines should be a statesman well acquainted with the different languages. But as I have said before the foundation should be laid by some Consul in Algiers whom the United States could depend on and then an American to come and conclude it. A good Consul is very requisite here.

We are much surprized at Mr. Lamb's ungentleman like behaviour whilst he was in Algiers and could hardly believe Congress would [have] sent such a man to negociate so important an affair as the making a peace with the Algerines where it required the most able Statesman and Politician.

The Count disapproved of his behaviour much and said he was a very uncapable man to treat for the redemption of us and worse for making the peace. A man that has no regularity in small affairs will have none in great ones. There is no Consul or man that has the least friendship for the Americans but says he was a very unable man and not the gentleman, which I believe Sir, when we can make such an observation on him we are sensible that a man of your abilities can have no great opinion of him.

Mr. Lamb's unguarded expressions, his hints, threats &c. despising the French and Spaniards, signifying their deciet and in fact every thing that he possibly could utter in the most vulgar language that it was with pain we see him so unworthy of his commission and the cloth he wore. His particular intimacy with Mr. Logie the British Consul, Mr. Lamb's bosom friend who I believe got all his secrets from him said often that the Americans had taken two forts on the Mississipi from the Spaniards and often in the hearing of some servants who spoke English that if the Spaniards did not assist the Americans in making their peace that we should take some of their territory from them. No doubt but the Count was informed of all this, for one of Mr. Lamb's servants is servant to the Count at present, and Mr. Lamb often said in my presence to Mr. Wolfe that he (meaning Mr. Wolfe) or the Count would have all the honor of laying the foundation of the peace.

Sir we are very sensible of your particular attention to us, and through your and Mr. Carmichaels care of us, we are indebted for the particular civility and attention of the Ct. D'Expilly and French Consul. But still it is impossible for us to be content whilst we are under the character of slaves, so disagreeable is confinement to the Land of Liberty. My crew go through the severities of slavery that is possible for men to endure. Capts. Stevens and Coffin have families and at present unknown how provided for. I have an aged mother, brother and sisters, that their whole dependance and subsistence was on me. Certainly the longer we stay here the greater expence we shall incur on our country. If we do not make our grievances known to you Sir I am sure who can we apply to. We have wrote to America when we were first taken, but not one of us has recieved a letter and cannot tell what our country has resolved on respecting us. We must submit to our hard fate and trust to God and our country to extricate us from Algiers. I hope Mr. Barclay will succeed with the Maroccians, their situation being more in the way of annoying us than the Algerines. I am surprized Mr. Lamb did not pay Mr. Logie the small sum of about 5 guineas which Mr. Logie paid to the marine for excluding us from it. Mr.

Lamb often insisted Mr. Logie to make some charge but at last Logie made a charge and Mr. Lamb did not pay him.

A Gentleman of the name of Mr. Basseline who rendered Mr. Lamb many services and lies much in his power to do many more, he being on the most friendly footing with the Micklassha &c., is here at present. When Mr. Lamb was on his return to Spain being confused in his affairs and wanted to leave Mr. Wolfe some money Bassaline gave Mr. Lamb about four hundred dollars in gold which Mr. Lamb gave to Mr. Wolfe to defray some expences. But as Bassaline was called to Spain he went on board the same vessel that Mr. Lamb did and during 17. days which they were together Mr. Bassaline signified to Mr. Lamb that he wanted the money. But Mr. Lamb evaded the matter from day to day and has not paid Bassaline or given him an order on any person for the money. Capt. Bassaline has returned to Algiers mentioned this affair to Mr. Wolfe &c. which has much surprized him of the behaviour of Mr. Lamb and I make no doubt but Mr. Bassaline wanted the money in Spain. His unpolitical behaviour in all his transactions is much against the honor and dignity of the United states. No doubt but Mr. Randall gave you a sketch of his behaviour. Not that I have any particular inveteracy against Mr. Lamb but prompted by a principle of honor and esteem for my country I mention Mr. Lamb's behaviour to you hoping that what I have mentioned will not escape your notice.

Mr. Wolfe will have occasion to write Mr. Carmichael respecting money he having orders from Mr. Lamb to supply the captives and nothing to do it with. Also Mr. Wolfe will give an account of our expences &c. The Cruisers are out at present. We are treated with the greatest civility by all the French and Spaniards here.

An account how we are situated and where.

4. of us at the house of Monsr. Ford

7. in the Dey's palace

9. in the marine

1. at the Swedish Consuls.

—RICHD O BRYEN

From Richard O'Bryen
SIR   Algiers July 12th. 1786

Since the arrival of Mr. Lamb at Algiers I wrote you several letters informing you of some particulars which came within my observation. Mr. Lamb has actually agreed with the Dey of Algiers for the redemption of us unfortunate captives. It is near three months since Mr. Lamb left Algiers and was to get the money in four months. I hope for our sakes, and the honor of his country, that he will not deviate from his word with the Dey of Algiers. We recieved a few lines from Mr. Lamb by the Spanish Brig. Mr. Lamb says he had stated our situation to you some months ago and that he had not recieved any answer from you or from Mr. Adams and therefore can not tell what will be determined on in our behalf.

He mentions in his letter that it was not in his power to redeem us as his orders were not to go higher than 200 dollars per man. I never blamed him for not redeeming us as there was so small a sum appropriated for that use, as he repeatedly told me and others. It is near one year since we are in the fetters of slavery without having any account from the Continent, and lately within the time that Mr. Lamb arrived here without any assurances from our Country or Countrymen, and Mr. Lamb's letter has struck us with the most poignant grief so that our gloomy unfortunate situation affects us beyond our expression or your Imagination. We try to administer consolation to our unfortunate crews; but poor fellows endure the severities of slavery. I am confident our Country must have resolved on something respecting us before this time. Certainly Liberty that is the basis of America will never let twenty one unfortunate citizens remain slaves to the Turkish yoke.

The other day when I was in the Dey's palace to see the boys, that belonged to my vessel, the next man to the Dey asked me when I had heard from Mr. Lamb, and asked me if I did not expect to go clear soon. I said I did not know, and he said that the American Ambassador had agreed with the Dey to give 50,000 dollars and to get the money in four months time which he often tells the boys.

The Algerines have taken several prizes this cruise. They went out the 27th. of May and to day the last of them returned into port.

A Russian ship of 700 ton loaded with wine   15 Men
A Leghorn ship of 20 Guns and   44 men
Two Genoa barks of the Coast.
One Neapolitan, but is returned being taken in a Spanish bay.
One Spaniard taken but the vessel returned.

A Brig under Imperial colours—all Genoese on board. A hard task to clear her but is given up, those people being much afraid of the Emperor. Four Portuguee fishing boats taken off Cape St. Vincent—15 Portuguese fishermen.

One of the Algerines went out of the coast of Portugal where they took the Fishermen off Cape St. Vincents.

We should be happy in hearing from you respecting our redemption or if it is our hard lot here to remain we must make the best of it.

I remain your most obedient & very unfortunate

—RICHD O BRYEN

෴

[Jay, in charge of foreign affairs, here writes in despair of the current form of the federal government, and complains of the difficulty—the near impossibility—of getting Congress to act on anything.]

From John Jay
DR SIR   New York 18th. August 1786

My last to you was dated the 14th. of last Month, since which I have received and laid before Congress your several Letters of 12th. 22d. 23d. two of 27th. and one of 31st. May last, with the Papers enclosed with them.

It has happened from various Circumstances, that several Reports on foreign Affairs still lay before Congress undecided upon. The want of an adequate Representation for long Intervals, and the Multiplicity of Business which pressed upon them when that was not the Case, has occasioned Delays and Omissions which however unavoidable are much to be regretted. It is painful to me to reflect that altho' my Attention to Business is unremitted yet I so often experience unseasonable Delays and successive Obstacles in obtaining the Decision and Sentiments of Congress, even on Points which require Dispatch. But so it is, and I must be content with leaving nothing undone that may depend upon me.

The consular Convention is now as it has long been, under the consideration of Congress, and I have Reason to hope they will soon enable me to send you full Instructions on that Subject.

I have long thought and become daily more convinced that the Construction of our fœderal Government is fundamentally wrong. To vest legislative, judicial and executive Powers in one and the same Body of Men, and that too in a Body daily changing its Members, can never be wise. In my Opinion those three great Departments of Sovereignty should be for ever separated, and so distributed as to serve as Checks on each other. But these are Subjects that have long been familiar to you and on which you are too well informed not to anticipate every Thing that I might say on them.

I enclose a late Ordinance of Congress for Indian Affairs, and their Requisition for the ensuing Year. Those Subjects have consumed much Time. They are however important ones and the Attention of Congress to them could not with Propriety have been postponed.

[I have advised Congress to renew your Commission as to certain Powers. Our Treasury is ill supplied; some States pay nothing and others very little. The Impost not yet established. The People generally uneasy in a certain Degree, but without seeming to discern the true Cause, vizt., want of Energy both in state and foederal Governments. It takes Time to make Sovereigns of Subjects.]

I am, Dr. Sir, with great Esteem & Regard, &c.

—JOHN JAY

❧

[This letter transmits to Jay the final results of Jefferson's work to obtain favorable trade agreements with the French, which he had been working on for a year. Much of the credit, as he here explains, belongs to Lafayette, whose committee pressed hard for the advantages here obtained. These agreements were the highlight of Jefferson's diplomatic career in Europe.]

To John Jay

SIR   Paris Oct. 23. 1786

In a letter of Jan. 2. I had the honor of communicating to you the measures which had been pursued here for the improvement of the commerce between the U.S. and France, the general view of that commerce which I had presented to the C. de Vergennes, the circumstance of the renewal of the farms which had obliged me to press separately and in the first place, the article of tobacco, and that which had also brought forward that of whale oil: and in my letters of May 27. and 31. I informed you of the result on the first of these articles. During the course of these proceedings a Committee had been established for considering the means of promoting the general commerce with America, and the M. de la Fayette was named of that committee. His influence in obtaining that establishment was valuable, but his labors and his perseverance as a member of it became infinitely more so. Immediately after the committee of Berni, of which my letter of May 27. gave an account, we thought it expedient to bring the general subject of the American commerce before the Committee; and as the members were much unacquainted with the nature and value of our Commercial productions, the Marquis proposed that in a letter to him as a member I should give as particular details of them as I could, as a ground for the committee to proceed on. I did so in the letter, a copy of which I have now the honour to inclose. The committee were well disposed, and agreed to report not only the general measures which they thought expedient to be adopted, but the form of the letter to be written by the Minister of finance to me, for the communication of those measures. I have received his letter this morning and have now the honour to inclose it. I accompany it with the one proposed by the committee, of which you will perceive that it is almost a verbal copy: it furnishes a proof of the disposition of the king and his ministers to produce a more intimate intercourse between the two nations. Indeed I must say that, as far as I am able to see, the friendship of the people of this country towards us is cordial and general, and that it is a kind of security for the friendship of ministers who cannot in any country be uninfluenced by the voice of the people. To this we may add that it is their interest as well as ours to multiply the bands of friendship between us. As the regulations stated in the minister's letter are immediately interesting to those concerned in our commerce, I send printed copies of it to the seaport towns of France. We may consider them as an ultimate settlement of the conditions of our commerce with this country: for tho the consolidation of ship duties and the encouragements for the importation of rice are not finally decided, yet the letter contains a promise of them so soon as necessary facts shall be known. With a view to come at the facts relative to the two last objects, I had proposed whenever I should receive the final decision now inclosed, to avail myself of the pause which that would produce, in order to visit the seaport towns with which we trade chiefly and to collect that kind of knowlege of our commerce, and of what may be further useful to it which can only be gathered on the spot, and suggested by one's own inspection. But the delay which has attended the obtaining the final determination has brought us to the entrance of winter, and will oblige me to postpone my journey to the spring. Besides the objects of public utility which induce me to make a tour of this kind, that of health will oblige me to pay more attention to exercise and change of air than I have hitherto done since my residence in Europe: and I am willing to hope that I may be permitted at times to absent myself from this place, taking occasions when there is nothing important on hand nor likely to arise.

The assistance of the M. de la Fayette in the whole of this business has been so earnest and so efficacious that I am in duty bound to place it under the eye of Congress, as worthy their notice on this occasion. Their thanks, or such other notice as they should think proper, would be grateful to him without doubt. He has richly deserved and will continue to deserve it whenever occasions shall arise of rendering service to the U.S. These occasions will continually occur. Tho the abolition of the monopoly of our tobaccoes can not be hoped under the present circumstances, changes are possible which may open that hope again. However jealous too this country is of foreign intercourse with their colonies, that intercourse is too essential to us to be abandoned as desperate. At this moment indeed it cannot be proposed: but by watching circumstances, occasion may arise hereafter, and I hope will arise. I know from experience what would in that case be the value of such an auxiliary.

I have the honour to be with sentiments of the most perfect esteem & respect Sir your most obedient & most humble servant,

—TH: JEFFERSON

[In the first paragraph of this letter, omitted here, Jefferson tells Madison about his damaged wrist; in the second, also omitted, he summarizes what he had just written to Jay about trade with France. Jefferson then proceeds to discuss the possibility of reforming the Articles of Confederation. Madison had attempted to do that in September, persuading Congress to call a convention designed to put trade under a single, federal power. The convention never took place, but its failure led to the wider convention we now know as the Constitutional Convention, which first met in May 1787.]

To James Madison
DEAR SIR   Paris Dec. 16. 1786

... I find by the public papers that your Commercial Convention failed in point of representation. If it should produce a full meeting in May, and a broader reformation, it will still be well. To make us one nation as to foreign concerns, and keep us distinct in Domestic ones, gives the outline of the proper division of powers between the general and particular governments. But to enable the Federal head to exercise the powers given it, to best advantage, it should be organized, as the particular ones are, into Legislative, Executive and Judiciary. The 1st. and last are already separated. The 2d should also be. When last with Congress, I often proposed to members to do this by making of the Committee of the states, an Executive committee during the recess of Congress, and during it's sessions to appoint a Committee to receive and dispatch all executive business, so that Congress itself should meddle only with what should be legislative. But I question if any Congress (much less all successively) can have self-denial enough to go through with this distribution. The distribution should be imposed on them then. I find Congress have reversed their division of the Western states, and proposed to make them fewer and larger. This is reversing the natural order of things. A tractable people may be governed in large bodies; but in proportion as they depart from this character, the extent of their government must be less. We see into what small divisions the Indians are obliged to reduce their societies. This measure, with the disposition to shut up the Missisipi give me serious

apprehensions of the severance of the Eastern and Western parts of our confederacy. It might have been made the interests of the Western states to
remain united with us, by managing their interests honestly and for their
own good. But the moment we sacrifice their interests to our own, they will
see it better to govern themselves. The moment they resolve to do this, the
point is settled. A forced connection is neither our interest nor within our
power.—The Virginia act for religious freedom [first proposed by Jefferson nearly
a decade before and one of the accomplishments he was most proud of] has been
received with infinite approbation in Europe and propagated with enthusiasm. I do not mean by the governments, but by the individuals which compose them. It has been translated into French and Italian, has been sent to
most of the courts of Europe, and has been the best evidence of the falshood of those reports which stated us to be in anarchy. It is inserted in the
new Encyclopedie, and is appearing in most of the publications respecting America. In fact it is comfortable to see the standard of reason at
length erected, after so many ages during which the human mind has
been held in vassalage by kings, priests and nobles; and it is honorable for
us to have produced the first legislature who has had the courage to declare
that the reason of man may be trusted with the formation of his own
opinions. I shall be glad when the revisal shall be got thro'. In the criminal law, the principle of retaliation is much criticized here, particularly in
the case of Rape. They think the punishment indecent and unjustifiable.
I should be for altering it, but for a different reason: that is on account of
the temptation women would be under to make it the instrument of
vengeance against an inconstant lover, and of disappointment to a rival.—
Are our courts of justice open for the recovery of British debts according
to the Septennial act? The principles of that act can be justified; but the
total stoppage of justice cannot. The removal of the negroes from New York
would only give cause for stopping some of the last payments, if the
British government should refuse satisfaction, which however I think
they will not do.

I thank you for your communications in Natural history. The several
instances of trees &c. found far below the surface of the earth, as in the case
of Mr. Hay's well, seem to set the reason of man at defiance. Another
Theory of the earth has been contrived by one Whitford, not absolutely rea-

sonable, but somewhat more so than any that has yet appeared. It is full of interesting facts; which however being inadequate to his theory, he is obliged to supply them from time to time by begging questions. It is worth your getting from London. If I can be useful to you in ordering books from London you know you may command me. You had better send me the duplicate volume of the Encyclopedie. I will take care to send you the proper one. I have many more livraisons for you and have made some other inconsiderable purchases for you in this way. But I shall not send them till the spring, as a winter passage is bad for books. I reserve myself till that time therefore to give you an account of the execution of your several commissions, only observing that the watch will not be finished till the spring and that it will be necessary for me to detain her some time on trial, because it often happens that a watch, looking well to the eye, and faithfully made, goes badly at first on account of some little circumstance which escapes the eye of the workman when he puts her together and which he could easily rectify .... [In the rest of this letter Jefferson discusses the difficulty of borrowing money in Europe for American commercial projects.]

—TH: JEFFERSON

ഔൗ

To Abigail Adams Smith   Paris Jan. 15. 1787

Mr. Jefferson has the honour to present his compliments to Mrs. Smith and to send her the two pair of Corsets she desired. He wishes they may be suitable, as Mrs. Smith omitted to send her measure. Times are altered since Mademoiselle de Sanson had the honour of knowing her. Should they be too small however, she will be so good as to lay them by a while. There are ebbs as well as flows in this world. When the mountain refused to come to Mahomet, he went to the mountain. Mr. Jefferson wishes Mrs. Smith a happy new year, and abundance of happier ones still to follow it. He begs leave to assure her of his esteem and respect, and that he shall always be happy to be rendered useful to her by being charged with her commands.

ഔൗ

[Louis XVI, the French king, called the Assembly of Notables—the cream, that is, of the French nobility—to deal with the near bankruptcy of his government. Much of France's national debt at the time stemmed from its participation in the American Revolution. The Assembly had last met in 1626; this time, little came of it. The tumult in America Jefferson refers to was Shays's Rebellion in western Massachusetts, of which little came as well. This letter contains Jefferson's most extreme remark on freedom of the press, and is famed for that reason. Carrington was a conservative Virginia planter, friend, and member of Congress.]

To Edward Carrington
DEAR SIR   Paris Jan. 16. 1787

Incertain whether you might be at New York at the moment of Colo. Frank's arrival, I have inclosed in my private letters for Virginia under cover to our delegation in general, which otherwise I would have taken the liberty inclose particularly to you, as best acquainted with the situation of the persons to whom they are addressed. Should this find you at New York, I will still ask your attention to them. The two large packages addressed to Colo. N. Lewis contain seeds, not valuable enough to pay postage, but which I would wish to be sent by the stage, or any similar quick conveyance. The letters to Colo. Lewis and Mr. Eppes (who take care of my affairs) are particularly interesting to me. The package for Colo. Richd. Cary our judge of Admiralty near Hampton, contains seeds and roots, not to be sent by post. Whether they had better go by the stage, or by water, you will be the best judge. I beg your pardon for giving you this trouble. But my situation and your goodness will I hope excuse it.

In my letter to Mr. Jay I have mentioned the meeting of the Notables appointed for the 29th inst. It is now put off to the 7th.or 8th. of next month. This event, which will hardly excite any attention in America, is deemed here the most important one which has taken place in their civil line during the present century. Some promise of their country great things from it, some nothing. Our friend de la fayette was placed on the list originally. Afterwards his name disappeared: but finally was reinstated. This shews that his character here is not considered as an indifferent one; and that it excites agitation. His education in our school has drawn on him a very jealous eye from a court whose principles are the most absolute despotism. But I hope he has nearly passed his crisis. The king, who is a good man, is favorably disposed towards him: and he is supported by powerful family connections, and by the public good will. He is the youngest man of the Notables, except one whose office placed him on the list.

The Count de Vergennes has within these ten days had a very severe attack of what is deemed an unfixed gout. He has been well enough however to do business to-day. But anxieties for him are not yet quieted. He is a great and good minister, and an accident to him might endanger the peace of Europe.

The tumults in America, I expected would have produced in Europe an unfavorable opinion of our political state. But it has not. On the contrary, the small effect of those tumults seems to have given more confidence in the firmness of our governments. The interposition of the people themselves on the side of government has had a great effect on the opinion here. I am persuaded myself that the good sense of the people will always be found to be the best army. They may be led astray for a moment, but will soon correct themselves. The people are the only censors of their governors: and even their errors will tend to keep these to the true principles of their institution. To punish these errors too severely would be to suppress the only safeguard of the public liberty. The way to prevent these irregular inter-positions of the people is to give them full information of their affairs thro' the channel of the public papers, and to contrive that those papers should penetrate the whole mass of the people. The basis of our governments being the opinion of the people, the very first object should be to keep that right; and were it left to me decide whether we should have a government without newspapers, or newspapers without a government, I should not hesitate a moment to prefer the latter. But I should mean that every man should receive those papers and be capable of reading them. I am convinced that those societies (as the Indians) which live without government enjoy in their general mass an infinitely greater degree of happiness than those who live under European governments. Among the former, public opinion is in the place of law, and restrains morals as powerfully as laws ever did any where. Among the latter, under pretence of governing they have divided their nations into two classes, wolves and sheep. I do not exaggerate. This is a true picture of Europe. Cherish therefore the spirit of our people, and keep alive their attention. Do not be too severe upon their errors, but reclaim them by enlightening them. If once they become inattentive to the public affairs, you and I, and Congress, and Assemblies, judges and governors shall all become wolves. It seems to be the law of our general nature, in spite of individual exceptions; and experience declares that man is the only animal which devours his own kind, for I can apply no milder term to the governments of Europe, and to the general prey of the rich on the poor. —The want of news had led me into disquisition instead of narration, forgetting you have every day enough of that. I shall be happy to hear from you some times, only observing that whatever passes thro' the post is read, and that when you write what should be read by myself only, you must be so good as to confide your letter to some passenger or officer of the packet. I will ask your permission to write to you sometimes, and to assure you of the esteem & respect with which I have the honour to be Dear Sir your most obedient & most humble servt.,

—TH: JEFFERSON

❧

[The following is also a well-known letter. Jefferson had been in France for two and a half years now, and was addressing a friend who had spent some time in Paris while he was there. We print her interesting reply directly after.]

To Anne Willing Bingham   Paris Feb. 7. 1787

I know, Madam, that the twelvemonth is not yet expired; but it will be, nearly, before this will have the honour of being put into your hands. You are then engaged to tell me truly and honestly whether you do not find the tranquil pleasures of America preferable to the empty bustle of Paris. For to what does that bustle tend? At eleven o'clock it is day chez Madame. The curtains are drawn. Propped on bolsters and pillows, and her head scratched into a little order, the bulletins of the sick are read, and the billets of the well. She writes to some of her acquaintance and receives the visits of others. If the morning is not very thronged, she is able to get out and hobble round the cage of the Palais royal: but she must hobble quickly, for the Coeffeur's turn is come; and a tremendous turn it is! Happy, if he does not make her arrive when dinner is half over! The torpitude of digestion a little passed, she flutters half an hour thro' the streets by way of paying visits, and then to the Spectacles. These finished, another half hour is devoted to dodging in and out of the doors of her very sincere friends, and away to supper. After supper cards; and after cards bed, to rise at noon the next day, and to tread, like a mill-horse, the same trodden circle over again. Thus the days of life are consumed, one by one, without an object beyond the present moment: ever flying from the ennui of that, yet carrying it with us; eternally in pursuit of happiness which keeps eternally before us. If death or a bankruptcy happen to trip us out of the circle, it is matter for the buz of the evening, and is completely forgotten by the next morning.

In America, on the other hand, the society of your husband, the fond cares for the children, the arrangements of the house, the improvements of the grounds fill every moment with a healthy and an useful activity. Every exertion is encouraging, because to present amusement it joins the promise of some future good. The intervals of leisure are filled by the society of real friends, whose affections are not thinned to cob-web by being spread over a thousand objects.—This is the picture in the light it is presented to my mind; now let me have it in yours. If we do not concur this year, we shall the next: or if not then, in a year or two more. You see I am determined not to suppose myself mistaken. To let you see that Paris is not changed in it's pursuits since it was honoured with your presence, I send you it's monthly history. But this relating only to the embellishments of their persons I must add that those of the city go well also. A new bridge, for example, is begun at the Place Louis Quinze; the old ones are clearing of the rubbish which encumbered them in the form of houses; new hospitals erecting; magnificent walls of inclosure and Custom houses at their entrance &c. &c. &c. —I know of no interesting change among those whom you honoured with your acquaintance, unless Monsr. De Saint James was of that number. His bankruptcy and taking asylum in the Bastile have furnished matter of astonishment. His garden at the Pont de Neuilly, where, on seventeen acres of ground he had laid out fifty thousand Louis, will probably sell for somewhat less money.—The workmen of Paris are making rapid strides towards English perfection. Would you believe that in the course of the last two years they have learnt even to surpass their London rivals in some articles?

Commission me to have you a Phaeton made, and if it is not as much hand-somer than a London one, as that is than a Fiacre, send it back to me. Shall I fill the box with caps, bonnets &c? not of my own chusing, but—I was going to say of Mademoiselle Bertin's, forgetting for the moment that she too is bankrupt. They shall be chosen then by whom you please; or, if you are altogether non plus-ed by her eclipse, we will call an assembleé des Notables to help you out of the difficulty, as is now the fashion. In short, honour me with your commands of any kind, and they shall be faithfully executed. The packets, now established from Havre to New York, furnish good opportunities of sending whatever you wish.

I shall end where I began, like a Paris day, reminding you of your engage-ment to write me a letter of respectable length, an engagement the more precious to me as it has furnished me the occasion, after presenting my respects to Mr. Bingham, of assuring you of the sincerity of those sentiments of esteem & respect with which I have the honour to be, dear Madam, your most obedient & most humble servt.,

—TH: JEFFERSON

⌘

From Anne Willing Bingham   [Philadelphia, 1 June 1787]

I am too much flattered by the Honor of your letter from Paris, not to acknowledge it by the earliest opportunity, and to assure you that I am very sensible of your attentions. The Candor with which you express your sentiments, merits a sincere declaration of mine.

I agree with you that many of the fashionable pursuits of the Parisian Ladies are rather frivolous, and become uninteresting to a reflective Mind; but the Picture you have exhibited, is rather overcharged. You have thrown a strong light upon all that is ridiculous in their Characters, and you have buried their good Qualities in the Shade. It shall be my Task to bring them forward, or at least to attempt it. The State of Society in different Countries requires corres-ponding Manners and Qualifications; those of the French Women are by no means calculated for the Meridian of America, neither are they adapted to render the Sex so amiable or agreable in the English acceptation, of those words.

But you must confess, that they are more accomplished, and understand the Intercourse of society better than in any other Country. We are irresistibly pleased with them, because they possess the happy Art of making us pleased with ourselves; their education is of a higher Cast, and by great cultivation they procure a happy variety of Genius, which forms their Conversation, to please either the Fop, or the Philosopher.

In what other country can be found a Marquise de Coigny, who, young and handsome, takes a lead in all the fashionable Dissipation of Life, and at more serious moments collects at her House an assembly of the Literati, whom she charms with her Knowledge and her bel Esprit. The Women of France interfere in the politics of the Country, and often give a decided Turn to the Fate of Empires. Either by the gentle Arts of persuasion, or by the commanding force of superior Attractions and Address, they have obtained that Rank and Consideration in society, which the Sex are intitled to, and which they in vain contend for in other Countries. We are therefore bound in Gratitude to admire and revere them, for asserting our Privileges, as much as the Friends of the Liberties of Mankind reverence the successful Struggles of the American Patriots.

The agreable resources of Paris must certainly please and instruct every Class of Characters. The Arts of Elegance are there considered essential, and are carried to a state of Perfection; the Mind is continually gratified with the admiration of Works of Taste. I have the pleasure of knowing you too well, to doubt of your subscribing to this opinion. With respect to my native Country, I assure you that I am fervently attached to it, as well as to my Friends and Connections in it; there is possibly more sincerity in Professions and a stronger desire of rendering real services, and when the Mouth expresses, the Heart speaks.

I am sensible that I shall tire you to Death from the length of this Letter, and had almost forgot that you are in Paris, and that every instant of your Time is valuable, and might be much better employed than I can possibly do it. However, I shall reserve a further examination of this subject to the Period, when I can have the happiness of meeting you, when we will again resume it. I feel myself under many obligations for your kind present of les Modes de Paris; they have furnished our Ladies with many Hints, for the decoration of their Persons, and I have informed them to whom they are indebted. I shall benefit by your obliging offer of service, whenever I shall have occasion for a fresh Importation of Fashions; at present I am well stocked having lately received a variety of Articles from Paris.

Be so kind as to remember me with affection to Miss Jefferson—tell her she is the envy of all the young Ladies in America, and that I should wish nothing so much as to place my little Girl, under her inspection and protection, should she not leave Paris before I re-visit it. I shall hope for the pleasure of hearing from you, and if you accompany another book of fashions, with any new Opera's or Comedies, you will infinitely oblige me. It is quite time I bad you adieu, but remember that this first of June I am constant to my former opinion, nor can I believe that any length of time will change it. I am determined to have some merit in your eyes, if not for taste and judgment, at least for consistency.

Allow me my dear Sir to assure that I am sincerely & respectfully yours &c.,

—A BINGHAM

CHAPTER FOUR

We'll Always Have Paris

T HOMAS JEFFERSON AND MARIA COSWAY MET IN MID-AUGUST 1786, DURING a slow period in his diplomatic work—he had just consulted with one of the Farmers-General on the price of tobacco—and a quiet time socially—many of his aristocratic friends were at their chateaus in the country. They met at the Halle aux Bleds, the new market with the great dome that had been built recently in Paris. The young American artist John Trumbull, recently arrived from London with a letter of introduction from Abigail Adams, contrived the meeting and introduced Jefferson to Maria Cosway and her husband, Richard. Trumbull knew the Cosways from London. They were both talented, successful artists, Richard having been taken under the wing of the Prince of Wales early in his career, while Maria painted landscapes and portraits for their aristocratic friends. Richard was a slight man, infamous for his extravagant dress, and was probably gay. Theirs was a marriage of convenience. He had in effect bought Maria from her mother, giving her what William Howard Adams calls "a generous settlement" at a time when her family was short of money. Maria, born in Florence to English innkeeper parents and raised there, had blue eyes and blond hair, and she was gorgeous. She spoke English with an Italian accent and was always more comfortable speaking Italian.

Jefferson fell in love with her on the spot, and the Cosways took to Jefferson, too. He was so smitten that he canceled his other engagements for the day in order to spend it with them. He had accepted an invitation to dine that evening with no less a personage than the Duchess d'Enville. He sent a messenger to tell her that pressing business had come up suddenly, and he would have to cancel.

Except for a few brief notes, the correspondence between them began after the Cosways had left London in early October, so what we know about the next few weeks we gather from hints in the letters, from the brief account Jefferson gave in his famous "Head and Heart" letter, reprinted in this chapter, and from outside sources. It's clear that they spent a great deal of time together. The two of them were often alone, taking excursions to the parks and woods outside Paris, to well-known sights like the architectural folies at the Desert de Retz, an estate near the Forest of Marly outside Paris, to the theater, and to concerts. Maria was a talented musician as well as an artist. Richard Cosway had work in Paris, which freed Maria to spend the time with Jefferson, but she was free in any case of her husband's control to a degree that would be surprising even today. She dropped in frequently on her own and without being announced to Jefferson's house. Their later correspondence gives every indication that this was a blissful time for Jefferson.

On September 18, in her company, Jefferson fell and broke his right wrist. Exactly how this happened we don't know. One account has him leaping a small puddle and slipping. Another has him jumping a fence. Whatever the case, he fell, it was misdiagnosed as a dislocation and badly set, and it troubled him for the rest of his life. The first letter in this chapter is from Maria to Jefferson, dated two days later. She is upset that they did not see each other that day. The next is dated October 5, from Jefferson to Maria. It is his first surviving letter to her. Pain, he writes, kept him awake all night. The Cosways left the next day for London and, despite his pain, Jefferson accompanied them out of town as far as St. Denis. He wrote his first letters to her with his left hand. It was months before he could write normally, with his right.

Their correspondence, as far as it goes, tells the rest of the story. The most remarkable of their letters is without question Jefferson's letter of a few weeks later, a dialogue between his head and his heart, which many historians think is the most personally revealing letter Jefferson ever wrote. But like the rest of their letters, it does not answer the question they would most like answered: Did Jefferson and Maria Cosway consummate this affair?

Lacking answers, historians have speculated endlessly on the question. Andrew Burstein, in his book The Inner Jefferson, notes that Jefferson was "playful to the point of hinting at amorous possibilities" in his relationships with women, "yet morally secure and nonthreatening." He doesn't believe that Jefferson and Maria Cosway were physically intimate. Joseph Ellis argues in his book American Sphinx that Jefferson was too bloodless, too much of an idealist, and too sentimentally inclined toward Romance with a capital R to have consummated the affair physically.

On one level this seems ridiculous. Jefferson had, after all, fathered five children by his wife, who had died in 1782, four years before, and he was still what we would call a relatively young man. Maria Cosway was a great, indeed a famous, beauty. Rumors of her having affairs were rife in London, and her husband's sexuality was compromised. The king himself called Richard Cosway a fop, at a time when the term was a slang term for gays. A year after Jefferson left Paris, in the summer of 1790, Maria Cosway had a child. There's no question that she, at least, was sexually active.

Then there's the business about Sally Hemings, who had arrived in Paris shortly before as a servant to Jefferson's little girl, Polly. Sally was hardly more than a girl herself, 14 years old at the time of her arrival, but she purportedly told her son Madison many years later that Jefferson was his father. Many historians, Joseph Ellis included, now accept it as highly probable, if not quite fact, that Jefferson did father at least some of Sally Hemings's children. The DNA evidence is equivocal. DNA samples have been taken from descendants of two of Sally Hemings's children. In one case it's clear that the Jeffersons were not involved. In the other, yes, a Jefferson was the father, but it was not necessarily Thomas Jefferson. At the time this child was born, Jefferson was 65 years old, and there were at least 20 other Jefferson males within walking distance of Monticello who might have been the father. Jefferson family tradition has it that one of his nephews, either Samuel Carr or his brother Peter—the nephew whose education Jefferson had sponsored—was the father. In a competing tradition, Jefferson's younger brother Randolph, known for visiting Monticello and spending the evening with the slaves, dancing, and making music, fathered some of Sally's children.

So did Thomas Jefferson sleep with Sally Hemings? We'll never know for sure. Opinions on the subject vary with the mindset of the historian in question.

Nor will we ever know whether he slept with Maria Cosway. She was a devout Roman Catholic. Later in life she devoted herself to good works and the church. She's hard to read, like Jefferson himself, and the problem, if that's the word for it, is complicated by the fact that the past as a whole is hard to read. We ourselves are obsessed with sexuality and have lost our understanding of the manners and style of older ways of life. In the times these two people lived, when marriages were still arranged, it was not at all uncommon to conduct not just affairs but elaborate flirtations outside marriage, especially in aristocratic circles, and to use the distance afforded by correspondence to make equally elaborate compliments to each other. Close friendships between men and women, furthermore, were easier then. One of Jefferson's closest friends during his years in Paris was Abigail Adams, John Adams's wife. He was also quite friendly with Abigail's daughter, Abby. They all wrote rather intimate letters to each other, letters that often contained a flirtatious undertone. Jefferson shopped for clothes for them in Paris, even for underclothes. He teases them about it in some of his letters. He must have felt like a member of their family. And quite clearly the correspondence is with them, the Adams women, and they carry it on without reference to John Adams.

Standard rules of decorum would have prevented either Maria Cosway or Jefferson from referring in their letters to any physical intimacy they might have had. We shall never know. She returned to Paris the following year, but we print very little from this period. She was there for months, and without her husband, who had not come with her, but Jefferson hardly saw her. She was always with company. She also had a new admirer, says George Green Shackelford in his book Thomas Jefferson's Travels in Europe, 1784-1789. He was the Duc de Lauzun, Armand Louis Gontaud, a rake and a spendthrift who had fought in the American Revolution and had been, or so he claimed, the lover of Marie Antoinette—who had many lovers. Shackelford notes that Jefferson gave Maria a small portrait of himself drawn by John Trumbull. Lauzun gave her "a life-size portrait bust of himself in marble." She left Paris that December without saying good-bye to Jefferson.

They corresponded, nevertheless, for the rest of their lives, although with less and less frequency. Jefferson's next "affair" was with one of her best friends, Angelica Schuyler Church, some of whose correspondence with Jefferson during the Paris years also appears in this section. She was an American, daughter of a general who served as an aide to Rochambeau during the Revolutionary War, and a great beauty in her own right. There's no indication in their correspondence or from other sources that these two wandered around the outskirts of Paris on romantic tours or that Jefferson felt the kind of passion for her that he felt for Maria Cosway, but that he was attracted to her there can be no doubt. She, too, was married—to a British businessman who had lived in America during the Revolution and served as commissary general to George Washington, then returned after the war to England with Angelica in tow and became, of all things, a member of Parliament. Angelica's sister was married to Alexander Hamilton. She herself was just as well connected in Europe as her sister in America. She knew Lafayette; she knew Talleyrand. Napoleon was greatly taken with her. Like Maria, she was an independent woman who traveled on her own. She met Jefferson in the winter of 1787, shortly after Maria Cosway left Paris for the second time. Her daughter Kitty was with Polly, Jefferson's recently arrived second daughter, at the same convent school.

And did they have a sexual relationship? The question gets sillier and sillier. As he had to Maria Cosway, Jefferson suggested to Angelica Schuyler Church that they travel home to America together and tour the country. Likewise they, too, maintained a correspondence for many years. But we cannot assume from this that sexual intimacy was the basis for what became lifelong friendship. The correspondence itself is the only reliable door into their world, which was so different from our own. These are people to whom it would never have occurred to descend in writing to the level of the explicit. So why should we? Why not let these mysteries lie unresolved, part of a past we can never fully recover even under the best of circumstances, the most complete documentation?

ↀ

From Maria Cosway   Parigi Mercoledi Sera [20 Sep. 1786]

[I hope] you dont always judge by appearances [or it wo]uld be Much to My disadvantage this day, without [my] deserving it; it has been the day of contradiction, I meant to have had the pleasure of seing you *Twice*, and I have appeard a Monster for not having sent to know how you was, *the whole day*. I have been More uneasy, Than I can express. This Morning My Husband kill'd My project, I had proposed to him, by burying himself among Pictures and forgeting the hours, though we were Near your House coming to see you, we were obliged to turn back, the time being much past that we were to be at St. Cloud to dine with the Duchess of Kingston; Nothing was to hinder us from Coming in the Evening, but Alas! My good intention prov'd only a disturbance to your Neighbours, and just late enough to break the rest of all your servants and perhaps yourself. I came home with the disapointment of not having been able to Make My appologies in *propria Persona.* I hope you feel my distress, instead of accusing me, the One I deserve, the other not. [We will] come to see you tomorrow Morning, [if nothing?] hapen to prevent it! Oh I wish you was well enough to come to us tomorrow to dinner and stay the Evening. I wont tell you what I shall have, Temptations now are too Cruel for your Situation. [*She was referring, of course, to his broken wrist.*] I only Mention my wish, if the executing them shou'd be possible, your Merit will be grater or my satisfaction the More flatter'd. I would Serve you and help you at dinner, and divert your pain after dinner by good Musik.

—MARIA COSWAY

❦

To Maria Cosway
TH: JEFFERSON TO MRS. COSWAY   Thursday [5 Oct. 1786]

I have passed the night in so much pain that I have not closed my eyes. It is with infinite regret therefore that I must relinquish your charming company for that of the Surgeon whom I have sent for to examine into the cause of this change. I am in hopes it is only the having rattled a little too freely over the pavement yesterday. If you do not go to day I shall still have the pleasure of seeing you again. If you do, god bless you wherever you go. Present me in the most friendly terms to Mr. Cosway, and let me hear of your safe arrival in England. Addio Addio.

Let me know if you do not go to day.

❦

From Maria Cosway   [5 Oct. 1786]

I am very, very sorry indeed, and [. . .] for having been the Cause of your pains in the [Night]; Why would you go? And why was I not more friendly to you and less to Myself by preventing your giving me the pleasure of your Company? You repeatedly said it wou'd do you no harm, I felt interested and did not insist. We shall go I believe this Morning, Nothing seems redy, but Mr. Cosway seems More dispos'd then I have seen him all this time. I shall write to you from England, it is impossible to be wanting to a person who has been so excesvely obliging. I dont attempt to make Compliments, they can be None for you, but I beg you will think us sensible to your kindness, and that it will be with infinite pleasure I shall remember the charming days we have past together, and shall long for next spring.

You will make me very happy, if you would send a line to the post restante at Antwerp, that I may know how you are. Believe me dr: Sir your Most obliged affectionate servant,

—MARIA COSWAY

⁊

[Jefferson wrote the following letter, his well-known "Head and Heart" dialogue, over the course of several days, and with his left hand. This letter remains the best source we have for what the two of them actually did during their time together in Paris. We know from Trumbull that they were together almost every day, that they visited all the picture galleries, and we know from this letter that the two of them liked to go off alone to visit spots around the city, the parks and sights like the Desert de Retz.]

To Maria Cosway
[MY DEAR] MADAM   Paris Octob. 12. 1786

Having performed the last sad office of handing you into your carriage at the Pavilion de St. Denis, and seen the wheels get actually into motion, I turned on my heel and walked, more dead than alive, to the opposite door, where my own was awaiting me. Mr. Danquerville was missing. He was sought for, found, and dragged down stairs. [We] were crammed into the carriage, like recruits for the Bastille, and not having [sou]l enough to give orders to the coachman, he presumed Paris our destination, [and] drove off. After a considerable interval, silence was broke with a 'je suis vraiment afflige du depart de ces bons gens.' This was the signal for a mutual confession [of dist]ress. We began immediately to talk of Mr. and Mrs. Cosway, of their goodness, their [talents], their amability, and tho we spoke of nothing else, we seemed hardly to have entered into matter when the coachman announced the rue St. Denis, and that we were opposite Mr. Danquerville's. He insisted on descending there and traversing a short passage to his lodgings. I was carried home. Seated by my fire side, solitary and sad, the following dialogue took place between my Head and my Heart.

Head. Well, friend, you seem to be in a pretty trim.

Heart. I am indeed the most wretched of all earthly beings. Overwhelmed with grief, every fibre of my frame distended beyond it's natural powers to bear, I would willingly meet whatever catastrophe should leave me no more to feel or to fear.

Head. These are the eternal consequences of your warmth and precipitation. This is one of the scrapes into which you are ever leading us. You confess your follies indeed: but still you hug and cherish them, and no reformation can be hoped, where there is no repentance.

Heart. Oh my friend! This is no moment to upbraid my foibles. I am rent into fragments by the force of my grief! If you have any balm, pour it into my wounds: if none, do not harrow them by new torments. Spare me in this awful moment! At any other I will attend with patience to your admonitions.

Head. On the contrary I never found that the moment of triumph with you was the moment of attention to my admonitions. While suffering under your follies you may perhaps be made sensible of them, but, the paroxysm over, you fancy it can never return. Harsh therefore as the medecine may be, it is my office to administer it. You will be pleased to remember that when our friend Trumbull used to be telling us of the merits and talents of these good people, I never ceased whispering to you that we had no occasion for new acquaintance; that the greater their merit and talents, the more dangerous their friendship to our tranquillity, because the regret at parting would be greater.

Heart. Accordingly, Sir, this acquaintance was not the consequence of my doings. It was one of your projects which threw us in the way of it. It was you, remember, and not I, who desired the meeting, at Legrand & Molinos. I never trouble myself with domes nor arches. The Halle aux bleds might have rotted down before I should have gone to see it. But you, forsooth, who are eternally getting us to sleep with your diagrams and crotchets, must go and examine this wonderful piece of architecture. And when you had seen it, oh! it was the most superb thing on earth! What you had seen there was worth all you had yet seen in Paris! I thought so too. But I meant it of the lady and gentleman to whom we had been presented, and not of a parcel of sticks and chips put together in pens. You then, Sir, and not I, have been the cause of the present distress.

Head. It would have been happy for you if my diagrams and crotchets had gotten you to sleep on that day, as you are pleased to say they eternally do. My visit to Legrand & Molinos had publick utility for it's object. A market is to be built in Richmond. What a commodious plan is that of Legrand & Molinos: especially if we put on it the noble dome of the Halle aux bleds. If such a bridge as they shewed us can be thrown across the Schuylkill at Philadelphia, the floating bridges taken up, and the navigation of that river opened, what a copious resource will be added, of wood and provisions, to warm and feed the poor of that city. While I was occupied with these objects, you were dilating with your new acquaintances, and contriving how to prevent a separation from them. Every soul of you had an engagement for the day. Yet all these were to be sacrificed, that you might dine together. Lying messengers were to be dispatched into every quarter of the city with apologies for your breach of engagement. You particularly had the effrontery [to] send word to the Dutchess Danville that, in the moment we were setting out to d[ine] with her, dispatches came to hand which required immediate attention. You [wanted] me to invent a more ingenious excuse; but I knew you were getting into a scrape, and I would have nothing to do with it. Well, after dinner to St. Cloud, from St. Cloud to Ruggieri's, from Ruggieri to Krumfoltz, and if the day had been as long as a Lapland summer day, you would still have contrived means, among you, to have filled it.

Heart. Oh! my dear friend, how you have revived me by recalling to my mind the transactions of that day! How well I remember them all, and that when I came home at night and looked back to the morning, it seemed to have been a month ago. Go on then, like a kind comforter, and paint to me the day we went to St. Germains. How beautiful was every object! the Port de Neuilly, the hills along the Seine, the rainbows of the machine of Marly, the terras of St. Germains, the chateaux, the gardens, the [statues] of Marly, the pavilion of Lucienne. Recollect too Madrid, Bagatelle, the King's garden, the Dessert. How grand the idea excited by the remains of such a column! The spiral staircase too was beautiful. Every moment was filled with something agreeable. The wheels of time moved on with a rapidity of which those of our carriage gave but a faint idea, and yet in the evening, when one took a retrospect of the day, what a mass of happiness had we travelled over! Retrace all those scenes to me, my good companion, and I will forgive the unkindness with which you were chiding me. The day we went to St. Germains was a little too warm, I think, was not it?

Head. Thou art the most incorrigible of all the beings that ever sinned! I reminded you of the follies of the first day, intending to deduce from thence some useful lessons for you, but instead of listening to these, you kindle at the recollection, you retrace the whole series with a fondness which shews you want nothing but the opportunity to act it over again. I often told you during it's course that you were imprudently engaging your affections under circumstances that must cost you a great deal of pain: that the persons indeed were of the greatest merit, possessing good sense, good humour, honest hearts, honest manners, and eminence in a lovely art: that the lady had moreover qualities and accomplishments, belonging to her sex, which might form a chapter apart for her: such as music, modesty, beauty, and that softness of disposition which is the ornament of her sex and charm of ours. But that all these considerations would increase the pang of separation: that their stay here was to be short: that you rack our whole system when you are parted from those you love, complaining that such a separation is worse than death, inasmuch as this ends our sufferings, whereas that only begins them: and that the separation would in this instance be the more severe as you would probably never see them again.

Heart. But they told me they would come back again the next year.

Head. But in the mean time see what you suffer: and their return too depends on so many circumstances that if you had a grain of prudence you would not count upon it. Upon the whole it is improbable and therefore you should abandon the idea of ever seeing them again.

Heart. May heaven abandon me if I do!

Head. Very well. Suppose then they come back. They are to stay here two months, and when these are expired, what is to follow? Perhaps you flatter yourself they may come to America?

Heart. God only knows what is to happen. I see nothing impossible in that supposition, and I see things wonderfully contrived sometimes to make us happy. Where could they find such objects as in America for the exercise of their enchanting art? especially the lady, who paints landscape so inimitably. She wants only subjects worthy of immortality to render her pencil immortal. The Falling spring, the Cascade of Niagara, the Passage of the Potowmac thro the Blue mountains, the Natural bridge. It is worth a voiage across the Atlantic to see these objects; much more to paint, and make them, and thereby ourselves, known to all ages. And our own dear Monticello, where has nature spread so rich a mantle under the eye? mountains, forests, rocks, rivers. With what majesty do we there ride above the storms! How sublime to look down into the workhouse of nature, to see her clouds, hail, snow, rain, thunder, all fabricated at our feet! And the glorious Sun, when rising as if out of a distant water, just gilding the tops of the mountains, and giving life to all nature!—I hope in god no circumstance may ever make either seek an asylum from grief! With what sincere sympathy I would open every cell of my composition to receive the effusion of their woes! I would pour my tears into their wounds: and if a drop of balm could be found at the top of the Cordilleras, or at the remotest sources of the Missouri, I would go thither myself to seek and to bring it. Deeply practised in the school of affliction, the human heart knows no joy which I have not lost, no sorrow of which I have not drank! Fortune can present no grief of unknown form to me! Who then can so softly bind up the wound of another as he who has felt the same wound himself? But Heaven forbid they should ever know a sorrow!—Let us turn over another leaf, for this has distracted me.

Head. Well. Let us put this possibility to trial then on another point. When you consider the character which is given of our country by the lying newspapers of London, and their credulous copyers in other countries; when you reflect that all Europe is made to believe we are a lawless banditti, in a state of absolute anarchy, cutting one another's throats, and plundering without distinction, how can you expect that any reasonable creature would venture among us?

Heart. But you and I know that all this is false: that there is not a country on earth where there is greater tranquillity, where the laws are milder, or better obeyed: where every one is more attentive to his own business, or meddles less with that of others: where strangers are better received, more hospitably treated, and with a more sacred respect.

Head. True, you and I know this, but your friends do not know it.

Heart. But they are sensible people who think for themselves. They will ask of impartial foreigners who have been among us, whether they saw or heard on the spot any instances of anarchy. They will judge too that a people occupied as we are in opening rivers, digging navigable canals, making roads, building public schools, establishing academies, erecting busts and statues to our great men, protecting religious freedom, abolishing sanguinary punishments, reforming and improving our laws in general, they will judge I say for themselves whether these are not the occupations of a people at their ease, whether this is not better evidence of our true state than a London newspaper, hired to lie, and from which no truth can ever be extracted but by reversing everything it says.

Head. I did not begin this lecture my friend with a view to learn from you what America is doing. Let us return then to our point. I wished to make you sensible how imprudent it is to place your affections, without reserve, on objects you must so soon lose, and whose loss when it comes must cost you such severe pangs. Remember the last night. You knew your friends were to leave Paris today. This was enough to throw you into agonies. All night you tossed us from one side of the bed to the other. No sleep, no rest. The poor crippled wrist too, never left one moment in the same position, now up, now down, now here, now there; was it to be wondered at if all it's pains returned? The Surgeon then was to be called, and to be rated as an ignoramus because he could not devine the cause of this extraordinary change.—In fine, my friend, you must mend your manners. This is not a world to live at random in as you do. To avoid these eternal distresses, to which you are for ever exposing us, you must learn to look forward before you take a step which may interest our peace. Everything in this world is matter of calculation. Advance then with caution, the balance in your hand. Put into one scale the pleasures which any object may offer; but put fairly into the other the pains which are to follow, and see which preponderates. The making an acquaintance is not a matter of indifference. When a new one is proposed to you, view it all round. Consider what advantages it presents, and to what inconveniencies it may expose you. Do not bite at the bait of pleasure till you know there is no hook beneath it. The art of life is the art of avoiding pain: and he is the best pilot who steers clearest of the rocks and shoals with which it is beset. Pleasure is always before us; but misfortune is at our side: while running after that, this arrests us. The most effectual means of being secure against pain is to retire within ourselves, and to suffice the only own happiness. Those, which depend on ourselves, are the only pleasures a wise man will count on: for nothing is ours which another may deprive us of. Hence the inestimable value of intellectual pleasures. Ever in our power, always leading us to something new, never cloying, we ride, serene and sublime, above the concerns of this mortal world, contemplating truth and nature, matter and motion, the laws which bind up their existence, and that eternal being who made and bound them up by these laws. Let this be our employ. Leave the bustle and tumult of society to those who have not talents to occupy themselves without them. Friendship is but another name for an alliance with the follies and the misfortunes of others. Our own share of miseries is sufficient: why enter then as volunteers into those of another? Is there so little gall poured into our own cup that we must needs help to drink that of our neighbor? A friend dies or leaves us: we feel as if a limb was cut off. He is sick: we must watch over him, and participate of his pains. His fortune is shipwrecked: ours must be laid under contribution. He loses a child, a parent or a partner: we must mourn the loss as if it was our own.

Heart. And what more sublime delight than to mingle tears with one whom the hand of heaven hath smitten! To watch over the bed of sickness, and to beguile it's tedious and it's painful moments! To share our bread with one to whom misfortune has left none! This world abounds indeed with misery: to lighten it's burthen we must divide it with one another. But let us now try the virtues of your mathematical balance, and as you have put into one scale the burthens of friendship, let me put it's comforts into the other. When languishing then under disease, how grateful is the solace of our friends! How are we penetrated with their assiduities and attentions! How much are we supported by their encouragements and kind offices! When Heaven has taken from us some object of our love, how sweet is it to have a bosom whereon to recline our heads, and into which we may pour the torrent of our tears! Grief, with such a comfort, is almost a luxury! In a life where we are perpetually exposed to want and accident, yours is a wonderful proposition, to insulate ourselves, to retire from all aid, and to wrap ourselves in the mantle of self-sufficiency! For assuredly nobody will care for him who cares for nobody. But friendship is precious not only in the shade but in the sunshine of life: and thanks to a benevolent arrangement of things, the greater part of life is sunshine. I will recur for proof to the days we have lately passed. On these indeed the sun shone brightly! How gay did the face of nature appear! Hills, vallies, chateaux, gardens, rivers, every object wore it's liveliest hue! Whence did they borrow it? From the presence of our charming companion. They were pleasing, because she seemed pleased. Alone, the scene would have been dull and insipid: the participation of it with her gave it relish. Let the gloomy Monk, sequestered from the world, seek unsocial pleasures in the bottom of his cell! Let the sublimated philosopher grasp visionary happiness while pursuing phantoms dressed in the garb of truth! Their supreme wisdom is supreme folly: and they mistake for happiness the mere absence of pain. Had they ever felt the solid pleasure of one generous spasm of the heart, they would exchange for it all the frigid speculations of their lives, which you have been vaunting in such elevated terms. Believe me then, my friend, that that is a miserable arithmetic which would estimate friendship at nothing, or at less than nothing. Respect for you has induced me to enter into this discussion, and to hear principles uttered which

I detest and abjure. Respect for myself now obliges me to recall you into the proper limits of your office. When nature assigned us the same habitation, she gave us over it a divided empire. To you she allotted the field of science, to me that of morals. When the circle is to be squared, or the orbit of a comet to be traced; when the arch of greatest strength, or the solid of least resistance is to be investigated, take you the problem: it is yours: nature has given me no cognisance of it. In like manner in denying to you the feelings of sympathy, of benevolence, of gratitude, of justice, of love, of friendship, she has excluded you from their controul. To these she has adapted the mechanism of the heart. Morals were too essential to the happiness of man to be risked on the incertain combinations of the head. She laid their foundation therefore in sentiment, not in science. That she gave to all, as necessary to all: this to a few only, as sufficing with a few. I know indeed that you pretend authority to the sovereign controul of our conduct in all it's parts: and a respect for your grave saws and maxims, a desire to do what is right, has sometimes induced me to conform to your counsels. A few facts however which I can readily recall to your memory, will suffice to prove to you that nature has not organised you for our moral direction. When the poor wearied souldier, whom we overtook at Chickahominy with his pack on his back, begged us to let him get up behind our chariot, you began to calculate that the road was full of souldiers, and that if all should be taken up our horses would fail in their journey. We drove on therefore. But soon becoming sensible you had made me do wrong, that tho we cannot relieve all the distressed we should relieve as many as we can, I turned about to take up the souldier; but he had entered a bye path, and was no more to be found: and from that moment to this I could never find him out to ask his forgiveness. Again, when the poor woman came to ask a charity in Philadelphia, you whispered that she looked like a drunkard, and that half a dollar was enough to give her for the ale-house. Those who want the dispositions to give, easily find reasons why they ought not to give. When I sought her out afterwards, and did what I should have done at first, you know that she employed the money immediately towards placing her child at school. If our country, when pressed with wrongs at the point of the bayonet, had been governed by it's heads instead of it's hearts, where should we have been now? hanging on a gallows as high as Haman's. You began to calculate and to compare wealth and numbers: we threw up a few pulsations of our warmest blood: we supplied enthusiasm against wealth and numbers: we put our existence to the hazard, when the hazard seemed against us, and we saved our country: justifying at the same time the ways of Providence, whose precept is to do always what is right, and leave the issue to him. In short, my friend, as far as my recollection serves me, I do not know that I ever did a good thing on your suggestion, or a dirty one without it. I do for ever then disclaim your interference in my province. Fill paper as you please with triangles and squares: try how many ways you can hang and combine them together. I shall never envy nor controul your sublime delights. But leave me to decide when and where friendships are to be contracted. You say I contract them at random, so you said the woman at Philadelphia was a drunkard. I receive no one into my esteem till I know they are worthy of it. Wealth, title, office, are no recommendations to my friendship. On the contrary great good qualities are requisite to make amends for their having wealth, title and office. You confess that in the present case I could not have made a worthier choice. You only object that I was so soon to lose them. We are not immortal ourselves, my friend; how can we expect our enjoiments to be so? We have no rose without it's thorn; no pleasure without alloy. It is the law of our existence; and we must acquiesce. It is the condition annexed to all our pleasures, not by us who receive, but by him who gives them. True, this condition is pressing cruelly on me at this moment. I feel more fit for death than life. But when I look back on the pleasures of which it is the consequence, I am conscious they were worth the price I am paying. Notwithstanding your endeavors too to damp my hopes, I comfort myself with expectations of their promised return. Hope is sweeter than despair, and they were too good to mean to deceive me. In the summer, said the gentleman; but in the spring, said the lady: and I should love her forever, were it only for that! Know then, my friend, that I have taken these good people into my bosom: that I have lodged them in the warmest cell I could find: that I love them, and will continue to love them thro life: that if fortune should dispose them on one side the globe, and me on the other, my affections shall pervade it's whole mass to reach them. Knowing then my determination, attempt not to disturb it. If you can at any time furnish matter for their amusement, it will be the office of a good neighbor to do it. I will in like manner seize any occasion which may offer to do the like good turn for you with Condorcet, Rittenhouse, Madison, La Cretelle, or any other of those worthy sons of science whom you so justly prize.

I thought this a favorable proposition whereon to rest the issue of the dialogue. So I put an end to it by calling for my nightcap. Methinks I hear you wish to heaven I had called a little sooner, and so spared you the ennui of such a tedious sermon. I did not interrupt them sooner because I was in a mood for hearing sermons. You too were the subject; and on such a thesis I never think the theme long; not even if I am to write it, and that slowly and awkwardly, as now, with the left hand. But that you may not be discoraged from a correspondence which begins so formidably, I will promise you on my honour that my future letters shall be of a reasonable length. I will even agree to express but half my esteem for you, for fear of cloying you with too full a dose. But, on your part, no curtailing. If your letters are as long as the bible, they will appear short to me. Only let them be brim full of affection. I shall read them with the dispositions with which Arlequin in les deux billets spelt the words 'je t'aime' and wished that the whole alphabet had entered into their composition.

We have had incessant rains since your departure. These make me fear for your health, as well as that you have had an uncomfortable journey. The same cause has prevented me from being able to give you any account of your friends here. This voiage to Fontainbleau will probably send the Count de Moutier and the Marquise de Brehan to America. [Here he refers to the count—as the French minister—going with his sister-in-law, the marquise, to the United States. The country was scandalized by the fact that although they were not married, they behaved as if they were.] Danquerville promised to visit me, but has not done it as yet. De latude comes sometimes to take family soupe with me, and entertains me with anecdotes of his five and thirty years imprisonment. [Delatude was a prisoner of the Bastille who had escaped more than once and became famous for it. Jefferson had befriended him.] How fertile is the mind of man which can make the Bastille and Dungeon of Vincennes yeild interesting anecdotes. You know this was for making four verses on Mme. de Pompadour. But I think you told me you did not know the verses. They were these. 'Sans esprit, sans sentiment, Sans etre belle, ni neuve, En France on peut avoir le premier amant: Pompadour en est l'epreuve.' I have read the memoir of his three escapes. As to myself my health is good, except my wrist which mends slowly, and my mind which mends not at all, but broods constantly over your departure. The lateness of the season obliges me to decline my journey into the South of France. Present me in the most friendly terms to Mr. Cosway, and receive me into your own recollection with a partiality and a warmth, proportioned, not to my own poor merit, but to the sentiments of sincere affection and esteem with which I have the honour to be, my dear Madam, your most obedient humble servant,

—TH: JEFFERSON

To Maria Cosway
MY DEAR MADAM   Paris Octob. 13. 1786

Just as I had sealed the inclosed I received a letter of a good length, dated Antwerp, with your name at the bottom. [*This was a letter from Trumbull.*] I prepared myself for a feast. I read two or three sentences: looked again at the signature to see if I had not mistaken it. It was visibly yours. Read a sentence or two more. Diable! Spelt your name distinctly. There was not a letter of it omitted. Began to read again. In fine after reading a little and examining the signature, alternately, half a dozen times, I found that your name was to four lines only instead of four pages. I thank you for the four lines however because they prove you think of me. Little indeed, but better a little than none. To shew how much I think of you I send you the inclosed letter of three sheets of paper, being a history of the evening I parted with you. But how expect you should read a letter of three mortal sheets of paper? I will tell you. Divide it into six doses of half a sheet each, and every day, when the toilette begins, take a dose, that is to say, read half a sheet. By this means it will have the only merit it's length and dulness can aspire to, that of assisting your coëffeuse to procure you six good naps of sleep. I will even allow you twelve days to get through it, holding you rigorously to one condition only, that is, that at whatever hour you receive this, you do not break the seal of the inclosed till the next toilette. Of this injunction I require a sacred execution. I rest it on your friendship, and that in your first letter you tell me honestly whether you have honestly performed it.—I send you the song I promised. Bring me in return it's subject, *Jours heureux!* Were I a songster I should sing it all to these words 'Dans ces lieux qu'elle tarde à se rendre'! Learn it I pray you, and sing it with feeling.—My right hand presents it's devoirs to you, and sees with great indignation the left supplanting it in a correspondence so much valued. You will know the first moment it can resume it's rights. The first exercise of them shall be addressed to you, as you had the first essay of it's rival. It will yet, however, be many a day. Present my esteem to Mr. Cosway, and believe me to be yours very affectionately,

—TH: JEFFERSON

⁂

[Jefferson kept his letters from Maria Cosway together. When they were found, they had all been damaged by mice; thus the somewhat mutilated state of the letter below.]

From Maria Cosway   [London, 30 Oct. 1786]

[How I wish I] could answer the Dialogue! But I hon[estly think my hear]t is invisable, and Mute, at this moment more than usual [it is] full or ready to burst with all the variety of Sentiments, wh[ich] a very feeling one is Capable of; sensible of My loss a[t] separating from the friends I left at Paris, I have hardly time to indulge a shamisly tribute; but My thoughts Must be contrasted by the joy of Meeting my friends in London. It is an excess which Must tear to peices a human Mind, when felt. You seem to be Such a Master on this subject, that whatever I may say will appear trifelling, not well express'd, faintly represented   but felt. Your letter could employ me for some time, an hour to Consider every word, to every sentence I could write a volume, but I could wish that my selfishness was not reproching to Me, for with difficulty do I find a line but after having admired it, I recolect some part concerns Me. Why do you say so Many kind things? Why present so many opportunities for my feeling undeserving of them, why not leave me a free consolation in admiring a friend, without the temptation […] to my Vanity? I wish your heart […] for it is too good. It expands to the Objects he […] too Much of his own, and blinds the reality of its demerit. [Hereupon she lapses into Italian to the end of the letter; we provide a translation as given in the Princeton edition of Papers of Thomas Jefferson, vol. 10, pp. 495–96.] But what am I doing, that I write so much English when I can write in my own language, and become a little less involved. I did not know what I was doing, I should like to write it over again. But do I not wish to send you the first sheet, the first lines written upon my arrival in London, let the consequences be what they may? Oh,

Sir, if my correspondence equalled yours how perfect it would be! I can only express my gratitude in your friendship. Forgive me if your orders were not obeyed regarding the time allotted me to read your letter. It was one of my first pleasures to find it and I could not resist the desire to read it at once, even at the cost of committing an act of disobedience. Forgive me, the crime merits it. Our voyage was a happy one, my health perfectly restored, the weather good except for those days preceding our departure from Paris, the Company of Mr. Trumbull [congenial] and pleasant. But London, the [unpleasant city ...] amid the fog and smoke, sadness seems [to reign] in every heart, if one is to judge from the physiognomies one meets; I must return as soon as possible to my occupations in order not to feel the rigor of the Melancholy which is inspired by this unpleasant climate. In the company of agreeable friends, practising the fine arts a little, one can often avoid sadness, even if something is lacking for perfect happiness. Everything is tranquil, quiet and gloomy, there are no Bells ringing to announce to us some festival, service or celebration; even when they call for a Deprofundis it is accompanied by the hope that that soul passed to a Better Life, is enjoying that blessed quiet which the World never grants in full: here at night you hear a voice at every hour which announces to us the fact that it has passed, which reminds us that it will never more return and often leaves us with the Mortifying sense that we have lost it. There are no Monasteries which contain men of God who at all hours pray for us and for all those who do not pray, all who are lost, either in the streets or gambling, in vice and Idleness. [...] you have begun to [write ... your letters] will never be long enough, when [...] in the long winter evenings there is left some idle moment, sacrifice it to me, to sending me news of yourself. I can hardly wait to receive a letter from your right Hand, it must be very inconvenient for you to write with your Left. This sacrifice will be received with so much gratitude as, putting faith in the promises made us for good actions, I shall invoke for your reward.

My Husband sends you a thousand Compliments, I beg you to present ours to Mr. Short, to Monr. D'ancherville when you see him. I shall never forget your attentions to us. Some times we shall mention our contemplated tour next year, either to Paris or to Italy. Many things can prevent its execution, but even greater impossibilities have been carried out. Accept my best wishes for your health and happiness and believe me your much obliged and affectionate Friend.

∾

To Maria Cosway   Paris Nov. 19. 1786

I begin, my dear Madam, to write a little with the right hand, and you are by promise, as well as by inclination entitled to it's first homage. But I write with pain and must be short. This is good news for you; for were the hand able to follow the effusions of the heart, that would cease to write only when this shall cease to beat. My first letter warned you of this danger. I became sensible myself of my transgression and promised to offend no more. Your goodness seems to have induced you to forgive, and even to flatter me. That was a great error. When sins are dear to us we are but too prone to slide into them again. The act of repentance itself is often sweetened with the thought that it clears our account for a repetition of the same sin. The friendly letter I have received from you might have been taken as a release from my promise: but you are saved by a cruel cramp in my hand which admonishes me in every line to condense my thoughts and words.

I made your excuses to Madame de Corny. She was as uneasy, as you had been, under the appearance of a failure in point of civility and respect. I knew the key to the riddle, and asked her on what day she had returned to town. She said on the 6th. of October. I told her you had left it on the 5th. Thus each stands excused in the eye of the other, and she will have the pleasure of seeing you in London. Nothing more will be necessary, for good people naturally grow together. I wish she could put me into her pocket, when she goes, or you, when she comes back.—Mercy, cramp! that twitch was too much. I am done, I am done.—Adieu ma chere madame: je ne suis plus à moi. Faites mes compliments a Monsieur Cosway, assurez le de mon amitié, et daignez d'agreer vous meme l'hommage d'un sincere & tendre attachement. Encore adieu.

∾

To Maria Cosway   Paris Nov. 29. 1786

My letters which pass thro' the post office either of this country or of England being all opened, I send thro' that channel only such as are very indifferent in their nature. This is not the character, my dear madam of those I write to you. The breathings of a pure affection would be profaned by the eye of a Commis of the poste. I am obliged then to wait for private conveniences. I wrote to you so long ago as the 19th. of this month by a gentleman who was to go to London immediately. But he is not yet gone. Hence the delay of which you express yourself kindly sensible in yours of the 17th. instant. [*Over time Maria complained repeatedly that she did not hear from Jefferson often enough. Many of her letters to him express real anger at this fact. What there is to make of this is anybody's guess. Here he makes his excuses.*] Could I write by the post, I should trouble you too often: for I am never happier than when I commit myself into dialogue with you, tho' it be but in imagination. Heaven has submitted our being to some unkind laws. When those charming moments were present which I passed with you, they were clouded with the prospect that I was soon to lose you: and now, when I pass the same moments in review, I recollect nothing but the agreeable passages, and they fill me with regret. Thus, present joys are damped by a consciousness that they are passing from us; and past ones are only the subjects of sorrow and regret. I am determined when you come next not to admit the idea that we are ever to part again. But are you to come again? I dread the answer to this question, and that my poor heart has been duped by the fondness of it's wishes. What a triumph for the head! God bless you! May your days be many and filled with sunshine! May your heart glow with warm affections, and all of them be gratified! Write to me often. Write affectionately, and freely, as I do to you. Say many kind things, and say them without reserve. They will be food for my soul. Adieu my dear friend!

P.S. No private conveiance occurring I must trust this thro' the post-office, disguising my seal and superscription.

✍

To Maria Cosway   Paris Dec. 24. 1786

Yes, my dear Madam, I have received your three letters, and I am sure you must have thought hardly of me, when at the date of the last, you had not yet received one from me. But I had written two. The second, by the post, I hope you got about the beginning of this month: the first has been detained by the gentleman who was to have carried it. I suppose you will receive it with this. I wish they had formed us like the birds of the air, able to fly where we please. I would have exchanged for this many of the boasted preeminencies of man. I was so unlucky when very young, as to read the history of Fortunatus. He had a cap of such virtues that when he put it on his head, and wished himself anywhere, he was there. I have been all my life sighing for this cap. Yet if I had it, I question if I should use it but once. I should wish myself with you, and not wish myself away again. En attendant the cap, I am always thinking of you. If I cannot be with you in reality, I will in imagination. But you say not a word of coming to Paris. Yet you were to come in the spring, and here is winter. It is time therefore you should be making your arrangements, packing your baggage &c. unless you really mean to disappoint us. If you do, I am determined not to suppose I am never to see you again. I will believe you intend to go to America, to draw the Natural bridge, the Peaks of Otter &c., that I shall meet you there, and visit with you all those grand scenes. I had rather be deceived, than live without hope. It is so sweet! It makes us ride so smoothly over the roughnesses of life. When clambering a mountain, we always hope the hill we are on is the last. But it is the next, and the next, and still the next. Think of me much, and warmly. Place me in your breast with those who you love most: and comfort me with your letters. Addio la mia Cara ed amabile amica!

After finishing my letter, the gentleman who brought yours sent me a roll he had overlooked, which contained songs of your composition. I am sure they are charming, and I thank you for them. The first words which met my eye on opening them, are I fear, ominous. 'Qua l'attendo, e mai non viene.'

✎

[The following letter was written the next year, when Maria had already come and gone, this time without saying goodbye. Whatever the nature of their affair, it was clear that it was now over.]

From Maria Cosway   London decembr Christmas day [1787]

How do you do My dear friend? You came to the invitation of my breakfast the Morning of my departure! and what did you think of Me? I did it to avoid the last taking leave, I went too early for any body to see Me. I cannot express

how Miserable I was in leaving Paris. How I regreted not having seen More
of you, and I cannot have even the Satisfaction to unburden My displeasure
of [it] by loading you with reproches. Your reasons Must be Sufficient, and My
forcing you would have [been] unkind and unfriendly as it woud be cruel to
pretend on what is totaly disagreable to you. Another reason keeps ever since
I am perfectly sure t'was My fault but my Misfortune, and then we can bear to
be Contradicted in our wishes with More resignation.

Have you seen yet the lovely Mrs. Church? You Must have seen her by
this time: what do you think of her? She Colls' me her Sister. I coll' her My
dearest Sister. If I did not love her so Much I should fear her rivalship, but no
I give you free permission to love her with all your heart, and I shall feel
happy if I think you keep me in a little corner of it, when you admit her even
to reing Queen.—I have not receivd any letter from you. I feel the loss of it.
Make it up by sending Me very long ones and tell Me all you do how you
pass your time. When you are at your Hermitage, all that regards you will be
interesting to me. Have you seen Any of the Gentlemen who I had the honor
to introduce to you and who received so politly. The Abbè Piatolli is a wor[thy
Man?] Mr. Niemicewiz a very Amiable gen[tleman ...] the Prince Charteressi
worthy of [...] Manners Custums and principles you [...] improve him in all
he has so far [...] Natural disposition and talent!

Again I request write to Me [...] My best Compliments to Mr. Short and
believe dear sir Yours Most Affly,

—MARIA COSWAY

ॐ

To Maria Cosway   Paris Jan. [31, 1788]

I went to breakfast with you according to promise, and you had gone off at
5. oclock in the morning. This spared me indeed the pain of parting, but it
deprives me of the comfort of recollecting that pain. Your departure was the
signal of distress to your friends. You know the accident which so long
confined the Princess to her room. Madame de Corny too was immediately
thrown into great alarm for the life of her husband. After being long at
death's door he is reviving. Mrs. Church seemed to come to participate of the

distress of her friend instead of the pleasures of Paris. I never saw her before: but I find in her all the good the world has given her credit for. I do not wonder at your fondness for each other. I have seen too little of her, as I did of you. But in your case it was not my fault, unless it be a fault to love my friends so dearly as to wish to enjoy their company in the only way it yeilds enjoiment, that is, en petite comite. You make every body love you. You are sought and surrounded therefore by all. Your mere domestic cortege was so numerous, et si imposante, that one could not approach you quite at their ease. Nor could you so unpremeditatedly mount into the Phaeton and hie away to the bois de Boulogne, St. Cloud, Marly, St. Germains &c. Add to this the distance at which you were placed from me. When you come again, you must be nearer, and move more extempore. You complain, my dear Madam, of my not writing to you, and you have the appearance of cause for complaint. But I have been above a month looking out for a private conveiance, without being able to find one, and you know the infidelity of the post office. Sometimes they mislay letters to pocket the frankmoney: and always they open those of people in office. As if your friendship and mine could be interesting to government! As if, instead of the effusions of a sincere esteem, we would fill our letters with the miserable trash called state secrets!—I am flattered by your attention to me in the affair of the tea vase. I like perfectly the form of the one Mrs. Church brought. But Mr. Trumbull and myself have seen one made for the count de Moutier, wherein the spout is suppressed, and the water made to issue at a pretty little ornament. When he returns he will explain this to you, and try to get me a vase of the size and form of Mrs. Church's, but with this improvement. In this business I shall beg leave to associate your taste with his. Present my compliments to Mr. Cosway. I am obliged to trust this letter through the post office, as I see no immediate chance of a private conveyance. Adieu, my dear Madam: think of me often and warmly, as I do of you.

❧

To Angelica Schuyler Church   Paris Sunday. Feb. 17. 1788

You speak, Madam, in your Note of Adieu, of civilities which I never rendered you. What you kindly call such were but the gratifications of my own heart: for indeed that was much gratified in seeing and serving you. The morning you left us, all was wrong. Even the sun shine was provoking, with which I never quarelled before. I took it into my head he shone only to throw light on our loss: to present a chearfulness not at all in unison with my mind. I mounted my horse earlier than common, and took by instinct the road you had taken. Some spirit whispered this to me: but he whispered by halves only: for, when I turned about at St. Denis, had he told me you were then broke down at Luzarches, I should certainly have spurred on to that place, and perhaps not have quitted you till I had seen the carriage perform it's office fully by depositing you at Boulogne. I went in the evening to Madame de Corny's, where we talked over our woes, and this morning I found some solace in going for Kitty [Angelica Church's daughter] and the girls. She is now here, just triste enough to shew her affection, and at the same time her discretion. I think I have discovered a method of preventing this dejection of mind on any future parting. It is this. When you come again, I will employ myself solely in finding or fancying that you have some faults, and I will draw a veil over all your good qualities, if I can find one large enough. I think I shall succeed in this. For, trying myself to-day, by way of exercise, I recollected immediately one fault in your composition. It is that you give all your attention to your friends, caring nothing about yourself. Now you must agree that I christian this very mildly when I call it a folly only. And I dare say I shall find many like it when I examine you with more sang froid.—I remember you told me, when we parted, you would come to see me at Monticello. Now tho' I believe this to be impossible, I have been planning what I would shew you: a flower here, a tree there; yonder a grove, near it a fountain; on this side a hill, on that a river. Indeed, madam, I know nothing so charming as our own country. The learned say it is a new creation; and I believe them; not for their reasons, but because it is made on an improved plan. Europe is a first idea, a crude production, before the maker knew his trade, or had made up his mind as to what he wanted. Let us go back to it together then. You intend it a visit; so do I. While you are indulging with your friends on the Hudson, I will go to see if Monticello remains in the same place. Or I will attend you to the falls of Niagara, if you will go on with me to the passage of the Patowmac, the Natural bridge &c. This done, we will come back together, you for a long, and I for a lesser time. Think of this plan, and when you come to pay your summer's visit to Kitty we will talk it over. In the mean time heavens bless you, Madam, fortify your health, and watch over your happiness. Your's affectionately,

—TH: J.

❧

From Angelica Schuyler Church   Down Place July 21. 88

I send my dear Sir the little urn so long promissed and so long delayed, and hope you will accept the gift for the sake of the giver; it will sometimes at Monticello remind you of your friend.—Madame de Corny tells me you are going to America next spring. I shall also make that desired voyage, and see what my family and friends are doing. If I should meet you their I should be so happy to see you, and to introduce you to my father. I am very certain that you would please each other. Mrs. Cosway and I are enjoying the quiet of the country, she plays and sings, and we very often wish that Mr. Jefferson was here, supposing that he would be indulgent to the exertions of two little women to please him, who are extremely vain of the pleasure of being permitted to write to him, and very happy to have some share of his favorable opinion.

Adieu my dear Sir accept the good wish of Maria and Angelica. Mr. Trumbull has given us each a picture of you. Mrs. Cosway's is a better likeness than mine, but then, I have a better elsewhere and so I console myself.

I beg my compliments to the Young Ladies, I hope your ward improves, I will not thank you for your care, I feel it, and sincerely your affectionate friend,

—ANGELICA CHURCH

❧

To Angelica Schuyler Church   Paris, July 27. 1788

Many motives, my dear Madam, authorize me to write to you, but none more than this that I esteem you infinitely. Yet I have thought it safe to get Kitty to write also, that her letter may serve as a passport to mine, and shed on it the *suave odeur* of those warm emotions it will excite in your breast. When we have long expected the visit of a dear friend, he is welcome when he comes, and all who come with him. I present myself then under the wing of Kitty, tho' she thinks herself under mine. She is here at this instant, well, chearful, and chattering French to her Doll, and her friend Polly. We want your presence to round the little family circle, to enliven the Sunday's dinner, which is not less a holiday to me than to the girls. We talk of you, we think of you, and try to enjoy your company by the force of imagination: and were the force of that very sufficient, you would be with me every day. Worn down every morning with writing on business, I sally at 12. o'clock into the bois de Boulogne, and unbend my labours by thinking on my friends: and could I write as I ride, and give them my thoughts warm as they flow from my heart, my friends would see what a foolish heart it is. Kitty tells me you are at London; but why do you not tell me so yourself? for, I had rather learn it from you than from any body in the world. I presume then you see Mr. Trumbull, and that he tells you that your boasted artists of London are unable to disencumber our charming vase of it's spout, which gives it more the air of a brandy tub than of a form of fancy. He will tell you too that after plaguing him a great deal with his caprice, I have at length desired him to leave the dunces to their own ways, and to send me the vase as it is, spout and all. Our friend Madame de Corny has been country-mad ever since you were here. I suspect you bit her; for I know that this is your rage also, and that tho' you are in London now, your heart is always in the country. I wish you would let it come here sometimes. Why cannot you take a trip of a fortnight now and then to see Kitty? A week of that indeed would be spent on the road, but there would be a week left for us. You might be of great service to your friends in the Chaussée d'Antin at this moment; because after an examination of a thousand country-houses, some of which had one fault and some another, one at length is found which pleases Madame, but not Monsieur, and the contest is, which shall permit the other to sacrifice their taste on this occasion. Your mediation might help them over the difficulty. Come then, my dear Madam, to the call of friendship, which does not issue from the Chaussee d'Antin alone. Your slender health, requires exercise, requires amusement, and to be comforted by seeing how much you are beloved every where. Do not be afraid of breakings down on the road. They never happen when you know your carriage. If you will install me your physician, I will prescribe to you a journey a month to Paris. En attendant I am with sentiments of infinite esteem & attachment, Dear Madam your sincere friend and humble servant,

—TH: JEFFERSON

∽

To Angelica Schuyler Church   Paris Aug. 17. 1788

The urn is well worth acceptance, my dear Madam, on it's own account, for it is a perfect beauty: but it is more flattering to me to accept it on account of the giver. I shall preserve it as sacred as I would the urns of my forefathers, had I all of them from Adam to the present day, and with this difference of estimation that it recalls to my mind a living friend. The memorial of me which you have from Trumbul is of the most worthless part of me. Could he paint my friendship to you, it would be something out of the common line. I should have been happy indeed to have made a third at Down-place with yourself and Mrs. Cosway. Your society would have been amusement enough for me. I never blame heaven so much as for having clogged the etherial spirit of friendship with a body which ties it to time and place. I am with you always in spirit: be you with me sometimes. I have in contemplation to visit America in the Spring, as Madame de Corny has mentioned to you. I have not as yet asked a Congé, because, till the new government is in activity, I know not to whom to address my request. I presume it will not be denied me. The project of carrying with me colonies of animals and plants for my native country, will oblige me to embark at Havre, as being the nearest port. This is but twenty hours distant from London. Can you, my dear madam, sacrifice twenty hours of your life to make my daughters and myself happy? In this event we might make our trips in concert. I allow myself all the months of April, May, and June, to find a good ship. Embarking in either of these months we shall avoid being out during the equinoxes and be sure of fine weather. Think of it then, my friend, and let us being a negociation on the subject. You shall find in me all the spirit of accomodation with which Yoric began his with the fair Piedmontese. We have a thousand inducements to wish it on our part. On yours perhaps you may find one in the dispositions we shall carry with us to serve and amuse you on the dreary voiage. Madme. de Corny talks of your brother coming to Europe for you. How much easier for him to meet you in Williamsburgh! Besides, I am your brother. Should this proposition be absolutely inadmissible, I will flatter myself with the hope of seeing you at New York, or even at Albany if I am master enough of my time. To see the country will be one motive: but to see you a much stronger, and to become acquainted with your father who must be good, because you are so. The fruit is a specimen of the tree. I had the honour of serving with him in Congress in the year 1775. but probably he does not remember me.

I have just deposited Kitty in good health in the Chaussée d'Antin. I had a consultation with Madame de Corny last night, the result of which was to insist on her being translated from the drawing mistress to the drawing master of the Convent. Write to me sometimes, and permit me to answer your letters. God bless you, my dear madam, your affectionate friend

—TH: JEFFERSON

[Jefferson continued to correspond with Angelica Church for many years thereafter.]

৵৹

To Maria Cosway   Paris May 21. 1789

I have not yet, my dear friend, received my leave of absence, but I expect it hourly, and shall depart almost in the hour of receiving it. My absence will be of about six months. I leave here a scene of tumult and contest. All is politics in this capital. Even love has lost it's part in conversation. This is not well, for love is always a consolatory thing. I am going to a country where it is felt in it's sublimest degree. In great cities it is distracted by the variety of objects. Friendship perhaps suffers there also from the same cause but I am determined to except from this your friendship for m[e], and to believe it distracted by neither time, distance, nor object. When wafting on the bosom of the ocean I shall pray it to be as calm and smooth as yours to me. What shall I say for you to our friend Mrs. Church? I shall see her assuredly, perhaps return with her. We shall talk a great deal of you. In fact you ought to have gone with her. We would have travelled a great deal together, we would have intruded our opinions into the choice of objects for your pencil and returned fraught with treasures of art, science and sentiment. Adieu, my very dear friend. Be our affections unchangeable, and if our little history is to last beyond the grave, be the longest chapter in it that which shall record their purity, warmth and duration.

CHAPTER FIVE

To the South of France

JEFFERSON LEFT PARIS FOR PROVENCE ON THE LAST DAY OF FEBRUARY 1787, intending to spend six weeks on the road. He was actually gone three and a half months. The stated reason for the trip was to investigate the agricultural production of France to see what he could learn about the possibilities for American farmers to break into the French market. He was especially interested in rice, which the French generally bought from farmers in the north of Italy. He decided in the midst of his journey to extend his travels into the area around Turin and Milan, to see whether the Italians knew things about rice that the Americans didn't.

He also wanted to find out everything he could about the making of wine. He hoped to establish wine grape vineyards in Virginia and bought cuttings for that purpose on this trip. He planned as well to take a long look at the Canal Royale de Languedoc (now the Canal du Midi), which crossed the south of France from the Rhone to Toulouse. Talk of canals was all the rage in America at the time. While he was in France, almost every letter Jefferson received from George Washington discussed various canal projects.

These were the ostensible reasons. His daughter suspected the real reason he wanted to go: for pleasure. Jefferson was a creature of the sun, a Southerner. He hated the dark and gloom of the Paris winters. And he loved to travel. He had been all over Virginia as a young lawyer, following the circuit judges around the state, and he had been to Philadelphia, New York, New England, and to most of the Southern states. But this trip to southern France and Italy would turn out to be the longest trip he ever took.

He clearly had a wonderful time. His letters written to his Paris friends and to William Short during the journey have a lightness about them, a gaiety, not always to be found. It must have been a relief to get away from the press of business and correspondence, the everlasting dinner parties, the boring, ritualistic levees at Versailles. He traveled incognito—not, that is, as Thomas Jefferson, minister to the French court, but as Thomas Jefferson, gentleman of Virginia. He hired a servant in Dijon who did not know who he was. He found the fellow suitable and kept him for the entire trip. He stayed at the inns that the French government had established along the post roads for the convenience of travelers. He took only a small trunk of clothes with him. He was a happy man.

Included here are the lengthy notes Jefferson made about the things he observed as well as the best of the letters he wrote back to Paris. His notes are full of detail about soils, landscapes, crops, the making of wine, various mechanical devices he saw, buildings he investigated, the lives led by the peasants, nightingales, olive trees, Roman ruins, and more. They could easily have served as the basis for a travel book—which, of course, he never wrote. In fact, it's hard to understand what he did plan to do with them. But he had an active, endlessly curious mind—he advised his daughter again and again never to be idle—and it may be that he was simply taking his own advice and keeping busy. Jefferson is almost always to be found out there, in the world, doing things, thinking about things. He is not visibly a self-reflective man. He does not agonize. Traveling the canal, he placed his little carriage on the canal boat, and when he was tired of walking beside the boat, got in the carriage, sat down, and read or wrote or looked at the countryside. When the boat stopped at the locks he asked the lock keepers about their work, talked to farmers, and made little side trips. Even in moments that might conduce to idleness, reverie, or thoughtfulness, in other words, he kept busy.

In the midst of his travels he still occasionally had business to perform. In Aix-en-Provence he met with a Brazilian who talked about the possibility of a revolution in Brazil, and would the United States help? He reported on the conversation to John Jay. He met with the American consuls in Marseilles and Bordeaux. On his trip to Italy he smuggled out samples of Italian rice, which he sent back to South Carolina to see whether it was really better than American rice and, if so, whether it could be grown there. He actually took some out in his pocket. Had he been caught, he would have faced the death penalty. The Italians wanted no competition for their rice. In Marseilles he wrote a man named Jean Baptiste Guide about the possibility of opening a direct trade between the United States and the Kingdom of Sardinia, which took in parts of Italy as well as the island of Sardinia.

Jefferson is not only always busy, he is also always conscientious. He had crossed the Alps into Italy: He was within reach of the Veneto and the villas of Palladio, the architect he most admired; he could have gone south to Florence, to Rome. He was steeped in Roman history, he loved Roman antiquities, but he did not go. He was afraid it would take him too long. He was not free to travel at will. He was the United States minister plenipotentiary to the court of France. His youngest child was on her way to Paris. He had business to take care of. Two years later he sponsored William Short's trip to Florence and Rome instead. It would have been interesting indeed if Jefferson had taken the time to go himself.

The letters contain by far the most personal comments and reactions, while the notes are relentlessly agricultural. The notes do have their interest, however, offering evidence of Jefferson's great devotion to facts, and to the useful. Among all the things he was, he was possibly most deeply a farmer. We know about his adoration of the Maison Carrée only from his letters. The notes he made in Nîmes don't even mention it.

It's worth noting that the rice he sent back to South Carolina didn't work out. The South Carolinians thought their own rice better. He also sent olive trees to the same state and to Georgia. Jefferson had an almost religious conviction about the value of olive trees, which seemed to grow in the worst soil and kept the poor people who lived on such soil alive. A few of his trees survived the trip across the Atlantic, but the United States never took to the production of olives or olive oil. Nor did his efforts to import vinifera grapes to Virginia come to anything. Jefferson continued the rest of his life to have to import his wines from France. But he had tried.

"The greatest service which can be rendered any country is," he once wrote, "to add a useful plant to its culture." That's largely what this journey was about.

✍

To William Short
DEAR SIR   Lyons Mar. 15. 1787

So far all is well. No complaints; except against the weathermaker, who has pelted me with rain, hail, and snow, almost from the moment of my departure to my arrival here. Now and then a few gleamings of sunshine to chear me by the way.

Such is this life: and such too will be the next, if there be another, and we may judge of the future by the past. My road led me about 60 miles through Champagne, mostly a corn [*the word for grain in the 18th century, not Indian corn*] country, lying in large hills of the colour and size of those in the neighborhood of Elkhill. The plains of the Yonne are of the same colour, that is to say, a brownish red; a singular circumstance to me, as our plains on the water side are always black or grey. The people here were ill clothed, and looked ill, and I observed the women performing the heavy labours of husbandry; an unequivocal proof of extreme poverty. In Burgundy and Beaujolois they do only light work in the feilds, being principally occupied within doors. In these counties they were well clothed and appeared to be well fed. Here the hills become mountains, larger than those of Champagne, more abrupt, more red and stony. I passed thro about 180 miles of Burgundy; it resembles extremely our red mountainous country, but is rather more stony, all in corn and vine. I mounted a bidet, put a peasant on another and rambled thro' their most celebrated vineyards, going into the houses of the labourers, cellars of the Vignerons, and mixing and conversing with them as much as I could. The same in Beaujolois, where nature has spread it's richest gifts in profusion. On the right we had fine mountain sides lying in easy slopes, in corn and vine, and on the left the rich extensive plains of the Saone in corn and pasture. This is the richest country I ever beheld. I passed some time at the Chateau de Laye Epinaye, a seignory of about 15,000 acres, in vine, corn, pasture and wood, a rich and beautiful scene. I was entertained by Madame de Laye with a hospitality, a goodness and an ease which was charming, and left her with regret. I beg of you to present to the good Abbés Chalut and Arnoud my thanks for their introduction to this family: indeed I should be obliged to you if you could see Monsr. de laye and express to him how sensible I am of my obligation to him for the letter to Madame de Laye, and of her attention and civilities. I have been much indebted here too for the letters from the Abbés, tho' the shortness of my stay does not give me time to avail myself of all their effect. A constant tempest confined me to the house the first day: the second, I determined to see every thing within my plan before delivering my letters, that I might do as much, in as little time, as possible. The third and fourth have been filled up with all the attentions they would admit, and I am now on the wing, as soon as this letter is closed. I enter into these details because they are necessary to justify me to the Abbés for the little time I had left to profit of the good dispositions of their friends. Six or seven hundred leagues still before me, and circumscribed in time, I am obliged to hasten my movements. I have not visited at all the manufactures of this place: because a knowledge of them would be useless, and would extrude from the memory other things more worth retaining. Architecture, painting, sculpture, antiquities, agriculture, the condition of the labouring poor fill all my moments. Hitherto I have derived as much satisfaction and even delight from my journey as I could propose to myself. The plan of having servants who know nothing of me, places me perfectly at my ease. I intended to have taken a new one at every principal city, to have carried him on to serve on the road to the next and there changed him. But the one I brought forward from Dijon is so good a one that I expect to keep him through the greater part of the journey, taking additionally a valet de place wherever I stay a day or two. You shall hear from me from Aix where I hope to meet letters from you giving me news both great and small. Present me affectionately to my friends and more particularly to Madame de Tessé and Madame de Tott: and accept assurances of my perfect esteem & friendship to yourself. Adieu.

—TH: JEFFERSON

❧

To Madame de Tessé   Nismes Mar. 20. 1787

Here I am, Madam, gazing at the Maison quarrée, like a lover at his mistress. [The Maison Carrée was the ancient Roman building, originally a temple, on which Jefferson based the design of the Virginia State Capitol. He chose the building on the basis of etchings of it and plans drawn up by Clerisseau. Here he actually sees it for the first time.] The stocking-weavers and silk spinners around it consider me as an hypochondriac Englishman, about to write with a pistol the last chapter of his history. This is the second time I have been in love since I left Paris. The first was with a Diana at the Chateau de Laye Epinaye in the Beaujolois, a delicious morsel of sculpture, by Michael Angelo Slodtz. This, you will say, was in rule, to fall in love with a fine woman: but with a house! It is out of all precedent! No, madam, it is not without a precedent in my own history. While at Paris, I was violently smitten with the hotel de Salm, and used to go to the Thuileries almost daily to look at it. The loueuse des chaises, inattentive to my passion, never had the complaisance to place a chair there; so that, sitting on the parapet, and twisting my neck round to see the object of my admiration, I generally left it with a torticollis. From Lyons to Nismes I have been nourished with the remains of Roman grandeur. They have always brought you to my mind, because I know your affection for whatever is Roman and noble. At Vienne I thought of you. But I am glad you were not there; for you would have seen me more angry than I hope you will ever see me. The Pretorian palace, as it is called, comparable for it's fine proportions to the Maison quarrée, totally defaced by the Barbarians who have converted it to it's present purpose; it's beautiful, fluted, Corithian columns cut out in part to make space for Gothic windows, and hewed down in the residue to the plane of the building. At Orange too I thought of you. I was sure you had seen with rapture the sublime triumphal arch at the entrance into the city. I went then to the Arenas. Would you believe Madam, that in [this 18th. centur]y, in France, und[er the reign of Louis XVI, they] are [at this mo]ment pulling down the circular wall of this superb remain [to pave a ro]ad? And that too from a hill which is itself an entire mass of stone just as fit, and more accessible. [The use of Roman ruins as quarries for cut stone was an old tradition in Europe. Portions of the Colosseum in Rome were used to build Renaissance palazzi.] A former Intendant, a Monsr. de Baville hs rendered his memory dear to travellers and amateurs by the pains he took to preserve and to restore these monuments of antiquity. The present one (I do not know who he is) is demolishing the object to make a good road to it. I thought of you again, and I was then in great good humour, at the Pont du Gard [the remains of a Roman aqueduct, still a famous tourist attraction], a sublime antiquity, and [well] preserved. But most of all here, where Roman taste, genius, and magnificence excite ideas analogous to yours at every step, I could no longer oppose the inclination to avail myself of your permission to write to you, a permission given with too much complaisance by you, taken advantage of with too much indiscretion by me. Madame de Tott too did me the same honour. But she being only the descendant of some of those puny heroes who boiled their own kettles before the walls of Troy, I shall write to her from a Graecian, rather than a Roman canton; when I shall find myself for example among her Phocean relations at Marseilles. Loving, as you do Madam, the precious remains of antiquity, loving architecture, gardening, a warm sun, and a clear sky,

I wonder you have never thought of moving Chaville to Nismes. This is not so impracticable as you may think. The next time a Surintendant des batiments du roi, after the example of M. Colbert, sends persons to Nismes to move the Maison [Car]rée to Paris, that they may not come empty-handed, desire them to bring Chaville with them to replace it. À propos of Paris, I have now been three weeks from there without knowing any thing of what has past. I suppose I shall meet it all [at Aix, where] I have directed my letters to be lodged poste restante. My journey has given me leisure to reflect on this Assemblée des Notables. Under a good and young king as the present, I think good may be m[ade of it.] I would have the deputies then by all means so conduct themselves as [to encorage] him to repeat the calls of this assembly. Their first step should be to get th[emselves] divided into two chambers, instead of seven, the Noblesse and the commons separately. The 2d. to persuade the king, instead of chusing the deputies of the commons himself, to summon those chosen by the people for the Provincial administrations. The 3d. as the Noblesse is too numerous to be all admitted into the assemblée, to obtain permission for that body to chuse it's own deputies. The rest would follow. Two houses so elected would contain a mass of wisdom which would make the people happy, and the king great; would place him in history where no other act can possibly place him. This is my plan Madam; but I wish to know yours, which I am sure is better.

[From a correspondent at N]ismes you will not expect news. Were I [to attempt to give you news, I shoul]d tell you stories a thousand years old. [I should detail to you the intrigue]s of the courts of the Caesars, how they [affect us here, the oppressions of their] Praetors, Praefects &c. I am immersed [in anti-quities from morning to night]. For me the city of Rome is actually [existing in all the splendor of it's] empire. I am filled with alarms for [the event of the irruptions dayly m]aking on us by the Goths, Ostrogoths, [Visigoths and Vandals, lest they shoul]d reconquer us to our original bar[barism. If I am sometimes ind]uced to look forward to the eighteenth [century, it is only when recalled] to it by the recollection of your goodness [and friendship, and by those sentiments of] sincere esteem and respect with which [I have the honor to be, Madam, your] most obedient & most humble servant,

—TH: JEFFERSON

෴

[The first half of this letter covered some of Jefferson's minor business and is omitted here.]

To William Short
DEAR SIR   Aix en Provence March. 27. 1787

... I am now in the land of corn, wine, oil, and sunshine. What more can man ask of heaven? If I should happen to die at Paris I will beg of you do send me here, and have me exposed to the sun. I am sure it will bring me to life again. It is wonderful to me that every free being who possesses cent ecus de rente, does not remove to the Southward of the Loire. It is true that money will carry to Paris most of the good things of this canton. But it cannot carry thither it's sunshine, nor procure any equivalent for it. This city is one of the cleanest and neatest I have ever seen in any country. The streets are straight, from 20. to 100 feet wide, and as clean as a parlour floor. Where they are of width sufficient they have 1. 2. or 4. rows of elms from 100 to 150 years old, which make delicious walks. There are no portes-cocheres, so that the buildings shew themselves advantageously on the streets. It is in a valley just where it begins to open towards the mouth of the Rhone, forming in that direction a boundless plain which is an entire grove of olive trees, and is moreover in corn, Lucerne, or vines, for the happiness of the olive tree is that it interferes with no superficial production. Probably it draws it's nourishment from parts out of the reach of any other plant. It takes well in every soil, but best where it is poorest, or where there is none. Comparing the Beaujolois with Provence, the former is of the richest soil, the latter richest in it's productions. But the climate of Beaujolois cannot be compared with this. I expect to find the situation of Marseilles still pleasanter; business will carry me thither soon, for a time at least. I can receive there daily the waters from this place, with no other loss than that of their warmth, and this can easily be restored to them. I computed my journey on leaving Paris to be of 1000 leagues. I am now over one fourth of it. My calculation is that I shall conclude it in the earlier half of June. Letters may come to me here till the last day of April, about which time I shall be vibrating by this place Westwardly.—In the long chain of causes and effects, it is droll sometimes to seize two distant links and to present the one as the consequence of the other. Of this nature are these propositions. The want of dung prevents the progress of luxury in Aix. The poverty of the soil makes it's streets clean. These are legitimate consequences from the following chain. The preciousness of the soil prevents it's being employed in grass. Therefore no cattle, no dung. Hence the dung-gatherers (a numerous calling here) hunt it as eagerly in the streets as they would diamonds. Every one therefore can walk cleanly and commodiously. Hence few carriages. Hence few assemblies, routs, and other occasions for the display of dress.— I thank M. Pio for his anxieties on my account. My ostensible purpose of traveling without a servant was only to spare Espagnol the pain of being postponed to another, as I was quite determined to be master of my own secret, and therefore to take a servant who should not know me. At Fontainebleau I could not get one: but at Dijon I got a very excellent one who will probably go through the journey with me. Yet I must say, it is a sacrifice to opinion, and that without answering any one purpose worth a moment's consideration. They only serve to insulate me from the people among whom I am. Present me in the most friendly terms to M. Pio, M. Mazzei and other friends and believe me to be with the most sincere esteem your affectionate friend & servant,

—TH: JEFFERSON

✑

[Once again, the business part of this letter is omitted.]

To William Short
DEAR SIR   Aix Mar. 29. 1787

... I did not see Mount Cenis. My plan was to have gone to Montbard which was on the left of my road, and then to have crossed again to the right to Mount Cenis. But there were no posts on these roads, the obtaining horses was difficult and precarious, and a constant storm of wind, hail, snow, and rain offered me little occasion of seeing any thing. I referred it therefore to some future excursion from Fontaineblu. The groupe of which M. de Laye spoke to you carries the perfection of the chissel to a degree of which I had no conception. It is the only thing in sculpture wich I have seen on my journey worthy of notice.

In painting I have seen good things at Lyons only. In Architecture nothing any where except the remains of antiquity. These are more in number, and less injured by time than I expected, and have been to me a great treat. Those at Nismes, both in dignity and preservation, stand first. There is however at Arles an Amphitheatre as large as that of Nismes, the external walls of which from the top of the arches downwards is well preserved. Another circumstance contrary to my expectation is the change of language. I had thought the Provençale only a dialect of the French; on the contrary the French may rather be considered as a dialect of the Provençale. That is to say, the Latin is the original. Tuscan and Spanish are degeneracies in the first degree. Piedmontese (as I suppose) in the 2d. Provençale in the 3d. and Parisian French in the 4th. But the Provençale stands nearer to the Tuscan than it does to the French, and it is my Italian which enables me to understand these people here, more than my French. This language, in different shades occupies all the country South of the Loire. Formerly it took precedence of the French under the name of la langue Romans. The ballads of it's Troubadours were the delight of the several courts of Europe, and it is from thence that the novels of the English are called Romances. Every letter is pronounced, the articulation is distinct, no nasal sounds disfigure it, and on the whole it stands close to the Italian and Spanish in point of beauty. I think it a general misfortune that historical circumstances gave a final prevalence to the French instead of the Provençale language. It loses it's ground slowly, and will ultimately disappear because there are few books written in it, and because it is thought more polite to speak the language of the Capital. Yet those who learn that language here, pronounce it as the Italians do. We were last night treated with Alexis and Justine, and Mazet, in which the most celebrated actress from Marseilles came to bear a part for the advantage of her friend whose benefit night it was. She is in the stile of Mde. Dugazon, has ear, voice, taste and action. She is moreover young and handsome: and has an advantage over Mde. Dugazon and some other of the celebrated ones of Paris, in being clear of that dreadful wheeze or rather whistle in respiration which resembles the agonizing struggles for breath in a dying person.—I thank you for your information of the health of my daughter. My respects to the family of Chaville are always to be understood if not expressed. To Mr. and Mde. de la Fayette also, Messrs. Mazzei, Pio and Crevecoeur, I wish to be presented. Be assured as to yourself that no person can more sincerely wish your prosperity and happiness, nor entertain warmer sentiments of esteem than Dear Sir your affectionate humble servant.

ℰℐ

To Chastellux   Marseilles Apr. 4. 1787

I must return you many thanks, my dear friend, for your kind attention in procuring me the acquaintance of Monsr. Bergasse, from whom I have received many civilities, and, what is more precious, abundance of information. To you and to him also I am indebted for an introduction to Monsr. Audibert, in whom I saw enough to make me regret that I could not see more of him. My journey from Paris to this place has been a continued feast of new objects, and new ideas. To make the most of the little time I have for so long a circuit, I have been obliged to keep myself rather out of the way of good dinners and good company. Had they been my objects, I should not have quitted Paris. I have courted the society of gardeners, vignerons, coopers, farmers &c. and have devoted every moment of every day almost, to the business of enquiry. M. de Bergasse however united for me all objects, a good dinner, good company, and information. I was unlucky in not having called on you before you went into the country, as I should have derived from you much useful counsel for my journey. I have still a favor to ask of you, which is, a letter to some one good person at Tours in Touraine, where I shall make a short stay of a day or two on my return about the latter part of May or beginning of June. The article Coquilles in the Questions Encyclopediques de Voltaire will inform you what is my object there. I have found the Abbés in general most useful acquaintances. They are unembarrassed with families, uninvolved in form and etiquette, frequently learned, and always obliging. If you know such a one at Tours you will oblige me infinitely by a letter to him: or if you know none yourself, perhaps some of your friends may. I will only beg to be announced but as a voyageur etranger simplement, and that it be addressed à Monsr. Jefferson à Tours, poste restante. This deception keeps me clear of those polite obligations to which I might otherwise be engaged, and leaves me the whole of the little time I have to pursue the objects that always delight me.—I have been concerned with the country I have passed thro hitherto. I could not help comparing it, en passant, with England, and found the comparison much more disadvantageous to the latter than I had expected. I shall have many interrogations to ask of you. These being too many for a letter, they shall therefore be reserved to some future conversation, when I can have the pleasure of returning you thanks in person for the multiplied instances of your goodness and partiality to me, and of assuring you how sincere those sentiments of esteem and friendship with which I have the honor to be Dear Sir, your affectionate friend & humble servant,

—TH: JEFFERSON

∽

To Madame de Tott   Marseilles Apr. 5. 1787

I thank you sincerely, Madam, for the favour of your letter on the subject of M. Drouay's picture. It has confirmed a part of my own ideas, given some which had escaped me, and corrected others wherein I had been wrong. The strong expression given to the countenance of Marius had absorbed all my attention, and made me overlook the slenderness of his frame, which you justly recall to my mind as faulty in that particular. Give me leave in return to rectify for you an opinion in another kind which I supposed you to entertain, because you have not yet had time to correct all the errors of the [human] mind. I presume that you think, as most people think, that a person cannot be in two places at one time. Yet is there no error more palpable than this. You know, for example, that you have been in Paris and it's neighborhood, constantly since I had the pleasure of seeing you there: yet I declare you have been with me above half my journey. I could repeat to you long conversations, word for word, and on a variety of subjects. When I find you fatigued wth conversation and sighing for your pallet and pencil, I permit you to return to Paris for a while, and amuse myself with philosophizing on the objects which occur. The plan of my journey, as well as of my life, being to take things by the smooth handle, few occur which have not something tolerable to offer me. [The Auberge] for instance in which I am obliged to take refuge at night, presents in the first moment nothing but noise, dirt, and disorder. But the auberge is not to be too much abused. True, it has not the charming gardens of Chaville without, nor it's decorations, nor it's charming society within. I do not seek therefore for the good things which it has not, but those which it has. 'A traveller, sais I, retired at night to his chamber in an Inn, all his effects contained in a single trunk, all his cares circumscribed by the walls of his apartment, unknown to all, unheeded, and undisturbed, writes, reads, thinks, sleeps, just in the moments when nature and the movements of his body and mind require. Charmed with the tranquility of his little cell, he finds how few are our real wants, how cheap a thing is happiness, how expensive a one pride. He views with pity the wretched rich, whom the laws of the world have submitted to the cumbrous trappings of rank: he sees him labouring through the journey of life like an ass oppressed under ingots of gold, little of which goes to feed, to clothe, or to cover himself; the rest gobbled up by harpies of various description with which he has surrounded himself. These and not himself, are it's real masters. He wonders that a thinking mind can be so subdued by opinion, and that he does not run away from his own crouded house, and take refuge in the chamber of an Inn.' Indeed I wonder so too, unless he has a Chaville to retire to, and a family composed like that of Chaville, where quiet and friendship can both be indulged. But between the society of real friends, and the tranquility of solitude the mind finds no middle ground.—Thus reconciled to my Auberge by night, I was still persecuted by day with the cruel whip of the postillion. How to find a smooth handle to this tremendous instrument? At length however I found it in the callous nerves of the horse, to which these terrible stripes may afford but a gentle and perhaps a pleasing irritation; like a pinch of snuff to an old snuff-taker.

Sometimes I amuse myself with physical researches. Those enormous boots, for instance, in which the postillion is incased like an Egyptian mummy, have cost me more pondering than the laws of planetary motion did to Newton. I have searched their solution in his physical, and in his moral constitution. I fancied myself in conversation with one of Newton's country-men, and asked him what he thought could be the reason of their wearing those boots? 'Sir, says he, it is because a Frenchman's heels are so light, that, without this ballast, he would turn keel up.' 'If so, Sir, sais I, it proves at least that he has more gravity in his head than your nation is generally willing to allow him.' I should go on, Madam, detailing to you my dreams and speculations; but that my present situation is most unfriendly to speculation. Four thousand three hundred and fifty market-women (I have counted them one by one) brawling, squabbling, and jabbering Patois, three hundred asses braying and bewailing to each other, and to the world, their cruel oppressions, four files of mule-carts passing in constant succession, with as many bells to every mule as can be hung about him, all this in the street under my window, and the weather too hot to shut it. Judge whether in such a situation it is easy to hang one's ideas together. Besides, writing from a colony of your own country, you would rather I should say less of myself and more of that. But, just dropped among them, how can I pretend to judge them with justice? Of beauty, you will say, one may judge on a single coup d'oeil. Of beauty then, Madam, they have a good share, as far as the public walks, the Spectacles, and the assembleé of Mademlle. Conil enable me to decide. But it is not a legitimate Graecian beauty. It is not such as yours. The reason I suppose is that yours is genuine, brought from the spot; [where]as theirs has been made here, and like all fabricated wares is sophisticated with foreign mixture. Perhaps you would rather I should write you news? Les Amandes sont de 22.^{tt}, Cacao 19s, Caffé 31., Cotton 130.^{tt}, huile 22.^{tt}, riz 21.^{tt}, savon 42.^{tt}, terebenthine 17.s &c. &c. This is not in the stile of Paris news; but I write from Marseilles, and it is the news of the place. I could continue it thro' the whole table of prices current; but that I am sure you have enough, and have already in your heart wished an end to my letter. I shall therefore annex but one preliminary condition; which is a permission to express here my respectful attachment to Madame and Monsieur de Tessé, and to assure yourself of those sentiments of perfect friendship & affection with which I have the honor to be sincerely & constantly, Madam, your most obedient & most humble servant,

—TH: JEFFERSON

෴

To William Short
DEAR SIR   Toulon April 7. 1787

... Having taken 40. douches, without any sensible benefit, I thought it useless to continue them. My wrist strengthens slowly: it is to time I look as the surest remedy, and that I believe will restore it at length. I set out tomorrow for Nice.

The information received at Marseilles encourages me in my researches on the subject of rice, and that I shall meet with rice fields and the machines for cleaning it just beyond the Alps. Unless they call me into the neighborhood of Turin I shall not go that far, having no object further eastward except the rice. Hitherto my journey has been a continued feast on objects of agriculture, new to me, and, some of them at least, susceptible of adoption in America. Nothing can be ruder or more savage than the country I am in, as it must have come from the hands of nature; and nothing more rich and variegated in the productions with which art has covered it. Marseilles is a charming place. All life and activity, and a useful activity like London and Philadelphia. As I shall receive no more of your letters till I get back to Aix you will hear from me less often: probably not at all while beyond the Alps. When I get back to Nice I shall be able to calculate to a day my return to Aix, and of course the term after which it will be proper to send my letters to another stage. Remember me to enquiring friends, and be assured of the sincere esteem with which I am Dear Sir your affectionate friend & servant,

—TH: JEFFERSON

⁊

To Lafayette   Nice Apr. 11. 1787

Your head, my dear friend, is full of Notable things; and being better employed, therefore, I do not expect letters from you. I am constantly roving about, to see what I have never seen before and shall never see again. In the great cities, I go to see what travellers think alone worthy of being seen; but I make a job of it, and generally gulp it all down in a day. On the other hand, I am never satiated with rambling through the fields and farms, examining the culture and cultivators, with a degree of curiosity which makes some take me to be a fool, and others to be much wiser than I am. I have been pleased to find among the people a less degree of physical misery than I had expected. They are generally well clothed, and have a plenty of food, not animal indeed, but vegetable, which is as wholesome. Perhaps they are over worked, the excess of the rent required by the landlord, obliging them to too many hours of labor, in order to produce that, and wherewith to feed and clothe themselves. The soil of Champagne and

Burgundy I have found more universally good than I had expected, and as I could not help making a comparison with England, I found that comparison more unfavorable to the latter than is generally admitted. The soil, the climate, and the productions are superior to those of England, and the husbandry as good, except in one point; that of manure. In England, long leases for twenty-one years, or three lives, to wit, that of the farmer, his wife, and son, renewed by the son as soon as he comes to the possession, for his own life, his wife's and eldest child's, and so on, render the farms there almost hereditary, make it worth the farmer's while to manure the lands highly, and give the landlord an opportunity of occasionally making his rent keep pace with the improved state of the lands. Here the leases are either during pleasure, or for three, six, or nine years, which does not give the farmer time to repay himself for the expensive operation of well manuring, and therefore, he manures ill, or not at all. I suppose, that could the practice of leasing for three lives be introduced in the whole kingdom, it would, within the term of your life, increase agricultural productions fifty per cent; or were any one proprietor to do it with his own lands, it would increase his rents fifty per cent, in the course of twenty-five years. But I am told the laws do not permit it. The laws then, in this particular, are unwise and unjust, and ought to give that permission. In the southern provinces, where the soil is poor, the climate hot and dry, and there are few animals, they would learn the art, found so precious in England, of making vegetable manure, and thus improving these provinces in the article in which nature has been least kind to them. Indeed, these provinces afford a singular spectacle. Calculating on the poverty of their soil, and their climate by its latitude only, they should have been the poorest in France. On the contrary, they are the richest, from one fortuitous circumstance. Spurs or ramifications of high mountains, making down from the Alps, and as it were, reticulating these provinces, give to the vallies the protection of a particular inclosure to each, and the benefit of a general stagnation of the northern winds produced by the whole of them, and thus countervail the advantage of several degrees of latitude. From the first olive fields of Pierrelate, to the orangeries of Hieres, has been continued rapture to me. I have often wished for you. I think you have not made this journey. It is a pleasure you have to come, and an improvement to be added to the many you have already made. It will be a great comfort to you to know, from your own inspection, the condition of all the provinces of your own country, and it will be interesting to them at some future day to be known to you. This is perhaps the only moment of your life in which you can acquire that knolege. And to do it most effectually you must be absolutely incognito, you must ferret the people out of their hovels as I have done, look into their kettles, eat their bread, loll on their beds under pretence of resting yourself, but in fact to find if they are soft. You will feel a sublime pleasure in the course of this investigation, and a sublimer one hereafter when you shall be able to apply your knolege to the softening of their beds, or the throwing a morsel of meat into the kettle of vegetables. You will not wonder at the subjects of my letter: they are the only ones which have been present to my mind for some time past, and the waters must always be what are the fountain from which they flow. According to this indeed I should have intermixed from beginning to end warm expressions of friendship to you: but according to the ideas of our country we do not permit ourselves to speak even truths when they may have the air of flattery. I content myself therefore with saying once for all that I love you, your wife and children. Tell them so and Adieu. Yours affectionately,

—TH: JEFFERSON

To William Short
DEAR SIR   Nice April 12. 1787

At Marseilles they told me I should encounter the ricefields of Piedmont soon after crossing the Alps. Here they tell me there are none nearer than Vercelli and Novarra, which is carrying me almost to Milan. I fear that this circumstance will occasion me a greater delay than I had calculated on. However I am embarked in the project and shall go through with it. Tomorrow I set out on my passage over the Alps, being to pursue it 93 miles to Coni on mules, as the snows are not yet enough melted to admit carriages to pass. I leave mine here therefore, proposing to return by water from Genoa. I think it will be three weeks before I get back to Nice.—I find this climate quite as superb as it has been represented. Hieres is the only place in France which may be compared with it. The climates are equal. In favor of this place are the circumstances of gay and dissipated society, a handsome city, good accommodations and some commerce. In favor of Hieres are environs of delicious and extensive plains, a society more contracted and therefore more capable of esteem, and the neighborhood of Toulon, Marseilles and other places to which excursions may be made. Placing Marseilles in comparison with Hieres, it has extensive society, a good theatre, freedom from military controul, and the most animated commerce. But it's winter climate far inferior.—I am now in the act of putting my baggage into portable form for my bat-mule; after praying you therefore to let my daughter know I am well and that I shall not be heard of again in three weeks. I take my leave of you for that time with assurances of the sincere esteem with which I am Dear Sir your friend & servt.,

—TH: JEFFERSON

♏

To Martha Jefferson
MY DEAR PATSY   Marseilles May 5. 1787

I got back to Aix the day before yesterday, and found there your letter of the 9th. of April, from which I presume you to be well tho' you do not say so. In order to exercise your geography I will give you a detail of my journey. You must therefore take your map and trace out the following places. Dijon, Lyons, Pont St. Esprit, Nismes, Arles, St. Remis, Aix, Marseilles, Toulon, Hieres, Frejus, Antibes, Nice, Col de Tende, Coni, Turin, Vercelli, Milan, Pavia, Tortona, Novi, Genoa, by sea to Albenga, by land to Monaco, Nice, Antibes, Frejus, Brignolles, Aix, and Marseille. The day after tomorrow I set out hence for Aix, Avignon, Pont du Gard, Nismes, Montpelier, Narbonne, along the Canal of Languedoc to Toulouse, Bourdeaux, Rochefort, Rochelle, Nantes, Lorient, Nantes, Tours, Orleans and Paris where I shall arrive about the middle of June, after having travelled something upwards of a thousand leagues. From Genoa to Aix was very fatiguing, the first two days having been at sea, and mortally sick, two more clambering the cliffs of the Appennine, sometimes on foot, sometimes on a mule according as a path was more or less difficult, and two others travelling thro' the night as well as day, without sleep. I am not yet rested, and shall therefore shortly give you rest by closing my letter, after mentioning that I have received a letter from your sister, which tho a year old, gave me great pleasure. I inclose it for your perusal, as I think it will be pleasing to you also. But take care of it, and return it to me when I shall get back to Paris, for trifling as it seems, it is precious to me. When I left Paris, I wrote to London to desire that your harpsichord might be sent during the months of April and May, so that I am in hopes it will arrive a little before I shall, and give me an opportunity of judging whether you have got the better of that want of industry which I had begun to fear would be the rock on which you would split. Determine never to be idle. No person will have occasion to complain of the want of time, who never loses any. It is wonderful how much may be done, if we are always doing. And that you may be always doing good, my dear, is the ardent prayer of yours affectionately,

—TH: JEFFERSON

To Martha Jefferson   May 21. 1787

I write to you, my dear Patsy, from the Canal of Languedoc, on which I am at present sailing, as I have been for a week past, cloudless skies above, limpid waters below, and on each hand a row of nightingales in full chorus. This delightful bird had given me a rich treat before at the fountain of Vaucluse. After visiting the tomb of Laura at Avignon, I went to see this fountain, a noble one of itself, and rendered for ever famous by the songs of Petrarch who lived near it. I arrived there somewhat fatigued, and sat down by the fountain to repose myself. It gushes, of the size of a river, from a secluded valley of the mountain, the ruins of Petrarch's chateau being perched on a rock 200 feet perpendicular above. To add to the enchantment of the scene, every tree and bush was filled with nightingales in full song. I think you told me you had not yet noticed this bird. As you have trees in the garden of the convent, there must be nightingales in them, and this is the season of their song. Endeavor, my dear, to make yourself acquainted with the music of this bird, that when you return to your own country you may be able to estimate it's merit in comparison with that of the mocking bird. The latter has the advantage of singing thro' a great part of the year, whereas the nightingale sings but 5. or 6. weeks in the spring, and a still shorter term and with a more feeble voice in the fall. I expect to be at Paris about the middle of next month. By that time we may begin to expect our dear Polly. It will be a circumstance of inexpressible comfort to me to have you both with me once more. The object most interesting to me for the residue of my life, will be to see you both developing daily those principles of virtue and goodness which will make you valuable to others and happy in yourselves, and acquiring those talents and that degree of science which will guard you at all times against ennui, the most dangerous poison of life. A mind always employed is always happy. This is the true secret, the grand recipe for felicity. The idle are the only wretched. In a world which furnishes so many emploiments which are useful, and so many which are amusing, it is our own fault if we ever know what ennui is, or if we are ever driven to the miserable resource of gambling, which corrupts our dispositions, and teaches us a habit of hostility against all mankind.—We are now entering the port of Toulouse, where I quit my bark; and of course must conclude my letter. Be good and be industrious, and you will be what I shall most love in this world. Adieu my dear child. Yours affectionately,

—TH: JEFFERSON

Notes of a Tour into the Southern Parts of France, &c.
[Memorandum taken on a journey from Paris into the Southern parts of France and Northern Italy, in the year 1787.]

CHAMPAGNE. MARCH 3. SENS TO VERMANTON. The face of the country is in large hills, not too steep for the plough, somewhat resembling the Elk hill and Beverdam hills of Virginia. The soil is generally a rich mulatto loam, with a mixture of coarse sand and some loose stone. The plains of Yonne are of the same colour. The plains are in corn, the hills in vineyard, but the wine not good. There are a few apple trees but none of any other kind, and no inclosures. No cattle, sheep, or swine. Fine mules.

Few chateaux. No farm houses, all the people being gathered in villages. Are they thus collected by that dogma of their religion which makes them believe that, to keep the Creator in good humor with his own works, they must mumble a mass every day? Certain is that they are less happy and less virtuous in villages than they would be insulated with their families on the grounds they cultivate. The people are illy clothed. Perhaps they have put on their worst clothes at this moment as it is raining. But I observe women and children carrying heavy burthens, and labouring with the hough. This is an unequivocal indication of extreme poverty. Men, in a civilised country, never expose their wives and children to labour above their force or sex, as long as their own labour can protect them from it. I see few beggars. Probably this is the effect of a police.

BURGUNDY. Mar. 4. LUCY LE BOIS. CUSSY LESS FORGES. ROUVRAY. MAISONNEUVE. VITTEAUX. LA CHALEURE. PONT DE PANIS. DIJON. The hills are higher and more abrupt. The soil a good red loam and sand, mixed with more or less grit, small stone, and sometimes rock. All in corn. Some forest wood here and there, broom, whins and holly, and a few inclosures of quick hedge. Now and then a flock of sheep.

The people are well clothed, but it is Sunday. They have the appearance of being well fed. The Chateau de Sevigny, near Cussy les forges is in a charming situation. Between Maison neuve and Vitteaux the road leads through an avenue of trees 8. American miles long in a right line. It is impossible to paint the ennui of this avenue. On the summit of the hills which border the valley in which Vitteaux is, there is a parapet of rock, 20. 30. or 40. feet perpendicular, which crowns the hills. The tops are nearly level and appear to be covered with earth. Very singular. Great masses of rock in the hills between la Chaleure and Pont de Panis, and a conical hill in the approach to the last place.

DIJON. The tavern price of a bottle of the best wine (e.g. of Vaune) is 4^{tt} The best round potatoes here I ever saw. They have begun a canal 30. feet wide, which is to lead into the Saone at. It is fed by springs. They are not allowed to take any water out of the riviere d'Ouche, which runs through this place on account of the mills on that river. They talk of making a canal to the Seine, the nearest navigable part of which at present is 15. leagues from hence. They have very light waggons here for the transportation of their wine. They are long and narrow, the fore wheels as high as the hind. Two peices of wine are drawn by one horse in one of these waggons. The road, in this part of the country, is divided into portions of 40. or 50. feet by stones, numbered, which mark the task of the labourers.

March 7. 8. FROM LA BARAQUE to CHAGNY. On the left are plains which extend to the Saone, on the right the ridge of mountains called the Cote. The plains are of a reddish-brown, rich loam, mixed with much small stone. The

Cote has for it's basis a solid rock on which is about a foot of soil, and small stone in equal quantities, the soil red and of midling quality. The plains are in corn, the Cote in vines. The former has no inclosures, the latter is in small ones of dry stone wall. There is a good deal of forest. Some small herds of small cattle and sheep. Fine mules which come from Provence and cost 20. Louis. They break them at 2. years old, and they last to 30.

The corn lands here rent for about 15^{tt} the arpent. They are now planting, pruning, and sticking their vines. When a new vineyard is made they plant the vines in gutters about 4. feet apart. As the vines advance they lay them down. They put out new shoots, and fill all the intermediate space till all trace of order is lost. They have ultimately about 1. foot square to each vine. They begin to yeild good profit at 5. or 6. years old and last 100. or 150. years. A vigneron at Voulenay carried me into his vineyard, which was of about 10. arpents. He told me that some years it produced him 60. peices of wine, and some not more than 3. peices. The latter is the most advantageous produce, because the wine is better in quality and higher in price in proportion as less is made: and the expences at the same time diminish in the same proportion. Whereas when much is made, the expences are increased, while the quality and price become less. In very plentiful years they often give one half the wine for casks to contain the other half. The cask for 250. bottles costs 6^{tt} in scarce years and 10^{tt} in plentiful. The FEUILLETTE is of 125. bottles, the PIECE of 250., and the QUEUE, or BOTTE of 500. An arpent rents for from 20.^{tt} to 60.^{tt} A farmer of 10. arpents has about three labourers engaged by the year. He pais 4. Louis to a man, and half as much to a woman, and feeds them. He kills one hog, and salts it, which is all the meat used in the family during the year. Their ordinary food is bread and vegetables. At Pommard and Voulenay I observed them eating good wheat bread; at Meursault, rye. I asked the reason of the difference. They told me that the white wines fail in quality much oftener than red, and remain on hand. The farmer therefore cannot afford to feed his labourers so well. At Meursault, only white wines are made, because there is too much stone for the red. On such slight circumstances depends the condition of man! —The wines which have given such celebrity to Burgundy grow only on the Cote, an extent of about 5 leagues long, and half a league wide. They begin at Chambertin, and go on through Vougeau, Romanie, Veaunne, Nuys, Beaune, Pommard, Voulenay, Meursault, and end at Monrachet. The two last are white;

the others red. Chambertin, Voujeau, and Veaune are strongest, and will bear transportation and keeping. They sell therefore on the spot for 1200.^{tt} the Queue, which is 48. sous the bottle. Voulenaye is the best of the other reds, equal in flavor to Chambertin &c. but being lighter, will not keep, and therefore sells for not more than 300^{tt} the Queue, which is 12. sous the bottle. It ripens sooner than they do and consequently is better for those who wish to broach at a year old. In like manner of the White wines, and for the same reason, Monrachet sells at 1200^{tt} the Queue (48s. the bottle) and (6s. the bottle). It is remarkable that the best of each kind, that is, of the Red and White, is made at the extremities of the line, to wit, at Chambertin and Monrachet. It is pretended that the adjoining vineyards produce the same qualities, but that, belonging to obscure individuals, they have not obtained a name, and therefore sell as other wines. The aspect of the Cote is a little South of the East. The Western side is also covered with vines, is apparently of the same soil; yet the wines are only the coarsest kinds. Such too are those which are produced in the Plains: but there the soil is richer and less stony. Vougeau is the property of the monks of Citeaux, and produces about 200 pieces. Monrachet contains about 50 arpents, and produces one year with another about 120 peices. It belongs to two proprietors only, Monsr. de Clermont, who leases to some wine merchants, and the Marquis de Sarsnet of Dijon, whose part is farmed to a Monsr. de la Tour whose family, for many generations, have thad the farm. The best wines are carried to Paris by land. The transportation costs 36^{tt} the peice. The more indifferent go by water. Bottles cost 4^{I}/2 sous each.

　　March 9. CHALONS. SENNECY. TOURNUS. ST. ALBIN. MACON. On the left are the fine plains of the Saone; on the right, high lands, rather waving than hilly, sometimes sloping gently to the plains, sometimes dropping down in precipices, and occasionally broken into beautiful vallies by the streams which run into the Saone. The Plains are dark rich loam, in pasture and corn; the heights more or less red or reddish, always gritty, of midling quality only; their sides in vines, and their summits in corn. The vineyards are inclosed with dry stone walls, and there are some quickhedges in the corn grounds. The cattle are few and indifferent. There are some good oxen however. They draw by the head. Few sheep, and small. A good deal of wood lands.

　　I passed three times the canal called le Charollois, which they are opening from Chalons on the Saone to Digoïn on the Loire. It passes near Chagny, and will be 23. leagues long. They have worked on it 3. years, and will finish it in 4. more. It will reanimate the languishing commerce of Champagne and Burgundy, by furnishing a water transportation for their wines to Nantes, which also will receive new consequence by becoming the emporium of that commerce. At some distance on the right are high mountains, which probably form the separation between the waters of the Saone and Loire.—Met a malefactor in the hands of one of the Marechaussée; perhaps a dove in the talons of the hawk. The people begin now to be in separate establishments, and not in villages. Houses are mostly covered with tile.

BEAUJOLOIS. Maison blanche. St. George. Chateau de Laye Epinaye. The face of the country is like that from Chalons to Macon. The Plains are a dark rich loam, the hills a red loam, of midling quality, mixed generally with more or less coarse sand and grit, and a great deal of small stone. Very little forest. The vineyards are mostly inclosed with dry stone wall. A few small cattle and sheep. Here, as in Burgundy, the cattle are all white.

This is the richest country I ever beheld. It is about 10. or 12. leagues in length, and 3. 4. or 5. in breadth; at least that part of it which is under the eye of the traveller. It extends from the top of a ridge of mountains running parallel with the Saone, and sloping down to the plains of that river scarcely any where too steep for the plough. The whole is thick sown with farm houses, chateaux, and the Bastides of the inhabitants of Lyons. The people live separately, and not in villages. The hillsides are in wine and corn: the plains in corn and pasture. The lands are farmed either for money, or on half-stocks. The rents of the corn lands farmed for money are about 10. or 12.^{tt} the arpent. A farmer takes perhaps about 150. arpents for 3. 6. or 9 years. The 1st. year they are in corn, the 2d. in other small grain, with which he sows red clover; the 3d. is for the clover. The spontaneous pasturage is of greenswerd, which they call formeteau. When lands are rented on half stocks, the cattle, sheep &c. are furnished by the landlord. They are valued and must be left of equal value. The increase of these, as well as the produce of the farm, are divided equally. These leases are only from year to year. They have a method of mixing beautifully the culture of vines, trees and corn. Rows of fruit trees are planted about 20. feet apart. Between the trees, in the row, they plant vines 4. feet apart and espalier them. The intervals are sowed alternately in corn, so as to be one year in corn the next in pasture, the 3d. in corn, the 4th in pasture &c. 100. toises of vines in length yeild generally about 4. peices of wine. In Dauphiné, I am told, they plant vines only at the roots of the trees and let cover the whole trees. But this spoils both the wine and the fruit. Their wine, when distilled, yeilds but one third it's quantity in brandy. The wages of a labouring man here are 5. Louis, of a woman one half. The women do not work with the hough: they only weed the vines, the corn, &c. and spin. They speak a Patois very difficult to understand. I passed some time at the chateau de Laye epinaye. Monsieur de Laye has a seignory of about 15,000 arpens, in pasture, corn, vines, and wood. He has over this, as is usual, a certain jurisdiction both criminal and civil. But this extends only to the first crude examination, which is before his judges. The subject is referred for final examination and decision to the regular judicatures of the country. The Seigneur is keeper of the peace on his domains. He is therefore subject to the expences of maintaining it. A criminal prosecuted to sentence and execution, costs M. de Laye about 5000.[tt] This is so burthensome to the Seigneurs, that they are slack in criminal prosecutions. A good effect from a bad cause. Thro' all Champagne, Burgundy and the Beaujolois, the husbandry seems good, except that they manure too little. This proceeds from the shortness of their leases. The people of Burgundy and Beaujolois are well clothed, and have the appearance of being well fed. But they experience all the oppressions which result from the nature of the general government, and from that of their particular tenures, and of the Seignorial government to which they are subject. What a cruel reflection that a rich country cannot long be a free one.—M. de Laye has a Diana and Endymion, a very superior morsel of sculpture by Michael Angelo Slodtz, done in 1740. The wild gooseberry is in leaf, the wild pear and sweet briar in bud.

LYONS. There are some feeble remains here of an amphitheatre of 200. feet diameter and of an aqueduct in brick. The Pont d'Ainay has 9. arches of 40. feet from center to center. The piers are of 6. feet.—The Almond is in bloom.

DAUPHINE. From St. Fond to Mornas. March 15. 16. 17. 18. The Rhone makes extensive plains, which lie chiefly on the Eastern side, and are often in two stages. Those of Montelimart are 3. or 4. miles wide, and rather good. Sometimes, as in the neighborhood of Vienne, the hills come in precipices to the river, resembling then very much our Susquehanna and it's hills, except that the Susquehanna is ten times as wide as the Rhone. The high lands are often very level.—The soil, both of hill and plain, where there is soil, is generally tinged, more or less, with red. The hills are sometimes mere masses of rock, sometimes a mixture of loose stone and earth. The plains are always stony and, as often as otherwise, covered perfectly with a coat of round stones of the size of the fist so as to resemble the remains of inundations from which all the soil has been carried away. Sometimes they are midling good, sometimes barren. In the neighborhood of Lyons there is more corn than wine, towards Tains more wine than corn. From thence the Plains, where best, are in corn, clover, almonds, mulberries, walnuts. Where there is still some earth they are in corn, almonds, and oaks; the hills are in vines.—There is a good deal of forest wood near Lyons, but not much afterwards. Scarcely any inclosures. There are a few small sheep before we reach Tains; there the number increases.

Nature never formed a country of more savage aspect than that on both sides the Rhone. A huge torrent, rushing like an arrow between high precipices often of massive rock, at other times of loose stone with but little earth. Yet has the hand of man subdued this savage scene, by planting corn where there is a little fertility, trees where there is still less, and vines where there is none. On the whole, it assumes a romantic, picturesque and pleasing air. The hills on the opposite side of the river, being high, steep, and laid up in terrasses, are of a singular appearance. Where the hills are quite in waste, they are covered in broom, whins, box, and some clusters of small pines. The high mountains of Dauphiné and Languedoc are now covered with snow. The Almond is in general bloom, and the willow putting out it's leaf. There were formerly OLIVES at Tains: but a great cold some years ago killed them, and they have not been replanted. I am told at Montelimart that an Almond tree yeilds about 3. livres profit a year. Supposing them 3. toises apart there will be 100 to the Arpent, which give 300.^{tt} a year, besides the corn growing in the same ground.—A league below Vienne, on the opposite side of the river COTE ROTIE. It is a string of broken hills, extending a league on the river from the village of Ampuys to the town of Condrieux. The soil is white, tinged a little, sometimes with yellow, sometimes with red, stony, poor and laid up in terrasses. Those parts of the hills only which look to the sun at Mid-day or the earlier hours of the afternoon produce wines of the first quality. 700 vines 3 feet apart, yeild a feuilette, which is about $2^{1}/2$ peices to the arpent. The best red wine is produced at the upper end in the neighborhood of Ampuys; the best white next to Condrieux. They sell of the first quality and last vintage at 150^{tt} the Piece, equal to 12.s the bottle. Transportation to Paris is 60.^{tt} and the bottle 4.s so it may be delivered at Paris in bottles at 20s. When old it costs

10. or 11. Louis the Piece. There is a quality which keeps well, bears transportation, and cannot be drunk under 4. years. Another must be drunk at a year old. They are equal in flavor and price. The best vintages of red wine are of Monsieur de la Condamine seigneur d'Ampuys, dans son fief de Monlis, le Marquis de Leusse dans son grand tupin, M. de Montjoli, M. du Vivier, and M. du Prunel. The best of white are at Chateau grillé by Madame la veuve Peyrouse.

The wine called HERMITAGE is made on the hills impending over the village of Tains; on one of which is the hermitage which gives name to the hills for about two miles, and to the wine made on them. There are but three of those hills which produce wine of the 1st. quality, and of these the middle regions only. They are about 300 feet perpendicular height, 3/4 of a mile in length and have a Southern aspect. The soil is scarcely tinged red, consists of small rotten stone, and, in it's most precious parts, without any perceptible mixture of earth. It is in sloping terrasses. They use a little dung. An Homme de vignes, which consist of 700 plants 3. feet apart, yeilds generally about 3/4 a peice, which is nearly 4 peices to the arpent. When new the Peice is sold at 225,^{tt} old at 300.^{tt} It cannot be drunk under 4. years, and improves fastest in a hot situation. There is so little White made in proportion to the red, that it is difficult to buy it separate. They make the White sell the Red. If bought separately it is from 15. to 18. Louis the peice, new, and 3^{tt} the bottle old. To give quality to the Red, they mix of white grapes. Portage to Paris is 72^{tt} the peice, weighing 600 lb. There are but about 1000. peices of both red and white of the 1st. quality made annually. They are made by M. Meus, seigneur of the place, M. de Loche avocat, M. Berger avocat, M. Chanoine Monron, M. Gaillet, M. de Beausace, M. Deure, M. Chalamelle, M. Monnet and two or three others. Vineyards are never rented here, nor are labourers in the vineyard hired by the year. They leave buds proportioned to the strenth of the vine: sometimes as much as 15. inches. The last Hermit died in 1751.

In the neighborhoood of Montelimart and below that they plant vines in rows 6. 8. or 10. feet apart, and 2. feet asunder in the row, filling the intervals with corn. Sometimes the vines are in double rows 2. feet apart. I saw single asses in ploughs proportioned to their strength. [Original included a drawing, here omitted.] The plough formed of three peices, thus a. is the beam, to which the share is fixed, b. a crooked bough of a tree sometimes single, sometimes forked, c. a crooked bough also to which the swingletree was fastened. Asses or mules, working in pairs, are coupled by square yokes in this form [illustration omitted] the side peices only sliding out to disengage the animal. There are a few chateaux in this province. The people too are mostly gathered into villages. There are however some scattering farm houses. These are made either of mud or of round stone and mud. They make inclosures also in both those ways. Day labourers receive 16.s or 18.s the day, and feed themselves. Those by the year receive, men 3. Louis and women half that, and are fed. They rarely eat meat; a single hog salted being the year's stock for a family. But they have plentiful of cheese, eggs, potatoes and other vegetables, and walnut oil with their sallad. It is a trade here to gather dung along the road for their vines. This proves they have few cattle. I have seen neither hares nor partridges since I left Paris, nor wild fowl on any of the rivers. The roads from Lyons to St. Rambert are neither paved nor gravelled. After that they are coated with broken flint. The ferry boats on the Rhone, and the Isere, are moved by the stream, and very rapidly. On each side of the river is a moveable stage, one end of which is on an axle and two wheels, which, according to the tide, can be advanced or withdrawn so as to apply to the gunwale of the boat. The Pretorian palace at Vienne is 44. feet wide, of the Corinthian order, 4. columns in front, and 4. in flank. It was begun the year 400. and finished by Charlemagne. The Sepulchral pyramid, a little way out of the town, has an order for it's basement, the pedestal of which from point to point of it's cap is 24.f 1.I At each angle is a column, engaged one fourth in the wall. The circumference of the three fourths disengaged is 4.f 4.I. Consequently the diameter is 23.I. The base of the column indicates it to be Ionic, but the capitals are not formed. The Cornice too is a bastard Ionic without modillions or dentils. Between the columns on each side is an arch of 8.f. 4.I opening, with a pilaster on each side of it. On the top of the basement is a zocle, in the plane of the frieze below. On that is the pyramid, it's base in the plane of the collanno of the pilaster below. The pyramid is a little truncated on it's top. This monument is inedited.

Mar. 18. PRINCIPALITY OF ORANGE. The plains on the Rhone here are 2. or 3. leagues wide, reddish, good, in corn, clover, almonds, olives. No forest. Here begins the country of olives, there being very few till we enter this principality. They are the only tree which I see planted among vines. Thyme growing wild here on the hills. Asses very small, sell here for 2. or 3. Louis. The high hills in Dauphiné are covered with snow. The remains of the

Roman aqueduct are of brick. A fine peice of Mosaic, still on it's bed, forming the floor of a cellar. 20 feet of it still visible. They are taking down the
circular wall of the Ampitheatre to pave a road.

March 19. to 23. LANGUEDOC. PONT ST. ESPRIT. BAGNOLS.
CONNAULT. VALIGNIERES. REMOULINS. ST. GERVASY. NISMES. PONT
D'ARLES. To Remoulins there is a mixture of hill and dale. Thence to Nismes,
hills on the right, on the left plains extending to the Rhone and the sea. The
hills are rocky. Where there is soil it is reddish and poor. The plains generally
reddish and good, but stony. When you approach the Rhone, going to Arles,
the soil becomes a dark grey loam, with some sand, and very good. The culture is corn, clover, St. foin, olives, vines, mulberries, willow, and some almonds.
There is no forest. The hills are inclosed in dry stone wall. Many sheep.

From the summit of the first hill after leaving Pont St. Esprit, there is a
beautiful view of the bridge at about 2. miles distance, and a fine landscape
of the country both ways. From thence an excellent road, judiciously conducted,
thro very romantic scenes. In one part, descending the face of a hill, it is laid
out in Serpentine, and not zig-zag, to ease the descent. In others it passes thro'
a winding meadow, from 50. to 100. yards wide, walled as it were on both sides
by hills of rock; and at length issues into plane country. The waste hills are
covered with thyme, box, and chenevert. Where the body of the mountains has
a surface of soil, the summit has sometimes a crown of rock, as observed in
Champagne. At Nismes the earth is full of limestone. They use square yokes
as in Dauphiné. The horses are shorn. They are now pruning the olive. A very
good tree produces 60.^{tt} of olives, which yield 15^{tt}. of oil: the best quality selling at 12.s the ^{tt} retail, and 10.s wholesale. The high hills of Languedoc still
covered with snow. The horse chestnut and mulberry are leafing; appletrees
and peas blossoming. The first butterfly I have seen. After the vernal equinox
they are often 6. or 8. months without any rain. Many separate farmhouses,
numbers of people in rags, and abundance of beggars. The Mine of wheat,
weighing 30.^{tt}. costs 4^{tt} 10.s, wheat bread 3.s the pound. Vin ordinaire, good
and of a strong body 2.s or 3.s the bottle. Oranges 1.s apeice. They are nearly
finishing at Nismes a grist mill worked by a steam engine, which pumps water
from a lower into an upper cistern, from whence two overshot wheels are supplied, each of which turns two pair of stones. The upper cistern being once
filled with water, it passes thro the wheels into the lower one from whence it

is returned into the upper by the pumps. A stream of water of $^1/4$ or $^1/2$ inch diameter supplies the wastes of evaporation, absorption, &c. This is furnished from a well by a horse. The arches of the pont St. Esprit are of 88 feet. Wild figs, very flourishing, grow out of the joints of the Pont du Gard. The fountain of Nismes is so deep, that a stone was 13" descending from the surface to the bottom.

March 24. FROM NISMES TO ARLES. The plains extending from Nismes to the Rhone in the direction of Arles is broken in one place by a skirt of low hills. They are red and stony at first, but as you approach the Rhone they are of a dark grey mould, with a little sand, and very good. They are in corn and clover, vines, olives, almonds, mulberries and willow. There are some sheep, no wood, no inclosures.

The high hills of Languedoc are covered with snow. At an antient church in the suburbs of Arles are perhaps some hundreds of antient stone coffins along the road side. The ground is thence called les champs elysées. In a vault in the church are some preciously wrought, and in a back yard are many antient statues, inscriptions &c. Within the town are a part of two Corinthian columns, and of the pediment with which they were crowned, very rich, having belonged to the antient Capitol of the place. But the principal monument here is an Ampitheatre, the external portico of which is tolerably compleat. How many of these porticoes there were, cannot be seen: but at one of the principal gates there are still 5. measuring from out to in 78f. 10I., the vault diminishing inwards. There are 64. arches, each of which is from center to center 20.f. 6.I. Of course the diameter is of 438. feet, or of 450. feet if we suppose the 4. principal arches a little larger than the rest. The ground floor is supported on innumerable vaults. The first story, externally, has a tall pedestal, like a pilaster; between every two arches: the upper story a column, the base of which would indicate it Corinthian. Every column is truncated as low as the impost of the arch, but the arches are all entire. The whole of the upper entablature is gone, and of the Attic, if there was one. Not a single seat of the internal is visible. The whole of the inside, and nearly the whole of the outside is masked by buildings. It is supposed there are 1000. inhabitants within the Ampitheatre. The walls are more entire and firm than those of the Ampitheatre at Nismes. I suspect it's plan and distribution to have been very different from that.

TERRASSON. The plains of the Rhone from Arles to this place are a league or two wide: the mould is of a dark grey, good, in corn and lucerne. Neither wood, nor inclosures. Many sheep.

ST. REMIS. From Terrasson to St. Remis is a plain of a league or two wide, bordered by broken hills of massive rock. It is grey and stony, mostly in olives. Some almonds, mulberries, willows, vines, corn, and lucerne. Many sheep. No forest, no inclosures.

A labouring man's wages here are 150^{tt}, a woman's the half, and fed. 280. lb. of wheat sells for 42.^{tt} They make no butter here. It costs, when brought, 15.s the lb. Oil is 10.s the lb. Tolerable good olive trees yeild one with another, about 20. lb. of oil. An olive tree must be 20 years old before it has paid it's own expences. It lasts for ever. In 1765. it was so cold that the Rhone was frozen over at Arles for 2. months. In 1767. there was a cold spell of a week which killed all the olive trees. From being fine weather in one hour there was ice hard enough to bear a horse. It killed people on the road. The old roots of the olive trees put out again. Olive grounds sell at 24^{tt} a tree, and lease at 24 sous the tree. The trees are 15. pieds apart. But Lucerne is a more profitable culture. An arpent yeilds 100. quintals of hay a year, worth 3^{tt} a quintal. It is cut 4. or 5. times a year. It is sowed in the broad cast and lasts 5. or 6. years. An arpent of ground for corn rents at 30.^{tt} to 36.^{tt} Their leases are for 6. or 9. years. They plant willow for fire wood, and for hoops to their casks. It seldom rains here in summer. There are some chateaux, many separate farm houses, good and ornamented in the small way, so as to shew that the tenant's whole time is not occupied in procuring physical necessaries.

March 25. ORGON. PONTROYAL. ST. CANNAT. From Orgon to Pontroyal, after quitting the plains of the Rhone, the country seems still to be a plain cut into compartments, by chains of mountains of massive rock running thro it in various directions. From Pontroyal to St. Cannat the land lies rather in basons. The soil is very various, Grey and clay, grey and stony, red and stony; sometimes good, sometimes midling, often barren. We find some golden willows. Towards Pontroyal the hills begin to be in vines, and afterwards is some pasture of green swerd and clover. About Orgon are some inclosures of quickset, others of conical yews planted close. Towards St. Cannat they begin to be of stone.

The high mountains are covered with snow. Some separate farm houses of mud. Near Pontroyal is a canal for watering the country. One branch goes to Terrasson, the other to Arles. At St. Cannat a hill covered with pines. There is no forest; many sheep.

March. 25. 26. 27. 28. AIX. The country is waving, in vines, pasture of green swerd and clover, much inclosed with stone, and abounding with sheep. On approaching Aix the valley which opens from thence towards the mouth of the Rhone and the sea is rich and beautiful: a perfect grove of olive trees, mixt among which is corn, lucerne and vines. The waste grounds throw out thyme and lavender. Wheat-bread is 3s. the lb., cow's milk 16s. the quart, sheep's milk 6s., butter of sheep's milk 20s. the lb., oil of the best quality 12s. the lb., and 16s. if it be virgin oil. This is what runs from the olive when put into the press, spontaneously: afterwards they are forced by the press and by hot water. Dung costs 10s. the 100 lb. Their fire wood is chene-vert and willow. The latter is lopped every three years. An ass sells for from 1. to 3. Louis; the best mules for 30. Louis. The best asses will carry 200. lb., the best horses 300 lb., the best mules 600 lb. The temperature of the mineral waters of Aix is 90.° of Farenheit's thermometer at the spout. A mule eats half as much as a horse. The allowance to an ass for the day is a handful of bran mixed with straw. The price of mutton and beef about $6^{1}/2$s the lb. The beef comes from Auvergne, is poor and bad. The mutton is small but of excellent flavor. The wages of a labouring man are 150^{tt} the year, a woman's 60^{tt} to 66^{tt} and fed. Their bread is half wheat, half rye, made once in 3. or 4. weeks to prevent too great a consumption. In the morning they eat bread with an anchovy, or an onion. Their dinner in the middle of the day is bread, soupe, and vegetables. Their supper the same. With their vegetables they have always oil and vinegar. The oil costs about 8s. the lb. They drink what is called Piquette. This is made after the grapes are pressed, by pouring hot water on the pumice. On Sunday they have meat and wine. Their wood for building comes mostly from the the Alps down the Durance and Rhone. A stick of pine 50. feet long, girting 6.f. 3.I at one end, and 2.f. 3.I at the other costs delivered here 54.^{tt} to 60.^{tt} 60 lb. of wheat cost 7.^{tt} One of their little asses will travel with his burthen about 5. or 6. leagues a day, and day by day: a mule from 6. to 8. leagues. (Note it is 20. American miles from Aix to Marseilles, and they call it 5. leagues. Their league then is of 4. American miles.)

Mar. 29. MARSEILLES. The country is hilly, intersected by chains of hills and mountains of massive rock. The soil is reddish, stony and indifferent where best. Whenever there is any soil it is covered with olives. Among these are vines, corn, some lucerne, mulberry, some almonds and willow. Neither inclosures, nor forest. A very few sheep.

On the road I saw one of those little whirlwinds which we have in Virginia. Also some gullied hill-sides. The people are in separate establisments. 10 morning observations of the thermometer, from the 20th. to the 31st. of March inclusive, made at Nismes, St. Remy, Aix and Marseilles give me an average of 52^{1}/$_{2}$° and 46° and 61° for the greatest and least morning heats. 9. afternoon observations yeild an average of 62^{2}/$_{3}$° and 57.° and 66.° the greatest and least. The longest day here from sunrise to sunset is 15H. 14.' The shortest is 8H.-46'. The latitude being. There are no tides in the Mediterranean. It is observed to me that the olive tree grows no where more than 30 leagues distant from that sea. I suppose however that both Spain and Portugal furnish proofs to the contrary, and doubt it's truth as to Asia, Africa and America.

There are 6. or 8. months at a time here without rain. The most delicate figs known in Europe are those growing about this place, called figues Marcelloises, or les veritables Marcelloises, to distinguish them from others of inferior quality growing here. These keep any length of time. All others exude a sugar in the spring of the year and become sour. The only process for preserving them is drying them in the sun, without putting any thing to them whatever. They sell at 15s. the lb. while there are others as cheap as the lb. I meet here a small dried grape from Smyrna without a seed. There are a few of the plants growing in this neighborhood. The best grape for drying known here is called des Panses. They are very large, with a thick skin and much juice. They are best against a wall of Southern aspect, as their abundance of juice requires a great deal of sun to dry it. Pretty good fig trees are about the size of the Apricot tree and yeild about 20. lb. of figs when dry, each. But the largest will yeild the value of a Louis. They are sometimes 15.1. diameter. It is said that the Marseilles fig degenerates when transplanted into another part of the country. The leaves of a Mulberry tree will sell for about 3,^{tt} the purchaser gathering them. The CAPER is a creeping plant. It is killed to the roots every winter. In the spring it puts out branches which creep to the distance of 3.f. from the center. The fruit forms on the stem as that extends itself, and must be gathered every day as it forms. This is the work of women. The pistache grows in this neighborhood also, but not very good. They eat them in their milky state. Monsieur de BERGASSE has a wine-cellar 240. pieds long, in which are 120. tons of from

50. to 100 peices each. These tons are 12. pieds diameter; the staves 4.I. thick, the heading $2^{1}/2$ pouces thick. The temperature of his cellar is of $9^{1}/2°$ of Reaumur. The best method of packing wine, when bottled, is to lay the bottles on their side, and cover them with sand. The 2d. of April the young figs are formed: the 4th. we have Windsor beans. They have had Asparagus ever since the middle of March. The 5th. I see strawberries and the Guelder rose in blossom. To preserve the raisin, it is first dipped into lye and then dried in the sun. The Aloe grows in the open ground. I measure a mule, not the largest, 5f. 2.I. high. Marseilles is in an amphitheatre, at the mouth of the Vaune, surrounded by high mountains of naked rock, distant 2. or 3. leagues. The country within that amphitheatre is a mixture of small hills, vallies and plains. The latter are naturally rich. The hills and vallies are forced into production. Looking from the chateau de Notre dame de la garde, it would seem as if there was a Bastide for every arpent. The plain lands sell for 100. Louis the Carterelle which is less than an acre. The ground of the arsenal in Marseilles sold for from 15. to 40. Louis the square verge, being nearly the square yard English. In the feilds open to the sea they are obliged to plant rows of canes every here and there to break the force of the wind. Saw at the Chateau Borelli pumps worked by the wind; the axis of the vanes vertical, the house open thus the radius 12.f. 5.I, external circumference 103. feet. 16 windows. The sails 4. feet wide and 12 feet high. [Illustration omitted.]

April 6. from MARSEILLES to AUBAGNE. A valley on the Vaune bordered on each side by high mountains of massive rock, on which are only some small pines. The interjacent valley is of small hills, vallies and plains, reddish, gravelly, and originally poor, but fertilised by art, and covered with corn, vines, olives, figs, almonds, mulberries, lucerne and clover. The river is 12. or 15. feet wide, 1. or 2. feet deep and rapid.

From Aubagne to Cuges, Beausset, Toulon. The road quitting the Vaune and it's wealthy valley, a little after Aubagne, enters those mountains of rock and is engaged with them about a dozen miles. Then it passes 6. or 8. miles thro' a country, still very hilly and stony, but laid up in terrasses, covered with olives, vines and corn. It then follows for 2. and 3. miles a hollow between two of those high mountains which has been found or made by a small stream. The mountains then reclining a little from their perpendicular and presenting a coat of soil, reddish and tolerably good has given place to the little village of Olioules, in the gardens of which are Oranges in the open ground. It continues hilly till we enter the plain of Toulon. On different parts of this road there are figs in the open fields. At Cuges is a plain of about 3/4 mile diameter, surrounded by high mountains of rock. In this the CAPER is principally cultivated. The soil is mulatto, gravelly, and of midling quality, or rather indifferent. The plants are set in quincunx about 8.f. apart. They have been covered during winter by a hill of earth a foot high. They are now uncovering, pruning and ploughing them.

TOULON. From Olioules to Toulon the figs are in the open fields. Some of them have stems of 15.I. diameter. They generally fork near the ground, but sometimes have a single stem of 5.f. long. They are as large as Apricot trees. The Olive trees of this day's journey are about the size of large apple trees. The people are in separate establishments. Toulon is in a valley at the mouth of the Goutier, a little river of the size of the Vaune; surrounded by high mountains of naked rock leaving some space between them and the sea. This space is hilly, reddish, gravelly, and of midling quality, in olives, vines, corn, almonds, figs, and capers. The capers are planted 8.f. apart. A bush yeilds, one year with another, 2. lb. worth 12s. the lb. Every plant then yeilds 24s.-1. sterling. An acre containing 676. plants would yeild 33£. 16s sterl. The fruit is gathered by women who can gather about 12. lb. a day. They begin to gather about the last of June and end about the middle of October. Each plant must be picked every other day. These plants grow equally well in the best or worst soil, or even in walls where there is no soil. They will last the life of a man or longer. The heat is so great at Toulon in summer as to occasion very great cracks in the earth. Where the caper is in a soil that will admit it, they plough it. They have peas here through the winter, sheltering them occasionally and they have had them ever since the 25 March without shelter.

April 6. HIERES. This is a plain of two or three miles diameter, bounded by the sea on one side and mountains of rock on the other. The soil is reddish, gravelly, tolerably good and well watered. It is in olives, mulberries, vines, figs, corn and some flax. There are also some cherry trees. From Hieres to the sea, which is 2. or 3. miles, is a grove of orange trees, olives, and mulberries. The largest orange tree is of 2.f. diameter one way and 1.f. the other (for the section of all the large ones would be an oval, not a round) and about 20.f. high. Such a tree will yeild about 6000. oranges a year. The garden of M. Fille has 15600 orange trees. Some years they yeild 40,000^{tt}, some only 10000^{tt}, but generally about 25,000.[^tt] The trees are from 8. to 10.f. apart. They are blossoming and bearing all the year, flowers and fruit, in every stage, at the same time, but the best fruit is that which is gathered in April and May. Hieres is a village of about 5000 inhabitants, at the foot of a mountain which covers it from the North and from which extends a plain of 2. or 3. miles to the sea shore. It has no port. Here are Palm trees 20. or 30.f. high, but they bear no fruit. There is also a botanical garden kept by the king. Considerable salt ponds here. Hieres is 6 miles from the public road. It is built on a narrow spur of the mountain. The streets in every direction are steep, or steps of stairs, and about 8 feet wide. No carriage of any kind can enter it. The wealthier inhabitants use chaises á porteurs. But there are few wealthy, the bulk of the inhabitants being labourers of the earth. At a league distance in the sea is an island, on which is the Chateau de Geans belonging to the Marquis de Pontoives. There is a causeway leading to it. The cold of the last November killed the leaves of a great number of the orange trees and some of the trees themselves.

From HIERES to CUERS, PIGNANS, LUC is mostly a plain with mountains on each hand at a mile or two distance. The soil is generally reddish, and the latter part very red and good. The growth is olives, figs, vines, mulberries, corn, clover and lucerne. The olive trees are from 3. to 4. diameter. There are hedges of pomegranates, sweetbriar and broom. A great deal of thyme growing wild. There are some enclosures of stone, some sheep and goats.

April 9. From LUC to VIDAUBAN, MUY, FREJUS the road leads thro vallies, and crosses occasionally the mountains which separate them. The vallies are tolerably good, always red, and stony, gravelly or gritty. Their produce as before. The mountains are barren.

LESTERELLE, NAPOULE. 18 miles of ascent and descent of a very high mountain. It's growth, where capable of any, two leaved pine, very small, and some chene-verte.

ANTIBES, NICE. From Napoule the road is generally near the sea, passing over little hills or strings of vallies, the soil stony and much below mediocrity in it's quality. Here and there is a good plain.

There is snow on the high mountains. The first frogs I have heard are of this day (the 9th). At Antibes are oranges in the open ground, but in small inclosures: palm trees also. From thence to the Var are the largest fig trees and olive trees I have seen. The fig trees are 18.I. diameter and 6.f. stem, the Olives some-times 6.f. diameter and as large heads as the largest low ground apple trees. This tree was but a shrub where I first fell in with it, and has become larger and larger to this place. The people are mostly in villages.—The several provinces, and even cantons are distinguished by the form of the women's hats, so that one may know of what canton a woman is by her hat. From Antibes to the Var it is shaped thus [illustration omitted] of straw, light and cool.

NICE. The pine bur is used here for kindling fires. The people are in separate establishments. With respect to the Orange there seems to be no climate on this side of the Alps sufficiently mild in itself to preserve it with-out shelter. At Olioules they are between 2. high mountains: at Hieres, covered on the North by a very high mountain, at Antibes and Nice covered by moun-tains, and also within small high inclosures. Qu. to trace the true line from East to West which forms the Northern and natural limit of that fruit? Saw an Elder tree (Sambucus) near Nice, 15.I. diameter and 8.f. stem. The wine made in this neighborhood is good, tho' not of the first quality. There are 1000 mules, loaded with merchandize, which pass every week between Nice and Turin, counting those coming as well as going.

April 13. SCARENA, SOSPELLO. There are no Orange trees after we leave the environs of Nice. We lose the Olive after rising a little above the village of Scarena on Mount Braus, and find it again on the other side a little before we get down to Sospello. But wherever there is soil enough, it is terrassed and in corn. The waste parts are either in two leaved pine and thyme, or of absolutely naked rock. Sospello is on a little torrent called Bevera which runs into the river Roia, at the mouth of which is Ventimiglia. The olive trees on the mountain are now loaded with fruit; while some at Sospella are in blossom. Fire wood here and at Scarena costs 15s. the quintal.

April 14. CIANDOLA. TENDE. In crossing Mount Brois we lose the Olive tree after getting to a certain height, and find it again on the other side at the village of Breglio. Here we come to the river Roia which, after receiving the branch on which is Sospello, leads to the sea at Ventimiglia. The Roia is about 12. yards wide and abounds with speckled trout. Were a road made from Breglio, along the side of the Roia, to Ventimiglia, it might turn the commerce of Turin to this last place instead of Nice; because it would avoid the moun-tains of Braus and Brois, leaving only that of Tende; that is to say it would avoid

more than half the difficulties of the passage. Further on, we come to the
Chateau di Saorgio, where a scene is presented, the most singular and picturesque I ever saw. The castle and village seem hanging to a cloud in front. On
the right is a mountain cloven through to let pass a gurgling stream; on the
left a river over which is thrown a magnificent bridge. The whole forms a bason,
the sides of which are shagged with rocks, olive trees, vines, herds &c. Near here
I saw a tub-wheel without a ream; the trunk descended from the top of the water
fall to the wheel in a direct line, but with the usual inclination. The produce
along this passage is most generally olives except on the heights as before
observed, also corn, vines, mulberry, figs, cherries and walnuts. They have
cows, goats and sheep. In passing on towards Tende, olives fail us ultimately
at the village of Fontan, and there the chesnut trees begin in good quantity.
Ciandola consists of only two houses, both taverns. Tende is a very inconsiderable village, in which they have not yet the luxury of glass windows: nor in
any of the villages on this passage have they yet the fashion of powdering the
hair. Common stone and limestone are so abundant that the apartments of every
story are vaulted with stone to save wood.

April 15. LIMONE. CONI. I see abundance of limestone as far as the earth
is uncovered with snow, i.e. to within half or three quarters of an hour's walk
of the top. The snows descend much lower on the Eastern than Western side.
Wherever there is soil there is corn, quite to the commencement of the snows,
and I suppose under them also. The waste parts are in two leaved pine,
lavender and thyme. From the foot of the mountain to Coni the road follows
a branch of the Po, the plains of which begin narrow, and widen at length into
a general plain country bounded on one side by the Alps. They are good,
dark-coloured, sometimes tinged with red, and in pasture, corn, mulberries and
some almonds. The hillsides bordering these plains are reddish, and, where
they admit of it, are in corn, but this is seldom. They are mostly in chesnut, and
often absolutely barren. The whole of the plains are plentifully watered from
the river, as is much of the hill side. A great deal of Golden willow all
along the rivers on the whole of this passage thro' the Alps. The Southern parts
of France, but still more the passage thro' the Alps, enables one to form a scale
of the tenderer plants, arranging them according to their several powers of
resisting cold. Ascending three different mountains, Braus, Brois, and Tende,
they disappear one after another; and, descending on the other side, they

shew themselves again one after another. This is their order, from the tenderest to the hardiest. Caper. orange. palm. aloe. olive. pomegranate. walnut. fig. almond. But this must be understood of the plant: for as to the fruit, the order is somewhat different. The caper, for example, is the tenderest plant; yet being so easily protected, it is the most certain in it's fruit. The almond, the hardiest plant, loses it's fruit the oftenest, on account of it's forwardness. The palm, hardier than the caper and the orange, never produces perfect fruit in these parts.—Coni is a considerable town, and pretty well built. It is walled.

April 16. CENTALE. SAVIGLIANO. RACCONIGI. POERINO. TURIN. The Alps, as far as they are in view from North to South, shew the gradation of climate by the line which terminates the snows lying on them. This line begins at their foot Northwardly, and rises, as they pass on to the South, so as to be half way up their sides on the most Southern undulations of the mountain, now in view. From the mountain to Turin we see no tree tenderer than the walnut. Of these, as well as of almonds and mulberries there are a few: somewhat more of vines, but most generally willows and poplars. Corn is sowed with all these. They mix with them also clover and small grass. The country is a general plain; the soil dark, sometimes, tho' rarely, reddish. It is rich. Much infested with wild onions. At Racconigi I see the tops and shucks of Maise, which prove it is cultivated here: but it can be in small quantities only, because I observe very little ground but what has already something else in it. Here and there are small patches prepared I suppose for maize. They have a method of planting the vine which I have not seen before. At intervals of about 8.f. they plant from 2. to 6. plants of vine in a cluster. At each cluster they fix a forked staff, the plane of the prongs of the fork at a right angle with the row of vines. Athwart these prongs they lash another staff, like a handspike, about 8.f. long, horizontally, 7. or 8. feet from the ground. Of course it crosses the rows at right angles. The vines are brought from the foot of the fork up to this cross peice, turned over it, and conducted along over the next, the next, and so on as far as they will extend, the whole forming an arbour 8.f. wide and high, and of the whole length of the row, little interrupted by the stems of the vines, which being close round the fork, pass up thro' hoops, so as to occupy a space only of small diameter. All the buildings in this country are of brick, sometimes covered with plaister, sometimes not. There is a very large and very handsome bridge of 7. arches over the torrent of Sangone. We cross the Po in swinging batteaux.

Two are placed side by side, and kept together by a plank floor, common to both, and lying on their gunwales. The carriage drives on this, without taking out any of the horses. About 150 yards up the river is a fixed stake, and a rope tied to it, the other end of which is made fast to one side of the batteaux so as to throw them oblique to the current. The stream then acting on them, as on an inclined plain, forces them across the current in the portion of a circle of which the rope is the radius. To support the rope in it's whole length, there are 2. intermediate canoes, about 50. yards apart, in the head of which is a short mast. To the top of this the rope is lashed, the canoes being free otherwise to concur with the general vibration in their smaller arks of circles. The Po is, there, about 50. yards wide, and about 100. in the neighborhood of Turin.

April 17. 18. TURIN. I observe them carrying very long beams on two pairs of wheels, which the beam connects together. The wheels with their hounds are placed thus (illustration omitted) and the beam is lashed from the hind to the fore axle. The first nightingale I have heard this year is to-day, (18th.). There is a red wine of Nebiule made in this neighbor-hood which is very singular. It is about as sweet as the silky Madeira, as astringent on the palate as Bordeaux, and as brisk as Champagne. It is a pleasing wine. At Moncaglieri, about 6 miles from Turin, on the right side the Po begins a ridge of mountains, which following the Po by Turin, after some distance, spreads wide and forms the dutchy of Montferrat. The soil is mostly red and in vines, affording a wine called Montferrat, which is thick and strong.

April 19. SETTIMO. CHIVASCO. CILIANO. S. GERMANO. VERCELLI. The country continues plain and rich, the soil black. The culture corn, pasture, maise, vines, mulberries, walnuts, some willow and poplar. The maize bears a very small proportion to the small grain. The earth is formed into ridges from 3. to 4.f. wide, and the maize sowed in the broad cast, on the higher parts of the ridge, so as to cover a third or half of the whole surface. It is sowed late in May. This country is plentifully and beautifully watered at present. Much of it is by torrents which are dry in summer. These torrents make a great deal of waste ground, covering it with sand and stones. These wastes are sometimes planted in trees, sometimes quite unemployed. They make hedges of willow, by setting the plants from 1. to 3.f. apart. When they are grown to the height of 8. or 10.f. they bend them down and interlace them one with another. I do not see any of these however which are become old. Probably therefore they soon die. The women here smite on the anvil, work with the mawl and the spade.

The people of this country are ill dressed in comparison with those of France, and there are more spots of uncultivated ground. The plough here is made with a single handle, which is a beam 12.f. long, 6.I. diameter, below, and tapered to about 2.I. at the upper end. They use goads for the oxen, not whips. The first SWALLOWS I have seen are to-day. There is a wine called Gatina made in the neighborhood of Vercelli, both red and white. The latter resembles Calcavallo. There is also a red wine of Salusola which is esteemed. It is very light. In the neighborhood of Vercelli begin the RICE fields. The water with which they are watered is very dear. They do not permit rice to be sown within 2. miles of the cities on account of the insalubrity. Notwithstanding this, when the water is drawn off the fields in August, the whole country is subject to agues and fevers. They estimate that the same measure of ground yields three times as much rice as wheat, and with half the labour. They are now sowing. As soon as sowed, they let on the water, 2. or 3.I. deep. After 6. weeks or 2. months they draw it off to weed: then let it on again, and it remains till August, when it is drawn off about 3. or 4. weeks before the grain is ripe. In September they cut it. It is first threshed: then beaten in the mortar to separate the husk; then by different siftings it is separated into 3. qualities. 12 rupes = 300. lb. of 12. oz. each, sell for 16.[ttt] money of Piedmont, where the livre is exactly the shilling of England. 12. rupes of maize sell for 9.[tt] The machine for separating the husk is thus made. In the axis of a water wheel are a number of arms inserted, which, as they revolve, catch the cog of a pestle, lift it to a certain height, and let it fall again. These pestles are $5^{1}/4$ I square, 10.f. long, and at their lower end formed into a truncated cone of 3.I. diameter where cut off. The conical part is covered with iron. The pestles are $10^{1}/2$ apart in the clear. They pass through two horizontal beams, which string them, as it were, together, and while the mortises in the beams are so loose as to let the pestle work vertically it restrains it to that motion. There is a mortar of wood, 12. or 15I. deep under each pestle, covered with a board, the hole of which is only large enough to let the pestle pass freely. There are two arms in the axis, for every pestil, so that the pestle gives two strokes for every revolution of the wheel. Poggio, a muletier, who passes every week between Vercelli and Genoa will smuggle a sack of rough rice for me to Genoa; it being death to export it in that form. They have good cattle in good number, mostly cream coloured, and some middle sized sheep. The streams furnish speckled trout.

April 20. NOVARA. BUFFALORA. SEDRIANO. MILAN. From Vercelli to Novara the fields are all in rice, and now mostly under water. The dams separating the several water plats, or ponds, are set in willow. At Novara there are some figs in the gardens, in situations well protected. From Novara to the Ticino it is mostly stony and waste, grown up in broom. From the Ticino to Milan it is all in corn. Among the corn are willows principally, a good many mulberries, some walnuts, and here and there an almond. The country still a plain, the soil black and rich, except between Novara and the Ticino as before mentioned. There is very fine pasture round Vercelli and Novara to the distance of 2. miles within which rice is not permitted. We cross the Sisto on the same kind of vibrating or pendulum boat as on the Po. The river is 80. or 90. yards wide; the rope fastened to an island 200. yards above, and supported by 5. intermediate canoes. It is about $1^{1}/_{2}$ I. in diameter. On these rivers they use a short oar of 12f. long, the flat end of which is hooped with iron shooting out a prong at each corner, so that it may be used occasionally as a setting pole. There is snow on the Appenines near Genoa. They have still another method here of planting the vine. Along rows of trees they lash poles from tree to tree. Between the trees are set vines which passing over the pole, are carried on to the pole of the next row, whose vines are in like manner brought to this, and twined together; thus forming the intervals between the rows of trees alternately into arbors, and open space. Another method also of making quickset hedges. Willows are planted from one to two feet apart, and thus interlaced [illustration omitted] so that every one is crossed by 3. or 4. others.

April 21. 22. MILAN. Figs and pomegranates grow here unsheltered, as I am told. I saw none, and therefore suppose them rare. They had formerly olives; but a great cold in 1709 killed them, and they have not been replanted. —Among a great many houses painted al fresco, the Casa Roma and Casa Candiani by Appiani, and Casa Belgioiosa by Martin are superior. In the second is a small cabinet, the cieling of which is in small hexagons, within which are Cameos and heads painted alternately, no two the same. The salon of the Casa Belgioiosa is superior to any thing I have seen. The mixture called Scaiola, of which they make their walls and floors, is so like the finest marble as to be scarcely distinguishable from it. The nights of the 20. and 21st. inst. the rice ponds freezed half an inch thick. Drowths of 2. or 3. months are not uncommon here in summer. About 5. years ago there was such a hail as to kill cats. The Count del Verme tells me of a pendulum Odometer for the wheel of a carriage. Leases here are mostly for 9. years. Wheat costs a Louis d'or the 140. lb. A labouring man receives 60.^{tt} and is fed and lodged. The trade of this country is principally rice, raw silk, and cheese.

April 23. CASINO. 5. miles from Milan. I examined another rice-beater of 6. pestles. They are 8f. 9.I. long. Their ends, instead of being a truncated cone, have 9. teeth of iron, bound closely together thus [illustration omitted]. Each tooth is a double pyramid, joined at the base. When put together they stand thus [illustration omitted], the upper ends placed in contact so as to form them into one great cone, and the lower end diverging. The upper are socketed into the end of the pestle, and the lower, when a little blunted by use, are not unlike the jaw-teeth of the Mammoth, with their studs. They say here that pestles armed with these teeth, clean the rice faster and break it less. The mortar too is of stone, which is supposed as good as wood, and more durable. One half of these pestles are always up. They rise about 21.I. Each makes 38. strokes in a minute. 100. Ib. of rough rice is put into the 6. mortars and beaten some-what less than a quarter of an hour. It is then taken out, put into a sifter of 4.f. diameter suspended horizontally; sifted there; shifted into another of the same size, sifted there, returned to the mortars, beaten a little more than a quarter of an hour, sifted again, and it is finished. The 6. pestles will clean 4000 lb. in 24 hours. The pound here is of 28. oz., the ounce equal to that of Paris. The best rice requires half an hour's boiling; a more indifferent kind some-what less. To sow the rice, they first plough the ground, then level it with a drag harrow, let on the water; when the earth is become soft they smooth it with a shovel under the water, and then sow the rice in the water.

ROZZANO. PARMESAN CHEESE. It is supposed this was formerly made at Parma, and took it's name thence, but none is made there now. It is made thro all the country extending from Milan 150. miles. The most is made about Lodi. The making of butter being connected with the making cheese, both must be described together. There are, in the stables I saw, 85. cows, fed on hay and grass, not on grain. They are milked twice in the 24. hours, 10 cows yeilding at the two milkings a brenta of milk, which is 24. of our gallons. The night's milk is scummed in the morning at day break, when the cows are milked again and the new milk mixed with the old. In 3. hours the whole mass is scummed a second time, the milk remaining in a kettle for cheese, and the cream being put into a cylindrical churn, shaped like a grindstone, 18.I. radius and 14.I. thick. In this churn there are three staves pointing inwardly endwise to break the current of the milk. Thro it's center passes an iron axis with a handle at each end. It is turned about an hour and an half by two men till the butter is produced. Then they pour off the buttermilk and put in some water which they agitate backwards and forwards about a minute, and pour it off. They take out the butter, press it with their hands into loaves, and stamp it. It has no other washing. 16 American gallons of milk yield 15 lb. of butter, which sells at 24 sous the lb.

The milk which after being scummed as before had been put into a copper kettle receives it's due quantity of rennet and is gently warmed if the season requires it. In about 4. hours it becomes a slip. Then the whey begins to separate. A little of it is taken out. The curd is then thoroughly broken by a machine like a chocolate mill. A quarter of an ounce of saffron is put to 7. brenta of milk to give colour to the cheese. The kettle is then moved over the hearth, and heated by a quick fire till the curd is hard enough, being broken into small lumps by continual stirring. It is moved off the fire, most of the whey taken out, the curd compressed into a globe by the hand, a linen cloth slipped under it, and it is drawn out in that. A loose hoop is then laid on a bench and the curd, as wrapped in the linen is put into the hoop. It is a little pressed by the hand, the hoop drawn tight, and made fast. A board 2.I. thick is laid on it, and a stone on that of about 20 lb. weight. In an hour the whey is run off and the cheese finished. They sprinkle a little salt on it every other day in summer and every day in winter for 6. weeks. 7. brentas of milk make a cheese of 50. lb., which requires 6. months to ripen, and is then dried to 45 lb. It sells on the spot for 88^{tt} the 100. lb. There are now 150. cheeses in this dairy. They are 19.I. diameter and 6.I. thick. They make a cheese a day in summer, and 2. in 3. days, or 1. in 2. days in winter.

The whey is put back into the kettle, the butter milk poured into it, and of this they make a poor cheese for the country people. The whey of this is given to the hogs. 8. men suffice to keep the cows and do all the business of this dairy. Mascarponi, a kind of curd, is made by pouring some butter milk into cream, which is thereby curdled, and is then pressed in a linen cloth.

The ICE-HOUSES at Rozzano are dug about 15.f. deep, and 20.f. diameter and poles are driven down all round. A conical thatched roof is then put over them 15f. high. Pieces of wood are laid at bottom to keep the ice out of the water which drips from it, and goes off by a sink. Straw is laid on this wood, and then the house filled with ice always putting straw between the ice and the walls, and covering ultimately with straw. About a third is lost by melting. Snow gives the most delicate flavor to creams; but ice is the most powerful congealer, and lasts longest. A tuft of trees surrounds these ice houses.

Round Milan, to the distance of 5. miles, is corn, pasture, gardens, mulberries, willows and vines, for in this state, rice-ponds are not permitted within 5. miles of the cities.

BINASCO. PAVIA. Near Cassino the rice ponds begin and continue to within 5. miles of Pavia, the whole ground being in rice, pasture, and willows. The pasture is in the rice grounds which are resting. In the neighborhood of Pavia again is corn, pasture &c. as round Milan. They gave me green peas at Pavia.

April 24. VOGHERA. TORTONA. NOVI. From Pavia to Novi corn, pasture, vines, mulberries, willows, but no rice. The country continues plain, except that the Appenines are approaching on the left. The soil, always good, is dark till we approach Novi, and then red. We cross the Po where it is 300 yards wide, on a pendulum boat. The rope is fastened to one side of the river 300 yards above, and supported by 8. intermediate canoes, with little masts in them to give a greater elevation to the rope. We pass in 11 minutes. Women, girls, and boys are working with the hoe, and breaking the clods with mauls.

Apr. 25. VOLTAGGIO. CAMPO MARONE. GENOA. At Novi the Appenines begin to rise. Their growth of timber is oak, tall, small, and knotty, and chesnut. We soon lose the walnut ascending, and find it again about one fourth of the way down on the South side. About half way down we find figs and vines, which continue fine and in great abundance. The Appenines are mostly covered with soil, and are in corn, pasture, mulberries and figs, in the parts before indicated. About half way from their foot at Campo marone to Genoa we find again the olive tree. Hence the produce becomes mixed of all the kinds before mentioned. The method of sowing the Indian corn at Campo-marone is as follows. With a hoe shaped like the blade of a trowel 2f. long and 6.I. broad at it's upper end, pointed below and a little curved, they make a trench. In that they drop the grains 6.I. apart. Then 2.f. from that they make another trench, throwing the earth they take out of that on the grain of the last one with a singular slight and quickness: and so through the whole peice. The last trench is filled with the earth adjoining.

Apr. 26. GENOA. Strawberries at Genoa. Scaffold poles for the upper parts of a wall, as for the 3d. story, rest on the window sills of the story below. Slate is used here for paving, for steps, for stairs (the rise as well as tread) and for fixed Venetian blinds. At the Palazzo Marcello Durazzo benches with strait legs, and bottoms of cane. At the Palazzo del prencipe Lomellino at Sestri a phaeton with a canopy. At the former, tables folding into one plane. At Nervi they have peas, strawberries &c. all the year round. The gardens of the Count Durazzo at Nervi exhibit as rich a mixture of the Utile dulci as I ever saw. All the environs of Genoa are in olives, figs, oranges, mulberries, corn and garden stuff. Aloes in many places, but they never flower.

April 28. NOLI. The Appenine and Alps appear to me to be one and the same continued ridge of mountains, separating every where the waters of the Adriatic gulph from those of the Mediterranean. Where it forms an elbow touching the Mediterranean, as a smaller circle touches a larger within which it is inscribed in the manner of a tangent, the name changes from Alps to Appenine. It is the beginning of the Appenine which constitutes the state of Genoa, the mountains there generally falling down in barren naked precipices into the sea. Wherever there is soil on the lower parts it is principally in olives and figs, in vines also, mulberries and corn. Where there are hollows well protected there are oranges. This is the case at Golfo de Laspeze, Sestri, Bugiasco, Nervi, Genoa,° Pegli, Savona, Finale, Oneglia (where there are abundance), St. Remo, Ventimiglia, Mantone, and Monaco. Noli, into which I was obliged to put by a change of wind is 40. miles from Genoa. There are 1200 inhabitants in the village, and many separate houses round about. One of the precipices hanging over the sea is covered with Aloes. But neither here, nor anywhere else where I have been, could I procure satisfactory information that they ever flower. The current of testimony is to the contrary. Noli furnishes many fishermen. Paths penetrate up into the mountains in several directions about 3/4 of a mile; but these are practicable only for asses and mules. I saw no cattle nor sheep in the settlement. The wine they make is white and indifferent. A curious cruet for oil and vinegar in one piece, and in this form [illustration omitted]. A bishop resides here whose revenue is 2000.^{tt} = 66 guineas. I heard a nightingale here.

April 29. ALBENGA. In walking along the shore from Louano to this place I saw no appearance of shells. The tops of the mountains are covered with snow, while there are olive trees &c. on their lower parts. I do not remember to have seen assigned any where the cause of the apparent colour of the sea. It's water is generally clear and colourless if taken up and viewed in a glass. That of the Mediterranean is remarkeably so. Yet in the mass, it assumes by reflection the colour of the sky or atmosphere, black, green, blue, according to the state of the weather.—If any person wished to retire from their acquaintance, to live absolutely unknown, and yet in the midst of physical enjoiments, it should be in some of the little villages of this coast, where air, earth and water concur to offer what each has most precious. Here are nightingales, beccaficas, ortolans, pheasants, partridges, quails, a superb climate, and the power of changing it from summer to winter at any moment, by ascending the mountains. The earth furnishes wine, oil, figs, oranges, and every production of the garden in every season. The sea yeilds lobsters, crabs, oysters, thunny, sardines, anchovies &c. Ortolans sell at this time at 30s = 1/ sterling the dozen. At this season they must be fattened. Through the whole of my route from Marseilles I observe they plant a great deal of cane or reed, which is convenient while growing as a cover from the cold and boisterous winds, and, when cut, it serves for espaliers to vines, peas &c. Thro' Piedmont, Lombardy, the Milanese and Genoese, the garden bean is a great article of culture, almost as much so as corn. At Albenga is a rich plain opening from between two ridges of mountains triangularly to the sea, and of several miles extent. It's growth is olives, figs, mulberries, vines, corn, beans and pasture. A bishop resides here whose revenue is 40,000.[tt] This place is said to be rendered unhealthy in summer by the river which passes thro the valley.

April 30. ONEGLIA. The wind continuing contrary, I took mules at Albenga for Oneglia. Along this tract are many of the tree called Carroubier, being a species of Locust. It is the Ceratonia siliqua of Linnaeus. It's pods furnish food for horses and even for the poor in times of scarcity. It abounds in Naples and Spain. Oneglia and Port Maurice, which are within a mile of each other are considerable places and in a rich country. At St. Remo are abundance of oranges and lemons and some palm trees.

May 1. VENTIMIGLIA. MENTON. MONACO. NICE. At Bordighera between Ventimiglia and Menton are extensive plantations of palms on the hill as well as in the plain. They bring fruit but it does not ripen. Some thing is made of the midrib which is in great demand at Rome on the Palm sunday, and which renders this tree profitable here. From Menton to Monaco there is more good land, and extensive groves of oranges and lemons. Orange water sells here at 40s = 16d. sterling the american quart. The distances on this coast are from

Laspeze, at the Eastern end of the territories of Genoa to Genoa 55. miles geometrical, to Savona 30. Albenga 30. Oneglia 20. Ventimiglia 25. Monaco 10. Nice 10. = 180. A superb road might be made along the margin of the sea from Laspeze where the champaign country of Italy opens, to Nice where the Alps go off Northwardly and the post roads of France begin, and it might even follow the margin of the sea quite to Cette. By this road travellers would enter Italy without crossing the Alps, and all the little insulated villages of the Genoese would communicate together, and in time form one continued village along that road.

May 3. LUC. BRIGNOLLES. TOURVES. POURCIEUX. LA GALI NIERE. Long small mountains very rocky, the soil reddish from bad to midling, in olives, grapes, mulberries, vines and corn. Brignolles is in an extensive plain, between two ridges of mountains and along a water course which continues to Tourves. Thence to Pourcieux we cross a mountain, low and easy. The country is rocky and poor. To la Galiniere are waving grounds bounded by mountains of rock at a little distance. There are some inclosures of dry wall from Luc to la Galiniere. Sheep and hogs. There is snow on the high mountains. I see no plumbs in the vicinities of Brignolles; which makes me conjecture that the celebrated plumb of that name is not derived from this place.

May 8. ORGON. AVIGNON. VAUCLUSE. AVIGNON. Orgon is on the Durance. From thence it's plain opens till it becomes common with that of the Rhone, so that from Orgon to Avignon is entirely a plain of rich dark loam, which is in willows, mulberries, vines, corn and pasture. A very few figs. I see no olives in this plain. Probably the cold winds have too much power here. From the Bac de Novo (where we cross the Durance) to Avignon is about 9. American miles; and from the same Bac to Vaucluse, 11. miles. In the valley of Vaucluse and on the hills impending over it are Olive trees. The stream issuing from the fountain of Vaucluse is about 20. yards wide, 4. or 5.f. deep and of such rapidity that it could not be stemmed by a canoe. They are now mowing hay, and gathering mulberry leaves. The high mountains, just back of Vaucluse, are covered with snow. Fine trout in the stream of Vaucluse, and the valley abounds peculiarly with nightingales. The vin blanc de M. de Rochegude of Avignon resembles dry Lisbon. He sells it at 6. years old for 22s. the bottle, the price of the bottle &c. included.

AVIGNON. REMOULINS. Some good plains, but generally hills, stony and poor, in olives, mulberries, vines and corn. Where it is waste the growth is chenevert, box, furze, thyme and rosemary.

May 10. NISMES. LUNEL. Hills on the right, plains on the left. The soil reddish, a little stony and of midling quality. The produce olives, mulberries, vines, corn, St. foin. No wood and few inclosures. Lunel is famous for it's vin de muscat blanc, thence called Lunel, or vin Muscat de Lunel. It is made from the raisin muscat, without fermenting the grape in the hopper. When fermented, it makes a red Muscat, taking that tinge from the dissolution of the skin of the grape, which injures the quality. When a red Muscat is required, they prefer colouring it with a little Alicant wine. But the white is best. The price of 240. bottles, after being properly drawn off from it's lees, and ready for bottling costs from 120. to 200.[tt] of the 1st. quality and last vintage. It cannot be bought old, the demand being sufficient to take it all the first year. There are not more than from 50. to 100. pieces a year made of the first quality. A setterie yields about one piece, and my informer supposes there are about two setteries in an arpent. Portage to Paris by land is 15.[tt] the quintal. The best recoltes are those of M. Bouquet and M. Tremoulet. The vines are in rows 4.f. apart every way.

May 11. MONTPELIER. Snow on the Cevennes, N.W. from hence. With respect to the Muscat grape, of which the wine is made, there are two kinds, the red and the white. The first has a red skin, but white juice. If it be fermented in the cuve, the colouring matter which resides in the skin, is imparted to the wine. If not fermented in the cuve, the wine is white. Of the white grape, only a white wine can be made.—The species of St. foin cultivated here by the name of SPARSETTE is the Hedysarum Onobryches. They cultivate a great deal of Madder (Garance) Rubia tinctorum here, which is said to be immensely profitable. M. de Gouan tells me that the pine, of which they use the burs for fuel, is the Pinus sativus, being two leaved. They use for an edging to the borders of their gardens the Santolina, which they call Garderobe. I find the yellow clover here in a garden: and the large pigeon succeeding well confined in a house.

May 12. FRONTIGNAN. Some tolerable good plains in olives, vines, corn, St. foin, and Luzerne. A great proportion of the hills are waste. There are some inclosures of stone, and some sheep.—The first four years of MADDER are unproductive. The 5th. and 6th. yields the whole value of the land. Then it must be renewed. The Sparsette is the common, or true St. foin. It lasts about 5. years. In the best land it is cut twice, in May and September, and yields 3000 lb. of dry hay to the Setterie the first cutting, and 500. lb. the second. The Setterie is of 75. dextres en tout sens, supposed about 2. arpens. Luzerne is the best of all forage. It is sowed here in the broad cast, and lasts about 12. or 14. years. It is cut 4. times a year and yeilds 6000 lb. of dry hay at the 4. cuttings to the Setterie. —The territory in which the vin muscat de FRONTIGNAN is made is about a league of 3000 toises long, and $^{1}/_{4}$ of a league broad. The soil is reddish and stony, often as much stone as soil. On the left it is a plain, on the right hills. There are made about 1000 pieces (of 250 bottles each) annually, of which 600 are of the first quality made on the coteaux. Of these Madame Soubeinan makes 200., M. Reboulle 90., M. Lambert, medecin de la faculte de Monpelier 60. M. Thomas notaire 50. M. Argilliers 50. M. Audibert 40. = 490. and there are some small proprietors who make small quantities. The 1st. quality is sold, brut, for 120.^{tt} the piece. But it is then thick, must have a winter and the fouet to render it potable and brilliant. The fouet is like a chocolate mill, the handle of iron, the brush of stiff hair. In bottles this wine costs 24.s the bottle &c. included. It is potable the April after it is made, is best that year, and after 10. years begins to have a pitchy taste resembling it to Malaga. It is not permitted to ferment more than half a day, because it would not be so liquorish. The best colour, and it's natural one, is the amber. By force of whipping it is made white but loses flavor. There are but 2. or 3. peices a year, of red Muscat, made, there being but one vineyard of the red grape, which belongs to a baker called Pascal. This sells in bottles at 30.s the bottle included. Rondette, negociant en vin, Porte St. Bernard fauxbourg St. Germain a Paris, buys 300. pieces of the 1st. quality, every year. The coteaux yeild about half a piece to the Setterie, the plains a whole piece. The inferior quality is not at all esteemed. It is bought by the merchants of Cette, as is also the wine of Bezieres, and sold by them for Frontignan of 1st. quality. They sell 30,000 pieces a year under that name. The town of Frontignan marks it's casks with a hot iron. An individual of that place, having two casks emptied, was offered 40.^{tt} for the empty cask by a merchant of Cette. The town of Frontignan contains about 2000 inhabitants. It is almost on the level of the ocean. Transportation to Paris is 15.^{tt} the quintal, and is 15 days going. The price of packages is about 8^{tt} —8 the 100 bottles. A setterie of good vineyard sells for from 350.^{tt} to 500.^{tt} and rents for 50.^{tt} A labouring man hires at 150.^{tt} the year, and is fed and lodged: a woman at half as much. Wheat sells at 10.^{tt} the settier, which weighs 100. Tbs. poids de table. They make some Indian corn here which is eaten by the poor. The olives do not extend Northward of this into the country above 12. or 15. leagues. In general the Olive country in Languedoc is about 15. leagues broad. More of the waste lands between Frontignan and Mirval are capable of culture: but it is a marshy country very subject to fever and ague, and generally unhealthy. Thence arises, as is said, a want of hands.

CETTE. There are in this town about 10,000 inhabitants. It's principal commerce is wine. It furnishes great quantities of grape pomice for making verdigriese. They have a very growing commerce, but it is kept under by the privileges of Marseilles.

May 13. AGDE. On the right of the Etang de Tau are plains of some width, then hills, in olives, vines, mulberry, corn and pasture. On the left a narrow sand bar separating the etang from the sea along which it is proposed to make a road from Cette to Agde. In this case the post would lead from Monpelier, by Cette and Agde to Bezieres, being leveller, and an hour, or an hour and a half nearer. Agde contains 6. or 8,000 inhabitants.

May 14. BEZIERES. Rich plains in corn, St. foin and pasture; hills at a little distance to the right in olives, the soil both of hill and plain is red, going from Agde to Bezieres. But at Bezieres the country becomes hilly, and is in olives, corn, St. foin, pasture, some vines and mulberries.

May 15. BEZIERES. ARGILIES. LE SAUMAL. From Argilies to Saumal are considerable plantations of vines. Those on the red hills to the right are said to produce good wine. No wood, no inclosures. There are sheep and good cattle. The Pyrenees are covered with snow. I am told they are so in certain parts all the year. The Canal of Languedoc along which I now travel is 6. toises wide at bottom, and 10 toises at the surface of the water, which is 1. toise deep. The barks which navigate it are 70. and 80. feet long, and 17. or 18. f. wide. They are drawn by one horse, and worked by 2. hands, one of which is generally a woman. The locks are mostly kept by women, but the necessary operations are much too laborious for them. The encroachments by the men on the offices proper for the women is a great derangement in the order of things. Men are shoemakers, tailors, upholsterers, staymakers, mantua makers, cooks, door-keepers, housekeepers, housecleaners, bedmakers. They coëffe the ladies, and bring them to bed: the women therefore, to live are obliged to undertake the offices which they abandon. They become porters, carters, reapers, wood cutters, sailors, lock keepers, smiters on the anvil, cultivators of the earth &c.

Can we wonder if such of them as have a little beauty prefer easier courses to get their livelihood, as long as that beauty lasts? Ladies who employ men in the offices which should be reserved for their sex, are they not bawds in effect? For every man whom they thus employ, some girl, whose place he has taken, is driven to whoredom.—The passage of the eight locks at Beziers, that is from the opening of the 1st. to the last gate, took 1. Hour 33'. The bark in which I go is about 35.f. long, drawn by one horse, and goes from 2. to 3. geographical miles an hour. The canal yeilds abundance of carp and eel. I see also small fish resembling our perch and chub. Some plants of white clover, and some of yellow on the banks of the canal near Capestan; Santolina also and a great deal of a yellow Iris. Met a raft of about 350 beams 40.f. long, and 12. or 15.I. diameter, formed into 14. rafts tacked together. The extensive and numerous fields of St. foin, in general bloom, are beautiful.

May 16. LE SAUMAL. MARSEILLETTE. May 17. MARSEILLETTE. CARCASSONNE. From Saumal to Carcassonne we have always the river Aube close on our left. This river runs in the valley between the Cevennes and Pyrenees, serving as the common receptacle for both their waters. It is from 50. to 150. yards wide, always rapid, rocky, and insusceptible of navigation. The canal passes in the side of the hills made by that river, overlooks the river itself, and it's plains, and has it's prospect ultimately terminated, on one side by mountains of rock overtopped by the Pyrenees, on the other by small mountains, sometimes of rock, sometimes of soil overtopped by the Cevennes. Marseillette is on a ridge which separates the river Aube from the etang de Marseillette. The canal, in it's approach to this village, passes the ridge, and rides along the front overlooking the etang and the plains on it's border; and having passed the village recrosses the ridge and resumes it's general ground in front of the Aube. The growth is corn, St. foin, pasture, vines, mulberries, willows, and olives.

May 18. CARCASSONNE. CASTELNAUDARI. Opposite to Carcassonne the canal receives the river Fresquel, about 30. yards wide, which is it's substantial supply of water from hence to Beziers. From Beziers to Agde the river Orb furnishes it, and the Eraut from Agde to the etang de Thau. By means of the ecluse ronde at Agde the waters of the Eraut can be thrown towards Bezieres to aid those of the Orb as far as the ecluse de Porcaraigne, 9 geometrical miles. Where the Fresquel enters the canal there is, on the opposite side, a waste, to let off the superfluous waters. The horse-way is continued over this waste by a bridge of stone of

18 arches. I observe them fishing in the canal with a skimming net of about 15. feet diameter, with which they tell me they catch carp. Flax in blossom. Neither strawberries nor peas yet at Carcassonne. The Windsor bean just come to table. From the ecluse de la Lande we see the last olive trees near a metairee or farm-house called la Lande. On a review of what I have seen and heard of this tree, the following seem to be it's Northern limits. Beginning on the Atlantic, at the Pyrenees, and along them to the meridian of la Lande, or of Carcassonne: up that Meridian to the Cevennes, as they begin just there to raise themselves high enough to afford it shelter. Along the Cevennes to the parallel of 45.° latitude, and along that parallel (crossing the Rhone near the mouth of the Isere) to the Alps, thence along the Alps and Appenines to what parallel of latitude I know not. Yet here the tracing of the line becomes the most interesting. For from the Atlantic so far, we see this production the effect of shelter and latitude combined. But where does it venture to launch forth, unprotected by shelter, and by the mere force of latitude alone? Where for instance does it's northern limit cross the Adriatic? — I learn that the olive tree resists cold to 8.° of Reaumur below the freezing point, which corresponds to 14° above zero, of Farenheit: and that the orange resists to 4.° below freezing of Reaumur, which is 23.° above zero of Farenheit.

May 19. CASTELNAUDARI. ST. FERIOL. ESCAMAZE. LAMPY. Some sheep and cattle. No inclosures. St. Feriol, Escamaze and Lampy are in the montagnes noires. The country almost entirely waste, some of it in shrubbery. The voute d'Escarmaze is of 135 yards. Round about Castelnaudari the country is hilly, as it has been constantly from Beziers. It is very rich. Where it is plain, or nearly plain, the soil is black: in general however it is hilly and reddish, and in corn. They cultivate a great deal of Indian corn here, which they call Millet. It is planted, but not yet up.

    May 20. CASTELNAUDARI. NAUROUZE. VILLEFRANCHE. BAZIEGE. At Naurouze is the highest ground which the canal had to pass between the two seas. It became necessary then to find water still higher, and to bring it here. The river Fresquel heading by it's two principal branches in the Montagnes noires, a considerable distance off to the Eastward, the springs of the most western one were brought together, and conducted to Naurouze, where it's waters are divided, part furnishing the canal towards the ocean, the rest towards the Mediterranean, as far as the ecluse de Fresquel where, as has been before noted, the Lampy12 branch, and the Alzau, under the name of the Fresquel, enter. They have found that a lock of 6. pieds is best. However, 8 pieds is well enough. Beyond this it is bad. Monsr. Pin tells me of a lock of 30. pieds made in Sweden, of which it was impossible to open the gates. They therefore divided it into 4. locks. The small gates of the locks of this canal have six square pieds of surface. They tried the machinery of the jack for opening them. They were more easily opened, but very subject to be deranged, however strongly made. They returned therefore to the original wooden screw, which is excessively slow and laborious. I calculate that 5. minutes are lost at every bason by this screw, which on the whole number of basons is one eighth of the time necessary to navigate the canal: and of course, if a method of lifting the gate at one stroke could be found, it would reduce the passage from 8. to 7. days, and the freight equally. I suggested to Monsr. Pin and others a quadrantal gate turning on a pivot, and lifted by a lever like a pump handle, aided by a windlass and cord, if necessary [illustration omitted]. He will try it and inform me of the success. The price of transportation from Cette to Bordeaux thro' the canal and Garonne is—— the quintal: round by the streights of Gibraltar is——. 240.barks, the largest of 2200 quintals (or say in general of 100 tons) suffice to perform the business of this canal, which is stationary, having neither increased nor diminished for many years. When pressed, they can pass and repass between Thoulouse and Beziers in 14. days: but 16. is the common period. The canal is navigated 10 months of the year; the other month and a half being necessary to lay it dry, cleanse it, and repair the works. This is done in July and August, when there would perhaps be a want of water.

May 21. BAZIEGE. TOULOUSE. The country continues hilly, but very rich. It is in mulberries, willows, some vines, corn, maize, pasture, beans, flax. A great number of chateaux and good houses in the neighborhood of the canal. The people partly in farm houses, partly in villages. I suspect that the farm houses are occupied by the farmer, while the labourers (who are mostly by the day) reside in the villages. Neither strawberries nor peas yet at Baziege or Toulouse. Near the latter are some feilds of yellow clover.

At Toulouse the canal ends. It has four communications with the Mediterranean. 1. Through the ponds of Thau, Frontignan, Palavas, Maguelone, and Manyo, the canal de la Radele aiguesmortes, le canal des salines de Pecair, and the arm of the Rhone called Bras de fer, which ends at Fourquet, opposite to Arles, and thence down the Rhone. 2. At Cette by a canal of a few hundred toises leading out of the etang de Thau into the sea. The vessels pass the etang, through a length of 9000 toises, with sails. 3. At Agde, by the river Eraut, 2500 toises. It has but 5. or 6. pieds of water at it's mouth. It is joined to the canal at the upper part of this communication by a branch of a canal 270 toises long. 4. At Narbonne by a canal they are now opening, which leads from the great canal near the Aquaeduct of the river Cesse, 2600 toises, into the Aude. This new canal will have 5 lock-basons of about 12. pieds fall each. Then you are to cross the Aude very obliquely, and descend a branch of it 6000. toises through 4. lock basons to Narbonne, and from Narbonne down the same branch 1200. toises into the etang de Sigen, across that etang 4000 toises, issuing at an inlet, called the Grau de la nouvelle into the gulf of Lyons. But only vessels of 30. or 40. tons can enter this inlet. Of these 4. communications, that of Cette only leads to a deep sea-port, because the exit is there by a canal and not a river. Those by the Rhone, Eraut, and Aude are blocked up by bars at the mouths of those rivers. It is remarkeable that all the rivers running into the Mediterranean are obstructed at their entrance by bars and shallows, which often change their position. This is the case with the Nile, the Tyber, the Po, the Lez, le Lyvron, the Orbe, the Gly, the Tech, the Tet &c. Indeed the formation of these bars seems not confined to the mouths of the rivers, tho' it takes place at them more certainly. Along almost the whole of the coast, from Marseilles towards the Pyrenees, banks of sand are thrown up, parallel with the coast, which have insulated portions of the sea, that is, formed them into etangs, ponds, or sounds, through which here and there, narrow and shallow inlets only are preserved by the currents of the rivers. These sounds fill up in time with the mud and sand deposited in them by the rivers. Thus the etang de Vendres, navigated formerly by vessels of 60 tons, is now nearly filled up by the mud and sand of the Aude. The Vistre and Vidourle which formerly emptied themselves into the Gulf of Lyons, are now received by the etangs de Manjo and Aiguesmortes, that is to say, the part of the gulf of Lyons which formerly received, and still receives, those rivers; is now cut off from the sea by a bar of sand which has been thrown up in it, and has formed it into sounds. Other proofs that the land gains there on the sea are that the towns of St. Gilles and Notre dame d'aspoets, formerly seaports, are now far from the sea, and that Aiguesmortes, where are still to be seen the iron rings to which vessels were formerly moored, and where St. Louis embarked for Palestine, has now in it's vicinities only ponds which cannot be navigated, and communicates with the sea by an inlet, called Grau du toy, through which only fishing barks can pass. It is pretty well established that all the Delta of Egypt has been formed by the depositions of the Nile and the alluvions of the sea, and probable that that operation is still going on. Has this peculiarity of the Mediterranean any connection with the scantiness of it's tides, which even at the Equinoxes, are of 2. or 3. feet only?

An accurate state of the locks, of their distances from each other, of their fall of water, and of the number of basons to each. [Here, omitted from this edition, Jefferson presented a detailed chart of the distance between, falling height of, and basin capacity of numerous canals, followed by a recapitulation that totaled the calculations.] The communication from the Western end of the canals to the ocean is by the river Garonne. This is navigated by flat boats of 800. quintals when the water is well but when it is scanty these boats can carry only 200. quintals till they get to the mouth of the Tarn. It has been proposed to open a canal that far from Toulouse along the right side of the river.

May 22. TOULOUSE. 23. AGEN. 24. CASTRES. BORDEAUX. The Garonne and rivers emptying into it make extensive and rich plains, which are in mulberries, willows, corn, maize, pasture, beans and flax. The hills are in corn, maize, beans and a considerable proportion of vines. There seems to be as much maize as corn in this country. Of the latter there is more rye than wheat. The maize is now up, and about 3.I. high. It is sowed in rows 2f. or $2^{1}/_{2}$ f. apart, and is pretty thick in the row. Doubtless they mean to thin it. There is a great deal of a forage they call Farouche. It is a species of red trefoil, with few leaves, a very coarse stalk, and a cylindrical blossom of 2.I. length and $^3/_4$ I. diameter, consisting of floscules exactly as does that of the red clover. It seems to be a coarse food, but very plentiful. They say it is for their oxen. These are very fine, large and cream coloured. The services of the farm and of transportation are performed chiefly by them. A few horses and asses, but no mules. Even in the city of Bordeaux we see scarcely any beasts of draught but oxen. When we cross the Garonne at Langon we find the plains entirely of sand and gravel, and they continue so to Bordeaux. Where they are capable of any thing they are in vines, which are in rows 4. 5. or 6. feet apart, and sometimes more. Near Langon is Sauterne, where the best white wines of Bordeaux are made. The waste lands are in fern, furze, shrubbery and dwarf trees. The farmers live on their farms at Agen, Castres, Bordeaux. Strawberries and peas are come to table; so that the country on the canal of Languedoc seems to have later seasons than that East and West of it. What can be the cause? To the Eastward the protection of the Cevennes makes the warm season advance sooner. Does the neighborhood of the Mediterranean cooperate? And does that of the Ocean mollify and advance the season to the Westward? There are Ortolans at Agen, but none at Bordeaux. The buildings on the Canal and the Garonne are mostly of brick; the size of the bricks the same with that of the antient Roman brick as seen in the remains of their buildings in this country. In those of a circus at Bordeaux, considerable portions of which are standing, I measured the bricks and found them 19. or 20. inches long, 11. or 12. inches wide, and from $1^{1}/_{2}$ to 2 inches thick. Their texture as fine, compact and solid as that of porcelaine. The bricks now made, tho' of the same dimensions, are not so fine. They are burnt in a kind of furnace, and make excellent work. The elm tree shews itself at Bordeaux peculiarly proper for being spread flat for arbours. Many are done in this way on the quay des Charterons. Strawberries, peas, and cherries at Bordeaux.

May 24. 25. 26. 27. 28. BORDEAUX. The cantons in which the most celebrated wines of Bordeaux are made are MEDOC down the river, GRAVE adjoining the city and the parishes next above; all on the same side of the river. In the first is made red wine principally, in the two last, white. In Medoc they plant the vines in cross rows of $3^{1}/_{2}$ pieds. They keep them so low that poles extended along the rows one way, horizontally, about 15. or 18.I. above the ground, serve to tye the vines to, and leave the cross row open to the plough. In Grave they set the plants in quincunx, i.e. in equilateral triangles of $3^{1}/_{2}$ pieds every side; and they stick a pole of 6. or 8. feet high to every vine separately. The vine stock is sometimes 3. or 4.f. high. They find these two methods equal in culture, duration, quantity and quality. The former however admits the alternative of tending by hand or with the plough. The grafting of the vine, tho a critical operation, is practised with success. When the graft has taken, they bend it into the earth and let it take root above the scar. They begin to yeild an indifferent wine at 3. years old, but not a good one till 25. years, nor after 80, when they begin to yield less, and worse, and must be renewed. They give three or four workings in the year, each worth 70.^{tt} or 75.^{tt}, the journal, which is of 840. square toises, and contains about 3000 plants. They dung a little in Medoc and Grave, because of the poverty of the soil; but very little; as more would affect the wine. The journal yeilds, communibus annis, about 3. pieces of 240. or 250 bottles each. The vineyards of first quality are all worked by their proprietors. Those of the

2d. rent for 300.^{tt} the journal: those of the 3d. at 200.^{tt} They employ a kind of overseer at four or five hundred livres the year, finding him lodging and drink; but he feeds himself. He superintends and directs, but is expected to work but little. If the proprietor has a garden the overseer tends that. They never hire labourers by the year. The day wages for a man are 30. sous, a woman's 15. sous, feeding themselves. The women make the bundles of sarment, weed, pull off the snails, tie the vines, gather the grapes. During the vintage they are paid high and fed well.

Of RED WINES, there are 4. vineyards of first quality, viz. 1. Chateau Margau, belonging to the Marquis d'Agicourt, who makes about 150. tonneaux of 1000 bottles each. He has engaged to Jernon a merchant. 2. La Tour de Segur, en Saint Lambert, belonging to Monsieur Mirosmenil, who makes 125. tonneaux. 3. Hautbrion, belonging is to M. le comte de Femelle, who has engaged to Barton a merchant, the other third to the Comte de Toulouse at Toulouse. The whole is 75. tonneaux. 4. Chateau de la Fite, belonging to the President Pichard at Bordeaux, who makes 175 tonneaux. The wines of the three first are not in perfection till 4 years old. Those [of] de la Fite, being somewhat lighter, are good at 3 years, that is, the crop of 1786 is good in the spring of 1789. These growths, of the year 1783 sell now at 2000.^{tt} the tonneau, those of 1784, on account of the superior quality of that vintage, sell at 2400,^{tt} those of 1785 at 1800,^{tt} those of 1786 at 1800,^{tt} tho they sold at first for only 1500.^{tt} RED WINES of the 2d. quality are ROZAN belonging to Madame de Rozan, Dabbadie, ou Lionville, la Rose, Quirouen, Durfort; in all 800 tonneaux, which sell at 1000.^{tt} new. The 3d. class are Calons, Mouton, Gassie, Arboete, Pontette, de Terme, Candale; in all, 2000 tonneaux at 8 or 900.^{tt} After these they are reckoned common wines and sell from 500.^{tt} down to 120.^{tt} the ton. All red wines decline after a certain age, losing colour, flavour, and body. Those of Bordeaux begin to decline at about 7. years old.

Of WHITE WINES, those made in the canton of Grave are most esteemed at Bordeaux. The best crops are 1. PONTAC, which formerly belonged to M. de Pontac, but now to M. de Lamont. He makes 40. tonneaux which sell at 400.^{tt} new. 2. ST. BRISE, belonging to M. de Pontac, 30 tonneaux at 350.^{tt} 3. DE CARBONIUS, belonging to the Benedictine monks, who make 50 tonneaux, and never selling till 3. or 4. years old, get 800.^{tt} the tonneau. Those made in the three parishes next above Grave, and more esteemed at Paris are

1. SAUTERNE. The best crop belongs to M. Diquem at Bordeaux, or to M. de Salus his son in law. 150. tonneaux at 300.^{tt} new and 600.^{tt} old. The next best crop is M. de Fillotte's 100. tonneaux sold at the same price. 2. PRIGNAC. The best is the President du Roy's at Bordeaux. He makes 175 tonneaux, which sell at 300.^{tt} new, and 600.^{tt} old. Those of 1784, for their extraordinary quality sell at 800.^{tt} 3. Barsac. The best belongs to the President Pichard, who makes 150. tonneaux at 280.^{tt} new and 600.^{tt} old. Sauterne is the pleasantest; next Prignac, and lastly Barsac; but Barsac is the strongest; next Prignac, and lastly Sauterne; and all stronger than Grave. There are other good crops made on the same paroisses of Sauterne, Prignac, and Barsac; but none as good as these. There is a Virgin wine, which tho' made of a red grape, is of a light rose colour, because, being made without pressure the colouring matter of the skin does not mix with the juice. There are other white wines from the preceding prices down to 75.^{tt} In general the white wines keep longest. They will be in perfection till 15. or 20. years of age. The best vintage now to be bought is of 1784, both of red and white. There has been no other good year since 1779.

The celebrated vineyards beforementioned are plains, as is generally the canton of Medoc, and that of Grave. The soil of Hautbrion particularly, which I examined, is a sand, in which is near as much round gravel or small stone, and a very little loam: and this is the general soil of Medoc. That of Pontac, which I examined also, is a little different. It is clayey, with a fourth or fifth of fine rotten stone; and of 2. feet depth it becomes all a rotten stone. M. de Lamont tells me he has a kind of grape without seeds, which I did not formerly suppose to exist, but I saw at Marseilles dried raisins from Smyrna, without seeds. I see in his farm at Pontac some plants of white clover and a good deal of yellow; also some small peach trees in the open ground. The principal English wine merchants at Bordeaux are Jernon, Barton, Johnston, Foster, Skinner, Copinger and McCartey. The chief French wine merchants are Feger, Nerac, Brunneau, Jauge, and du Verget. Desgrands, a wine broker, tells me they never mix the wines of first quality: but that they mix the inferior ones to improve them. The smallest wines make the best brandy. They yield about a fifth or sixth.

May 28. 29. From BORDEAUX to BLAYE the country near the river is hilly, chiefly in vines, some corn some pasture. Further out are plains, boggy and waste. The soil in both cases clay and grit. Some sheep on the waste. To ETAULIERE we have sometimes boggy plains, sometimes waving grounds and sandy, always poor, generally waste in fern and furze, with some corn however interspersed. To MIRAMBEAU and ST. GENIS it is hilly, poor and mostly waste. There is some corn and maize however, and better trees than usual. Towards Pons it becomes a little red, mostly rotten stone. There are vines, corn, and maize, which is up. At PONS we approach the Charenton: the country becomes better, a blackish mould mixed with a rotten chalky stone, a great many vines, corn, maize and farouche. From LAJART to SAINTES and ROCHEFORT the soil is reddish, it's foundation a chalky rock at about a foot depth, in vines, corn, maize, clover, lucerne and pasture. There are more and better trees than I have seen in all my journey; a great many apple and cherry trees. Fine cattle, and many sheep.

May 30. From Rochefort to LE ROCHER it is sometimes hilly and red with a chalky foundation, midling good in corn, pasture, and some waste. Sometimes it is reclaimed marsh in clover and corn, except the parts accessible to the tide which are in wild grass. About ROCHELLE it is a low plain. Towards USSEAU and half way to Marans level highlands, red, mixed with an equal quantity of broken chalk, mostly in vines, some corn and pasture: then to MARANS and half way to St. Hermines it is reclaimed marsh, dark, tolerably good and all in pasture: there we rise to plains a little higher, red, with a chalky foundation boundless to the eye and altogether in corn and maize. May 31. At ST. HERMINES the country becomes very hilly, a red clay mixed with chalky stone, generally waste in furze and broom, with some patches of corn and maize and so it continues to CHANTENAY, and ST. FULGENT. Thro the whole of this road from Bordeaux are frequent hedge rows and small patches of forest wood, not good, yet better than I had seen in the preceding part of my journey. Towards Montaigu the soil mends a little, the cultivated parts in corn and pasture, the uncultivated in broom. It is in very small inclosures of ditch and quickset. On approaching the Loire to NANTES the country is leveller, the soil from Rochelle to this place may be said to have been sometimes red, but oftener grey and always on a chalky foundation. The last census, of about 1770. made 120,000 inhabitants at Nantes. They conjecture there are now 150,000 which equals it to Bordeaux.

June 1. 2. The country from Nantes to LORIENT is very hilly and poor, the soil grey. Nearly half is waste, in furze and broom, among which is some poor grass. The cultivated parts are in corn, some maize, a good many apple trees, no vines. All is in small inclosures of quick hedge and ditch. There are patches and hedge-rows of forest wood, not quite deserving the name of timber. The people are mostly in villages, they eat rye bread and are ragged. The villages announce a general poverty as does every other appearance. Women smite on the anvil, and work with the hoe, and cows are yoked to labour. There are great numbers of cattle, insomuch that butter is their staple. Neither asses nor mules, yet it is said that the fine mules I have met with on my journey are raised in Poictou. There are but few chateaux here. I observe mill ponds, and hoes with long handles. Have they not, in common with us, derived these from England, of which Bretagne is probably a colony? Lorient is supposed to contain 25,000 inhabitants. They tell me here that to make a reasonable profit on potash and pearl ash, as bought in America, the former should sell at 30.[tt] the latter 36.[tt] the quintal. Of turpentine they make no use in their vessels. Bayonne furnishes pitch enough. But tar is in demand, and ours sells well. The tower of Lorient is 65. pi. above the level of the sea, 120. pi. high, 25. pi. diameter; the stairs 4. feet radius, and cost 30,000.[tt] besides the materials of the old tower.

June 3. 4. 5. The country and productions from Lorient to RENNES, and Rennes to Nantes, are precisely similar to those from Nantes to Lorient. About Rennes it is somewhat leveller, perhaps less poor, and almost entirely in pasture. The soil always grey. Some small separate houses which seem to be the residence of labourers, or very small farmers; the walls frequently of mud, and the roofs generally covoured with slate. Great plantations of walnut, and frequent of pine. Some apple trees and sweet briar still in bloom, and broom generally so. I have heard no nightingale since the last day of May. There are gates in this country made in the form here represented [illustration omitted]. The top rail of the gate overshoots backwards the hind post so as to counterpoise the gate and prevent it's swagging.

NANTES. Vessels of 8.f. draught only can come to Nantes. Those which are larger lie at Point boeuf, 10. leagues below Nantes, and 5. leagues above the mouth of the river. There is a continued navigation from Nantes to Paris thro' the Loire, the canal de Briare and the Seine. Carolina rice is preferred to that of Lombardy for the Guinea trade because it requires less water to boil it.

June 6. 7. 8. NANTES. ANCENIS. ANGERS. TOURS. Ascending the Loire from Nantes, the road, as far as Angers, leads over the hills, which are grey, oftener below than above mediocrity, and in corn, pasture, vines, some maise, flax and hemp. There are no waste lands. About the limits of Bretagne and Anjou, which are between Loriottiere and St. George, the lands change for the better. Here and there we get views of the plains on the Loire, of some extent and good appearance, in corn and pasture. After passing Angers, the road is raised out of the reach of inundations, so as at the same time to ward them off from the interior plains. It passes generally along the river side; but sometimes leads thro' the plains, which, after we pass Angers, become extensive and good, in corn, pasture, some maize, hemp, flax, peas and beans; many willows also, poplars and walnuts. The flax is near ripe. Sweetbriar in general bloom. Some broom here still, on which the cattle and sheep browze in winter and spring when they have no other green food: and the hogs eat the blossoms and pods in spring and summer. This blossom, tho' disagreeable when smelt in a small quantity, is of delicious fragrance when there is a whole field of it. There are some considerable vineyards in the river plains, just before we reach les trois volées, (which is at the 136th. mile stone) and after that, where the hills on the left come into view, they are mostly in vines. Their soil is clayey and stoney, a little reddish and of Southern aspect. The hills on the other side of the river, looking to the North, are not in vines. There is very good wine made on these hills; not equal, indeed to the Bordeaux of best good quality, but to that of good quality and like it. It is a great article of exportation from Anjou and Touraine, and probably is sold abroad under the name of Bordeaux. They are now mowing the first crop of hay. All along both hills of the Loire is a mass of white stone, not durable, growing black with time, and so soft that the the people cut their houses out of the solid with all the partitions, chimnies, doors &c. The hill sides resemble coney burrows, full of inhabitants. The borders of the Loire are almost a continued village. There are many chateaux, many cattle, sheep, and horses; some asses.

TOURS is at the 119th. mile stone. Being desirous of enquiring here into a fact stated by Voltaire in his Questions encyclopediques. art. Coquilles, relative to the growth of shells unconnected with animal bodies at the chateau of Monsr. de la Sauvagiere near Tours, I called on M. Gentil premier Secretaire de l'Intendance, to whom the Intendant had written on my behalf at the request of the Marquis de Chastellux. I stated to him the fact as advanced by Voltaire and found he was, of all men, the best to whom I could have addressed myself. He told me he had been in correspondence with Voltaire on that very subject, and was perfectly acquainted with M. dela Sauvagiere, and the Faluniere where the fact is said to have taken place. It is at the Chateau de Grille mont, 6. leagues from

Tours on the road to Bordeaux, belonging now to M. d'Orcai. He sais that de la Sauvagiere was a man of truth, and might be relied on for whatever facts he stated as of his own observation: but that he was overcharged with imagination, which, in matters of opinion and theory, often led him beyond his facts: that this feature in his character had appeared principally in what he wrote on the antiquities of Touraine: but that as to the fact in question he believed him. That he himself indeed had not watched the same identical shells, as Sauvagiere had done, growing from small to great: but that he had often seen such masses of those shells of all sizes, from a point to full size, as to carry conviction to his mind that they were in the act of growing: that he had once made a collection of shells for the Emperor's cabinet, reserving duplicates of them for himself; and that these afforded proofs of the same fact: that he afterwards gave those duplicates to a M. du Verget, a physician of Tours of great science and candour, who was collecting on a larger scale, and who was perfectly in sentiment with M. de la Sauvagiere: that not only the Faluniere, but many other places about Tours, would convince any unbiassed observer that shells are a fruit of the earth, spontaneously produced: and he gave me a copy of de la Sauvagiere's Recueil de dissertations, presented him by the author, wherein is one Sur la vegetation spontanee des coquilles du chateau des Places. So far I repeat from him. What are we to conclude? That we have not materials enough yet to form any conclusion. The fact stated by Sauvagiere is not against any law of nature, and is therefore possible: but it is so little analogous to her habitual processes that, if true, it would be extraordinary: that, to command our belief therefore, there should be such a suite of observations as that their untruth would be more extraordinary than the existence of the fact they affirm. The bark of trees, the skin of fruits and animals, the feathers of birds receive their growth and nutriment from the internal circulation of a juice thro' the vessels of the individual they cover. We conclude from analogy then that the shells of the testaceous tribe receive also their growth from a like internal circulation. If it be urged that this does not exclude the possibility of a like shell being produced by the passage of a fluid thro the pores of the circumjacent body, whether of earth, stone, or water; I answer that it is not within the usual oeconomy of nature to use two processes for one species of production. While I withold my assent however from this hypothesis, I must deny it to every other I have ever seen by which their authors pretend to account for the origin of shells in high places. Some of these are against the laws of nature and therefore impossible: and others are built on positions more difficult to assent to than that of de la Sauvagiere. They all suppose these shells to have covered submarine animals, and have then to answer the question How came they 15,000 feet above the level of the sea? and they answer it by demanding what cannot be conceded. One therefore who had rather have no opinion, than a false one, will suppose this question one of those beyond the investigation of human sagacity; or wait till further and fuller observations enable him to decide it.

CHANTELOUP. I heard a nightingale to-day at Chanteloup. The gardener sais it is the male, who alone sings, while the female sits; and that when the young are hatched, he also ceases. In the Boudoir at Chanteloup is an ingenious contrivance to hide the projecting steps of a stair-case. 3 steps were of necessity to project into the Boudoir. They are therefore made triangular steps; and instead of being rested on the floor as usual, they are made fast at their broad end to the stair door, swinging out and in with that. When it shuts, it runs them under the other steps; when open, it brings them out to their proper place. In the kitchen garden are three pumps worked by one horse. The pumps are placed in an equilateral triangle, each side of which is about 35.f. In the center is a post 10. or 12.f. high and 1.f. diameter. in the top of this enters the bent end of a lever thus [illustration omitted] of about 12. or 15.f. long with a swingle tree at the other end. About 3.f. from the bent end it receives, on a pin, three horizontal bars of iron, which at their other end lay hold of one corner of a quadrantal crank (like a bell crank) moving in a vertical plane, to the other corner of which is hooked the vertical handle of the pump: thus [illustration omitted]. This crank turns on it's point as a center, by a pin or pivot passing thro' it at (a), the horse moving the lever horizontally in a circle; every point in the lever describes a horizontal circle. That which receives the three bars at (b) in the diagram, describes a circle of 6.f. diameter. It gives a stroke then of 6.f. to the handle of each pump, at each revolution [illustration omitted].

BLOIS. ORLEANS. June 9. 10. At Blois the road leaves the river, and traverses the hills, which are mostly reddish, sometimes grey, good enough, in vines, corn, St. foin. From Orleans to the river Juines at ESTAMPES, it is a continued plain of corn and St. foin, tolerably good, sometimes grey, sometimes red. From Estampes to ESTRECHY the country is mountainous and rocky, resembling that of Fontainebleau. Question. if it may not be the same vein?

∾

To Maria Cosway   Paris July 1. 1787

You conclude, Madam, from my long silence that I am gone to the other world. Nothing else would have prevented my writing to you so long. I have not thought of you the less. But I took a peep only into Elysium. I entered it at one door, and came out at another, having seen, as I past, only Turin, Milan, and Genoa. I calculated the hours it would have taken to carry me on to Rome. But they were exactly so many more than I had to spare. Was not this provoking? In thirty hours from Milan I could have been at the espousals of the Doge and Adriatic. But I am born to lose every thing I love. Why were you not with me? So many enchanting scenes which only wanted your pencil to consecrate them to fame. Whenever you go to Italy you must pass at the Col de Tende. You may go in your chariot in full trot from Nice to Turin, as if there were no mountain. But have your pallet and pencil ready: for you will be sure to stop in the passage, at the chateau de Saorgio. Imagine to yourself, madam, a castle and village hanging to a cloud in front. On one hand a mountain cloven through to let pass a gurgling stream; on the other a river, over which is thrown a magnificent bridge; the whole formed into a bason, it's sides shagged with rocks, olive trees, vines, herds, &c. I insist on your painting it.

How do you do? How have you done? and when are you coming here? If not at all, what did you ever come for? Only to make people miserable at losing you. Consider that you are but 4. days from Paris. If you come by the way of St. Omers, which is but two posts further, you will see a new and beautiful country. Come then, my dear Madam, and we will breakfast every day a l'Angloise, hie away to the Desert, dine under the bowers of Marly, and forget that we are ever to part again. I received, in the moment of my departure your favor of Feb. 15. and long to receive another: but lengthy, warm, and flowing from the heart, as do the sentiments of friendship & esteem with which I have the honor to be, dear Madam, your affectionate friend & servant,

—TH: JEFFERSON

CHAPTER SIX

Between Two Revolutions

J EFFERSON RETURNED FROM THE SOUTH OF FRANCE TO FIND THREE AND A HALF
months of work waiting for him in Paris. Soon after he got back, his youngest
daughter, Polly, showed up at the door of John and Abigail Adams in London, in the
care of the captain of the ship that had brought her to Europe. Because of his work load,
Jefferson sent Petit, the French servant who ran his household, to get her. Polly was eight
years old when she crossed the Atlantic Ocean. The nurse who came with her—Sally
Hemings—was herself only fourteen or fifteen, and had probably never traveled before
more than a few miles from home. Eighteenth-century children grew up faster than today's.

The work facing Jefferson was largely routine. The negotiation of the consular
convention between the two countries lay ahead of him; the work of finalizing trade agreements with France was over. Along the latter lines he had done pretty much everything
he could. In July he wrote Montmorin—the minister of foreign affairs after the death
of Vergennes—another long, detailed complaint about the tobacco monopoly. The
letter is at the same time an eloquent plea for free trade. It had little if any effect. The
United States's indebtedness to France and to the Dutch bankers remained a serious
and difficult problem, but, considering the powerlessness of the United States government under the Confederacy and the deeply embarrassing emptiness of the United
States treasury, he could only make more promises. All hopes of freeing the United States
citizens being held in Algiers as captives were in abeyance. There was no money to pay
their ransom price. Jefferson still believed that war was the only answer, and he went
on believing that until he became President—and could begin one.

For the next eight or nine months, then, as far as his mission to France was concerned, Jefferson was largely spinning his wheels. John Adams was in an even worse situation in England, where the government would hardly speak to him, and he longed to go home. He had been spending his time writing the second volume of his Defense of the Constitutions of the United States, an analysis of the various state constitutions. He sent Jefferson a copy as soon as it was printed. Adams had himself written the Massachusetts Constitution. In the spring of 1788, before he left for America, Adams made a quick trip to Holland to negotiate new loans for the United States from the Dutch bankers, and Jefferson met him there to help and to learn. Jefferson freely admitted that he was far less competent than Adams on the subject of the nation's credit. Rather than returning to Paris at once, he made a short trip through Holland and Germany. That trip is the subject of the next chapter in this collection.

In the meantime, what occupied Jefferson's closest attention were the revolutions going on in France and America. In France, of course, Jefferson was witnessing, with high hopes, the run-up to the French Revolution that would break out in violence in 1789. In America, the Revolution was more peaceful. All that summer of 1787 the Constitutional Convention had been meeting in Philadelphia. His friend and protégé, James Madison, was not only in attendance; he was its prime mover, its father— if the convention could be said to have a single father—and the entire Atlantic world was waiting to see what emerged. It had been agreed at the beginning that the proceedings would be secret. Nobody knew what sort of government the convention would propose. Jefferson was one of the first in Europe to find out, when the Convention finally issued its draft in late September 1787. He and Madison were soon in correspondence about it. One of the great letters of this period, printed in this chapter, is Madison's letter of October 24, 1787, to Jefferson explaining the reasoning behind the Constitution's provisions. It is all by itself a short course in the history of the making of the document and a vade mecum to constitutional law. Jefferson's letters in response to Madison are also highly interesting and revealing. Jefferson was shocked when he first read the constitution—and somewhat appalled. It took him months, and a lot of thought to come around; and he was never entirely comfortable with all its provisions. Those thoughts surface in these letters.

The two men's opinions differed on other matters as well. Early in 1787 Shays's Rebellion had disturbed the peace of Massachusetts. This uprising of poor farmers, overburdened with debt and taxes, in the western part of the state, didn't amount to much of a rebellion and was quickly dispersed, but it generated alarm all over the country and confirmed to British conservatives that Americans were incapable of self-government.

Madison was one of those who took fright at the event, calling the rebels "traitors" and considering their rebellion a hanging offense. Jefferson took quite another tack, as the letters here reveal. Not only was he not concerned about this rebellion—he also thought an occasional rebellion was good for the country.

We forget how radical Jefferson really was. His experience in France had taught him to fear power in all its forms, whatever checks upon it might exist. He understood the need to rethink the Articles of Confederation, but only as they pertained to foreign affairs. He wrote Madison before the convention met that "to make us one nation as to foreign concerns and keep us distinct in Domestic ones, gives the outline of the proper division of powers between the general and particular governments." For him, the less government there was, the better. Madison had a much more thoroughgoing reform in mind, together with a much less sanguine view of human nature and its capacity to act in a disinterested fashion for the good of the whole. He was more like John Adams in some respects than Thomas Jefferson. One of the more entertaining letters in this section is the one from Adams on October 9, 1787, in which he talks about an unidentified "disgrace" and then weighs in at length on the weakness of human nature in general. Adams may be referring to the actions of the Georgia branch of the Society of the Cincinnati when they made a son of Nathaniel Greene, the late Revolutionary War general, an honorary member. The proposals after the war to make that society a hereditary organization raised alarms all over the country. The fear was that the society could become the germ of an American hereditary aristocracy.

Given his initial objections to the Constitution, it's interesting to wonder what the document might have become if Jefferson had been in America, attending the convention. His physical distance from America and the psychological distance his years in France inevitably provided gave him, certainly, a perspective that would have been lacking had he been on the spot. We now are blessed by the event. That selfsame distance created the opportunity for him and Madison to correspond on the subject. It is a correspondence that continued until the end of Jefferson's stay in France, and it is collectively one of the greatest series of letters on government and its principles that we now possess. Later in this anthology we shall see the two men arguing the advantages and disadvantages of a Bill of Rights, bringing this particular discussion to an end.

Jefferson in the meantime was left hanging between the old government and the new, which would not form until the constitution was ratified and elections could be held. Nobody knew how long that would take. Madison reported on December 20, 1787, that "the Treasury Board seem to be in despair of maintaining the shadow of Government much longer." That meant that Jefferson would not get any kind of compensation for his outfit, that even the interest on the national debt could not be paid, and that the credit, in every sense of the word, of the United States would become even more of a problem for Jefferson as his mission continued.

ॐ

From Abigail Adams
MY DEAR SIR   London July 6. 1787

If I had thought you would so soon have sent for your dear little Girl, I should have been tempted to have kept her arrival here, from you a secret. I am really loth to part with her, and she last evening upon Petit's arrival, was thrown into all her former distresses, and bursting into Tears, told me it would be as hard to leave me as it was her Aunt Epps. She has been so often deceived that she will not quit me a moment least she should be carried away. Nor can I scarcly prevail upon her to see Petit. Tho she says she does not remember you, yet she has been taught to consider you with affection and fondness, and depended upon your comeing for her. She told me this morning, that as she had left all her Friends in virginia to come over the ocean to see you, she did think you would have taken the pains to have come here for her, and not have sent a man whom she cannot understand. I express her own words. I expostulated with her upon the long journey you had been, and the difficulty you had to come and upon the care kindness and attention of Petit, whom I so well knew. But she cannot yet hear me. She is a child of the quickest sensibility, and the maturest understanding, that I have ever met with for her years. She had been 5 weeks at sea, and with men only, so that on the first day of her arrival, she was as rough as a little sailor, and then she been decoyed from the ship, which made her very angry, and no one having any Authority over her; I was apprehensive I should meet with some trouble. But where there are such materials to work upon as I have found in her, there is no danger. She listend to my admonitions, and attended to my advice and in two days, was restored to the amiable lovely Child which her Aunt had formed her. In short she is the favorite of every creature in the House, and I cannot but feel Sir, how many pleasures you must lose by committing her to a convent. Yet situated as you are, you cannot keep her with you. The Girl she has with her, wants more care than the child, and is wholy incapable of looking properly after her, without some superiour to direct her.

As both Miss Jefferson and the maid had cloaths only proper for the sea, I have purchased and made up for them, such things as I should have done had they been my own, to the amount of Eleven or 12 Guineys. The particulars I will send by Petit.

Captain Ramsey has said that he would accompany your daughter to Paris provided she would not go without him, but this would be putting you to an expence that may perhaps be avoided by Petits staying a few days longer. The greatest difficulty in familiarizing her to him, is on account of the language. I have not the Heart to force her into a Carriage against her will and send her from me almost in a Frenzy; as I know will be the case, unless I can reconcile her to the thoughts of going and I have given her my word that Petit shall stay untill I can hear again from you. Books are her delight, and I have furnished her out a little library, and she reads to me by the hour with great distinctness, and comments on what she reads with much propriety.

Mrs. Smith desires to be remembered to you, and the little Boy his Grandmama thinks is as fine a Boy as any in the Kingdom. I am my dear sir with Sentiments of Esteem Your Friend and Humble Servant,

—A ADAMS

⁊

To Mary Jefferson Bolling
DEAR SISTER   Paris July 23. 1787

I received with great pleasure your letter of May 3. informing me of your health and of that of your family. Be assured that it is and ever has been among the most interesting things to me. Letters of business claiming their rights before those of affection, we often write seldomest to those whom we love most. The distance to which I am removed has given a new value to all I valued before in my own country, and the day of my return to it will be the happiest I expect to see in this life. When it will come is not yet decided as far as depends on myself. My dear Polly is safely arrived here and in good health. She had got so attached to Captn. Ramsay that they were obliged to decoy her from him. She staid three weeks in London with Mrs. Adams, and had got such an attachment to her that she refused to come with the person I sent for her. After some days, she was prevailed on to come. She did not know either her sister or myself, but soon renewed her acquaintance and attachment. She is now in the same convent with her sister, and will come to see me once or twice a week. It is a house of education altogether the best in France, and at which the best masters attend. There are in it as many protestants as Catholics, and not a word is ever spoken to them on the subject of religion. Patsy enjoys good health, and longs much to return to her friends. We shall doubtless find much change when we do get back; many of our older friends withdrawn from the stage, and our younger ones grown out of our knowledge. I suppose you are now fixed for life at Chesnut grove: I take a part of the misfortune to myself, as it will prevent my seeing you as often as would be practicable at Lickinghole. It is still a greater loss to my sister Carr. We must look to Jack for indemnification, as I think it was the plan that he should live at Lickinghole. I suppose he is now become the father of a family, and that we may hail you as grandmother. As we approach that term it becomes less fearful. You mention Mr. Bolling's being unwell, so as not to write to me. He has just been sick enough all his life to prevent his writing to any body. My prayer is therefore only that he may never be worse. Were he to be so, no body would feel it more sensibly than myself, as nobody has a more sincere esteem for him than myself. I find as I grow older, that I love those most whom I loved first. Present me to him in the most friendly terms, to Jack also, and my other nephews and neices of your fire side and be assured of the sincere love with which I am, dear sister, your affectionate brother,

—TH: JEFFERSON

ℒℴ

To George Washington
DEAR SIR   Paris Aug. 14. 1787

I was happy to find by the letter of Aug. 1. 1786. which you did me the honour to write me, that the modern dress for your statue would meet your approbation. I found it strongly the sentiment of West, Copeley, Trumbul and Brown in London, after which it would be ridiculous to add that it was my own. I think a modern in an antique dress as just an object of ridicule as an Hercules or Marius with a periwig and chapeau bras.

I remember having written to you while Congress sat at Annapolis on the water communications between ours and the Western country, and to have mentioned particularly the information I had received of the plain face of the country between the sources of Big beaver and Cayohoga, which made me hope that a canal of no great expence might unite the navigations of L. Erie and the Ohio. You must since have had occasion of getting better information on this subject and, if you have, you would oblige me by a communication of it. I consider this canal, if practicable, as a very important work.

I remain in hopes of great and good effects from the decisions of the assembly over which you are presiding. To make our states one as to all foreign concerns, preserve them several as to all merely domestic, to give to the federal head some peaceable mode of enforcing their just authority, to organize that head into Legislative, Executive, and Judiciary departments are great desiderata in our federal constitution. Yet with all it's defects, and with all those of our particular governments, the inconveniencies resulting from them are so light in comparison with those existing in every other government on earth, that our citizens may certainly be considered as in the happiest political situation which exists.—The assemblée des Notables has been productive of much good in this country. The reformation of some of the most oppressive laws has taken place and is taking place. The allotment of the state into subordinate governments, the administration of which is committed to persons chosen by the people, will work in time a very beneficial change in their constitution. The expence of the trappings of monarchy too are lightening. Many of the useless officers, high and low, of the king, queen, and princes are struck off. Notwithstanding all this the discovery of the abominable abuses of public money by the late comptroller general, some new expences of the court, not of a peice with the projects of reformation, and the imposition of new taxes, have in the course of a few weeks raised a spirit of discontent in this nation, so great and so general, as to threaten serious consequences. The Parliaments in general, and particularly that of Paris put themselves at the head of this effervescence, and direct it's object to the calling the states general, who have not been assembled since 1614. The object is to fix a constitution, and to limit expences. The king has been obliged to hold a bed of justice to enforce the registering the new taxes: the parliament on their side propose to issue a prohibition against their execution. Very possibly this may bring on their exile. The mild and patriotic character of the new ministry is the principal dependance against this extremity.

The turn which the affairs of Europe will take is not yet decided. The Emperor, on his return to Vienna, disavowed the retrocessions made by his governors general in the low countries. He at the same time called for deputies to consult on their affairs. This, which would have been the sole measure of a wise sovereign, was spoiled by contrary indications resulting from his Thrasonic character. The people at first refused to send deputies. At last however they sent them without powers, and go on arming. I think there is little doubt but the Emperor will avail himself of these deputies to tread back his steps. He will do this the rather that he may be in readiness to take part in the war likely to be produced by the Dutch differences. The kings of England and Prussia were abetting the cause of the Stadholder, France that of the Patriots: but negotiations were going on to settle them amicably, when all of a sudden, the Princess of Orange, undertaking a secret journey to the Hague to incite an insurrection of the people there, is stopped on the road, writes an inflammatory letter to her brother, he without consulting England, or even his own council, or any thing else but his own pride, orders 20,000 men to march into the neighborhood of Holland. This has been followed by the sailing of the English squadron somewhere Westwardly, and that will be followed by a squadron from Brest, and an army to the confines of Holland from this country. Appearances therefore are within a few days past more like war than they had been. Still however the negotiations are going on, and the finances both of France and England are so notoriously incompetent to war, that the arrest of hostile movements and an amicable adjustment are not yet altogether despaired of. A war, wherein France, Holland and England should be parties, seems prima facie to promise much advantage to us. But in the first place no war can be safe for us which threatens France with an unfavourable issue. And in the next, it will probably embark us again into the ocean of speculation, engage us to overtrade ourselves, convert us into Sea-rovers under French and Dutch colours, divert us from Agriculture which is our wisest pursuit, because it will in the end contribute most to real wealth, good morals and happiness. The wealth acquired by speculation and plunder is fugacious in it's nature and fills society with the spirit of gambling. The moderate and sure income of husbandry begets permanent improvement, quiet life, and orderly conduct both public and private. We have no occasion for more commerce than to take off our superfluous produce, and tho people complain that some restrictions prevent this, yet the price of articles with us in general shew the contrary. Tobacco indeed is low, not because we cannot carry it where we please, but because we make more than the consumption requires. Upon the whole I think peace advantageous to us, necessary for Europe, and desireable for humanity. A few days will decide probably whether all these considerations are to give way to the bad passions of kings and those who would be kings. I have the honour to be with very sincere esteem and respect dear Sir Your most obedient & most humble servant,

—TH: JEFFERSON

P. S. Aug. 15. The Parliament is exiled to Troyes this morning.

∽

[At this time it was not generally known in Europe, or even in America, who had actually written the Declaration of Independence. In the next letter, Jefferson sets the record straight, giving credit for the document not to Dickinson but to a committee. He does not mention the names of anyone on this committee, including his own, but he must have reckoned that the letter contained enough information to identify him as the author, so not only did he not sign it, he did not send it, either.]

To the Editor of the Journal de Paris
SIR   Paris Aug. 29. 1787

I am a citizen of the United states of America, and have passed in those states almost the whole of my life. When young, I was passionately fond of reading books of history, and travels. Since the commencement of the late revolution which separated us from Great Britain, our country too has been thought worthy to employ the pens of historians and travellers. I cannot paint to you, Sir, the agonies which these have cost me, in obliging me to renounce these favorite branches of reading and in discovering to me at length that my whole life has been employed in nourishing my mind with fables and falshoods. For thus I reason. If the histories of d'Auberteuil and of Longchamps, and the travels of the Abbé Robin can be published in the face of the world, and can be read and believed by those who are cotemporary with the events they pretend to relate, how may we expect that future ages shall be better informed? Will those rise from their graves to bear witness to the truth, who would not, while living, lift their voices against falshood? If cotemporary histories are thus false, what will future compilations be. And what are all those of preceding times? In your Journal of this day, you announce and criticize a book under the title of 'les ligues Acheenne, Suisse, and Hollandoise, et revolution des etats unis de l'Amerique par M. de Mayer.' I was no part of the Achaeen Swiss or Dutch confederacies and have therefore nothing to say against the facts related of them. And you cite only one fact from his account of the American revolution. It is in these words, 'Monsieur Mayer assure qu'une seule voix, un seul homme, prononça l'independance des Etats unis. "Ce fut, dit il, John Dickinson, un des Deputés de la Pensilvanie au Congrées. Le veille, il avoit voté pour la soumission. L'egalité des suffrages avoit suspendu la resolution; s'il eut persisté, le Congrés ne deliberoit point. Il fut foible: il cede aux instances de ceux qui avoient plus d'energie, plus d'eloquence, et plus de lumieres; il donna sa voix: l'Amerique lui doit une reconnoissance eternelle; c'est Dickinson qui l'a affranchie."' The modesty and candour of Mr. Dickinson himself, Sir, would disavow every word of this paragraph, except these 'il avoit voté pour la soumission.' These are true, every other tittle false. I was on the spot, and can relate to you this transaction with precision. On the 7th. of June 1776. the delegates from Virginia moved, in obedience to instructions from their constituents, that Congress should declare the 13. united colonies to be independant of Great Britain, that a Confederation should be formed to bind them together, and measures be taken for procuring the assistance of foreign powers. The house ordered a punctual attendance of all their members the next day at ten o'clock, and then resolved themselves into a Committee of the whole and entered on the discussion. It appeared in the course of the debates that 7. states, viz. N. Hampshire, Massachusets, Rhodeisland, Connecticut, Virginia, North Carolina and Georgia were decided for a separation, but that 6. others still hesitated, to wit, New York, New Jersey, Pennsylvania, Delaware, Maryland and South Carolina. Congress, desirous of unanimity, and seeing that the public mind was advancing rapidly to it, referred the further discussion to the 1st. of July, appointing in the mean time a Committee to prepare a declaration of independance, a second to form Articles for the confederation of the states, and a third to propose measures for obtaining foreign aid. On the 28th. of June the Declaration of Independance was reported to the house, and was laid on the table for the consideration of the members. On the 1st. day of July they resolved themselves into a committee of the whole, and resumed the consideration of the motion of June 7. It was debated through the day, and at length was decided in the affirmative by the votes of 9. states, viz. New Hampshire, Massachusets, Rhode island, Connecticut, N. Jersey, Maryland, Virginia, North Carolina and Georgia. Pennsylvania and South Carolina voted against it. Delaware, having but two members present, was divided. The delegates from New York declared they were for it, and their constituents also: but that the instructions against it, which had been given them a twelvemonth before, were still unrepealed; that their convention was to meet in a few days, and they asked leave to suspend their vote till they could obtain a repeal of their instructions. Observe that all this was in committee of the whole Congress, and that according to the mode of their proceedings the Resolution of that Committee to declare themselves independant was to be put to the same persons re-assuming their form as a Congress. It was now evening, the members exhausted by a debate of 9 hours, during which all the powers of the soul had been distended with the magnitude of the object without refreshment, without a pause; and the delegates of S. Carolina desired that the final decision might be put off to the next morning that they might still weigh in their own minds their ultimate vote. It was put off, and in the morning of the 2d. of July they joined the other nine states in voting for it. The members of the Pennsylvania delegation too, who had been absent the day before, came in and decided the votes of their state in favor of Independance, and a 3d member of the state of Delaware, who, hearing of the division of the sentiments of his two collegues, had travelled post to arrive in time, now came in and decided the vote of that state also for the resolution. Thus twelve states voted for it at the time of it's passage, and the delegates of New York, the 13th. state received instructions within a few days to add theirs to the general vote: so that, instead of the 'egalité des suffrages' spoken of by Mr. Mayer, there was not a dissenting voice. Congress proceeded immediately to consider the Declaration of Independence which had been reported by their committee on the 28th. of June. The several paragraphs of that were debated for three days. viz. the 2d. 3d. and 4th. of July. In the evening of the 4th. they were finally closed, and the instrument approved by an unanimous vote, and signed by every member, *except* Mr. Dickinson. Look into the Journals of Congress of that day, Sir, and you will see the instrument, and the names of the signers, and that Mr. Dickinson's name is not among them. Then read again those words of your paper. 'Il (Mr. Mayer) assure qu'une seule voix, un seul homme, prononça l'independance des etats unis. "Ce fut John Dickinson. L'Amerique lui doit une reconnoissance eternal; c'est Dickinson qui l'a affranchie."' With my regrets, and my Adieus to History, to Travels, to Mayer, and to you, Sir, permit me to mingle assurances of the great respect with which I have the honor to be, Sir, your most obedient & most humble servant,

—AN AMERICAN

❧

[Minor business matters have been omitted from the beginning of this letter.]

To John Adams
DEAR SIR   Paris Aug. 30. 1787

... From the separation of the Notables to the present moment has been perhaps the most interesting interval ever known in this country. The propositions of the Government, approved by the Notables, were precious to the nation and have been in an honest course of execution, some of them being carried into effect, and others preparing. Above all the establishment of the Provincial assemblies, some of which have begun their sessions, bid fair to be the instrument for circumscribing the power of the crown and raising the people into consideration. The election given to them is what will do this. Tho' the minister who proposed these improvements seems to have meant them as the price of the new supplies, the game has been so played as to secure the improvements to the nation without securing the price. The Notables spoke softly on the subject of the additional supplies, but the parliament took them up roundly, refused to register the edicts for the new taxes, till compelled in a bed of justice and prefered themselves to be transferred to Troyes rather than withdraw their opposition. It is urged principally against the king, that his revenue is 130. millions more than that of his predecessor was, and yet he demands 120. millions further. You will see this well explained in the 'Conference entre un ministre d'etat et un Conseiller au parlement' which I send you with some other small pamphlets. In the mean time all tongues in Paris (and in France as it is said) have been let loose, and never was a license of speaking against the government exercised in London more freely or more universally. Caracatures, placards, bon mots, have been indulged in by all ranks of people, and I know of no well attested instance of a single punishment. For some time mobs of 10; 20; 30,000 people collected daily, surrounded the parliament house, huzzaed the members, even entered the doors and examined into their conduct, took the horses out of the carriages of those who did well, and drew them home. The government thought it prudent to prevent these, drew some regiments into the neighborhood, multiplied the guards, had the streets constantly patrolled by strong parties, suspended privileged places, forbad all clubs, &c. The mobs have ceased: perhaps this may be partly owing to the absence of parliament. The Count d'Artois, sent to hold a bed of justice in the Cour des Aides, was hissed and hooted without reserve by the populace; the carriage of Madame de (I forget the name) in the queen's livery was stopped by the populace under a belief that it was Madame de Polignac's whom they would have insulted, the queen going to the theater at Versailles with Madame de Polignac was received with a general hiss. The king, long in the habit of drowning his cares in wine, plunges deeper and deeper; the queen cries but sins on. The Count d'Artois is detested, and Monsieur the general favorite. The Archbishop of Thoulouse is made Ministre principale, a virtuous, patriotic and able character. The Marechal de Castries retired yesterday notwithstanding strong sollicitations to remain in office. The Marechal de Segur retired at the same time, prompted to it by the court. Their successors are not yet known. M. de St. Prist goes Ambassador to Holland in the room of Verac transferred to Switzerland, and the Count de Moustier goes to America in the room of the Chevalier de la Luzerne who has a promise of the first vacancy. These nominations are not yet made formally, but they are decided on and the parties are ordered to prepare for their destination. As it has been long since I have had a confidential conveiance to you, I have brought together the principal facts from the adjournment of the Notables to the present moment which, as you will perceive from their nature, required a confidential conveyance. I have done it the rather because, tho' you will have heard many of them and seen them in the public papers, yet floating in the mass of lies which constitute the atmospheres of London and Paris, you may not have been sure of their truth: and I have mentioned every truth of any consequence to enable you to stamp as false the facts pretermitted. I think that in the course of three months the royal authority has lost, and the rights of the nation gained, as much ground, by a revolution of public opinion only, as England gained in all her civil wars under the Stuarts. I rather believe too they will retain the ground gained, because it is defended by the young and the middle aged, in opposition to the old only. The first party increases, and the latter diminishes daily from the course of nature. You may suppose that under this situation, war would be unwelcome to France. She will surely avoid it if not forced by the courts of London and Berlin. If forced, it is probable she will change the system of Europe totally by an alliance with the two empires, to whom nothing would be more desireable. In the event of such a coalition, not only Prussia but the whole European world must receive from them their laws. But France will probably endeavor to preserve the present system if it can be done by sacrifising to a certain degree the pretensions of the patriotic party in Holland. But of all these matters you can judge, in your position, where less secrecy is observed, better than I can. I have news from America as late as July 19. Nothing had then transpired from the Federal convention. I am sorry they began their deliberations by so abominable a precedent as that of tying up the tongues of their members. Nothing can justify this example but the innocence of their intentions, and ignorance of the value of public discussions. I have no doubt that all their other measures will be good and wise. It is really an assembly of demigods. Genl. Washington was of opinion they should not separate till October. I have the honour to be with every sentiment of friendship and respect Dear Sir Your most obedient & most humble servant,

—TH: JEFFERSON

∾

From James Madison
DEAR SIR   Philada. Sepr. 6. 1787

My last was intended for the Augst. Packet and put into the hands of Commodore Paul Jones. Some disappointments prevented his going, and as he did not know but its contents might be unfit for the ordinary conveyance, he retained it. The precaution was unnecessary. For the same reason the delay has been of little consequence. The rule of secrecy in the Convention rendered that as it will this letter barren of those communications which might otherwise be made. As the Convention will shortly rise I should feel little scruple in disclosing what will be public here, before it could reach you, were it practicable for me to guard by Cypher against an intermediate discovery. But I am deprived of this resource by the shortness of the interval between the receipt of your letter of June 20. and the date of this. This is the first days which has been free from Committee service both before and after the hours of the House, and the last that is allowed me by the time advertised for the sailing of the Packet.

The Convention consists now as it has generally done of Eleven States. There has been no intermission of its Sessions since a house was formed; except an interval of about ten days allowed a Committee appointed to detail the general propositions agreed on in the House. The term of its dissolution cannot be more than one or two weeks distant. A Government will probably be submitted to the people of the states consisting of a [President] cloathed with executive power; a Senate chosen by the Legislatures, and another house chosen by the people of the states jointly possessing the legislative power and a regular judiciary establishment. The mode of constituting the executive is among the few points not yet finally settled. The Senate will consist of two members from each State and appointed sexennially: The other, of members appointed biennially by the people of the states in proportion to their number. The Legislative power will extend to taxation, trade and sundry other general matters. The powers of Congress will be distributed according to their nature among the several departments. The States will be restricted from paper money and in a few other instances. These are the outlines. The extent of them may perhaps surprize you. I hazard an opinion nevertheless that the plan should it be adopted will neither effectually answer its national object nor prevent the local mischiefs which every where excite disgusts against the state governments. The grounds of this opinion will be the subject of a future letter.

I have written to a friend in Congress intimating in a covert manner the necessity of deciding and notifying the intentions of Congress with regard to their foreign Ministers after May next, and have dropped a hint on the communications of Dumas.

Congress have taken some measures for disposing of their public land, and have actually sold a considerable tract. Another bargain I learn is on foot for a further sale.

Nothing can exceed the universal anxiety for the event of the Meeting here. Reports and conjectures abound concerning the nature of the plan which is to be proposed. The public however is certainly in the dark with regard to it. The Convention is equally in the dark as to the reception which may be given to it on its publication. All the prepossessions are on the right side, but it may well be expected that certain characters will wage war against any reforms whatever. My own idea is that the public mind will now or in a very little time receive any thing that promises stability to the public Councils and security to private rights, and that no regard ought to be had to local prejudices or temporary considerations. If the present moment be lost it is hard to say what may be our fate.

Our information from Virginia is far from being agreeable. In many parts of the Country the drouth has been extremely injurious to the corn. I fear, tho' I have no certain information, that Orange and Albemarle [Madison's and Jefferson's home counties, respectively, in Virginia] share in the distress. The people also are said to be generally discontented. A paper emission is again a topic among them. So is an instalment of all debts in some places and the making property a tender in others. The taxes are another source of discontent. The weight of them is complained of, and the abuses in collecting them still more so. In several Counties the prisons and Court Houses and Clerks offices have been wilfully burnt. In Green Briar the course of Justice has been mutinously stopped, and associations entered into against the payment of taxes. No other County has yet followed the example. The approaching meeting of the Assembly will probably allay the discontents on one side by measures which will excite them on another.

Mr. Wythe has never returned to us. His lady whose illness carryed him away, died some time after he got home. The other deaths in Virga. are Col. A. Cary, and a few days ago, Mrs. Harrison, wife of Benjn. Harrison Junr. and sister of J. F. Mercer. Wishing you all happiness I remain Dear Sir Yrs. affecty.,

—JS. MADISON JR.

❧

From John Adams
DEAR SIR   Grosvenor Square Oct. 9. 1787

I sent you a copy of my second volume by Mr. Barthelemy the French Chargé here now Minister, with a Letter about Money matters. In your favour of

Sept. 28. you dont mention the receipt of them.—I have indeed long thought with Anxiety of our Money in the hands of our Friends, whom you mention, and have taken the best Precaution in my Power, against Accidents. I do not consider the Game as up. But a disgrace has happened, which is not easy to get rid of.—Disgrace is not easily washed out, even with blood. Lessons my dear Sir, are never wanting. Life and History are full. The Loss of Paradise, by eating a forbidden apple, has been many Thousand years a Lesson to Mankind; but not much regarded. Moral Reflections, wise Maxims, religious Terrors, have little Effect upon Nations when they contradict a present Passion, Prejudice, Imagination, Enthusiasm or Caprice. Resolutions never to have an hereditary officer will be kept in America, as religiously as that of the Cincinnati was in the Case of General Greens son. Resolutions never to let a Citizen ally himself with Kings will be kept untill an Opportunity presents to violate it. If the Duke of Angoleme, or Burgundy, or especially the Dauphin should demand one of your beautiful and most amiable Daughters in Marriage, all America from Georgia to New Hampshire would find their Vanity and Pride, so agreably flattered by it, that all their Sage Maxims would give way; and even our Sober New England Republicans would keep a day of Thanksgiving for it, in their hearts. If General Washington had a Daughter, I firmly believe, she would be demanded in Marriage by one of the Royal Families of France or England, perhaps by both, or if he had a Son he would be invited to come a courting to Europe.—The Resolution not to call in foreign Nations to settle domestic differences will be kept until a domestic difference of a serious nature shall break out.—I have long been settled in my own opinion, that neither Philosophy, nor Religion, nor Morality, nor Wisdom, nor Interest, will ever govern nations or Parties, against their Vanity, their Pride, their Resentment or Revenge, or their Avarice or Ambition. Nothing but Force and Power and Strength can restrain them. If Robert Morris should maintain his Fortune to the End, I am convinced that some foreign Families of very high rank will think of Alliances with his Children. If the Pen Family [presumably the Penns related to William Penn of Pennsylvania] should go to America, and engage in public affairs and obtain the Confidence of the People, you will see Connections courted there. A Troop of Light Horse from Philadelphia meeting Dick Pen in New Jersey, will strike the Imaginations of Princes and Princesses. How few Princes in Europe could obtain a Troop of Light Horse to make them a Compliment of Parade. In short my dear Friend you and I have been indefatigable Labourers through our whole Lives for a Cause which will be thrown away in the next generation, upon the Vanity and Foppery of Persons of whom we do not now know the Names perhaps.—The War that is now breaking out will render our Country, whether she is forced into it, or not, rich, great and powerful in comparison of what she now is, and Riches Grandeur and Power will have the same effect upon American as it has upon European minds. We have seen enough already to be sure of this. A Covent Garden Rake will never be wise enough to take warning from the Claps caught by his Companions. When he comes to be poxed himself he may possibly repent and reform. Yet three out of four of them become even by their own sufferings, more shameless instead of being penitent.

Pardon this freedom. It is not Melancholly: but Experience and believe me without reserve your Friend,

—JOHN ADAMS

O tempora—oh mores

✍

From Edward Carrington

DEAR SIR   New York 23 Oct. 1787

I have been honoured with your favor of the 4th. of August. Inclosed you will receive a Copy of the report of our late federal Convention, which presents, not amendments to the old Confederation, but an entire new Constitution. This work is short of the ideas I had the honor to communicate to you in June, in no other instance than an absolute negative upon the State laws.

When the report was before Congress, it was not without its direct opponents, but a great majority were for giving it a warm approbation. It was thought best, however, by its friends, barely to recommend to the several Legislatures the holding of Conventions for its consideration, rather than send it forth with, even, a single negative to an approbatory act. The people do not scrutinize terms; the unanimity of Congress in recommending a measure to their consideration, naturally implies approbation: but any negative to a direct approbation would have discovered a dissention, which would have been used to favor divisions in the States. It certainly behoved Congress to give a measure of such importance, and respectable birth, a fair chance in the deliberations of the people, and I think the step taken in that body well adapted to that idea.

The project is warmly received in the Eastern States, and has become pretty generally a subject of consideration in Town-meetings and other Assemblies of the people, the usual result whereof are declarations for its adoption. In the Middle States appearances are generally for it, but not being in habits of assembling for public objects, as is the case to the Eastward, the people have given but few instances of collective declarations. Some symptoms of opposition have appeared in New York and Pensylvania; in the former, only in individual publications, which are attended with no circumstances evidencing the popular regard; the Governor holds himself in perfect silence, wishing, it is suspected, for a miscarriage, but is not confident enough to commit himself in an open opposition: in the latter the opposition has assumed a form somewhat more serious, but under circumstances which leave it doubtful whether it is founded in objection to the project or the intemperance of its more zealous friends. The [Pennsylvania] Legislature was in session in Philada. when the Convention adjourned. 42 Members were for immediately calling a Convention before the measure had received the consideration of Congress, and were about to prepare a vote for that purpose. 19 Seceded and broke up the House, and although they, afterwards, added to their protest against the intemperance of the majority, some objections against the report, yet it is to be doubted whether they would have set themselves in opposition to it, had more moderation been used. The next morning the resolution of Congress arrived, upon which the 42, wanting 2 to compleat a House for business, sent their Sergeant for so many of the Seceders, who were brought by force, whereupon an Act was passed for calling a Convention in November. The Seceders are from the upper Counties, have carried their discontents home with them, and some of them being men of influence, will occasion an inconvenience, but Gentlemen well acquainted with the Country are of opinion, that their opposition will have no extensive effect, as there is, in general, a Coalescence of the two parties which have divided that State ever since the birth of her own Constitution, in support of the new Government. From the Southern States we are but imperfectly informed. Every member from the Carolina's and Georgia, as well in Convention, as Congress, are warm for the new Constitution; and when we consider the ascendency possessed by Men of this description over the people in those States, it may well be concluded, that the reception will be favorable. In Virginia there may be some difficulty. Two of her members in Convention whose characters entitle them to the public confidence, refused to sign the report. These were Colo. Mason and Governor Randolph, nor was that State without its dissentients, of the same description, in Congress. These were Mr. R. H. Lee and Mr. Grayson, but upon very opposite principles—the former because it is too strong, the latter because it is too weak. The Governor has declared that his refusal to sign, shall not be followed by hostility against the measure, that his wish is to get the exceptional parts altered if practicable, but if not that he will join in its support from the necessity of the Case.

Mr. Madison writes you fully upon the objections from Virginia, and therefore I will not impose on your patience by repeating them; one, however, being merely local, and an old source of jealousy I will present to your consideration my opinion upon. This is the ability of a bare majority in the federal Government, to regulate Commerce. It is supposed that a Majority of the Union are carriers, and that it will be for the interest, and in the power, of that majority to form regulations oppressing, by high freights, the agricultural States. It does not appear to me that this objection is well founded. In the first place it is not true that the Majority are carriers, for Jersey and Connecticut who fall into the division are by means such and New York and Pensylvania, who also are within that division, are as much agricultural as Carrying States: but, admitting the first position to be true, I do not see that the supposed consequences would follow. No regulation could be made on other than general and uniform principles. In that case every created evil would effect its own cure. The Southern States possess more materials for shipping than the Eastern, and if they do not follow the carrying business, it is because they are occupied in more lucrative pursuits. A rate of freight would make that an object, and they would readily turn to it; but the Competition amongst the eastern States themselves, would be sufficient to correct every abuse. A Navigation Act ought doubtless to be passed for giving exclusive benefits to American ships. This would of course serve the eastern States, and such, in justice ought to be the case, as it may perhaps be shown, that no other advantage can result to them from the Revolution. Indeed, it is important to the interests of the Southern states that the growth of a Navy be promoted, for the security of that wealth which is to be derived from their agriculture.

My determination to join in the adoption results from a Compound consideration of the measure itself, the probable issue of another attempt, and the critical state of our affairs. It has in my mind great faults, but the formers of it met under powers and dispositions which promised greater accommodation in their deliberations than can be expected to attend any future convention. The particular interests of States are exposed and future deputations, would be clogged with instructions and biassed by the presentiments of their constituents. Hence, it is fairly to be concluded that this is a better scheme than can be looked for from another experiment; on these considerations, I would clearly be for closing with it, and relying upon the correction of its faults, as experience may dictate the necessary alterations. But when I extend my view to that approaching anarchy which nothing but the timely interposition of a new government can avert, I am doubly urged in my wishes for the adoption.

Some Gentlemen apprehend that this project is the foundation of a Monarchy, or at least an oppressive Aristocracy; but my apprehensions are rather from the inroads of the democracy. It is true there is a preposterous combination of powers in the President and Senate, which may be used improperly, but time is to discover whether the tendency of abuse, will be to strengthen or relax. At all events this part of the constitution must be exceptionable. But when we consider the degree of democracy of which the scheme itself partakes, with the addition of that which will be constantly operating upon it, it clearly appears to my mind, that the prevailing infractions are to be expected from thence. As State acts can go into effect without the direct controul of the General Government, having clearly defined the objects of their legislation, will not secure the federal ground against their encroachments. A disposition to encroach must, in the nature of the thing exist, and the democratic branch in the federal legislature, will be more likely to cover their approches, than resist them. [The remaining portion of this letter covers arrangements made for governing the Western territories beyond the Appalachians.]
—ED. CARRINGTON

❧

From James Madison
DEAR SIR   New York Octr. 24. 1787

My two last, though written for the two last Packets, have unluckily been delayed till this conveyance. The first of them was sent from Philada. to

Commodore Jones in consequence of information that he was certainly to go by the packet then about to sail. Being detained here by his business with Congress, and being unwilling to put the letter into the mail without my approbation, which could not be obtained in time, he detained the letter also. The second was sent from Philada. to Col. Carrington, with a view that it might go by the last packet at all events in case Commodore Jones should meet with further detention here. By ill luck he was out of Town, and did not return till it was too late to make use of the opportunity. Neither of the letters were indeed of much consequence at the time and are still less so now. I let them go forward nevertheless as they may mention some circumstances not at present in my recollection, and as they will prevent a chasm on my part of our correspondence which I have so many motives to cherish by an exact punctuality.

Your favor of June 20. has been already acknowledged. The last packet from France brought me that of August 2d. I have received also by the Mary Capt. Howland the three Boxes for W. H. B. F. and myself. The two first have been duly forwarded. The contents of the last are a valuable addition to former literary remittances and lay me under additional obligations, which I shall always feel more strongly than I express. The articles included for Congress have been delivered and those for the two Universities and for General Washington have been forwarded, as have been the various letters for your friends in Virginia and elsewhere. The parcel of rice referred to in your letter to the Delegates of S. Carolina has met with some accident. No account whatever can be gathered concerning it. It probably was not shipped from France. Ubbo's book I find was not omitted as you seem to have apprehended. The charge for it however is, which I must beg you to supply. The duplicate volume of the Encyclopedie, I left in Virginia, and it is uncertain when I shall have an opportunity of returning it. Your Spanish duplicates will I fear be hardly vendible. I shall make a trial wherever a chance presents itself. A few days ago I received your favor of the 15 of Augst. via L'Orient and Boston. The letters inclosed along with it were immediately sent on to Virga.

You will herewith receive the result of the Convention, which continued its session till the 17th of September. I take the liberty of making some observations on the subject which will help to make up a letter, if they should answer no other purpose.

It appeared to be the sincere and unanimous wish of the Convention to cherish and preserve the Union of the States. No proposition was made, no suggestion was thrown out in favor of a partition of the Empire into two or more Confederacies.

It was generally agreed that the objects of the Union could not be secured by any system founded on the principle of a confederation of sovereign States. A voluntary observance of the federal law by all the members could never be hoped for. A compulsive one could evidently never be reduced to practice, and if it could, involved equal calamities to the innocent and the guilty, the necessity of a military force both obnoxious and dangerous, and in general, a scene resembling much more a civil war, than the administration of a regular Government.

Hence was embraced the alternative of a government which instead of operating, on the States, should operate without their intervention on the individuals composing them: and hence the change in the principle and proportion of representation.

This ground-work being laid, the great objects which presented themselves were 1. to unite a proper energy in the Executive and a proper stability in the Legislative departments, with the essential characters of Republican Government. 2. To draw a line of demarkation which would give to the General Government every power requisite for general purposes, and leave to the States every power which might be most beneficially administered by them. 3. To provide for the different interests of different parts of the Union. 4. To adjust the clashing pretensions of the large and small States. Each of these objects was pregnant with difficulties. The whole of them together formed a task more difficult than can be well conceived by those who were not concerned in the execution of it. Adding to these considerations the natural diversity of human opinions on all new and complicated subjects, it is impossible to consider the degree of concord which ultimately prevailed as less than a miracle.

The first of these objects as it respects the Executive, was peculiarly embarrassing. On the question whether it should consist of a single person, or a plurality of co-ordinate members, on the mode of appointment, on the duration in office, on the degree of power, on the re-eligibility, tedious and reiterated discussions took place. The plurality of co-ordinate members had finally but few advocates. Governour Randolph was at the head of them. The modes of appointment proposed were various, as by the people at large—by electors chosen by the people—by the Executives of the States—by the Congress, some preferring a joint ballot of the two Houses—some a separate concurrent ballot allowing to each a negative on the other house—some a nomination of several canditates by one House, out of whom a choice should be made by the other. Several other modifications were started. The expedient at length adopted seemed to give pretty general satisfaction to the members. As to the duration in office, a few would have preferred a tenure during good behaviour—a considerable number would have done so in case an easy and effectual removal by impeachment could be settled. It was much agitated whether a long term, seven years for example, with a subsequent and perpetual ineligibility, or a short term with a capacity to be re-elected, should be fixed. In favor of the first opinion were urged the danger of a gradual degeneracy of re-elections from time to time, into first a life and then a hereditary tenure, and the favorable effect of an incapacity to be reappointed, on the independent exercise of the Executive authority. On the other side it was contended that the prospect of necessary degradation would discourage the most dignified characters from aspiring to the office, would take away the principal motive to the faithful discharge of its duties the hope of being rewarded with a reappointment would stimulate ambition to violent efforts for holding over the constitutional term, and instead of producing an independent administration, and a firmer defence of the constitutional rights of the department, would render the officer more indifferent to the importance of a place which he would soon be obliged to quit for ever, and more ready to yield to the incroachments of the Legislature of which he might again be a member.—The questions concerning the degree of power turned chiefly on the appointment to offices, and the controul on the Legislature. An absolute appointment to all offices—to some offices—to no offices, formed the scale of opinions on the first point. On the second, some contended for an absolute negative, as the only possible mean of reducing to practice, the theory of a free government which forbids a mixture of the Legislative and Executive powers. Others would be content with a revisionary power to be overruled by three fourths of both Houses. It was warmly urged that the judiciary department should be associated in the revision. The idea of some was that a separate revision should be given to the two departments—that if either objected two thirds; if both three fourths, should be necessary to overrule.

In forming the Senate, the great anchor of the Government, the questions as they came within the first object turned mostly on the mode of appointment, and the duration of it. The different modes proposed were, 1. by the House of Representatives, 2. by the Executive, 3 by electors chosen by the people for the purpose, 4. by the State Legislatures. On the point of duration, the propositions descended from good behavior to four years, through the intermediate terms of nine, seven, six and five years. The election of the other branch was first determined to be triennial, and afterwards reduced to biennial.

The second object, the due partition of power, between the General and local Governments, was perhaps of all, the most nice and difficult. A few contended for an entire abolition of the States; Some for indefinite power of Legislation in the Congress, with a negative on the laws of the States, some for such a power without a negative, some for a limited power of legislation, with such a negative: the majority finally for a limited power without the negative. The question with regard to the Negative underwent repeated discussions, and was finally rejected by a bare majority. As I formerly intimated to you my opinion in favor of this ingredient, I will take this occasion of explaining myself on the subject. Such a check on the States appears to me necessary 1. to prevent encroachments on the General authority, 2. to prevent instability and injustice in the legislation of the States.

1. Without such a check in the whole over the parts, our system involves the evil of imperia in imperio. If a compleat supremacy some where is not necessary in every Society, a controuling power at least is so, by which the general authority may be defended against encroachments of the subordinate authorities, and by which the latter may be restrained from encroachments on each other. If the supremacy of the British Parliament is not necessary as has been contended, for the harmony of that Empire, it is evident I think that without the royal negative or some equivalent controul, the unity of the system would be destroyed. The want of some such provision seems to have been mortal to the antient Confederacies, and to be the disease of the modern. Of the Lycian Confederacy little is known. That of the Amphyctions is well known to have been rendered of little use whilst it lasted, and in the end to have been destroyed by the predominance of the local over the federal authority. The same observation may be made, on the authority of Polybius, with regard to the Achman League. The Helvetic System scarcely amounts to a confederacy and is distinguished by too many peculiarities to be a ground of comparison. The case of the United Netherlands is in point. The authority of a Statholder,

the influence of a standing army, the common interest in the conquered possessions, the pressure of surrounding danger, the guarantee of foreign powers, are not sufficient to secure the authority and interests of the generality, against the antifederal tendency of the provincial sovereignties. The German Empire is another example. A Hereditary chief with vast independent resources of wealth and power, a federal Diet, with ample parchment authority, a regular Judiciary establishment, the influence of the neighbourhood of great and formidable Nations, have been found unable either to maintain the subordination of the members, or to prevent their mutual contests and encroachments. Still more to the purpose is our own experience both during the war and since the peace. Encroachments of the States on the general authority, sacrifices of national to local interests, interferences of the measures of different States, form a great part of the history of our political system. It may be said that the new Constitution is founded on different principles, and will have a different operation. I admit the difference to be material. It presents the aspect rather of a feudal system of republics, if such a phrase may be used, than of a Confederacy of independent States. And what has been the progress and event of the feudal Constitutions? In all of them a continual struggle between the head and the inferior members, until a final victory has been gained in some instances by one, in others, by the other of them. In one respect indeed there is a remarkable variance between the two cases. In the feudal system the sovereign, though limited, was independent; and having no particular sympathy of interests with the great Barons, his ambition had as full play as theirs in the mutual projects of usurpation. In the American Constitution The general authority will be derived entirely from the subordinate authorities. The Senate will represent the States in their political capacity, the other House will represent the people of the States in their individual capacity. The former will be accountable to their constituents at moderate, the latter at short periods. The President also derives his appointment from the States, and is periodically accountable to them. This dependence of the General, on the local authorities seems effectually to guard the latter against any dangerous encroachments of the former: Whilst the latter within their respective limits, will be continually sensible of the abridgment of their power, and be stimulated by ambition to resume the surrendered portion of it. We find the representatives of counties and corporations in the Legislatures of the States, much more disposed to sacrifice the aggregate interest, and even authority, to the local views of their Constituents, than the latter to the former. I mean not by these remarks to insinuate that an esprit de corps will not exist in the national Government, that opportunities may not occur of extending its jurisdiction in some points. I mean only that the danger of encroachments is much greater from the other side, and that the impossibility of dividing powers of legislation, in such a manner, as to be free from different constructions by different interests, or even from ambiguity in the judgment of the impartial, requires some such expedient as I contend for. Many illustrations might be given of this impossibility. How long has it taken to fix, and how imperfectly is yet fixed the legislative power of corporations, though that power is subordinate in the most compleat manner? The line of distinction between the power of regulating trade and that of drawing revenue from it, which was once considered as the barrier of our liberties, was found on fair discussion, to be absolutely undefinable. No distinction seems to be more obvious than that between spiritual and temporal matters. Yet wherever they have been made objects of Legislation, they have clashed and contended with each other, till one or the other has gained the supremacy. Even the boundaries between the Executive, Legislative and Judiciary powers, though in general so strongly marked in themselves, consist in many instances of mere shades of difference. It may be said that the Judicial authority under our new system will keep the States within their proper limits, and supply the place of a negative on their laws. The answer is that it is more convenient to prevent the passage of a law, than to declare it void after it is passed; that this will be particularly the case where the law aggrieves individuals, who may be unable to support an appeal against a State to the supreme Judiciary, that a State which would violate the Legislative rights of the Union, would not be very ready to obey a Judicial decree in support of them, and that a recurrence to force, which in the event of disobedience would be necessary, is an evil which the new Constitution meant to exclude as far as possible.

2. A Constitutional negative on the laws of the States seems equally necessary to secure individuals against encroachments on their rights. The mutability of the laws of the States is found to be a serious evil. The injustice of them has been so frequent and so flagrant as to alarm the most stedfast friends of Republicanism. I am persuaded I do not err in saying that the evils issuing from these sources

contributed more to that uneasiness which produced the Convention, and prepared the public mind for a general reform, than those which accrued to our national character and interest from the inadequacy of the Confederation to its immediate objects. A reform therefore which does not make provision for private rights, must be materially defective. The restraints against paper emissions, and violations of contracts are not sufficient. Supposing them to be effectual as far as they go, they are short of the mark. Injustice may be effected by such an infinitude of legislative expedients, that where the disposition exists it can only be controuled by some provision which reaches all cases whatsoever. The partial provision made, supposes the disposition which will evade it. It may be asked how private rights will be more secure under the Guardianship of the General Government than under the State Governments, since they are both founded on the republican principle which refers the ultimate decision to the will of the majority, and are distinguished rather by the extent within which they will operate, than by any material difference in their structure. A full discussion of this question would, if I mistake not, unfold the true principles of Republican Government, and prove in contradiction to the concurrent opinions of theoretical writers, that this form of Government, in order to effect its purposes must operate not within a small but an extensive sphere. I will state some of the ideas which have occurred to me on this subject. Those who contend for a simple Democracy, or a pure republic, actuated by the sense of the majority, and operating within narrow limits, assume or suppose a case which is altogether fictitious. They found their reasoning on the idea, that the people composing the Society enjoy not only an equality of political rights; but that they have all precisely the same interests and the same feelings in every respect. Were this in reality the case, their reasoning would be conclusive. The interest of the majority would be that of the minority also; the decisions could only turn on mere opinion concerning the good of the whole of which the major voice would be the safest criterion; and within a small sphere, this voice could be most easily collected and the public affairs most accurately managed. We know however that no Society ever did or can consist of so homogeneous a mass of Citizens. In the savage State indeed, an approach is made towards it; but in that state little or no Government is necessary. In all civilized Societies, distinctions are various and unavoidable. A distinction of property results from that very protection which a free Government gives to unequal faculties of acquiring it. There will be rich and poor; creditors and debtors; a landed interest, a monied interest, a mercantile interest, a manufacturing interest. These classes may again be subdivided according to the different productions of different situations and soils, and according to different branches of commerce and of manufactures. In addition to these natural distinctions, artificial ones will be founded on accidental differences in political, religious and other opinions, or an attachment to the persons of leading individuals. However erroneous or ridiculous these grounds of dissention and faction may appear to the enlightened Statesman, or the benevolent philosopher, the bulk of mankind who are neither Statesmen nor Philosophers, will continue to view them in a different light. It remains then to be enquired whether a majority having any common interest, or feeling any common passion, will find sufficient motives to restrain them from oppressing the minority. An individual is never allowed to be a judge or even a witness in his own cause. If two individuals are under the biass of interests or enmity against a third, the rights of the latter could never be safely referred to the majority of the three. Will two thousand individuals be less apt to oppress one thousand, or two hundred thousand, one hundred thousand? Three motives only can restrain in such cases. 1. A prudent regard to private or partial good, as essentially involved in the general and permanent good of the whole. This ought no doubt to be sufficient of itself. Experience however shews that it has little effect on individuals, and perhaps still less on a collection of individuals, and least of all on a majority with the public authority in their hands. If the former are ready to forget that honesty is the best policy; the last do more. They often proceed on the converse of the maxim: that whatever is politic is honest. 2. Respect for character. This motive is not found sufficient to restrain individuals from injustice, and loses its efficacy in proportion to the number which is to divide the praise or the blame. Besides as it has reference to public opinion, which is that of the majority, the standard is fixed by those whose conduct is to be measured by it. 3. Religion. The inefficacy of this restraint on individuals is well known. The conduct of every popular assembly, acting on oath, the strongest of religious ties, shews that individuals join without remorse in acts against which their consciences would revolt, if proposed to them separately in their closets. When Indeed Religion is kindled into enthusiasm, its force like that of other passions is increased by the sympathy of a multitude. But enthusiasm is only a temporary state of Religion, and whilst it lasts will hardly be seen with pleasure at the helm. Even in its coolest state, it has been much oftener a motive to oppression than a restraint from it. If then there must be different interests and parties in Society; and a majority when united by a common interest or passion can not be restrained from oppressing the minority, what remedy can be found in a republican Government, where the majority must ultimately decide, but that of giving such an extent to its sphere, that no common interest or passion will be likely to unite a majority of the whole number in an unjust pursuits. In a large Society, the people are broken into so many interests and parties, that a common sentiment is less likely to be felt, and the requisite concert less likely to be formed, by a majority of the whole. The same security seems requisite for the civil as for the religious rights of individuals. If the same sect form a majority and have the power, other sects will be sure to be depressed. Divide et impera, the reprobated axiom of tyranny, is under certain qualifications, the only policy, by which a republic can be administered on just principles. It must be observed however that this doctrine can only hold within a sphere of a mean extent. As in too small a sphere oppressive combinations may be too easily formed against the weaker party; so in too extensive a one a defensive concert may be rendered too difficult against the oppression of those entrusted with the administration. The great desideratum in Government is, so to modify the sovereignty as that it may be sufficiently neutral between different parts of the Society to controul one part from invading the rights of another, and at the same time sufficiently controuled itself, from setting up an interest adverse to that of the entire Society. In absolute monarchies, the Prince may be tolerably neutral towards different classes of his subjects, but may sacrifice the happiness of all to his personal ambition or avarice. In small republics, the sovereign will is controuled from such a sacrifice of the entire Society, but it is not sufficiently neutral towards the parts composing it. In the extended Republic of the United States, the General Government would hold a pretty even balance between the parties of particular States, and be at the same time sufficiently restrained by its dependence on the community, from betraying its general interests.

Begging pardon for this immoderate digression, I return to the third object abovementioned, the adjustment of the different interests of different parts of the Continent. Some contended for an unlimited power over trade including exports as well as imports, and over slaves as well as other imports; some for such a power, provided the concurrence of two thirds of both Houses were required; some for such a qualification of the power, with an exemption of exports and slaves, others for an exemption of exports only. The result is seen in the Constitution. S. Carolina and Georgia were inflexible on the point of the slaves.

The remaining object, created more embarrassment, and a greater alarm for the issue of the Convention than all the rest put together. The little States insisted on retaining their equality in both branches, unless a compleat abolition of the State Governments should take place; and made an equality in the Senate a sine qua non. The large States on the other hand urged that as the new Government was to be drawn principally from the people immediately and was to operate directly on them, not on the States; and consequently as the States would lose that importance which is now proportioned to the importance of their voluntary compliances with the requisitions of Congress, it was necessary that the representation in both Houses should be in proportion to their size. It ended in the compromise which you will see, but very much to the dissatisfaction of several members from the large States.

It will not escape you that three names only from Virginia are subscribed to the Act. Mr. Wythe did not return after the death of his lady. Docr. MClurg left the Convention some time before the adjournment. The Governour and Col. Mason refused to be parties to it. Mr. Gerry was the only other member who refused. The objections of the Govr. turn principally on the latitude of the general powers, and on the connection established between the President and the Senate. He wished that the plan should be proposed to the States with liberty to them to suggest alterations which should all be referred to another general Convention to be incorporated into the plan as far as might be judged expedient. He was not inveterate in his opposition, and grounded his refusal to subscribe pretty much on his unwillingness to commit himself so as not to be at liberty to be governed by further lights on the subject. Col. Mason left Philada. in an exceeding ill humour indeed. A number of little circumstances arising in part from the impatience which prevailed towards the close of the business, conspired to whet his acrimony. He returned to Virginia with a fixed disposition to prevent the adoption of the plan if possible. He considers the want of a Bill of Rights as a fatal objection. His other objections are to the substitution of the Senate in place of an Executive Council and to the powers vested in that body—to the powers of the Judiciary—to the vice President being made President of the Senate—to the smallness of the number of Representatives—to the restriction on the States with regard to ex post facto laws—and most of all probably to the power of regulating trade, by a majority only of each House. He has some other lesser objections. Being now under the necessity of justifying his refusal to sign, he will of course, muster every possible one. His conduct has given great umbrage to the County of Fairfax, and particularly to the Town of Alexandria. He is already instructed to promote in the Assembly the calling a Convention, and will probably be either not deputed to the Convention, or be tied up by express instructions. He did not object in general to the powers vested in the National Government, so much as to the modification. In some respects he admitted that some further powers could have improved the system. He acknowledged in particular that a negative on the State laws, and the appointment of the State Executives ought to be ingredients; but supposed that the public mind would not now bear them and that experience would hereafter produce these amendments.

The final reception which will be given by the people at large to this proposed System can not yet be decided. The Legislature of N. Hampshire was sitting when it reached that State and was well pleased with it. As far as the sense of the people there has been expressed, it is equally favorable. Boston is warm and almost unanimous in embracing it. The impression on the country is not yet known. No symptoms of disapprobation have appeared. The Legislature of that State is now sitting, through which the sense of the people at large will soon be promulged with tolerable certainty. The paper money faction in Rh. Island is hostile. The other party zealously attached to it. Its passage through Connecticut is likely to be very smooth and easy. There seems to be less agitation in this state than any where. The discussion of the subject seems confined to the newspapers. The principal characters are known to be friendly. The Governour's party which has hitherto been the popular and most numerous one, is supposed to be on the opposite side; but considerable reserve is practiced, of which he sets the example. N. Jersey takes the affirmative side of course. Meetings of the people are declaring their approbation, and instructing their representatives. Penna. will be divided. The City of Philada., the Republican party, the Quakers, and most of the Germans espouse the Constitution. Some of the Constitutional leaders, backed by the western Country will oppose. An unlucky ferment on the subject in their assembly just before its late adjournment has irritated both sides, particularly the opposition, and by redoubling the exertions of that party may render the event doubtful. The voice of Maryland I understand from pretty good authority, is, as far as it has been declared, strongly in favor of the Constitution. Mr. Chase is an enemy, but the Town of Baltimore which he now represents, is warmly attached to it, and will shackle him as far as they can. Mr. Paca will probably be, as usually, in the politics of Chase. My information from Virginia is as yet extremely imperfect. I have a letter from Genl. Washington which speaks favorably of the impression within a circle of some extent, and another from Chancellor Pendleton which expresses his full acceptance of the plan, and the popularity of it in his district. I am told also that Innis and Marshall are patrons of it. In the opposite scale are Mr. James Mercer, Mr. R. H. Lee, Docr. Lee and their connections of course, Mr. M. Page according to Report, and most of the Judges and Bar of the general Court. The part which Mr. Henry will take is unknown here. Much will depend on it. I had taken it for granted from a variety of circumstances that he would be in the opposition, and still think that will be the case. There are reports however which favor a contrary supposition. From the States South of Virginia nothing has been heard. As the deputation from S. Carolina consisted of some of its weightiest characters, who have returned unanimously zealous in favor of the Constitution, it is probable that State will readily embrace it. It is not less probable, that N. Carolina will follow the example unless that of Virginia should counterbalance it. Upon the whole, although, the public mind will not be fully known, nor finally settled for a considerable time, appearances at present augur a more prompt, and general adoption of the plan than could have been well expected.

When the plan came before Congress for their sanction, a very serious report was made by R. H. Lee and Mr. Dane from Masts. to embarrass it. It was first contended that Congress could not properly give any positive countenance to a measure which had for its object the subversion of the Constitution under which they acted. This ground of attack failing, the former gentleman urged the expediency of sending out the plan with amendments, and proposed a number of them corresponding with the objections of Col. Mason. This experiment had still less effect. In order however to obtain unanimity it was necessary to couch the resolution in very moderate terms.

Mr. Adams has received permission to return with thanks for his services. No provision is made for supplying his place, or keeping up any representation there. Your reappointment for three years will be notified from the office of F. Affairs. It was made without a negative, eight states being present. Connecticut however put in a blank ticket, the sense of that state having been declared against embassies. Massachusetts betrayed some scruple on like ground. Every personal consideration was avowed and I believe with sincerity to have militated against these scruples. It seems to be understood that letters to and from the foreign Ministers of the U.S. are not free of postage: but that the charge is to be allowed in their accounts.

The exchange of our French for Dutch Creditors has not been countenanced either by Congress or the Treasury Board. The paragraph in your last letter to Mr. Jay, on the subject of applying a loan in Holland to the discharge of the pay due to the foreign officers has been referred to the Board since my arrival here. No report has yet been made. But I have little idea that the proposition will be adopted. Such is the state and prospect of our fiscal department that any new loan however small that should now be made, would probably subject us to the reproach of premeditated deception. The balance of Mr. Adams' last loan will be wanted for the interest due in Holland, and with all the income here, will, it is feared, not save our credit in Europe from further wounds. It may well be doubted whether the present Government can be kept alive thro' the ensuing year, or untill the new one may take its place.

Upwards of 100,000 Acres of the surveyed lands of the U.S. have been disposed of in open market. Five million of unsurveyed have been sold by private contract to a N. England Company, at $2/3$ of a dollar per acre, payment to be made in the principal of the public securities. A negociation is nearly closed with a N. Jersey Company for two million more on like terms, and another commenced with a Company of this City for four million. Col. Carrington writes more fully on this subject.

You will receive herewith the desired information from Alderman Broome in the case of Mr. Burke. Also the Virga. Bill on crimes and punishments. Sundry alterations having been made in conformity to the sense of the House in its latter stages, it is less accurate and methodical than it ought to have been. To these papers I add a speech of Mr. C. P. on the Mississippi business. It is printed under precautions of secrecy, but surely could not have been properly exposed to so much risk of publication. You will find also among the pamplets and papers I send by Commodore Jones, another printed speech of the same

Gentleman. The Musaeum Magazine, and Philada. Gazettes, will give you a tolerable idea of the objects of present attention.

The summer crops in the Eastern and Middle States have been extremely plentiful. Southward of Virga. They differ in different places. On the whole I do not know that they are bad in that region. In Virginia the drought has been unprecedented, particularly between the falls of the Rivers and the Mountains. The Crops of Corn are in general alarmingly short. In Orange I find there will be scarcely subsistence for the inhabitants. I have not heard from Albemarle. The crops of Tobacco are every where said to be pretty good in point of quantity, and the quality unusually fine. The crops of wheat were also in general excellent in quality and tolerable in quantity.

Novr. 1. Commodore Jones having preferred another vessel to the packet, has remained here till this time. The interval has produced little necessary to be added to the above. The Legislature of Massts. has it seems taken up the Act of the Convention and have appointed or probably will appoint an early day for its State Convention. There are letters also from Georgia which denote a favorable disposition. I am informed from Richmond that the new Election-law from the Revised Code produced a pretty full House of Delegates, as well as a Senate, on the first day. It had previously had equal effect in producing full meetings of the freeholders for the County elections. A very decided majority of the Assembly is said to be zealous in favor of the New Constitution. The same is said of the Country at large. It appears however that individuals of great weight both within and without the Legislature are opposed to it. A letter I just have from Mr. A. Stuart names Mr. Henry, Genl. Nelson, W. Nelson, the family of Cabels, St. George Tucker, John Taylor and the Judges of the General Court except P. Carrington. The other opponents he described as of too little note to be mentioned, which gives a negative information of the Characters on the other side. All are agreed that the plan must be submitted to a Convention.

We hear from Georgia that that State is threatened with a dangerous war with the Creek Indians. The alarm is of so serious a nature, that law-martial has been proclaimed, and they are proceeding to fortify even the Town of Savannah. The idea there is that the Indians derive their motives as well as their means from their Spanish neighbours. Individuals complain also that their fugitive slaves are encouraged by East Florida. The policy of this is explained by supposing that it is considered as a discouragement to the Georgians to form settlements near the Spanish boundaries.

There are but few States on the spot here which will survive the expiration of the federal year; and it is extremely uncertain when a Congress will again be formed. We have not yet heard who are to be in the appointment of Virginia for the next year.

With the most affectionate attachment I remain Dear Sr. Your obed friend & servant,

—JS. MADISON JR.

To John Adams
DEAR SIR   Paris Nov. 13. 1787

... How do you like our new constitution? I confess there are things in it which stagger all my dispositions to subscribe to what such an assembly has proposed. The house of federal representatives will not be adequate to the management of affairs either foreign or federal. Their President seems a bad edition of a Polish king. He may be reelected from 4. years to 4. years for life. Reason and experience prove to us that a chief magistrate, so continuable, is an officer for life. When one or two generations shall have proved that this is an office for life, it becomes on every succession worthy of intrigue, of bribery, of force, and even of foreign interference. It will be of great consequence to France and England to have America governed by a Galloman or Angloman. Once in office, and possessing the military force of the union, without either the aid or check of a council, he would not be easily dethroned, even if the people could be induced to withdraw their votes from him. I wish that at the end of the 4. years they had made him for ever ineligible a second time. Indeed I think all the good of this new constitution might have been couched in three or four new articles to be added to the good, old, and venerable fabrick, which should have been preserved even as a religious relique.—Present me and my daughters affection- ately to Mrs. Adams. The younger one continues to speak of her warmly. Accept yourself assurances of the sincere esteem and respect with which I have the honour to be, Dear Sir, your friend & servant,

—TH: JEFFERSON

∽

[The following letter contains Jefferson's notorious approval of Shays's Rebellion, with the accompanying statement, often quoted, about the tree of liberty's being watered from time to time by the blood of martyrs.]

To William Stephens Smith

DEAR SIR   Paris Nov. 13. 1787

I am now to acknolege the receipt of your favors of October the 4th. 8th. and 26th. In the last you apologize for your letters of introduction to Americans coming here. It is so far from needing apology on your part, that it calls for thanks on mine. I endeavor to shew civilities to all the Americans who come here, and who will give me opportunities of doing it: and it is a matter of comfort to know from a good quarter what they are, and how far I may go in my attentions to them.—Can you send me Woodmason's bills for the two copying presses for the M. de la fayette, and the M. de Chastellux? The latter makes one article in a considerable account, of old standing, and which I cannot present for want of this article.—I do not know whether it is to yourself or Mr. Adams I am to give my thanks for the copy of the new constitution. I beg leave through you to place them where due. It will be yet three weeks before I shall receive them from America. There are very good articles in it: and very bad. I do not know which preponderate. What we have lately read in the history of Holland, in the chapter on the Stadtholder, would have sufficed to set me against a Chief magistrate eligible for a long duration, if I had ever been disposed towards one: and what we have always read of the elections of Polish kings should have forever excluded the idea of one continuable for life. Wonderful is the effect of impudent and persevering lying. The British ministry have so long hired their gazetteers to repeat and model into every form lies about our being in anarchy, that the world has at length believed them, the English nation has believed them, the ministers themselves have come to believe them, and what is more wonderful, we have believed them ourselves. Yet where does this anarchy exist? Where did it ever exist, except in the single instance of Massachusets? And can history produce an instance of a rebellion so honourably conducted? I say nothing of it's motives. They were founded in ignorance, not wickedness. God forbid we should ever be 20. years without such a rebellion. The people can not be all, and always, well informed. The part which is wrong will be discontented in proportion to the importance of the facts they misconceive. If they remain quiet under such misconceptions it is a lethargy, the forerunner of death to the public liberty. We have had 13. states independant 11. years. There has been one rebellion. That comes to one rebellion in a century and a half for each state. What country before ever existed a century and half without a rebellion? And what country can preserve it's liberties if their rulers are not warned from time to time that their people preserve the spirit of resistance? Let them take arms. The remedy is to set them right as to facts, pardon and pacify them. What signify a few lives lost in a century or two? The tree of liberty must be refreshed from time to time with the blood of patriots and tyrants. It is it's natural manure. Our Convention has been too much impressed by the insurrection of Massachusets: and in the spur of the moment they are setting up a kite to keep the hen yard in order. I hope in god this article will be rectified before the new constitution is accepted.—You ask me if any thing transpires here on the subject of S. America? Not a word. I know that there are combustible materials there, and that they wait the torch only. But this country probably will join the extinguishers.—The want of facts worth communicating to you has occasioned me to give a little loose to dissertation. We must be contented to amuse, when we cannot inform. Present my respects to Mrs. Smith, and be assured of the sincere esteem of Dear Sir Your friend & servant,

—TH: JEFFERSON

෴

From John Adams
DEAR SIR   London Decr. 6. 1787

The Project of a new Constitution, has Objections against it, to which I find it difficult to reconcile my self, but I am so unfortunate as to differ somewhat from you in the Articles, according to your last kind Letter.

You are afraid of the one—I, of the few. We agree perfectly that the many should have a full fair and perfect Representation.—You are Apprehensive of Monarchy; I, of Aristocracy. I would therefore have given more Power to the President and less to the Senate. The Nomination and Appointment to all offices I would have given to the President, assisted only by a Privy Council of his own Creation, but not a Vote or Voice would I have given to the Senate or any Senator, unless he were of the Privy Council. Faction and Distraction are the sure and certain Consequence of giving to a Senate a vote in the distribution of offices.

You are apprehensive the President when once chosen, will be chosen again and again as long as he lives. So much the better as it appears to me. —You are apprehensive of foreign Interference, Intrigue, Influence. So am I. —But, as often as Elections happen, the danger of foreign Influence recurs. The less frequently they happen the less danger.—And if the Same Man may be chosen again, it is probable he will be, and the danger of foreign Influence will be less. Foreigners, seeing little Prospect will have less Courage for Enterprize.

Elections, my dear sir, Elections to offices which are great objects of Ambition, I look at with terror. Experiments of this kind have been so often tryed, and so universally found productive of Horrors, that there is great Reason to dread them.

Mr. Littlepage who will have the Honour to deliver this will tell you all the News. I am, my dear Sir, with great Regard,

—JOHN ADAMS

ɔ∫ɔ

[The following letter to William Carmichael, American chargé d' affaires in Madrid, discussed other matters, but only passages pertaining to the Constitution are included here.]

To William Carmichael
DEAR SIR   Paris Dec. 15. 1787

Our new constitution is powerfully attacked in the American newspapers. The objections are that it's effect would be to form the 13. states into one: that proposing to melt all down into one general government they have fenced the people by no declaration of rights, they have not renounced the power of keeping a standing army, they have not secured the liberty of the press, they have reserved a power of abolishing trials by jury in civil cases, they have proposed that the laws of the federal legislature shall be paramount the laws and constitutions of the states, they have abandoned rotation in office: and particularly their president may be re-elected from 4. years to 4. years for life, so as to render him a king for life, like a king of Poland, and have not given him either the check or aid of a council. To these they add calculations of expence &c. &c. to frighten the people. You will perceive that these objections are serious, and some of them not without foundation. The constitution however has been received with a very general enthusiasm, and as far as can be judged from external demonstrations the bulk of the people are eager to adopt it. In the Eastern states the printers will print nothing against it unless the writer subscribes his name. Massachusets and Connecticut have called conventions in January to consider of it. In New York there is a division. The Governor (Clinton) is known to be hostile to it. Jersey it is thought will certainly accept it. Pennsylvania is divided, and all the bitterness of her factions has been kindled anew on it. But the party in favor of it is strongest both in and out of the legislature. This is the party antiently of Morris, Wilson &c. Delaware will do what Pennsylvania shall do. Maryland is thought favourable to it: yet it is supposed Chase and Paca will oppose it. As to Virginia two of her delegates in the first place refused to sign it. These were Randolph the governor, and George Mason. Besides these Henry, Harrison, Nelson, and the Lees are against it. Genl. Washington will be for it, but it is not in his character to exert himself much in the case. Madison will be it's main pillar: but tho an immensly powerful one, it is questionable whether he can bear the weight of such a host. So that the presumption is that Virginia will reject it. We know nothing of the disposition of the states South of this. Should it fall thro', as is possible notwithstanding the enthusiasm with which it was received in the first moment, it is probable that Congress will propose that the objections which the people shall make to it being once known, another Convention shall be assembled to adopt the improvements generally accept-able, and omit those found disagreeable. In this way union may be produced under a happy constitution, and one which shall not be too energetic, as are the constitutions of Europe. I give you these details, because possibly you may not have received them all. The sale of our Western lands is immensly succesful. 5. millions of acres had been sold at private sale for a dollar an acre in certificates, and at the public sales some of them had sold as high as 2 4/10 dollars the acre. The sale had not been begun two months by these means, taxes &c. our domestic debt, originally 28. millions of dollars. was reduced by the 1st. day of last October to 12. millions and they were then in treaty for 2. millions of acres more at a dollar private sale. Our domestic debt will thus be soon paid off, and that done, the sales will go on for money, at a cheaper rate no doubt, for the paiment of our foreign debt. The petite guerre always waged by the Indians seems not to abate the ardor of purchase or emigration. Kentucky is now counted at 60,000. Frankland [*i.e., Tennessee*] is also growing fast.

—TH: JEFFERSON

ॐ

To James Madison

DEAR SIR   Paris Dec. 20. 1787

... The season admitting only of operations in the Cabinet, and these being in a great measure secret, I have little to fill a letter. I will therefore make up the deficiency by adding a few words on the Constitution proposed by our Convention. I like much the general idea of framing a government which should go on of itself peaceably, without needing continual recurrence to the state legislatures. I like the organization of the government into Legislative, Judiciary and Executive. I like the power given the Legislature to levy taxes; and for that reason solely approve of the greater house being chosen by the people directly. For tho' I think a house chosen by them will be very illy qualified to legislate for the Union, for foreign nations &c. yet this evil does not weigh against the good of preserving inviolate the fundamental principle that the people are not to be taxed but by representatives chosen immediately by themselves. I am captivated by the compromise of the opposite claims of the great and little states, of the latter to equal, and the former to proportional influence. I am much pleased too with the substitution of the method of voting by persons, instead of that of voting by states: and I like the negative given to the Executive with a third of either house, though I should have liked it better had the Judiciary been associated for that purpose, or invested with a similar and separate power. There are other good things of less moment. I will now add what

I do not like. First the omission of a bill of rights providing clearly and without the aid of sophisms for freedom of religion, freedom of the press, protection against standing armies, restriction against monopolies, the eternal and unremitting force of the habeas corpus laws, and trials by jury in all matters of fact triable by the laws of the land and not by the law of Nations. To say, as Mr. Wilson does that a bill of rights was not necessary because all is reserved in the case of the general government which is not given, while in the particular ones all is given which is not reserved might do for the Audience to whom it was addressed, but is surely gratis dictum, opposed by strong inferences from the body of the instrument, as well as from the omission of the clause of our present confederation which had declared that in express terms. It was a hard conclusion to say because there has been no uniformity among the states as to the cases triable by jury, because some have been so incautious as to abandon this mode of trial, therefore the more prudent states shall be reduced to the same level of calamity. It would have been much more just and wise to have concluded the other way that as most of the states had judiciously preserved this palladium, those who had wandered should be brought back to it, and to have established general right instead of general wrong. Let me add that a bill of rights is what the people are entitled to against every government on earth, general or particular, and what no just government should refuse, or rest on inference. The second feature I dislike, and greatly dislike, is the abandonment in every instance of the necessity of rotation in office, and most particularly in the case of the President. Experience concurs with reason in concluding that the first magistrate will always be re-elected if the constitution permits it. He is then an officer for life. This once observed it becomes of so much consequence to certain nations to have a friend or a foe at the head of our affairs that they will interfere with money and with arms. A Galloman or an Angloman will be supported by the nation he befriends. If once elected, and at a second or third election outvoted by one or two votes, he will pretend false votes, foul play, hold possession of the reins of government, be supported by the states voting for him, especially if they are the central ones lying in a compact body themselves and separating their opponents: and they will be aided by one nation of Europe, while the majority are aided by another. The election of a President of America some years hence will be much more interesting to certain nations of Europe than ever the election of a king of Poland was. Reflect on all the instances in history antient and modern, of elective monarchies, and say if they do not give foundation for my fears, the Roman emperors, the popes, while they were of any importance, the German emperors till they became hereditary in practice, the kings of Poland, the Deys of the Ottoman dependancies. It may be said that if elections are to be attended with these disorders, the seldomer they are renewed the better. But experience shews that the only way to prevent disorder is to render them uninteresting by frequent changes. An incapacity to be elected a second time would have been the only effectual preventative. The power of removing him every fourth year by the vote of the people is a power which will not be exercised. The king of Poland is removeable every day by the Diet, yet he is never removed.—Smaller objections are the Appeal in fact as well as law, and the binding all persons Legislative, Executive and Judiciary by oath to maintain that constitution. I do not pretend to decide what would be the best method of procuring the establishment of the manifold good things in this constitution, and of getting rid of the bad. Whether by adopting it in hopes of future amendment, or, after it has been duly weighed and canvassed by the people, after seeing the parts they generally dislike, and those they generally approve, to say to them 'We see now what you wish. Send together your deputies again, let them frame a constitution for you omitting what you have condemned, and establishing the powers you approve. Even these will be a great addition to the energy of your government.'—At all events I hope you will not be discouraged from other trials, if the present one should fail of it's full effect.—I have thus told you freely what I like and dislike: merely as a matter of curiosity for I know your own judgment has been formed on all these points after having heard every thing which could be urged on them. I own I am not a friend to a very energetic government. It is always oppressive. The late rebellion in Massachusets has given more alarm than I think it should have done. Calculate that one rebellion in 13 states in the course of 11 years, is but one for each state in a century and a half. No country should be so long without one. Nor will any degree of power in the hands of government prevent insurrections. France with all it's despotism, and two or three hundred thousand men always in arms has had three insurrections in the three years I have been here in every one of which greater numbers were engaged than in Massachusets and a great deal more blood was spilt. In Turkey, which Montesquieu supposes more despotic, insurrections are the events of every day. In England, where the hand of power is lighter than here, but heavier than with us they happen every half dozen years. Compare again the ferocious depredations of their insurgents with the order, the moderation and the almost self extinguishment of ours.—After all, it is my principle that the will of the Majority should always prevail. If they approve the proposed Convention in all it's parts, I shall concur in it chearfully, in hopes that they will amend it whenever they shall find it work wrong. I think our governments will remain virtuous for many centuries; as long as they are chiefly agricultural; and this will be as long as there shall be vacant lands in any part of America. When they get piled upon one another in large cities, as in Europe, they will become corrupt as in Europe. Above all things I hope the education of the common people will be attended to; convinced that on their good sense we may rely with the most security for the preservation of a due degree of liberty. I have tired you by this time with my disquisitions and will therefore only add assurances of the sincerity of those sentiments of esteem and attachment with which I am Dear Sir your affectionate friend & servant,

—TH: JEFFERSON

P.S. The instability of our laws is really an immense evil. I think it would be well to provide in our constitutions that there shall always be a twelvemonth between the ingrossing a bill and passing it: that it should then be offered to it's passage without changing a word: and that if circumstances should be thought to require a speedier passage, it should take two thirds of both houses instead of a bare majority.

৩৯৯

From Francis Hopkinson
DEAR SIR   Philada. April 6th. 1788

It is a very long Time indeed since I have had the Satisfaction of a Line from you. Mr. Rittenhouse had a Letter last Fall in which you mention some Books to have been forwarded for him in a Package address'd either to me or Dr. Franklin, but those Books have not come to hand. I have another Gathering of Magazines, Museums, and News Papers for you, waiting a suitable oppor- tunity.—We are in a high political Fermentation about our new proposed federal Constitution. There are in every State People who have Debts to pay, Interests to support, or Fortunes to make. These wish for scrambling Times, paper Money Speculations or partial Commercial advantages. An effective general Government will not suit their Views, and of Course there are great oppositions made to the new Constitution, but this opposition chiefly arises from a few leading Party Men in the Towns and Cities who have been very industrious in holding it up as a political Monster to the multitude who know nothing of Government and have gained many Proselytes in the back Counties.—The Lees and Mr. Mason have so exerted themselves in Virginia as to make the Determination of that State doubtful. Maryland is infected with a Mr. Martin, but I am told the Constitution will be adopted there. We shall know in a few Weeks. The Convention met in New Hampshire and adjourned to sometime in June. The City of New York is federal, but the Country much opposed, under the Influence of Govr. Clinton. Altho' Pennsylvania has long since adopted the proposed System, yet in no State have the People behaved so scandalously as here. George Bryan and his Party (formerly called the Constitutional Party) have been moving Heaven and Earth against the Establishment of a federal Government. Our Papers teem with the most opprobrious Recitings against the System and against all who befriend it. These Scriblers begin with Arguments against the proposed Plan such Arguments as would stand with equal Force against every or any Government that can be devised. They were Arguments against Government in general as an Infringement upon natural Liberty. They then poured forth a torrent of abuse against the Members of the late general Convention personally and individually. You will be surprized when I tell you that our public News Papers have announced General Washington to be a Fool influenced and lead by that Knave Dr. Franklin who is a public Defaulter for Millions of Dollars, that Mr. Morris has defrauded the Public out of many Millions as you please and that they are to cover their frauds by this new Government. What think you of this. Some of the Authors of these inflamatory Publications have been traced, and found to be men of desperate Circumstances. I had the Luck to discover and bring forward into public View on sufficient Testimony the Writer of a Series of abominable abuse, under the Signature Philadelphiensis. He is an Irishman who came from Dublin about 3 Years ago and got admitted as a Tutor in Arithmetic in our University. I am now under the Lash for this Discovery, scarce a Day passes without my Appearance in the News Paper in every scandalous Garb that scribling Vengeance can furnish. I wrote also a Piece stiled The new Roof which had a great Run. I would send you a Copy but for the Postage. You will probably see it in some of the Papers as it was reprinted in I believe every state.

I am sorry to tell you that our friend Mr. Rittenhouse is anti-federal. However we never touch upon Politics. Dr. Franklin is as well as usual.

My Mother desires her Love to your Daughter, to which add my affectionate Regards.

I have long had it in Contemplation to establish a Wax Chandlery here and if I can get some Gentleman to join me in the Scheme, as I believe I shall, I will make the Trial. My Circumstances require some Exertion. I know of nothing so promising. Let me have your Opinion. If I determine upon it I shall request you to send over a Master Workman to superintend the Factory. Be so good as to enquire and inform me, what Capital would be requisite for such a Project, in the large Way. I shall depend much on your Encouragement. Yours ever,

—F. HOPKINSON

CHAPTER SEVEN

A Little Tour in Holland and Germany

U NLIKE HIS TRIP THROUGH THE SOUTH OF FRANCE, JEFFERSON'S EXCURSION into Holland and Germany in the spring of 1788 was unplanned. It grew, more or less on the spot, out of his hurried trip to The Hague to intercept John Adams and try to put the American foreign debt into order before Adams left for America. In addition to his position as the United States minister to the Court of St. James, Adams had also been formally posted to Holland as U.S. minister there, and he was crossing the Channel to make his formal good-byes. For Jefferson, the situation represented a crisis. Adams had handled money matters with the Dutch bankers who financed most of the debt of the United States, negotiating loans with them, something which Jefferson freely admitted was not in his line. Years later in his Autobiography he wrote that "I had no powers, no instructions, no means, and no familiarity with the subject." This was a man, after all, who could barely manage his own debts.

And the situation was getting worse. The Confederation Congress, a lame duck institution in any case after the drafting of the new Constitution, had run out of money. No additional money was to be expected until the new federal government met, which was a year away, and the Paris banker who managed the funds on which Jefferson drew to pay his own expenses was refusing any further advances. The French government had not only never been paid a cent of principal on their own advances to the United States during the Revolution, but also now Congress had no money even to pay the interest on this debt. That interest was due in June. It was now March. The Dutch bankers let it be known that if the United States forfeited on this payment, Europe would regard the country as bankrupt. No European banker thereafter would have any inclination to lend the United States money. Its credit would be destroyed. Jefferson could not let this happen.

It was, happily, not that hard to renegotiate the American loans with the bankers. Adams and Jefferson met at The Hague and made their way to Amsterdam, where they were able to borrow enough money to stabilize the foreign debt of the United States and provide for interest payments on it through 1790, which would be after the new government had taken power and could finally raise money through taxes. The bankers, it's worth noting, were almost all members of the Patriot party in Holland—antiroyalists, in other words—and were sympathetic to the United States. The prospect of a new, much more powerful and stabler United States government raised the country's credit rating even as the Constitution was in the process of achieving ratification. It took several weeks to work out the details, during which Adams returned to London—he would leave London to take ship for Boston on March 30—while Jefferson cooled his heels in Amsterdam, shopped, visited the local sights, and decided to return to Paris the long way round.

That proved to be through Holland to Germany and up the Rhine to Strasbourg, thence west to Paris. He took the post roads, changing horses for his cabriolet at the postes along the way. Except for Espagnol, a French servant, he was alone. It is the closest to a trip for pure pleasure that Jefferson ever took. The route may have been suggested to him by his friend John Trumbull, the young artist who had introduced him to Maria Cosway and had made this journey himself two years before, but in the opposite direction.

Trumbull's account of his trip is full of the minor adventures of European travel at the time, along with numerous comments on the artwork he saw. Jefferson confines most of his comments, once again, to agricultural matters. He inquires into the cultivation of vinifera grapes, he checks out soils, and he describes how bridges work, counting the number of small boats the bridges rest on, how long they are, and how they work to let river traffic move past them. It was during this trip that he began to think seriously about plows and the shapes of moldboards; eventually he designed his own plow and achieved renown for its inventiveness. He notes the prices of everything and compares them with prices elsewhere. He is a great measurer of things. When he finds a new kind of bedstead in an inn, he draws a diagram of it and measures it. He must have had a ruler or some kind of tape measure with him wherever he went.

Jefferson left Amsterdam at the end of March and was back in Paris by April 23. In Frankfurt he met up with Baron Geismar, an old friend who had fought with the

British during the Revolution. At Saratoga, Geismar had been taken prisoner along with the Hessian troops under him and housed in the area of Monticello to wait out the end of the war. Jefferson had treated him as a guest, and the two had become close friends. Geismar was one of the very few people close enough to Jefferson to call him "mon cher." They spent three or four days together seeing the sights around Frankfurt, particularly the vineyards.

Jefferson also went to see some of the same art that Trumbull had seen, although his comments on it are sparse. In the paintings gallery belonging to the Elector of Dusseldorf, he reserved his greatest enthusiasm for the works of Adrian van der Werff, a minor figure from the late 17th century. That gallery was then full of van Dycks, Gerard Dous, a Raphael (now attributed to someone else), an Annibale Caracci, two Rembrandts, and one of the finest collections in existence of the paintings of Rubens. Jefferson dismissed the Rubens and never mentioned the others. Trumbull says about the van der Werffs in this gallery, "of all the celebrated pictures I have ever seen, [these] appear to me to be the very worst." Jefferson liked them for their subject matter. He mentioned them in a letter to Maria Cosway when he got back to Paris. Jefferson had said elsewhere that, while architecture was a useful subject for an American to study, paintings were not. The country was too young, he thought, too little developed, for someone to pursue arts like painting and poetry. It was another of his many contradictions. During the six weeks he spent with Maria Cosway in Paris, they had visited paintings galleries almost every day. He had written one of his friends about staring at a painting, totally enthralled, for half an hour.

Two weeks after his return, Jefferson wrote his "Hints on European Travel," a little guidebook of sorts that expands on his own trip and offers suggestions for Americans on how to navigate European roads, avoid the worst inns, hire guides, and travel through Europe without getting cheated, while at the same time gathering as much useful information as possible along the way. He sent it to John Rutledge, Jr., yet another young American he had befriended on his grand tour, who had just left Paris with Thomas Lee Shippen, the same Shippen he had introduced to the court at Versailles on their way to Italy.

It's a delightful text, included here, along with the notes of his trip and a few letters pertaining to it and to the American debt. He was already thinking of leaving France. His work there was mostly done. He had become comfortable in Paris, he had a great many friends, he liked the people and the life, but he was now mostly just an observer of Paris life. But what a time to be an observer in Paris! The French Revolution was about to break out.

To John Adams

DEAR SIR   Paris Mar. 2. 1788. Sunday

I received this day a letter from Mrs. Adams of the 26th. ult. informing me you would set out on the 29th. for the Hague. Our affairs at Amsterdam press on my mind like a mountain. I have no information to go on but that of the Willincks and Van Staphorsts, and according to that something seems necessary to be done. I am so anxious to confer with you on this, and to see you and them together, and get some effectual arrangement made in time that I determined to meet you at the Hague. I will set out the moment some repairs are made to my carriage. It is promised me at 3. oclock tomorrow; but probably they will make it night, and that I may not set out till Tuesday morning. In that case I shall be at the Hague Friday night. In the mean time you will perhaps have made all your bows there. I am sensible how irksome this must be to you in the moment of your departure, but it is a great interest of the U.S. which is at stake and I am sure you will sacrifice to that your feelings and your interest. I hope to shake you by the hand within 24. hours after you receive this, and in the mean time am with much esteem & respect Dear Sir Your affectionate friend & humble servt,

—TH: JEFFERSON

෴

To John Jay, with Enclosures

SIR   Amsterdam March 16. 1788

In a letter of the 13th. inst. which I had the honor of addressing you from this place, I mentioned in general terms the object of my journey hither and that I should enter into more particular details by the confidential conveiance which would occur thro' Mr. Adams and Colo. Smith.

The board of Treasury had, in the month of December, given notice to our bankers here that it would be impossible for them to make any remittances to Europe for the then ensuing year, and that they must therefore rely altogether on the progress of the late loan. But this, in the mean time, after being about one third filled, had ceased to get forward. The bankers, who had been referred to me for advice by Mr. Adams, stated these circumstances, and pressed their apprehensions for the ensuing month of June, when 270,000 florins would be wanting for interest. In fine, they urged an offer of the holders of the former bonds to take all those now remaining on hand, provided they might retain out of them the interest on a part of our domestic debt, of which they had also become the holders. This would have been 180,000 florins. To this proposition I could not presume any authority to listen. Thus pressed between the danger of failure on one hand, and an impossible proposition on the other, I heard of Mr. Adams's being gone to the Hague to take leave. His knoledge of the subject was too intimate to be neglected under the present difficulty, and it was the last moment in which we could be availed of it. I set out therefore immediately for the Hague, and we came on to this place together, in order to see what could be done. It was easier to discover, than to remove the causes which obstructed the progress of the loan. Our affairs here, like those of other nations, are in the hands of particular bankers. These employ particular brokers; and they have their particular circle of money lenders. These money lenders, as I have before mentioned, while placing a part of their money in our foreign loans, had at the same time employed another part in a joint speculation to the amount of 840,000 dollars of our domestic debt. A year's interest was becoming due on this, and they wished to avail themselves of our want of money for the foreign interest, to obtain paiment of the domestic. Our first object was to convince our bankers that there was no power on this side the Atlantic which could accede to this proposition, or give it any countenance. They at length therefore, but with difficulty receded from this ground, and agreed to enter into conferences with the brokers and lenders, and to use every exertion to clear the loan from the embarrasment in which this speculation had engaged it. What will be the result of these conferences is not yet known. We have hopes however that it is not desperate, because the bankers consented yesterday to pay off, and did actually pay off the capital of 51,000 florins which had become due to the house of Fizeaux and company on the first day of January, and which had not yet been paid.

We have gone still further. The Treasury board gives no hope of remittances till the new government can procure them. For that government to be adopted, it's legislature assembled, it's system of taxation and collection arranged, the money gathered from the people into their treasury, and then remitted to

Europe, must enter us considerably into the year 1790. To secure our credit then for the present year only, is but to put off the evil day to the next. What remains of the last, even when it shall be filled up, will little more than clear us of present demands, as may be seen by the estimate inclosed. We thought it better therefore to provide at once for the years 1789. and 1790. also; and thus to place the government at it's ease and our credit in security during that trying interval. The same estimate will shew that another million of florins will be necessary to effect this. We stated this to our bankers, who concurred in our views, and that to ask the whole sum at once would be better than to make demands from time to time so small as that they betray to the money holders the extreme feebleness of our own resources. Mr. Adams therefore has executed bonds for another million of florins: which however are to remain unissued till Congress shall have ratified the measure; so that this transaction is something or nothing at their pleasure. We suppose it's expediency so apparent as to leave little doubt of it's ratification. In this case much time will have been saved by the execution of the bonds at this moment, and the proposition will be presented here under a more favorable appearance according to the opinion of the bankers. Mr. Adams is under a necessity of setting out tomorrow morning: but I shall stay two or three days longer, to attend to, and to encourage the efforts of the bankers to judge and to inform you whether they will ensure us a safe passage over the month of June .... [The rest of the letter concerns the possibility of war breaking out in Europe.]

—TH: JEFFERSON

❧

Notes of a Tour through Holland and the Rhine Valley

MEMORANDUMS ON A TOUR FROM PARIS TO AMSTERDAM, STRASBURG AND BACK TO PARIS. 1788. MARCH. 3.

AMSTERDAM. Joists of houses placed, not with their sides horizontally and perpendicular[ly] but diamond-wise thus ◊ first for greater strength, 2. to arch between with brick thus [illustration omitted]. Windows opening so that they admit air, and not rain. The upper sash opens on [a hori]zontal axis, or pins in the center of the sides thus [illustration omitted]. The lower sash slides up.

Manner of fixing a flag staff, or the mast of a vessel [illustration omitted]. a. is the bolt on which it turns. b. a bolt which is taken in and out to fasten it or to let it down. When taken out, the lower end of the staff is shoved out of it's case, and the upper end being heaviest brings itself down. A rope must have been previously fastened to the butt end, to pull it down again when you want to raise the flag end.

Peat costs about 1. doit each, or 12$^{1}/_{2}$ stivers the 100. 100. makes 7. cubic feet, and to keep a tolerably comfortable fire for a study or chamber takes about 6. every hour and a half.

A machine for drawing light empty boats over a dam at Amsterdam. It is an Axis in peritrochio [i.e., a capstan] fixed on the dam. From the dam each way is a sloping stage. The boat is presented to this, the rope of the axis made fast to it, and it is drawn up. The water [on one] side of the dam is about 4.f. higher than on the other.

The Camels used for lightering ships over the Pampus will raise the ship 8. fe[et.] [A camel was a kind of pontoon.] There are beams passing through the ship's sides, projecting to the off side of the Came[l] and resting on it. Of course that alone would keep the Camel close to the ship. Besides this there are a great number of windlasses on the Camels, the ropes of which are made fast to the gunwale of the ship. The Camel is shaped to the ship on the near side, and straight on the off one. When placed alongside, water is let into it, so as nearly to sink it. In this state it receives the beams &c. of the ship: and then the water is pumped out.

Wind saw mills. See the plans detailed in the Moolen book which I bought. A circular foundation of brick is raised about 3. or 4. feet high, and covered with a curb or [sill] of wood, and has little rollers under it's sill which make it turn easily on the cu[rb. A] hanging bridge projects at each end about 15. or 20. feet beyond the circular area thus horizontally, and thus [illustrations omitted] in the profile to increase the play of the timbers on the frame. The wings are at one side, as at a. There is a shelter over the hanging bridges, [b]ut of plank, with scarce any frame, very light.

A bridge across a canal formed by two scows which open each to the opposite shore, and let boats pass.

A lanthern over the street door which gives light equally into the antichamber and the street. It is a hexagon, and occupies the place of the middle pane of [gla]ss in the circular top of the street door.

[A] bridge on a canal, turning on a swivel, by which means it is arranged along the [side] of the canal, so as not to be in the way of boats when not in use. When used it is turned across the canal. It is of course a little more than double the width of the canal.

Hedges of beach, which not losing the old leaf till the new bud pushes it off, has the effect of an evergreen, as to cover.

Mr. Ameshoff merchant at Amsterdam. The distribution of his aviary worthy notice. Each kind of the large birds has it's coop 8.f. wide and 4.f. deep. The middle of the front is occupied by a broad glass window, on one side of which is a door for the keeper to enter at, and on the other a little trap door for the birds to pass in and out. The floor strowed with clean hay. Before each coop is a court of 8. by 16.f. with wire in front, and netting above if the fowls be able to fly. For such as require it there are bushes of evergreen growing in their court for them to lay their eggs under. The coops are frequently divided into two stories, the upper for those birds which perch, such as pigeons &c. the lower for those which feed on the ground, as pheasants, partridges &c. The court is in common for both stories, because the birds do no injury to each other. For the waterfowl there is a pond of water passing thro' the courts, with a moveable separation. While they are breeding they must be separate. Afterwards they may come together. The small birds [are some] of them in a common aviary, and some in cages.

Mr. Hermen Hend Damen, merchant-broker of Amsterdam tells me that the emigrants to America come from the Palatinate down the Rhine and take shipping from Amsterdam. Their passage is 10. guineas if paid here, and 11. if paid in America. He says they might be had in any number to go to America and settle lands as tenants on half stocks or metairies. Perhaps they would serve their employer one year as an indemnification for the passage, and then be bound to remain on his lands 7. years. They would come to Amsterdam at their own expence. He thinks they would employ more than 50. acres each. But qu[?}especially if they have 50. acres for their wife also?

Hodson the best house. Stadhouderian. His son in the government. Friendly, but old and very infirm.

Hope. The first house in Amsterdam. His first object England: but it is supposed he would like to have the American business also. Yet he would probably make our affairs subordinate to those of England.

Vollenhoven. An excellent old house, connected with no party.

Sapportus. A broker. Very honest and ingenuous. Well disposed. Acts for Hope; but will say with truth what he can do for us. The best person to consult with as to the best house to undertake a piece of business. He has brothers in London in business.

Jacob Van Staphorst tells me there are about 14. millions of florins, new money, placed in loans in Holland every year, being the savings of individuals out of their annual revenue &c. Besides this there are every year reimbursements of old loans from some quarter or other, to be replaced at interest in some new loan.

1788. March 16. Baron Steuben has been generally suspected of having suggested the first idea of the self-styled order of Cincinnati. But Mr. Adams tells me that in the year 1776. he had called at a tavern in the state of N. York to dine, just at the moment when the British army was landing at Frog's neck. Genls. Washington, Lee, Knox, and Parsons came to the same tavern. He got into conversation with Knox. They talked of antient history, of Fabius who used to raise the Romans from the dust, of the present contest &c. and Genl. Knox, in the course of the conversation, said he should wish for some ribbon to wear in his hat, or in his button hole, to be transmitted to his descendants as a badge and a proof that he had fought in defence of their liberties. He spoke of it in such precise terms as shewed he had revolved it in his mind before. Mr. Adams says he and Knox were standing together in the door of the tavern, and does not recollect whether Genl. Washington and the others were near enough to hear the conversation, or were even in the room at that moment. Baron Steuben did not arrive in America till above a year after that. Mr. Adams is now 53. years old; i.e. 9. more than I am.

HOPE'S HOUSE NEAR HARLAEM. [Illustration omitted.] It is said this house will cost 4 tons of silver, [or] 40,000. £ sterl. The separation between the middle building and wings in the upper story has a capricious appearance, yet a pleasing one. The right wing of the house (which is the left in the plan) extends back to a great length so as to make the ground plan in the form of an L. The parapet has a pannel of wall, and a pannel of balusters alternately, which lighten it. There is no portico, the columns being backed against the wall of the front.

Mar. 30. 31. AMSTERDAM, UTRECHT, NIMEGUEN. The lower parts of the low countries seem partly to have been gained from the sea, and partly to be made up of the plains of the Yssel, the Rhine, the Maese and the Schelde united. To Utrecht nothing but plain is seen, a rich black mould, wet, lower than the level of the waters which intersect it; almost entirely in grass; few or no farm houses, as the business of grazing requires few labourers. The canal is lined with country houses which bespeak the wealth and cleanliness of the country; but generally in an uncouth state and exhibiting no regular architecture. After passing Utrecht the hills N.E. of the Rhine come into view, and gather in towards the river till, at Wyck Dursted they are within 3. or 4. miles and at Amelengen they join the river. The plains, after passing Utrecht become more sandy; the hills are very poor and sandy, generally waste in broom, sometimes a little corn. The plains are in corn, grass and willow. The plantations of the latter are immense, and give it the air of an uncultivated country. There are now few chateaux. Farm houses abound, built generally of brick, and covered with tile or thatch. There are some apple trees, but no forest. A few inclosures of willow wattling. In the gardens are hedges of beach 1. foot apart, which, not losing it's old leaves till they are pushed off in the spring by the young ones, gives the shelter of evergreens. The Rhine is here about 300. yards wide, and the road to Nimeguen passing it a little below Wattelingen leaves Hetern in sight on the left. On this side, the plains of the Rhine, the Ling, and the Waal unite. The Rhine and Waal are crossed on vibrating boats, the rope supported by a line of 7. little barks. The platform by which you go on to the ferry boat is supported by boats. The view from the hill at Gress [Grebbe] is sublime. It commands the Waal, and extends far up the Rhine. That also up and down the Waal from the Bellevue of Nimeguen is very fine. The chateau here is pretended to have lodged Julius Caesar. This is giving it an antiquity of at least 18. centuries, which must be apocryphal. Some few sheep to-day, which were feeding in turnep-patches.

Apr. 1. CRANENBURG. CLEVES. SANTEN. REYNBERG. HOOGSTRAAT. The transition from ease and opulence to extreme poverty is remarkeable on crossing the line between the Dutch and Prussian territory. The soil and climate are the same. The governments alone differ. With the poverty, the fear also of slaves is visible in the faces of the Prussian subjects. There is an improvement however in the physiognomy, especially could it be a little brightened up. The road leads generally over the hills, but sometimes thro' skirts of the plains of the Rhine. These are always extensive and good. They want manure, being visibly worn down. The hills are almost always sandy, barren, uncultivated, and insusceptible of culture, covered with broom and moss. Here and there a little indifferent forest, which is sometimes of beach. The plains are principally in corn, some grass and willow. There are no chateaux, nor houses that bespeak the existence even of a middle class. Universal and equal poverty overspreads the whole. In the villages too, which seem to be falling down, the overproportion of women is evident. The cultivators seem to live on their farms. The farmhouses are of mud, the better sort of brick, all covered with thatch. Cleves is little more than a village. If there are shops or magazines of merchandize in it, they shew little. Here and there at a window some small articles are hung up within the glass. The gooseberry beginning to leaf.

Apr. 2. Passed the Rhine at ESSENBERG. It is there about $^1/_4$ of a mile wide, or 500 yds. It is crossed in a scow with sails. The wind being on the quarter we were 8. or 10' only in the passage. Duysberg is but a village, in fact, walled in; the buildings mostly of brick. No new ones which indicate a thriving state. I had understood that near that were remains of the encampment of Varus, in which he and his legions fell by the arms of Arminius (in the time of Tiberius I think it was) [Jefferson has mistaken the place where Varus lost the battle; it was in the Teutoburg Forest, well east of this site.] but there was not a person to be found in Duysberg who could understand either English, French, Italian or Latin. So I could make no enquiry.

From DUYSBERG to DUSSELDORP the road leads sometimes over the hills, sometimes thro' the plains of the Rhine, the quality of which are as before described. On the hills however are considerable groves of oak, of spontaneous growth, which seems to be of more than a century: but the soil barren, the trees, tho' high, are crooked and knotty. The undergrowth is broom and moss. In the plains is corn entirely, as they are become rather sandy for grass. There are no inclosures on the Rhine at all. The houses are poor and ruinous, mostly of brick and scantling mixed, a good deal of rape cultivated.

DUSSELDORP. The gallery of paintings is sublime, particularly the room of Vander Werff. The plains from Dusseldorp to Cologne are much more extensive, and go off in barren downs at some distance from the river. These downs extend far, according to appearance. They are manuring the plains with lime. We cross at Cologne on a pendulum boat. I observe the hog of this country (Westphalia) of which the celebrated ham is made, is tall, gaunt, and with heavy lop ears. Fatted at a year old, would weigh 100. or 120. lb. at 2 years old 200 lb. Their principal food is acorns. The pork fresh sells @ $2^{1}/_{2}$d sterl. the lb. The ham ready made @ $5^{1}/_{2}$d sterl. the lb. 106. lb. of this country is equal to 100. lb of Holland. About 4. lb of fine Holland salt is put on 100. lb. of pork. It is smoked in a room which has no chimney. Well informed people here tell me there is no other part of the world where the bacon is smoked. They do not know that we do it. Cologne is the principal market of exportation. They find that the small hog makes the sweetest meat.

COLOGNE is a sovereign city, having no territory out of it's walls. It contains about 60.000. inhabitants; appears to have much commerce, and to abound with poor. It's commerce is principally in the hands of protestants, of whom there are about 60. houses in the city. They are extremely restricted in their operations, and otherwise oppressed in every form by the government which is catholic, and excessively intolerant. Their Senate some time ago, by a majority of 22. to 18. allowed them to have a church: but it is believed this privilege will be revoked. There are about 250. catholic churches in the city. The Rhine is here about 400. yds. wide. This city is in 50.° Lat. wanting about 6.' Here the vines begin, and it is the most Northern spot on the earth on which wine is made. Their first grapes came from Orleans, since that from Alsace, Champagne &c. It is 32. years only since the first vines were sent from Cassel, near Mayence, to the Cape of good hope, of which the Cape wine is now made. Afterwards new supplies were sent from the same quarter. That I suppose is the most Southern spot on the globe where wine is made and it is singular that the same vine should have furnished two wines as much opposed to each other in quality, as in situation.

Apr. 4. COLOGNE. BONNE. ANDERNACH. COBLENTZ. I see many walnut trees to-day in the open fields. It would seem as if this tree and wine required the same climate. The soil begins now to be reddish, both on the hills and in the plains. These from Cologne to Bonne extend about 3. miles from the river on each side: but, a little above Bonne, they become contracted, and continue from thence to be from 1. mile to nothing, comprehending both sides of the river. They are in corn, some clover, and rape, and many vines. These are planted in rows 3. feet apart both ways. The vine is left about 6. or 8.f. high, and stuck with poles 10. or 12.f. high. To these poles they are tied in two places, at the height of about 2. and 4.f. They are now performing this operation. The hills are generally excessively steep, a great proportion of them barren, the rest in vines principally, sometimes small patches of corn. In the plains, tho' rich, I observe they dung their vines plentifully; and it is observed here, as elsewhere, that the plains yield much wine, but bad. The good is furnished from the hills. The walnut, willow, and appletree beginning to leaf.

ANDERNACH is the port on the Rhine to which the famous millstones of Cologne are brought, the quarry, as some say, being at Mendich, 3. or 4. leagues from thence. I suppose they have been called Cologne millstones because the merchants of that place having the most extensive correspondence, have usually sent them to all parts of the world. I observed great collections of them at Cologne. This is one account.

Apr. 5. COBLENTZ, NASSAU. Another account is that these stones are cut at Triers, and brought down to Moselle. I could not learn the price of them at the quarry; but I was shewn a grindstone, of the same stone, 5.f. diam. which cost at Triers 6. florins. It was but of half the thickness of a millstone. I suppose therefore that two millstones would cost about as much as 3. of these grindstones, i.e. about a guinea and a half. This country abounds with slate.

The best Moselle wines are made about 15. leagues from hence, in an excessively mountainous country. The 1st. quality (without any comparison) is that made on the mountain of Brownberg, adjoining to the village of Dusmond, and the best crop is that of the Baron Breidbach Burrhesheim grand chambellan et grand Baillif de Coblentz. His Receveur, of the name of Mayer, lives at Dusmond. The last fine year was 1783. which sells now at 50. Louis the foudre, which contains 6 aumes of 170 bottles each = about 1100. bottles. This is about 22. sous Tournois the bottle. In general the Baron Burresheim's crop will sell as soon as made, say at the vintage, for 130. 140. 150. ecus the foudre (the ecu is $1^{1}/_{2}$ florin of Holland) say 200f. 2. Vialen is the 2d. quality, and sells new at 120. ecus the futre. 3. Crach, Bisport are the 3d. and sell for about 105. ecus. I compared Crach of 1783. with Baron Burrhesheim's of the same year. That latter is quite clear of acid, stronger, and very sensibly the best. 4. Selting, which sells at 100. ecus. 5. Kous, Berncastle the 5th. quality sells at 80. or 90. After this there is a gradation of qualities down to 30. ecus.

These wines must be 5. or 6. years old before they are quite ripe for drinking. 1000. plants yeild a foudre of wine a year in the most plentiful vineyards. In other vineyards it will take 2000. or 2500. plants to yield a foudre. The culture of 1000. plants costs about 1. Louis a year. A day's labour of a man is paid in Winter 20 kreitzers (i.e. 1/3 of a florin) in Summer 26. A woman's is half that. The red wines of this country are very indifferent and will not keep. The Moselle is here from 100. to 200. yds. wide, the Rhine 300. to 400. A jessamine in the Ct. de Moustier's garden in leaf.

In the Elector of Treves' palace at Coblentz, are large rooms very well warmed by warm air conveyed from an oven below through tubes which open into the rooms. An oil and vinegar cruet in this form [illustration omitted]. At Coblentz we pass the river on a pendulum boat, and the road to Nassau is over tremendous hills, on which is here and there a little corn, more vines, but mostly barren. In some of these barrens are forests of beach and oak, tolerably large, but crooked and knotty, the undergrowth beach brush, broom and moss. The soil of the plains, and of the hills where they are cultivable, is reddish. Nassau is a village the whole rents of which should not amount to more than a hundred or two guineas, yet it gives the title of Prince to the house of Orange to which it belongs.

Apr. 6. NASSAU, SCHWELBACH, WISBADEN, HOCHHEIM, FRANK-FORT. The road from Nassau to Schwelbach is over hills, or rather mountains, both high and steep; always poor, and above half of them barren in beach and oak. At Schwelbach there is some chesnut. The other parts are either in winter grain, or preparing for that of the Spring. Between Schwelbach and Wisbaden we come in sight of the plains of the Rhine, which are very extensive. From hence the lands, both high and low are very fine, in corn, vines, and fruit trees. The country has the appearance of wealth, especially in the approach to Frankfurt.

Apr. 7. FRANCFORT. Among the poultry, I have seen no turkies in Germany till I arrive at this place. The Stork, or Crane, is very commonly tame here. It is a miserable, dirty, ill-looking bird. The Lutheran is the reigning religion here and is equally intolerant to the Catholic and Calvinist, excluding them from the free corps.

Apr. 8. FRANCFORT, HANAU. The road goes thro' the plains of the Maine, which are mulatto and very fine. They are well cultivated till you pass the line between the republic and the Landgraviate of Hesse, when you immediately see the effect of the difference of government, notwithstanding the tendency which the neighborhood of such a commercial town as Francfort has to counteract the effects of tyranny in it's vicinities, and to animate them in spite of oppression. In Francfort all is life, bustle and motion. In Hanau the silence and quiet of the mansions of the dead. Nobody is seen moving in the streets; every door is shut; no sound of the saw, the hammer, or other utensil of industry. The drum and fife is all that is heard. The streets are cleaner than a German floor, because nobody passes them. At Williamsbath, near Hanau, is a country seat of the Landgrave. There is a ruin which is clever. It presents the remains of an old castle. [*Jefferson is now in the company of Baron Geismar.*] The upper story in this, a circular room of 31^1/2 f. diameter within [*illustrations omitted*]. The 4. little square towers, at the corners, finish at the floor of the upper story, so as to be only platforms to walk out on. Over the circular room is platform also, which is covered by the broken parapet which once crowned the top, but is now fallen off in some parts, whilst the other parts remain. I like better however the form of the ruin at Hagley in England. A centry box here covered over with bark, so as to look exactly like the trunk of an old tree. This is a good idea, and may be of much avail in a garden. There is a hermitage in which is a good figure of a hermit in plaister, coloured to the life, with a table and book before him, in the attitude of reading and contemplation. In a little cell is his bed, in another his books, some tools &c., in another his little provision of fire wood &c. There is a monument erected to the son of the present landgrave in the form of a pyramid, the base of which is 18^1/2f. The side declines from the perpendicular about 22^1/2°. An arch is carried through it both ways so as to present a door in each side. In the middle of this, at the crossing of the two arches, is a marble monument with this inscription 'ante tempus.' He died at 12. years of age. Between Hanau and Frankfort, in sight of the road, is the village of Bergen, where was fought the battle of Bergen in the war before last.—Things worth noting here are 1. a folding ladder, 2. manner of packing china cups and saucers, the former in a circle within the latter. 3. the marks of different manufactures of china. 4. the top rail of the waggon supported by the washers on the ends of the axle-trees.

Apr. 10. FRANKFORT, HOCHEIM, MAYENCE. The little tyrants round about having disarmed their people, and made it very criminal to kill game, one knows when they quit the territory of Frankfort by the quantity of game which is seen. In the Republic, every body being allowed to be armed, and to hunt on their own lands, there is very little game left in it's territory. The hog hereabouts resembles extremely the little hog of Virginia, round like that, a small head, and short upright ears. This makes the ham of Mayence, so much esteemed at Paris.

We cross the Rhine at Mayence on a bridge 1840. feet long, supported by 47. boats. It is not in a direct line, but curved up against the stream, which may strengthen it, if the difference between the upper and lower curve be sensible, if the planks of the floor be thick, well jointed together, and form-ing sectors of circles, so as to act on the whole as the stones of an arch. But it has by no means this appearance. Near one end, one of the boats has an Axis in peritrochio and a chain, by which it may be let drop down stream some distance, with the portion of the floor belonging to it, so as to let a vessel through. Then it is wound up again into place, and to consolidate it the more with adjoining parts, the loose section is a little higher, and has at each end a folding stage, which folds back on it when it moves down, and when brought up again into place, these stages are folded over on the bridge. This whole operation takes but 4. or 5. minutes. In the winter the bridge is taken away entirely, on account of the ice, and then every thing passes on the ice, thro' the whole winter.

Apr. 11. MAYENCE. RUDESHEIM. JOHANSBERG. MARKEBRONN. The women do everything here. They dig the earth, plough, saw, cut, and split wood, row, tow the batteaux &c. In a small but dull kind of batteau, with two hands rowing with a kind of large paddle, and a square sail but scarcely a breath of wind we went down the river at the rate of 5. miles an hour, making it $3^{1}/_{2}$ hours to Rudesheim. The floats of wood which go with the current only, go $1^{1}/_{2}$ mile an hour. They go night and day. There are 5. boatmills abreast here. Their floats seem to be about 8.f. broad. The Rhine yields salmon, carp, pike, and perch, and the little rivers running into it yield speckled trout. The plains from Maintz to Rudesheim are good and in corn: the hills mostly in vines. The banks of the river are so low that, standing up in the batteau, I could generally see what was in the plains, yet they are seldom overflowed.

Though they begin to make wine, as has been said, at Cologne, and continue it up the river indefinitely, yet it is only from Rudesheim to Hocheim, that wines of the very first quality are made. The river happens there to run due East and West, so as to give to it's hills on that side a Southern aspect, and even in this canton, it is only Hocheim, Johansberg, and

Rudesheim that are considered as of the very first quality. Johansberg is a little mountain (berg signifies mountain) wherein is a religious house, about 15. miles below Mayence, and near the village of Vingel. It has a Southern aspect, the soil a barren mulatto clay, mixed with a good deal of stone, and some slate. This wine used to be but on a par with Hocheim and Rudesheim; but the place having come to the Bp. Of Fulda, he improved it's culture so as to render it stronger, and since the year 1775. it sells at double the price of the other two. It has none of the acid of the Hocheim and other Rhenish wines. There are about 60. tons made in a good year, which sell, as soon as of a drinkable age, at 1000.f. each. The ton here contains $7^{1/2}$ aumes of 170. bottles each. Rudesheim is a village about 18. or 20. miles below Mayence. It's fine wines are made on the hills about a mile below the village, which look to the South, and on the middle and lower parts of them. They are terrassed. The soil is grey, about one half of slate and rotten stone, the other half of barren clay, excessively steep. Just behind the village also is a little spot, called hinder house, belonging to the Counts of Sicken and Oschstein, wherein each makes about a ton of wine of the first quality. This spot extends from the bottom to the top of the hill. The vignerons of Rudesheim dung their vines about once in 5. or 6. years putting a one-horse tumbrel load of dung on every 12.f. square. 1000 plants yield about 4. aumes in a good year.

[A list of the best crops and their annual yield, along with an illustration of a tower, are omitted here.] These wines begin to be drinkable at about 5. years old. The proprietors sell them old or young, according to the price offered, and according to their own want of money. There is always a little difference between different casks, and therefore when you chuse and buy a single cask, you pay 3, 4, 5, or 600. florins for it. They are not at all acid, and to my taste much preferable to Hocheim, tho' but of the same price. Hocheim is a village about 3. miles above Mayence, on the Maine where it empties into the Rhine. The spot whereon the good wine is made is the hill side from the church down to the plain, a gentle slope of about $^{1/4}$ of a mile wide and extending half a mile towards Mayence. It is of South Western aspect, very poor, sometimes grey, sometimes mulatto, with a moderate mixture of small broken stone. The vines are planted 3.f. apart, and stuck with sticks about 6.f. high. The vine too is cut at that height. They are dunged once in 3. or 4. years. 1000 plants yield from 1. to 2. aumes a year. They begin to yield a little at 3. years old, and continue to 100. years, unless sooner killed by a cold winter. Dick, keeper of the Rothen-house tavern at Francfort, a great wine merchant, who has between 3. and 400. tons of wine in his cellars, tells me that Hocheim of the year 1783. sold, as soon as it was made at 90. florins the aume, Rudesheim of the same year, as soon as made at 115. florins, and Markebronn 70. florins. But a peasant of Hocheim tells me that the best crops of Hocheim in the good years, when sold new, sell but for 32. or 33. florins the aume: but that it is only the poorer proprietors who sell new. [Another list of fine crops is omitted here.]

Markebronn (bronn signifies a spring, and is probably of affinity with the Scotch word, burn) is a little canton in the same range of hills, adjoining to the village of Hagenheim, about 3. miles above Johansberg, subject to the elector of Mayence. It is a sloping hill side of Southern aspect, mulatto, poor, and mixed with some stone. This yields wine of the 2d. quality.

Apr. 12. MAYENCE. OPPENHEIM. WORMS. MANHEIM. On the road between Mayence and Oppenheim are three cantons which are also esteemed as yielding wines of the 2d. quality. These are Laudenheim, Bodenheim, and Nierstein. Laudenheim is a village about 4. or 5. miles from Mayence. It's wines are made on a steep hill side, the soil of which is grey, poor and mixed with some stone. The river happens there to make a short turn to the S.W. so as to present it's hills to the S.E. Bodenheim is a village 9. miles, and Nierstein another 10. or 11. miles from Mayence. Here too the river is N.E. and S.W. so as to give to the hills between these villages a S.E. aspect; and at Nierstein a valley making off, brings the face of the hill round to the South. The hills between these villages are almost perpendicular, of a vermillion red, very poor, and having as much rotten stone as earth. It is to be observed that these are the only cantons on the South side of the river which yield good wine, the hills on this side being generally exposed to the cold winds, and turned from the sun. The annexed bill of prices current will give an idea of the estimation of these wines respectively.

With respect to the grapes in this country, there are three kinds in use for making white wine (for I take no notice of the red wines as being absolutely worthless.) 1. The Klemperien, of which the inferior qualities of Rhenish wines are made, and is cultivated because of it's hardness. The wines of this grape descend as low as 100. florins the ton of 8. aumes. 2. The Rhysslin grape which grows only from Hocheim down to Rudesheim. This is small and delicate, and therefore succeeds only in this chosen spot. Even at Rudesheim, it yields a fine wine only in the little spot called Hinder-house before mentioned: the mass of good wines made at Rudesheim below the village being of the 3d. kind of grape, which is called the Orleans grape.

To Oppenheim the plains of the Rhine and Maine are united. From that place we see the commencement of the Berg-strasse, or mountains which separate at first the plains of the Rhine and Maine, then cross the Neckar at Heidelberg, and from thence forms the separation between the plains of the Neckar and Rhine, leaving those of the Rhine about 10. and 12. miles wide. These plains are some-times black, sometimes mulatto, always rich. They are in corn, potatoes, and some willow. On the other side again, that is, on the West side, the hills keep at first close to the river. They are 150. or 200.f. high, sloping, red, good, and mostly in vines. Above Oppenheim, they begin to go off till they join the mountains of Lorraine and Alsace, which separate the waters of the Moselle and Rhine, leaving to the whole valley of the Rhine about 20. or 25. miles breadth. About Worms these plains are sandy, poor, and often covered only with small pine.

April 13. MANHEIM. There is a bridge over the Rhine here supported on 39. boats, and one over the Neckar on 11. boats. The bridge over the Rhine is $21^{1}/_{2}$f. wide from rail to rail. The boats are 4.f. deep, 52.f. long, and 9f. 8I. broad. The space between boat and boat is 18f. 10I. From these data the length of the bridge should be 9f. – 8I + 18f – 10I x 40 = 1140. feet. In order to let vessels pass through, two boats well framed together, with their flooring are made to fall down stream together.—Here too they make good ham. It is fattened on round potatoes and Indian corn. The farmers smoke what is for their own use in their chimnies. When it is made for sale, and in greater quantities than the chimney will hold, they make the smoke of the chimney pass into an adjoining loft or apartment from which it has no issue; and here they hang their hams.   .

An economical curtain bedstead. The bedstead is 7.f. by 4.f.2 I. From each leg there goes up an iron rod $^3/_8$ I. diam. Those from the legs at the foot of the bed meeting at top as in the margin, and those from the head meet-ing in like manner, so that the two at the foot form one point, and the two at the head another. On these points lays an oval iron rod, whose long diameter is 5.f. and short one 3f. 1.I. There is a hole through this rod at each end, by which it goes on firm on the point of the upright rods. Then a nut screws it down firmly. 10. breadths of stuff 2.f. 10I. wide and 8.f. 6.I. long form the curtains. There is no top nor vallons. The rings are fastened within 2$^{1}/_{2}$ or 3.I. of the top of the inside, which 2$^{1}/_{2}$I. or 3.I. stand up and are an ornament somewhat like a ruffle.

I have observed all along the Rhine that they make the oxen draw by the horns. A pair of very handsome chariot horses, large, bay, and 7. years old sell for 50. Louis. 1 lb of beef sells for 8 kreitzers (i.e. 8/60 of a florin) 1 lb of mutton or veal 6. kreitzers, 1 lb of pork 7$^{1}/_{2}$ kr., of ham 12. kr., of fine wheat bread 2. kr., of butter 20. kr. 160 lb wheat 6 f. 160 lb maize 5.f. 160 lb potatoes 1 f. 100. lb hay 1 f. a cord of wood (which is 4. 4. and 6.f.) 7 f. A labourer by the day recieves 24. kr. and feeds himself. A journee or arpent of land (which is 8. by 200. steps) such as the middling plains of the Rhine will sell for 200. f. There are more souldiers here than other inhabitants, to wit, 6000. souldiers and 4000. males of full age of the citizens, the whole number of whom is reckoned at 20,000.

Apr. 14. MANHEIM. DOSSENHEIM. HEIDELBERG. SCHWET-ZINGEN. MANHEIM. The elector placed in 1768. 2. male and 5. females of the Angora goat at Dossenheim, which is at the foot of the Bergstrasse mountains. He sold 25. last year, and has now 70. They are removed into the mountains 4. leagues beyond Dossenheim. Heidelberg is on the Neckar just where it issues from the Bergstrasse mountains, occupying the first skirt of a plain which it forms. The Chateau is up the hill a considerable height. The gardens lie above the Chateau, climbing up the mountain in terrasses. This chateau is the most noble ruin I have ever seen, having been reduced to that state by the French in the time of Louis XIV. 1693. Nothing remains under cover but the chapel. The situation is romantic and pleasing beyond expression. It is on a great scale much like the situation of Petrarch's chateau at Vaucluse on a small one. The climate too is like that of Italy. The apple, the pear, cherry, peach, apricot and almond are all in bloom. There is a station in the garden to which the chateau re-echoes distinctly 4. syllables. The famous ton [i.e., tun] of Heidelberg was new built in 1751. and made to contain 30. foudres more than the antient one. It is said to contain 236. foudres of 1200. bottles each. I measured it, and found it's length external to be 28.f. 10.I. it's diameter at the end 20.f. 3.I. the thickness of the staves 7$^{1}/_{2}$I. thickness of the hoops 7$^{1}/_{2}$I. besides a great deal of external framing. There is no wine in it now. The gardens at Schwetzingen shew how much money may be laid out to make an ugly thing. What is called the English quarter however relieves the eye from the strait rows of trees, round and square basons which constitute the great mass of the garden. There are some tolerable morsels of Graecian architecture, and a good ruin. The Aviary too is clever. It consists of cells of about 8.f. wide, arranged round, and looking into, a circular area of about 40. or 50.f. diameter. The cells have doors both of wire and glass, and have small shrubs in them. The plains of the Rhine on this side are 12. miles wide, bounded by the Bergstrasse mountains. These appear to be 800. or 1000.f. high; the lower part in vines, from which is made what is called the vin de Nichar; the upper in chesnut. There are some cultivated spots however quite to the top. The plains are generally mulatto, in corn principally; they are planting potatoes in some parts, and leaving others open for Maize and tobacco. Many peach and other fruit trees on the lower part of the mountain. The paths on some parts of these mountains are somewhat in the style represented in the margin.

MANHEIM. KAEFERTHAL. MANHEIM. Just beyond Kaerferthal is an extensive sandy waste planted in pine, in which the elector has about 200 sangliers [a kind of boar], tamed. I saw about 50. The heaviest I am told would weigh about 300 lb. They are fed on round potatoes and range in an extensive forest of small pines. At the village of Kaeferthal is a plantation of Rhubarb begun in 1769 by a private company. It contains 20 arpens or journees, and it's culture costs about 4. or 500f. a year. It sometimes employs 40 to 50 labourers at a time. The best age to sell the Rhubarb at is the 5th. or 6th. year; but the sale being dull they keep it sometimes to the 10th. year. They find it best to let it remain in the earth, because when taken out it is liable to the worm. At about 10. years old however it begins to rot in the ground. They sell about 200 quintals a year at 2 or 3f. a lb. and could sell double that quantity from this ground if they could find a market. The apothecaries of Frankfort and of England are the principal buyers. It is in beds resembling lettuce beds, the plants 4. 5 or 6I. apart. When dug, a thread is passed thro' every peice of root and it is hung separate in a kind of rack. When dry it is rasped. What comes off is given to the cattle.

Apr. 15. MANHEIM. SPIRE. CARLSRUH. The valley preserves it's width, extending on each side of the river about 10. or 12. miles. But the soil loses much in it's quality, becoming sandy and lean, often barren and overgrown with pine thicket. At Spire is nothing remarkeable. Between that and Carlsruh we pass the Rhine in a common Skow with oars where it is between 3. and 400. yards wide. Carlsruh is the residence of the Margrave of Baden, a sovereign prince. His chateau is built in the midst of a natural forest of several leagues diameter, and of the best trees I have seen in these countries. They are mostly oak, and would be deemed but indifferent in America. A great deal of money has been spent to do more harm than good to the ground, cutting a number of straight allies through the forest. He has a pheasantry of the gold and silver kind, the latter very tame, but the former excessively shy. A little inclosure of stone $2^{1/2}$f. high and 30.f. diameter in which are two tamed beavers. There is a pond of 15.f. diameter in the center and at each end a little cell for them to retire into, which is stowed with boughs and twigs with leaves on them which are their principal food. They eat bread also. Twice a week the water is changed. They cannot get over this wall.—Some cerfs of a peculiar kind, spotted like fawns. The horns remarkeably long, small and sharp, with few points. I am not sure there were more than two to each main beam, and I saw distinctly there came out a separate and subordinate beam from the root of each. 8 Ancora goats, beautiful animals, all white. This town is only an appendage of the Chateau, and but a moderate one. It is a league from Durlach, halfway between that and the river.—I observe they twist the funnels of their stoves about in any form, for ornament merely, without fearing their smoking.

Apr. 16. CARLSRUH. RASTADT. SCHOLHOVEN. BISCHOFHEIM. KEHL. STRASBOURG. The valley of the Rhine still preserves it's width, but varies in quality, sometimes a rich mulatto loam, sometimes a poor sand, covered with small pine. The culture is generally corn. It is to be noted that thro the whole of my route through the Netherlds. and the valley of the Rhine there is a little red clover every here and there, and a great deal of rape cultivated. The seed of this is sold to be made into oil. The rape is now in blossom. No inclosures. The fruit trees are generally blossoming thro' the whole valley. The high mountains of the Bergstrasse as also of Alsace are crowned with snow within this day or two. The every day dress of the country women here is black. Rastadt is a seat also of the Margrave of Baden. Scholhoven and Kehl are in his territory but not Bischofheim. I see no beggars since I enter his government nor is the traveller obliged to ransom himself every moment by a chaussée gold. The roads are excellent, and made so I presume out of the coffers of the prince. From Cleves till I enter the Margravate of Baden the roads have been strung with beggars, in Hesse the most, and the road tax very heavy. We pay it chearfully however through the territory of Frankfort and thence up the Rhine, because fine gravelled roads are kept up. But through the Prussian and other parts of the road below Frankfort the roads are only as made by the carriages, there not appearing to have been ever a day's work employed on them.—At Strasburg we pass the Rhine on a wooden bridge.

At Brussell and Antwerp the fuel is pit-coal, dug in Brabant. Thro' all Holland it is turf. From Cleves to Cologne it is pit coal brought from Engld. They burn it in open stoves. From thence it is wood burnt in close stoves, till you get to Strasbourg, where the open chimney comes again into use.

April 16. 17. 18. STRASBOURG. The Vin de paille is made in the neighborhood of Colmar in Alsace about—— from this place. It takes it's name from the circumstance of spreading the grapes on straw where they are preserved till spring, and then made into wine. The little juice then remaining in them makes a rich sweet wine, but the dearest in the world without being the best by any means. They charge 9 the bottle for it in the taverns of Strasbourg. It is the caprice of wealth alone which continues so losing an operation. This wine is sought because dear, while the better wine of Frontignan is rarely seen at a good table because it is cheap.

STRASBOURG. SAVERNE. PHALSBOURG. As far as Saverne, the country is in waving hills and hollows, red, rich enough, mostly in small grain, but some vines. A little stone. From Saverne to Phalsbourg we cross a considerable mountain which takes an hour to rise it.

April 19. PHALSBOURG. FENESTRANGE. MOYENVIC. NANCY. Asparagus to-day at Moyenvic. The country is always either mountainous or hilly, red, tolerably good, and in small grain. On the hills about Fenestrange, Moyenvic and Nancy are some small vineyards where a bad wine is made. No inclosures. Some good sheep, indifferent cattle and small horses. The most forest I have seen in France, principally of beech, pretty large. The houses, as in Germany are of scantling, filled in with wicker and morter, and covered either with thatch or tiles. The people too here, as there, gathered in villages. Oxen plough here with collars and hames. The awkward figure of their mould board leads one to consider what should be it's form. The offices of the mouldboard are to receive the sod after the share has cut under it, to raise it gradually and reverse it. The fore end of it then should be horizontal to enter under the sod, and the hind end perpendicular to throw it over, the intermediate surface changing gradually from the horizontal to the perpendicular.

It should be as wide as the furrow, and of a length suited to the construction of the plough. [Jefferson's description of how to make the moldboard is omitted here. His design evolved from the one described here.]—The women here, as in Germany do all sorts of work. While one considers them as useful and rational companions, one cannot forget that they are also objects of our pleasures. Nor can they ever forget it. While employed in dirt and drudgery some tag of a ribbon, some ring or bit of bracelet, earbob or necklace, or something of that kind will shew that the desire of pleasing is never suspended in them. How valuable is that state of society which allots to them internal emploiments only, and external to the men. They are formed by nature for attentions and not the hard labour. A woman never forgets one of the numerous train of little offices which belong to her; a man forgets often.

Apr. 20. NANCY. TOULE. VOID. LIGNY EN BARROIS. BAR LE DUC. ST. DIZIER. Nancy itself is a neat little town, and it's environs very agreeable. The valley of the little branch of the Moselle on which it is, is about a mile wide. The road then crossing the head waters of the Moselle, the Maes, and the Marne, the country is very hilly, and perhaps a third of it poor and in forests of beach. The other two thirds from poor up to midling, red, and stony, almost entirely in corn, now and then only some vines on the hills. The Moselle at Toul is 30 or 40 yds. wide, the Maese near Void about half that, that Marne at St. Dizier about 40. yds. They all make good plains of from a quarter of a mile to a mile wide. The hills of the Maese abound with chalk. The rocks coming down from the tops of the hills on all the road of this day at regular intervals like the ribs of an animal, have a very singular appearance. Considerable flocks of sheep and asses, and in the approach to St. Dizier great plantations of apple and cherry trees. Here and there a peach tree, all in general bloom. The roads thro' Lorraine are strung with beggars.

Apr. 21. ST. DIZIER. VITRY. LE FRANÇAIS. CHALONS SUR MARNE. EPERNAY. The plains of the Marne and the Sault uniting, appear boundless to the eye till we approach their confluence at Vitry where the hills come in on the right. After that the plains are generally about a mile, mulatto, of middling quality sometimes stony. Sometimes the ground goes off from the river so sloping, that one does not know whether to call it high or low land. The hills are mulatto also but whitish, occasioned by the quantity of chalk which seems to constitute their universal base. They are poor and principally in vines.

The streams of water are of the colour of milk, occasioned by the chalk also. No inclosures. Some flocks of sheep. Children gathering dung in the roads. Here and there a chateau, but none considerable.

Apr. 22. EPERNAY. The hills abound with chalk. Of this they make lime, not so strong as stone lime, and therefore to be used in greater proportion. They cut the blocks into regular forms also like stone and build houses of it. The common earth too, well impregnated with this, is made into mortar, moulded in the form of brick, dried in the sun, and houses built of them which last 100 or 200 years. The plains here are a mile wide, red, good, in corn, clover, Luzerne, St. foin. The hills are in vines, and this being precisely the canton where the most celebrated wines of Champagne are made details must be entered into. Remember however that they will relate always to the white wines unless where the red are expressly mentioned. The reason is that their red wines, tho much esteemed on the spot, are by no means esteemed elsewhere equally with their white, nor do they merit it ....

Soil. Meagre mulatto clay mixt with small broken stones, and a little hue of chalk. Very dry.

Aspect. The hills from Aij to Cumieres are generally about 250f. high. The good wine is made only in the middle region. The lower region however is better than the upper because this last is exposed to cold winds and a colder atmosphere.

Culture. The vines are planted 2f. apart. Afterwards they are multiplied (provignés) when a stock puts out two shoots they lay them down, spread them open and cover them with earth so as to have in the end about a plant for every square foot. This operation is performed with the aid of a hook 9.I. long which being stuck in the ground holds down the main stock while the labourer separates and covers the new shoots. They leave two buds above the ground. When the vine has shot up high enough, they stick it with oak sticks of the size and length of our tobacco sticks and tie the vine to them with straw. These sticks cost 2 the hundred and will last 40. years. An arpent, one year with another in the fine vineyards gives 12. peices and in the inferior vineyards 25. pieces. Each piece is of 200. bottles. An arpent of the first quality sells for 3000 and there have been instances of 7200 (the arpent contains 100 verges of 22 pieds square). The arpent of inferior quality sells at 1000. They plant the vines in a hole about a foot deep, and fill that hole with good mould to make the plant take. Otherwise it would perish. Afterwards if ever they put dung it is very little. During wheat harvest there is a month or 6. weeks that nothing is done in the vineyards. That is to say from the 1st. Aug. to the beginning of vintage. The vintage commences early in Sep. and lasts a month. A day's work of a labourer in the busiest season is 20s. and he feeds himself. In the least busy season it is 15s. Cornlands are rented from 4^{tt} to 24,^{tt} but vinelands never rented. The three façons of an arpent of vines cost 15.^{tt} The whole year's expence of an arpent is worth 100.^{tt}

Grapes. The bulk of their grapes are purple, which they prefer for making even white wine. They press them very lightly (without treading them or permitting them to ferment at all) for about an hour, so that it is the beginning of the running only which makes the bright wine. What follows the beginning is of a straw colour and therefore not placed on a level with the first; the last part of the juice produced by strong pressure is red and ordinary. They chuse the bunches with as much care to make wine of the very 1st. quality as if to eat. Not above one eighth of the whole grapes will do for this purpose. The white grape, tho not so fine for wine as the red, when the red can be produced, and more liable to rot in a moist season, yet grows better if the soil be excessively poor, and therefore in such a soil it is preferred: because there indeed the red would not grow at all.

Wines. The white wines are either 1. mousseux (sparkling) or 2. non mousseux (still). The sparkling are little drank in France but are alone known and drank in foreign countries. This makes so great a demand and so certain a one that it is the dearest by about an eigth and therefore they endeavour to make all sparkling if they can. This is done by bottling in the spring from the beginning of March to June. If it succeeds they lose abundance of bottles from $^{1}/_{10}$ to $^{1}/_{3}$. This is another cause encreasing the price. To make the still wine they bottle in September. This is only done when they know from some circumstance that the wine will not be brisk. So if the spring bottling fails to make a brisk wine, they decant it into other bottles in the fall and it then makes the very best still wine. In this operation it loses from $^{1}/_{10}$ to $^{1}/_{20}$ by sediment. They let it stand in the bottles in this case 48. hours with only a napkin spread over their mouths, but no cork. The best sparkling wine decanted in this manner makes the best still wine and which will keep much longer than that originally made still by being bottled in September. The brisk wines lose their briskness the older they are, but they gain in quality with age to a certain length. These wines are in perfection from 2. to 10. years old, and will even be very good to 15. 1766 was the best year ever known. 1775. and 1776 next to that. 1783 is the last good year, and that not to be compared with those. These wines stand icing very well.

Aij. M. Dorsay makes 1100 peices which sell as soon as made at 300. and in good years 400 in the cask. I paid in his cellar to M. Louis his homme d'affaires for the remains of the year 1783. 3^{tt}-10 the bottle. Brisk champaigne of the same merit would have cost 4. (The piece and demiqueue are the same. The feuillette is 100. bouteilles) M. le Duc 400 to 500 pieces. M. de Villermont 300. pieces. Mr. Janson 250. pieces. All of the 1st. quality, red and white in equal quantities.

Auvillij. Les moines Benedictins, 1000 peices red and white but three fourths red. Both of the first quality. The king's table is supplied by them. This enables them to sell at 550 the piece tho' their white is hardly as good as Dorsay's, and their red is the best. L'Abbatiale belonging to the bishop of the place 1000 to 1200 pieces red and white, three fourths red at 400. to 550. because neighbors to the monks.

Cumieres is all of a 2d quality. Both red and white 150^{tt} to 200^{tt} the piece.

Epernay. Mde. Jermont 200 pieces @ 300.^{tt}–M. Patelaine 150 pieces. M. Marc 200 peices. M. Chertems 60 pieces. M. Lauchay 50 peices. M. Cousin 100 pieces (Aubergiste de l'hotel de Rohan á Epernay.) M. Pierrot 100 pieces. Les Chanoines regulieres d'Epernay 200. pieces. Mesdames les Urselines religieuses 100. pieces. M. Gilette 200. p. All of the 1st. quality red and white in equal quantities.

Pierrij. M. Casotte 500 pieces. M. de la Motte 300 pieces. M. de Failli 300 pieces. I tasted his wine of 1779 which was really very good, tho not equal to that of M. Dorsay of 1783. He sells it at 2-10 to merchants and 3.^{tt} to individuals. Les Semnaristes 150.p. M. Hoquart 200.p. all of 1st. quality, white and red in equal quantities. At Cramont also there are some wines of 1st. quality made. At Avize also, and Aucy, Le Meni, Mareuil, Verzy-Verzenni. This last place (Verzy Verzenni) belongs to the M. de Sillery, the wines are carried to Sillery and there stored, whence they are called Vins de Sillery, tho not made there.

All these wines of Epernay and Pierrij sell almost as dear as M. Dorsay's, their quality being nearly the same. There are many small proprietors who might make all wines of the 1st. quality if they would cull their grapes: but they are too poor for this. Therefore the proprietors beforenamed, whose names are established buy of the poorer ones the right to cull their vineyards, by which means they increase their quantity, as they find about $^1/_3$ of the grapes fit to make wine of the 1st. quality.

The lowest priced wines of all the 30 the peice, red or white. They make brandy of the pumice. In very bad years when their wines become vinegar they are sold for 6 the peice and made into brandy. They yield $^1/_{10}$ brandy.

White Champaigne is good in proportion as it is silky and still. Many circumstances derange the scale of wines. The proprietor of the best vineyard, in the best year, having bad weather come upon while he is gathering his grapes, makes a bad wine, while his neighbor holding a more indifferent vineyard, which happens to be ingathering while the weather is good, makes a better. The M. de Casotte at Pierrij formerly was the first house. His successors by some imperceptible change of culture have degraded the quality of their wines. Their cellars are admirably made, being about 6. 8. or 10f. wide vaulted and extending into the ground in a kind of labyrinth to a prodigious distance, with an air hole of 2.f. diameter every 50. feet. From the top of the vault to the surface of the earth is from 15. to 30f. I have no where seen cellars comparable to these. In packing their bottles they lay a row on their side, then across them at each end they lay laths, and on these another row of bottles, heads and points on the others. By this means they can take out a bottle from the bottom of where they will.

Apr. 23. EPERNAY. CHATEAU THIERY. ST. JEAN. MEAUX. VERGALANT. PARIS. From Epernay to St. Jean the road leads over hills which in the beginning are indifferent, but get better towards the last. The plains wherever seen are inconsiderable. After passing St. Jean the hills become good and the plains increase. The country about Vert-galant is pretty. A skirt of a low ridge which runs in on the extensive plains of the Marne and Seine is very picturesque. The general bloom of fruit trees proves there are more of them than I had imagined from travelling in other seasons when they are less distinguishable at a distance from the Forest trees.

❧

To William Short
DEAR SIR   Frankfort on the Maine April 9. 1788

I arrived here on the 6th. inst. having been overtaken at Cleves by the commencement of a storm of rain hail and snow which lasted to this place, with intermissions now and then. The roads however continued good to Bonne, where beginning to be clayey and to be penetrated with the wet they became worse than imagination can paint for about 100 miles which brought me to the neighborhood of this place where the chaussee began. My old friend the Baron de Geismar met me here, on a letter I had written him from Amsterdam, and has been my Cicerone. It happens to be the moment of the fair of Frankfort which is very great. Yesterday we made an excursion up the Maine to Hanau, passing the ground where the battle of Bergen was fought in the war before last. Tomorrow we shall go to the vineyards of Hocheim, and perhaps to Rudesheim and Johannesberg, where the most celebrated wines are made. Then I shall pass on to Mayence, Worms, Manheim, Heidelberg and Spires, and from this last place to Strasburg. Unless I find there any thing from you which may call me to Paris directly, I shall probably go a little circuitously, perhaps by the way of Reims in Champagne, so that I am unable to say exactly when I shall be at Paris. I guess about the 20th. I met at Hanau with many acquaintances, the officers who had been stationed in Albemarle while in captivity. I have seen much good country on the Rhine, and bad whenever I got a little off of it. But what I have met with the most wonderful in nature is a set of men absolutely incorruptible by money, by fair words or by foul: and that this should, of all others, be the class of postillions. This however is the real character of German postillions whom nothing on earth can induce to go out of a walk. This has retarded me not a little: so that I shall be glad to be delivered over to the great jack boots.

The neighborhood of this place is that which has been to us a second mother country. It is from the palatinate on this part of the Rhine that those swarms of Germans have gone, who, next to the descendants of the English, form the greatest body of our people. I have been continually amused by seeing here the origin of whatever is not English among us. I have fancied myself often in the upper parts of Maryland and Pennsylvania. I have taken some measures too for realizing a project which I have wished to execute for 20 years past without knowing how to go about it. I am not sure but that you will enter into similar views when I can have the pleasure of explaining them to you at Paris. Being too long for a letter, and having already given you a sufficiency of egoismes, for want of other subjects I shall conclude with assurances of the esteem & attachment with which I am Dear Sir your affectionate friend & servt.,

—TH: JEFFERSON

⁓

To Maria Cosway   Paris Apr. 24. 1788

I arrived here, my dear friend, the last night, and in a bushel of letters presented me by way of reception, I saw that one was of your handwriting. It is the only one I have yet opened, and I answer it before I open another. I do not think I was in arrears in our epistolary account when I left Paris. In affection I am sure you were greatly my debtor. I often determined during my journey to write to you: but sometimes the fatigue of exercise, and sometimes a fatigued attention hindered me. At Dusseldorp I wished for you much. I surely never saw so precious a collection of paintings. Above all things those of Van der Werff affected me the most. His picture of Sarah delivering Agar to Abraham is delicious. I would have agreed to have been Abraham though the consequence would have been that I should have been dead five or six thousand years. Carlo Dolce became also a violent favorite. I am so little of a connoisseur that I preferred the works of these two authors to the old faded red things of Rubens. I am but a son of nature, loving what I see and feel, without being able to give a reason, nor caring much whether there be one. At Heidelberg I wished for you too. In fact I led you by the hand thro' the whole garden. I was struck with the resemblance of this scene to that of Vaucluse as seen from what is called the chateau of Petrarch. Nature has formed both on the same sketch, but she has filled up that of Heidelberg with a bolder hand. The river is larger, the mountains more majestic and better clothed. Art too has seconded her views. The chateau of Petrarch is the ruin of a modest country house, that of Heidelbourg would stand well along side the pyramids of Egypt. It is certainly the most magnificent ruin after those left us by the antients. At Strasbourg I sat down to write to you. But for my soul I could think of nothing at Strasbourg but the promontory of noses, of Diego, of Slawkenburgius his historian, and the procession of the Strasburgers to meet the man with the nose. Had I written to you from thence it would have been a continuation of Sterne upon noses, and I knew that nature had not formed me for a Continuator of Sterne: so I let it alone till I came here and received your angry letter. It is a proof of your esteem, but I love better to have soft testimonials of it. You must therefore now write me a letter teeming with affection; such as I feel for you. So much I have no right to ask.—Being but just arrived I am not au fait of the small news respecting your acquaintance here. I know only that the princess Lubomirski is still here, and that she has taken the house that was M. de Simoulin's. When you come again therefore you will be somewhat nearer to me, but not near enough: and still surrounded by a numerous cortege, so that I shall see you only by scraps as I did when you were here last. The time before we were half days, and whole days together, and I found this too little. Adieu! God bless you! Your's affectionately,

—TH: JEFFERSON

ॐ

[The following was sent June 19, 1788, to Thomas Lee Shippen and John Rutledge, Jr., traveling together on a grand tour of Europe, partly in Jefferson's footsteps. The two young men were already on the road. The first part of this document expands on Jefferson's own trip up the Rhine and is well worth reading. We omit only very small portions of it and include the entire second section, which contains general advice to travelers. The third portion, which picks up on the route Jefferson took in the south of France, is omitted in its entirety, as it adds little to the material in chapter five.]

HINTS TO AMERICANS TRAVELLING IN EUROPE
Old Louis or Dutch Ducats are the best money to take with you.

AMSTERDAM to UTRECHT. Go in the Track scout on account of the remarkeable pleasantness of the canal. You can have the principal cabin to yourselves for 52 stivers. At Amsterdam I lodged at the Wapping van Amsterdam. I liked the Valet de place they furnished me. He spoke French, and was sensible and well informed, his name was Guillaume or William.

UTRECHT. The best tavern Aubelette's. A steeple remarkeable for it's height.

NIMEGUEN. Chez un Anglois au Place royale. The Belle-vue here is well worth seeing. The Chateau also. At this place you must bribe your horse hirer to put as few horses to your carriage as you think you can travel with. Because with whatever number of horses you arrive at the first post house in Germany, with that they will oblige you to go on through the whole empire. I paid the price of four horses on condition they would put but three to my chariot. On entering the Prussian dominions remark the effect of despotism on the people.

CLEVES. The Posthouse. The road most used is by Xanten and Hochstrass. But that by Wesel and Duysberg is perhaps as short. Near Duysberg is the place where Varus and his legions were cut off by the Germans. I could find no body in the village however who could speak any language I spoke, and could not make them understand what I wished to see. I missed my object therefore, tho' I had taken this road on purpose. The Posthouse is the best tavern.

DUSSELDORFF. Zwey brukker Hoff. Chez Zimmerman. The best tavern I saw in my whole journey. In the palace is a collection of paintings equal in merit to any thing in the world. That of Dresden is said to be as good. This will be worth repeated examination. On the road from Dusseldorff to Cologne is a chateau of the elector, worth seeing. There is a famous one at Bensberg, which is off the road. I do not know whether it is best to go to it from Dusseldorff or Cologne.

COLOGNE. At the Holy ghost. Chez Ingel. A good tavern. This place and it's commerce is to be noted. A good deal is carried on to America. It's quai resembles, for the number of vessels, a seaport town. From hence the Cologne millstones are sent.

BONNE. The court of England. The palace here is to be seen.

COBLENTZ. The Wildman or l'Homme sauvage. A very good tavern. The tavern keeper furnished me with the Carte des postes d'Allemagne. I paid his bill without examining it. When I looked into it, after my departure I found he had forgot to insert the Map, and I had no sure opportunity of sending him the price. Pray pay him for me with this apology, and I shall reimburse it with thankfulness. He is very obliging. He accompanied me to a gentleman well acquainted with the vineyards and wines of the Moselle about which I wished to inform myself. He will recollect me from that circumstance.

Here call for Moselle wine, and particularly that of Brownberg and of the Grand Chambellan's crop of 1783. that you may be acquainted with the best quality of Moselle wine. The Elector's palace here is worth visiting, and note the manner in which the rooms are warmed by tubes coming from an oven below. The Chateau over the river to be visited. Remarkeably fine bread here, particularly the roll for breakfast, from which the Philadelphians derive what they call the French roll, which does not exist in France, but has been carried over by the Germans.

From Coblentz to Mayence or Frankfort the post road goes by Nassau, Nastaden, Schwalbach, and Wisbaden. It is as mountainous as the passage of the Alps, and entirely a barren desert. Were I to pass again, I would hire horses to carry me along the Rhine as far as a practicable road is to be found. Then I would embark my carriage on a boat to be drawn by a horse or horses till you pass the cliffs which intercept the land communication. This would be only for a few miles, say half a dozen or a dozen. You will see what I am told are the most picturesque scenes in the world, and which travelers go express to see, and you may be landed at the first village on the North East side of the river after passing the cliffs, and from thence hire horses to Mayence. Stop on the road at the village of Rudesheim, and the Abbaye of Johansberg to examine their vineyards and vines. The latter is the best made on the Rhine without comparison ....

MAYENCE. Hotel de Mayence. Good and reasonable. The ham of Mayence is next to that of Westphalia for celebrity ....

FRANKFORT. The Rothen house, or Red house chez Monsr. Dick. The son of the Tavern keeper speaks English and French, has resided some time in London, is sensible and obliging ....

Francfort is a considerable place and worth examining in detail.

Major de Geismer may happen to be here. If he be, present yourselves to him in my name. If you shew him this note, it will serve to ensure you all the attentions you need. He can tell what there is worth seeing ....

MANHEIM. Cour du Palatin. Good tavern. At this place you must propose to make some stay. Buy the pamphlet which mentions the curiosities of the town and country. The gallery of paintings is more considerable than that of Dusseldorp, but has not so many precious things. The Observatory worth seeing.

Excursion to KAEFERTHALL to see the plantation of Rhubarb and herd of wild boars.

Excursion to Dossenheim to see the Angora goats. They are in the mountains a few leagues beyond Dossenheim.

Excursion to HEIDELBERG. The chateau is the most imposing ruin of modern ages. It's situation is the most romantic and the most delightful possible. I should have been glad to have passed days at it. The situation is, on a great scale, what that of Vaucluse is on a small one.

Excursion to SCHWETZINGEN to see the garden. They are not to be compared to the English gardens, but they are among the best of Germany ....

CARLSRUH. This place is not noted in the post map, but it is a post station, and well worth staying at a day or two. The posts leading to it are Spire and Craben.

Carlsruh is the seat of the Margrave of Baden, an excellent sovereign if we may judge of him from the appearance of his dominions. The town seems to be only an appendage to his palace.

The tavern is (au Prince hereditaire) good and reasonable. Visit the palace and particularly it's tower. Visit the gardens minutely. You will see in it some deer of an uncommon kind, Angora goats, tamed beavers, and a fine collection of pheasants.

STRASBURGH. a l'Esprit. The Cardinal de Rohan's palace to be seen. The steeple of the Cathedral which I believe is the highest in the world, and the handsomest. Go to the very top of it; but let it be the last operation of the day, as you will need a long rest after it.

KOENIG, bookseller here has the best shop of classical books I ever saw. Basker-ville's types I think are in this town. Beaumarchais' editions of Voltaire are printing here.

Here you will take a different route from mine. [One of the two was planning to descend the Danube to Vienna and then go on to Istanbul, but abandoned this plan when war broke out in eastern Europe.] The rivers Rhine and Danube will be the best guides in general. You will probably visit the falls of Schaffhausen.

At ULM, if you find it eligible, you can embark on the Danube and descend it to Vienna.

From VIENNA to TRIESTE. Examine carefully where you first meet with the Olive tree, and be so good as to inform me of it. This is a very interesting enquiry, for South Carolina and Georgia particularly. I have now orders from S. Carolina to send a large quantity of olive trees there, as they propose to endeavour to introduce the culture of that precious tree.

GENERAL OBSERVATIONS

Buy Dutens. Buy beforehand the map of the country you are going into. On arriving at a town, the first thing is to buy the plan of the town, and the book noting it's curiosities. Walk round the ramparts when there are any. Go to the top of a steeple to have a view of the town and it's environs.

When you are doubting whether a thing is worth the trouble of going to see it, recollect that you will never again be so near it, that you may repent the not having seen it, but can never repent having seen it. But there is an opposite extreme too. That is, the seeing too much. A judicious selection is to be aimed at, taking care that the indolence of the moment have no influence on the decision. Take care particularly not to let the porters of churches, cabinets &c. lead you thro' all the little details in their possession, which will load the memory with trifles, fatigue the attention and waste that and your time. It is difficult to confine these people to the few objects worth seeing and remembering. They wish for your money, and suppose you give it more willingly the more they detail to you.

When one calls in the taverns for the vin du pays they give you what is natural and unadulterated and cheap: when vin etrangere is called for, it only gives a pretext for charging an extravagant price for an unwholsome stuff, very often of their own brewing.

The people you will naturally see the most of will be tavern keepers, Valets de place, and postillions. These are the hackneyed rascals of every country. Of course they must never be considered when we calculate the national character.

Before entering Italy buy Addison's travels [Joseph Addison, Remarks on Several Parts of Italy]. He visited that country as a classical amateur, and it gives infinite pleasure to apply one's classical reading on the spot. Besides it aids our future recollection of the place.

Buy the Guide pour le voyage d'Italie en poste. The latest edition. It is the post book of Italy.

The theatres, public walks and public markets to be frequented. At these you see the inhabitants from high to low.

OBJECTS OF ATTENTION FOR AN AMERICAN

1. Agriculture. Every thing belonging to this art, and whatever has a near relation to it. Useful or agreeable animals which might be transported to America. New species of plants for the farm or garden, according to the climate of the different states.

2. Mechanical arts, so far as they respect things necessary in America, and inconvenient to be transported thither ready made. Such are forges, stonequarries, boats, bridges (very specially) &c. &c.

3. Lighter mechanical arts and manufactures. Some of these will be worth a superficial view. But circumstances rendering it impossible that America should become a manufacturing country during the time of any man now living, it would be a waste of attention to examine these minutely.

4. Gardens. Peculiarly worth the attention of an American, because it is the country of all others where the noblest gardens may be made without expence. We have only to cut out the superabundant plants.

5. Architecture worth great attention. As we double our numbers every 20 years we must double our houses. Besides we build of such perishable materials that one half of our houses must be rebuilt in every space of 20 years. So that in that term, houses are to be built for three fourths of our inhabitants. It is then among the most important arts: and it is desireable to introduce taste into an art which shews so much.

6. Painting, statuary. Too expensive for the state of wealth among us. It would be useless therefore and preposterous for us to endeavor to make ourselves connoisseurs in those arts. They are worth seeing, but not studying.

7. Politics of each country. Well worth studying so far as respects internal affairs. Examine their influence on the happiness of the people: take every possible occasion of entering into the hovels of the labourers, and especially at the moments of their repast, see what they eat, how they are cloathed, whether they are obliged to labour too hard; whether the government or their landlord takes from them an unjust proportion of their labour; on what footing stands the property they call their own, their personal liberty &c.

8. Courts. To be seen as you would see the tower of London or Menagerie of Versailles with their Lions, tigers, hyaenas and other beasts of prey, standing in the same relation to their fellows. A slight acquaintance with them will suffice to shew you that, under the most imposing exterior, they are the weakest and worst part of mankind. Their manners, could you ape them, would not make you beloved in your own country, nor would they improve it could you introduce them there to the exclusion of that honest simplicity now prevailing in America, and worthy of being cherished.

At Venice, Mr. Shippen will of course call on his relation the Countess Barziza.

CHAPTER EIGHT

The Last Year

W HEN JEFFERSON RETURNED TO PARIS IN LATE APRIL 1788, ONLY ONE MAJOR
piece of diplomatic work awaited him, and that was the consular convention
with France that Congress wanted him to renegotiate. Benjamin Franklin had negotiated the original convention, which was heartily disliked in America for the concessions granted to French nationals living in America, concessions that went much too
far and, many believed, impinged on American sovereignty. It was not a task Jefferson
looked forward to with any pleasure, but he attacked it with the energy he habitually
brought to official work. By August he and Montmorin had reached agreement on all
points, and the two men signed it. The old Confederation no longer existed by that time,
however, and the new American government had yet to meet. It was not until Jefferson
himself had become secretary of state in 1790 that the United States ratified the convention. As it happened, the consular convention was the first foreign agreement the United
States entered into. Thus in his official capacity as secretary of state, Jefferson had the
satisfaction of certifying a document he himself had negotiated in France.

The French government, to be sure, had changed by then as well. The new government repudiated the convention, and it never went into effect.

Other official business also came his way. In the fall of 1788, the French, in a moment
of inattention, banned the importation of all foreign whale oil, after having specifically
exempted this American export in the past from any such ban. That exemption had been
one of Jefferson's few trade victories, and he had to scramble to undo the damage. The ban

was aimed at the English, but the Americans had been included, and Jefferson had to go to Montmorin and have it reversed. In the process he put together a comprehensive and deeply knowledgable report on the whaling business, so substantial that he had it printed and distributed it to his own government (such as it was at that moment) and to the French ministers. It did the trick: The ban on American whale oil was rescinded, and Jefferson later gloated over the results. The British whaling fleet was reduced as a result of the ban by a little less than 30 percent, while American whaling flourished.

The whale oil business occupied Jefferson's time into the late fall of 1788. He had already written to ask Congress, no longer meeting, to grant him a six-month leave of absence. He had been away for four years and had personal affairs to attend to. He needed, for one thing, to take his daughters home so they could be raised to be American girls. According to Jefferson family tradition, his oldest daughter, Patsy, after years in the convent school in Paris, had expressed an interest in becoming a nun. Jefferson took both his daughters out of the school in April, some five months before he left. He also had to deal with numerous debts on his family estate and needed to check out the conditions of his possessions and his people at Monticello.

He did not expect to leave Paris permanently. He thought he would probably return in the same capacity for two or three more years of service. The old Congress had extended his commission. It seems not to have occurred to him that he would be wanted at home in the new government. Furthermore he liked Paris, liked the French, liked the life there, and he was watching close up what he thought would be a replay of the American Revolution, but without the bloodshed. For it had become obvious by the summer of 1788 that the current government of France could not last, that indeed the whole structure of the French government was collapsing. And he knew most of the people involved. Lafayette was one of his most intimate friends. The men and women of the aristocracy with the most liberal views were people with whom he regularly dined and exchanged ideas. As a minister of a foreign government, he was enjoined from participating in events, but he could watch, he could listen, and in an informal way he could advise. The French were about to make history on a grand scale, and he wanted to see it happen.

Back home, in the meantime, a new government was forming. The summer of 1788 saw the ratification of the Constitution. By June nine states had voted to adopt it, and that was enough. In late June his own state, Virginia, came in, and then New York. Only North Carolina and Rhode Island—"Rogue Island," as contemporaries called it—were holding out. Jefferson watched this happen through letters from Madison and other friends, a few of which are included below. He became unwittingly and unwillingly involved in the ratification process when, in the Virginia ratifying convention, opponents of the Constitution used extracts from his early letters to argue against approval. He had already changed his mind about most of these provisions, but it was a sign of his prestige in Virginia that he would become a factor in the debate even in absentia.

The only objections Jefferson now had to the Constitution were the lack of a Bill of Rights, and of what we now call term limits in the Presidency and the Senate. He was not alone in thinking that without some limit to the term, the Presidency could easily devolve into a monarchy. Since George Washington was slated to become the first President, however, this did not become a defining issue. Respect for Washington was universal then; no one believed he was in any way corruptible, or would be tempted to raise himself to the level of a hereditary monarch.

The matter of a Bill of Rights was altogether different. One of the most interesting exchanges in this chapter is that between him and Madison on the subject of such a bill, and why it was necessary. These letters are still important. If one wants to know what the original intent of the founders was, which is the main focus of debate today about the Constitution and the appointment of Supreme Court justices, this is one place to look. Madison was initially not in favor of a Bill of Rights. He believed that it was unnecessary, that all rights not explicitly granted to the government belonged to the people. It would be a mistake, therefore, to enumerate them; that would seem to limit them. Jefferson disagreed; he thought it would be a stronger defense of human rights to list them, to make rights explicit, based in text. Jefferson's arguments helped bring Madison around, and his letter to Madison of March 15, 1789, some historians believe, helped to inspire Madison's powerful June speech on the subject to the new Congress, a speech that was to a great degree instrumental in the speedy adoption of the Bill of Rights.

Human rights were also very much on the minds of the French liberals, the party called the Patriots, in 1789. Indeed Lafayette, Jefferson, and Thomas Paine had discussed the subject over dinner at Jefferson's house as early as the spring of 1788, along with a fourth gentleman, Dr. Gem, who was attending Jefferson's daughters. The subject was the debate over the American Constitution, which aroused almost as much interest in Europe as it did in America, and the three of them, sometimes with Dr. Gem as the fourth, talked it over "in a convention of our own," said Lafayette, "as earnestly as if we were to decide upon it." A little over a year later, Lafayette would be participating in such a decision.

It must have been a breathtaking experience to be in Paris during the French Revolution. Jefferson's letters to John Jay are models of reporting. They thoroughly explain the sequence of events, and you can feel at the same time the underlying excitement of the occasion. In a quite literal sense Jefferson was in the thick of things. In early July 1789, at a moment when the conservative party among the aristocrats had maneuvered the King into sending foreign troops (i.e., mercenaries) to Paris to confront the citizenry, a hundred German cavalry drew up in the Place Louis XV (now the Place de la Concorde). "This drew people to the spot," Jefferson wrote in his Autobiography years later, "who thus accidentally found themselves in front of the troops, merely at first as spectators; but as their numbers increased their indignation rose. They retired a few steps, and posted themselves on and behind large piles of stones, large and small, collected in that place for a bridge, which was to be built adjacent to it. In this position, happening to be in my carriage on a visit, I passed through the lane they had formed, without interruption. But the moment after I had passed, the people attacked the cavalry with stones. They charged, but the advantageous position of the people, and the showers of stones, obliged the horse to retire, and quit the field altogether …. This was the signal for universal insurrection."

The people surged through Paris, arming themselves. The date was July 12. On July 14, the Bastille fell. Over the coming days Jefferson went to the Bastille to watch the crowd tear it down, stone by stone. He no doubt saw the heads of de Launay and de Flesselles—the prison's governor and the royal keeper of arms in Paris, who had misled the crowd in its quest for arms—raised on pikes. When Ethiel de Corny came back to his house after serving as the head of the delegation that had requested arms from de Launay on July 14, Jefferson happened to be there, "and received from him a narrative of these transactions." That night the Duke de Liancourt forced his way into the king's bedchamber to tell him what had happened at the Bastille. This was the same duke whose wife was William Short's mistress and who was Jefferson's good friend.

This is not the place to describe the events of the French Revolution. In his correspondence, Jefferson writes clearly enough not to need further explanation. The correspondence serves indeed as a kind of mini-history of that time, including the events that led up to the decisive summer of 1789—the bad harvest of the previous summer, which left the population of France without bread over the following winter (even at the dinner parties of the elite in Paris that winter, guests were asked to bring their own bread); the great cold of that winter, when the temperature dropped well below zero degrees Fahrenheit and the government was forced to light huge bonfires at street corners to keep people warm; the unrest, the cold, and the famine experienced by the people; the meetings of the État-général in May, the machinations of the conservatives among the aristocrats to control it, the Tennis Court oath that united the third estate, the refusal of French troops to fire on their own people; and the virtual bankruptcy of the French government. There was no shortage of causes for what happened that summer.

Years later, in his Autobiography, Jefferson was thinking of the French declaration of the rights of man—a document he had a part in generating—and of the movement toward liberty in the world at large, which he regarded as irresistible. It occurred to him with a sense of wonder how it had all started with such a little thing—a tax on tea. "So inscrutable is the arrangement of causes and consequences in this world," he wrote, "that a two-penny duty on tea, unjustly imposed in a sequestered part of it, changes the condition of all its inhabitants." The British duty on tea, in other words, which led to the revolt of its American colonies, had come to this—millions of people, everywhere in the world, imbued with the spirit of liberty.

The role he played in the French Revolution, small but significant, came to an end when he finally received official permission from his own government to return home. That came in September 1789, and our selections conclude with the full text of his letter to Madison of September 6, suggesting that the Earth belongs in usufruct to the living. Like so many letters in this volume, it is famous. Jefferson's time in France, although it did not accomplish much in the way of diplomatic gains, gave him occasions to write letters home, and we are the beneficiaries. He was seldom less than eloquent, and he thought hard and deeply about things. To read the correspondence from his years in France is to watch history happen, to be in the midst of it in all its confusion, its compelling mix of the squalid and the splendid. It is deeply compelling. The correspondence included below omits information on other matters, to convey something of what must have been the intensity of the experience. Not wanting to get in the way of the text's immediacy, I have added very little in the way of annotation.

❧

To Anne Willing Bingham
DEAR MADAM   Paris May 11. 1788

A gentleman going to Philadelphia furnishes me the occasion of sending you some numbers of the Cabinet des modes and some new theatrical peices. These last have had great success on the stage, where they have excited perpetual applause. We have now need of something to make us laugh, for the topics of the times are sad and eventful. The gay and thoughtless Paris is now become a furnace of Politics. All the world is run politically mad. Men, women, children talk nothing else; and you know that naturally they talk much, loud and warm. Society is spoilt by it, at least for those who, like myself, are but lookers on.—You too have had your political fever. But our good ladies, I trust, have been too wise to wrinkle their foreheads with politics. They are contented to soothe and calm the minds of their husbands returning ruffled from political debate. They have the good sense to value domestic happiness above all other, and the art to cultivate it beyond all others. There is no part of the earth where so much of this is enjoyed as in America. You agree with me in this: but you think that the pleasures of Paris more than supply it's want: in other words that a Parisian is happier than an American. You will change your opinion, my dear Madam, and come over to mine in the end. Recollect the women of this capital, some on foot, some on horses, and some in carriages hunting pleasure in the streets, in routs and assemblies, and forgetting that they have left it behind them in their nurseries; compare them with our own countrywomen occupied in the tender and tranquil amusements of domestic life, and confess that it is a comparison of Amazons and Angels.—You will have known from the public papers that Monsieur de Buffon, the father, is dead: and you have known long ago that the son and his wife are separated. They are pursuing pleasure in opposite directions. Madame de Rochambeau is well: so is Madame de la Fayette. I recollect no other Nouvelles de societé interesting to you, and as for political news of battles and sieges, Turks and Russians, I will not detail them to you, because you would be less handsome after reading them. I have only to add then, what I take a pleasure in repeating, tho' it be to the thousandth time that I have the honour to be with sentiments of very sincere respect & attachment, dear Madam, Your most obedient & most humble servant,

—TH: JEFFERSON

❧

To Edward Carrington
DEAR SIR   Paris May 27. 1788

I have received with great pleasure your friendly letter of Apr. 24. It has come to hand after I had written my letters for the present conveiance, and just in time to add this to them. I learn with great pleasure the progress of the new Constitution. Indeed I have presumed it would gain on the public mind, as I confess it has on my own. At first, tho I saw that the great mass and groundwork was good, I disliked many appendages. Reflection and discussion have cleared off most of these. You have satisfied me as to the query I had put to you about the right of direct taxation. My first wish was that 9 states would adopt it in order to ensure what was good in it, and that the others might, by holding off, produce the necessary amendments. But the plan of Massachusets is far preferable, and will I hope be followed by those who are yet to decide. There are two amendments only which I am anxious for. 1. A bill of rights, which it is so much the interest of all to have, that I conceive it must be yielded. The 1st. amendment proposed by Massachusets will in some degree answer this end, but not so well. It will do too much in some instances and too little in others. It will cripple the federal government in some cases where it ought to be free, and not restrain it in some others where restraint would be right. The 2d. amendment which appears to me essential is the restoring the principle of necessary rotation, particularly to the Senate and Presidency: but most of all to the last. Re-eligibility makes him an officer for life, and the disasters inseparable from an elective monarchy, render it preferable, if we cannot tread back that step, that we should go forward and take refuge in an hereditary one. Of the correction of this article however I entertain no present hope, because I find it has scarcely excited an objection in America. And if it does not take place ere long, it assuredly never will. [In fact, the U.S. Presidency was limited to two terms by the 22nd Amendment, ratified in 1951.] The natural progress of things is for liberty to yeild, and government to gain ground. As yet our spirits are free. Our jealousy is only put to sleep by the unlimited confidence we all repose in the person to whom we all look as our president. After him inferior characters may perhaps succeed and awaken us to the danger which his merit has led us into. For the present however, the general adoption is to be prayed for, and I wait with great anxiety for the news from Maryland and S. Carolina which have decided before this, and wish that Virginia, now in session, may give the 9th. vote of approbation. There could then be no doubt of N. Carolina, N. York, and New Hampshire. But what do you propose to do with Rhode island? As long as there is hope, we should give her time. I cannot conceive but that she will come to rights in the long run. Force, in whatever form, would be a dangerous precedent ....

—TH: JEFFERSON

❧

To James Madison
DEAR SIR   Paris July 31. 1788

[The first half of this letter contained European political gossip] ... I sincerely rejoice
at the acceptance of our new constitution by nine states. It is a good canvas, on
which some strokes only want retouching. What these are, I think are sufficiently
manifested by the general voice from North to South, which calls for a bill of
rights. It seems pretty generally understood that this should go to Juries,
Habeas corpus, Standing armies, Printing, Religion and Monopolies. I conceive
there may be difficulty in finding general modification of these suited to the
habits of all the states. But if such cannot be found then it is better to establish
trials by jury, the right of Habeas corpus, freedom of the press and freedom of
religion in all cases, and to abolish standing armies in time of peace, and
Monopolies, in all cases, than not to do it in any. The few cases wherein these
things may do evil, cannot be weighed against the multitude wherein the want
of them will do evil. In disputes between a foreigner and a native, a trial by jury
may be improper. But if this exception cannot be agreed to, the remedy will be
to model the jury by giving the medietas linguae in civil as well as criminal cases.
Why suspend the Hab. Corp. in insurrections and rebellions? The parties who
may be arrested may be charged instantly with a well defined crime. Of course
the judge will remand them. If the publick safety requires that the government
should have a man imprisoned on less probable testimony in those than in other
emergencies; let him be taken and tried, retaken and retried, while the necessity
continues, only giving him redress against the government for damages.
Examine the history of England: see how few of the cases of the suspension of
the Habeas corpus law have been worthy of that suspension. They have been
either real treasons wherein the parties might as well have been charged at once,
or sham-plots where it was shameful they should ever have been suspected. Yet
for the few cases wherein the suspension of the hab. corp. has done real good,
that operation is now become habitual, and the minds of the nation almost
prepared to live under it's constant suspension. A declaration that the federal
government will never restrain the presses from printing any thing they please,
will not take away the liability of the printers for false facts printed. The

declaration that religious faith shall be unpunished, does not give impunity to criminal acts dictated by religious error. The saying there shall be no monopolies lessens the incitements to ingenuity, which is spurred on by the hope of a monopoly for a limited time, as of 14. years; but the benefit even of limited monopolies is too doubtful to be opposed to that of their general suppression. If no check can be found to keep the number of standing troops within safe bounds, while they are tolerated as far as necessary, abandon them altogether, discipline well the militia, and guard the magazines with them. More than magazine-guards will be useless if few, and dangerous if many. No European nation can ever send against us such a regular army as we need fear, and it is hard if our militia are not equal to those of Canada or Florida. My idea then is, that tho' proper exceptions to these general rules are desireable and probably practicable, yet if the exceptions cannot be agreed on, the establishment of the rules in all cases will do ill in very few. I hope therefore a bill of rights will be formed to guard the people against the federal government, as they are already guarded against their state governments in most instances.

The abandoning the principle of necessary rotation in the Senate, has I see been disapproved by many; in the case of the President, by none. I readily therefore suppose my opinion wrong, when opposed by the majority as in the former instance, and the totality as in the latter. In this however I should have done it with more complete satisfaction, had we all judged from the same position.

—TH: JEFFERSON

To John Jay
SIR   Paris Sep. 3. 1788

In my letter of the 20th. I informed you of the act of public bankruptcy which has taken place here. The effect of this would have been a forced loan of about 180. millions of livres in the course of the present and ensuing year. But it did not yeild a sufficient immediate relief. The treasury became literally monyless, and all purposes depending on this mover came to a stand. The archbishop was hereupon removed, with Monsieur Lambert, the Comptroller general, and

Mr. Neckar was called in as Director general of the finance. To soften the Archbishop's dismission, a cardinal's hat is asked for him from Rome, and his nephew promised the succession to the Archbishopric of Sens. The public joy on this change of administration was very great indeed. The people of Paris were amusing themselves with trying and burning the Archbishop in effigy, and rejoicing on the appointment of Mr. Neckar. The commanding officer of the city guards undertook to forbid this, and not being obeyed, he charged the mob with fixed bayonets, killed two or three and wounded many. This stopped their rejoicings for that day: but enraged at being thus obstructed in amusements wherein they had committed no disorder whatever, they collected in great numbers the next day, attacked the guards in various places, burnt 10. or 12. guardhouses, killed two or three of the guards, and had about 6. or 8. of their own number killed. The city was hereupon put under martial law, and after a while the tumult subsided, and peace was restored. The public stocks rose 10. per cent on the day of Mr. Neckar's appointment; he was immediately offered considerable sums of money, and has been able so far to waive the benefit of the act of bankruptcy as to pay in cash all demands except the remboursements des capitaux. For these and for a sure supply of other wants he will depend on the States general, and will hasten their meeting, as thought. No other change has yet taken place in administration. The minister of war however must certainly follow his brother, and some think, and all wish that Monsr. de Lamoignon, the garde des sceaux, may go out also. The administration of justice is still suspended. The whole kingdom seems tranquil at this moment .... [The rest of the letter contains more European political news.]

—TH JEFFERSON

ॐ

From James Madison
DEAR SIR   New York Ocr. 17. 1788

[The first portion of this letter concerns Jefferson's outfit, and the impossibility of the old Congress taking the subject up. Italics indicate language in code.] ...The States which have adopted the new Constitution are all proceeding to the arrangements for putting it into action in March next. Pennsylva. alone has as yet actually appointed deputies; and that only for the Senate. My last mentioned that these were Mr. R. Morris and a Mr. McClay. How the other elections there and else-where will run is matter of uncertainty. The Presidency alone unites the con-jectures of the public. The vice president is not at all marked out by the general voice. As the President will be from a Southern State, it falls almost of course for the other part of the Continent to supply the next in rank. South Carolina may however think of Mr. Rutledge unless it should be previously discovered that votes will be wasted on him. The only candidates in the Northern States brought forward with their known consent are *Hancock and Adams and between these it seems probable the question will lie. Both of them are objectionable and would I think be postponed by the general suffrage to several others if they would accept the place. Hancock is weak, ambitious, a courtier of popularity given to low intrigue and lately reunited by a factious friendship with S. Adams.—J. Adams has made himself obnoxious to many particularly in the Southern states by the political principles avowed in his book. Others recolecting his cabal during the war against General Washington, knowing his extravagant self importance and considering his preference of an unprofitable dignity to some place of emolument better adapted to private fortune as a proof of his having an eye to the presidency conclude that he would not be a very cordial second to the General and that an impatient ambition might even intrigue for a premature advancement. The danger would be the greater if particular factious characters, as may be the case, should get into the public councils. Adams it appears, is not unaware of some of the obstacles to his wish and thro a letter to Smith has thrown out popular sentiments as to the proposed president.*

The little pamphlet herewith inclosed will give you a collective view of the alterations which have been proposed for the new Constitution. Various and numerous as they appear they certainly omit many of the true grounds of oppo-sition. The articles relating to Treaties, to paper money, and to contracts, created more enemies than all the errors in the System positive and negative put together. It is true nevertheless that not a few, particularly in Virginia have contended for the proposed alterations from the most honorable and patriotic motives; and that among the advocates for the Constitution there are some who wish for further guards to public liberty and individual rights. As far as these may consist of a constitutional declaration of the most essential rights, it is probable they will be added; though there are many who think such addition unnecessary, and not a few who think it misplaced in such a Constitution. There is scarce any point on which the party in opposition is so much divided as to its importance and its propriety. My own opinion has always been in favor of a bill of rights; provided it be so framed as not to imply powers not meant to be included in the enumeration. At the same time I have never thought the omission a material defect, nor been anxious to supply it even by subsequent amendment, for any other reason than that it is anxiously desired by others. I have favored it because I supposed it might be of use, and if properly executed could not be of disservice. I have not viewed it in an important light. 1. Because I conceive that in a certain degree, though not in the extent argued by Mr. Wilson, the rights in question are reserved by the manner in which the federal powers are granted. 2. Because there is great reason to fear that a positive declaration of some of the most essential rights could not be obtained in the requisite latitude. I am sure that the rights of conscience in particular, if submitted to public definition would be narrowed much more than they are likely ever to be by an assumed power. One of the objections in New England was that the Constitution by prohibiting religious tests opened a door for Jews Turks and infidels. 3. Because the limited powers of the federal Government and the jealousy of the subordinate Governments, afford a security which has not existed in the case of the State Governments, and exists in no other. 4. Because experience proves the inefficacy of a bill of rights on those occasions when its controul is most needed. Repeated violations of these parchment barriers have been committed by overbearing majorities in every State. In Virginia I have seen the bill of rights violated in every instance where it has been opposed to a popular current. Notwithstanding the explicit provision contained in that instrument for the rights of Conscience it is well known that a religious establishment would have taken place in that State, if the legislative majority had found as they expected, a majority of the people in favor of the measure; and I am persuaded that if a majority of the people were now of one sect, the measure would still take place and on narrower ground than was then proposed, notwithstanding the additional obstacle which the law has since created. Wherever the real power in a Government lies, there is the danger of oppression. In our Governments the real power lies in the majority of the Community, and the invasion of private rights is chiefly to be apprehended, not from acts of Government contrary to the sense of its constituents, but from acts in which the Government is the mere instrument of the major number of the constituents. This is a truth of great importance, but not yet sufficiently attended to: and is probably more strongly impressed on my mind by facts, and reflections suggested by them, than on yours which has contemplated abuses of power issuing from a very different quarter. Wherever there is an interest and power to do wrong, wrong will generally be done, and not less readily by a powerful and interested party than by a powerful and interested prince. The difference, so far as it relates to the superiority of republics over monarchies, lies in the less degree of probability that interest may prompt abuses of power in the former than in the latter; and in the security in the former against oppression of more than the smaller part of the Society, whereas in the former it may be extended in a manner to the whole. The difference so far as it relates to the point in question—the efficacy of a bill of rights in controuling abuses of power—lies in this: that in a monarchy the latent force of the nation is superior to that of the Sovereign, and a solemn charter of popular rights must have a great effect, as a standard for trying the validity of public acts, and a signal for rousing and uniting the superior force of the community; whereas in a popular Government, the political and physical power may be considered as vested in the same hands, that is in a majority of the people, and consequently the tyrannical will of the sovereign is not to be controuled by the dread of an appeal to any other force within the community. What use then it may be asked can a bill of rights serve in popular Governments? I answer the two following which though less essential than in other Governments, sufficiently recommend the precaution. 1. The political truths declared in that solemn manner acquire by degrees the character of fundamental maxims of free Government, and as they become incorporated with the national sentiment, counteract the impulses of interest and passion. 2. Altho' it be generally true as above stated that the danger of oppression lies in the interested majorities of the people rather than in usurped acts of the Government, yet there may be occasions on which the evil may spring from the latter sources; and on such, a bill of rights will be a good ground for an appeal to the sense of the community. Perhaps too there may be a certain degree of danger, that a succession of artful and ambitious rulers, may by gradual and well-timed advances, finally erect an independent Government on the subversion of liberty. Should this danger exist at all, it is prudent to guard against it, especially when the precaution can do no injury. At the same time I must own that I see no tendency in our governments to danger on that side. It has been remarked that there is a tendency in all Governments to an augmentation of power at the expence of liberty. But the remark as usually understood does not appear to me well founded. Power when it has attained a certain degree of energy and independence goes on generally to further degrees. But when below that degree, the direct tendency is to further degrees of relaxation, until the abuses of liberty beget a sudden transition to an undue degree of power. With this explanation the remark may be true; and in the latter sense only is it in my opinion applicable to the Governments in America. It is a melancholy reflection that liberty should be equally exposed to danger whether the Government have too much or too little power, and that the line which divides these extremes should be so inaccurately defined by experience.

Supposing a bill of rights to be proper the articles which ought to compose it, admit of much discussion. I am inclined to think that absolute restrictions in cases that are doubtful, or where emergencies may overrule them, ought to be avoided. The restrictions however strongly marked on paper will never be regarded when opposed to the decided sense of the public; and after repeated violations in extraordinary cases, they will lose even their ordinary efficacy. Should a Rebellion or insurrection alarm the people as well as the Government, and a suspension of the Hab. Corp. be dictated by the alarm, no written prohibitions on earth would prevent the measure. Should an army in time of peace be gradually established in our neighbourhood by Britn: or Spain, declarations on paper would have as little effect in preventing a standing force for the public safety. The best security against these evils is to remove the pretext for them. With regard to Monopolies they are justly classed among the greatest nuisances in Government. But is it clear that as encouragements to literary works and ingenious discoveries, they are not too valuable to be wholly renounced? Would it not suffice to reserve in all cases a right to the public to abolish the privilege at a price to be specified in the grant of it? Is there not also infinitely less danger of this abuse in our Governments than in most others? Monopolies are sacrifices of the many to the few. Where the power is in the few it is natural for them to sacrifice the many to their own partialities and corruptions. Where the power, as with us, is in the many not in the few, the danger can not be very great that the few will be thus favored. It is much more to be dreaded that the few will be unnecessarily sacrificed to the many.

I inclose a paper containing the late proceedings in Kentucky. I wish the ensuing Convention may take no step injurious to the character of the district, and favorable to the views of those who wish ill to the U. States. One of my late letters communicated some circumstances which will not fail to occur on perusing the objects of the proposed Convention in next month. Perhaps however there may be less connection between the two cases than at first one is ready to conjecture. I am Dr. Sir with the sincerest esteem & affectn. Yours,

—JS. MADISON JR

∾

To Francis Hopkinson
DEAR SIR   Paris Mar. 13. 1789

... I hope that by this time you have ceased to make wry faces about your vinegar, and that you have received it safe and good. You say that I have been dished up to you as an antifederalist, and ask me if it be just. My opinion was never worthy enough of notice to merit citing: but since you ask it I will tell it you. I am not a Federalist, because I never submitted the whole system of my opinions to the creed of any party of men whatever in religion, in philosophy, in politics, or in any thing else where I was capable of thinking for myself. Such an addiction is the last degradation of a free and moral agent. If I could not go to heaven but with a party, I would not go there at all. Therefore I protest to you I am not of the party of federalists. But I am much farther from that of the Antifederalists. I approved from the first moment, of the great mass of what is in the new constitution, the consolidation of the government, the organisation into Executive, legislative and judiciary, the subdivision of the legislative, the happy compromise of interests between the great and little states by the different manner of voting in the different houses, the voting by persons instead of states, the qualified negative on laws given to the Executive which however I should have liked better if associated with the judiciary also as in New York, and the power of taxation. I thought at first that the latter might have been limited. A little reflection soon convinced me it ought not to be. What I disapproved from the first moment also was the want of a bill of rights to guard liberty against the legislative as well as executive branches of the government, that is to say to secure freedom in religion, freedom of the press, freedom from monopolies, freedom from unlawful imprisonment, freedom from a permanent military, and a trial by jury in all cases determinable by the laws of the land. I disapproved also the perpetual re-eligibility of the President. To these points of disapprobation I adhere. My first wish was that the 9. first conventions might accept the constitution, as the means of securing to us the great mass of good it contained, and that the 4. last might reject it, as the means of obtaining amendments. But I was corrected in this wish the moment I saw the much better plan of Massachusets and which had never occurred to me. With respect to the declaration of rights I suppose the majority of the United states are of my opinion: for I apprehend all the anti-federalists, and a very respectable proportion of the federalists think that such a declaration should now be annexed. The enlightened part of Europe have given us the greatest credit for inventing this instrument of security for the rights of the people, and have been not a little surprised to see us so soon give it up. With respect to the re-eligibility of the president, I find myself differing from the major-ity of my countrymen, for I think there are but three states of the 11. which have desired an alteration to this. And indeed, since the thing is established, I would wish it not to be altered during the life of our great leader, whose executive talents are superior to those I believe of any man in the world, and who alone by the authority of his name and the confidence reposed in his perfect integrity, is fully qualified to put the new government so under way as to secure it against the efforts of opposition. But having derived from our error all the good there was in it I hope we shall correct it the moment we can no longer have the same person at the helm. These, my dear friend, are my sentiments, by which you will see I was right in saying I am neither federalist nor antifederalist; that I am of neither party, nor yet a trimmer between parties. These my opinions I wrote within a few hours after I had read the constitution, to one or two friends in America. I had not then read one single word printed on the subject. I never had an opinion in politics or religion which I was afraid to own. A costive reserve on these subjects might have procured me more esteem from some people, but less from myself. My great wish is to go on in a strict but silent performance of my duty: to avoid attracting notice and to keep my name out of newspapers, because I find the pain of a little censure, even when it is unfounded, is more acute than the pleasure of much praise. The attaching circumstance of my present office is that I can do it's duties unseen by those for whom they are done.—You did not think, by so short a phrase in your letter, to have drawn on yourself such an egoistical dissertation. I beg your pardon for it, and will endeavor to merit that pardon by the constant sentiments of esteem & attachment with which I am Dear Sir, Your sincere friend & servant,

—TH: JEFFERSON

P.S. Affectionate respects to Dr. Franklin Mr. Rittenhouse, their and your good families.

∽

To James Madison

DEAR SIR   Paris Mar. 15. 1789

I wrote you last on the 12th. of Jan. since which I have received yours of Octob. 17. Dec. 8 and 12. That of Oct. 17. came to hand only Feb. 23. How it happened to be four months on the way, I cannot tell, as I never knew by what hand it came. Looking over my letter of Jan. 12th. I remark an error of the word 'probable' instead of 'improbable,' which doubtless however you had been able to correct. Your thoughts on the subject of the Declaration of rights in the letter of Oct. 17. I have weighed with great satisfaction. Some of them had not occurred to me before, but were acknoleged just in the moment they were presented to my mind. In the arguments in favor of a declaration of rights, you omit one which has great weight with me, the legal check which it puts into the hands of the judiciary. This is a body, which if rendered independent, and kept strictly to their own department merits great confidence for their learning and integrity. In fact what degree of confidence would be too much for a body composed of such men as Wythe, Blair, and Pendleton? On characters like these the 'civium ardor prava jubentium' would make no impression. I am happy to find that on the whole you are a friend to this amendment. The Declaration of rights is like all other human blessings alloyed with some inconveniences, and not accomplishing fully it's object. But the good in this instance vastly overweighs the evil. I cannot refrain from making short answers to the objections which your letter states to have been raised. 1. That the rights in question are reserved by the manner in which the federal powers are granted. Answer. A constitutive act may certainly be so formed as to need no declaration of rights. The act itself has the force of a declaration as far as it goes: and if it goes to all material points nothing more is wanting. In the draught of a constitution which I had once a thought of proposing in Virginia, and printed afterwards, I endeavored to reach all the great objects of public liberty, and did not mean to add a declaration of rights. Probably the object was imperfectly executed: but the deficiencies would have been supplied by others in the course of discussion. But in a constitutive act which leaves some precious articles unnoticed, and raises implications against others, a declaration of rights becomes necessary by way of supplement. This is the case of our new federal constitution. This instrument forms us into one state as to certain objects, and gives us a legislative and executive body for these objects. It should therefore guard us against their abuses of power within the feild submitted to them. 2. A positive declaration of some essential rights could not be obtained in the requisite latitude. Answer. Half a loaf is better than no bread. If we cannot secure all our rights, let us secure what we can. 3. The limited powers of the federal government and jealousy of the subordinate governments afford a security which exists in no other instance. Answer. The first member of this seems resolvable into the 1st. objection before stated. The jealousy of the subordinate governments is a precious reliance. But observe that those governments are only agents. They must have principles furnished them whereon to found their opposition. The declaration of rights will be the text whereby they will try all the acts of the federal government. In this view it is necessary to the federal government also: as by the same text they may try the opposition of the subordinate governments. 4. Experience proves the inefficacy of a bill of rights. True. But tho it is not absolutely efficacious under all circumstances, it is of great potency always, and rarely inefficacious. A brace the more will often keep up the building which would have fallen with that brace the less. There is a remarkeable difference between the characters of the Inconveniencies which attend a Declaration of rights, and those which attend the want of it. The inconveniences of the Declaration are that it may cramp government in it's useful exertions. But the evil of this is short-lived, moderate, and reparable. The inconveniencies of the want of a Declaration are permanent, afflicting and irreparable: they are in constant progression from bad to worse. The executive in our governments is not the sole, it is scarcely the principal object of my jealousy. The tyranny of the legislatures is the most formidable dread at present, and will be for long years. That of the executive will come in it's turn, but it will be at a remote period. I know there are some among us who would now establish a monarchy. But they are inconsiderable in number and weight of character. The rising race are all republicans. We were educated in royalism: no wonder if some of us retain that idolatry still. Our young people are educated in republicanism. I am much pleased with the prospect that a declaration of rights will be added: and hope it will be done in that way which will not endanger the whole frame of the government, or any essential part of it .... [The remainder of the letter pertains to European political matters.]

—TH: JEFFERSON

⁊

[Portions of this letter covering European political affairs have been omitted.]

To John Jay

SIR   Paris May 9. 1789

Since my letter of Mar. 1. by the way of Havre and those of March 12th. and 15th. by the way of London no opportunity of writing has occurred till the present to London....

The revolution of this country has advanced thus far without encountering any thing which deserves to be called a difficulty. There have been riots in a few instances in three or four different places, in which there may have been a dozen or twenty lives lost. The exact truth is not to be got at. A few days ago a much more serious riot took place in this city, in which it became necessary for the troops to engage in regular action with the mob, and probably about 100 of the latter was killed. Accounts vary from 20. to 200. They were the most abandoned banditti of Paris, and never was a riot more unprovoked and unpitied. They began under a pretence that a paper manufacturer had proposed in an assembly to reduce their wages to 15. sous a day. They rifled his house, destroyed every thing in his magazines and shops, and were only stopped in their career of micheif by the carnage above mentioned. Neither this nor any other of the riots have had a professed connection with the great national reformation going on. They are such as have happened every year since I have been here, and as will continue to be produced by common incidents. The States general were opened on the 4th.

instant by a speech from the throne, one by the Garde des sceaux and one from Mr. Neckar. I hope they will be printed in time to send you herewith. Lest they should not, I will observe that that of Mr. Neckar stated the real and ordinary deficit to be 56. millions, and that he shewed that this could be made up without a new tax by economies and bonifications which he specified. Several articles of the latter are liable to the objection that they are proposed on branches of the revenue of which the nation has demanded a suppression. He tripped too slightly over the great articles of constitutional reformation these being not as clearly enounced in this Discourse as they were in his Rapport au roy which I sent you some time ago. On the whole his Discourse has not satisfied the patriotic party. It is now for the first time that their revolution is likely to receive a serious check, and begins to wear a fearful appearance. The progress of light and liberality in the order of the Noblesse has equalled expectation in Paris only and it's vicinities. The great mass of deputies of that order which come from the country shew that the habits of tyranny over the people are deeply rooted in them. They will consent indeed to equal taxation. But five sixths of that chamber are thought to be decidedly for voting by orders. So that had this great preliminary question rested on this body which formed theretofore the sole hope, that hope would have been completely disappointed. Some aid however comes in from a quarter whence none was expected. It was imagined the ecclesiastical elections would have been generally in favor of the higher clergy. On the contrary the lower clergy have obtained five sixths of these deputations. These are the sons of peasants who have done all the drudgery of the service for 10, 20, 30 guineas a year, and whose oppressions and penury contrasted by the pride and luxury of the higher clergy had rendered them perfectly disposed to humble the latter. They have done it in many instances with a boldness they were thought insusceptible of. Great hopes have been formed that these would concur with the tiers etat in voting by persons. In fact about half of them seem as yet so disposed: but the bishops are intrigueing and drawing them over with the address which has ever marked ecclesiastical intrigue. The deputies of the Tiers etat seem almost to a man inflexibly determined against the vote by orders. This is the state of parties as well as can be judged from conversation only during the fortnight they have been now together. But as no business has been yet begun, no votes as yet taken, this calculation can not be considered as sure. A middle proposition is talked of, to form the two privileged orders into one chamber. It is thought more possible to bring them into it than the tiers etat. Another proposition is to distinguish questions, referring those of certain descriptions to a vote by persons, others to a vote by orders. This seems to admit of endless altercation, and the Tiers etat manifest with no respect for that or any other modification whatever. Were this single question accomodated, I am of opinion there would not occur the least difficulty in the great and essential points of constitutional reformation. But on this preliminary question the parties are so irreconcileable that it is impossible to foresee what issue it will have. The Tiers etat, as constituting the nation, may propose to do the business of the nation either with or without the minorities in the houses of clergy and nobles which side with them. In that case, if the king should agree to it, the majorities in those two houses would secede, and might resist the taxgatherers. This would bring on a civil war. On the other hand, the privileged orders, offering to submit to equal taxation, may propose to the king to continue the government in it's former train, resuming to himself the power of taxation. Here the taxgatherers might be resisted by the people. In fine it is but too possible that between parties so animated, the king may incline the balance as he pleases. Happy that he is an honest unambitious man, who desires neither money nor power for himself; and that his most operative minister, tho he has appeared to trim a little, is still in the main a friend to public liberty.

I mentioned to you in a former letter the construction which our bankers at Amsterdam had put on the resolution of Congress appropriating the last Dutch loan, by which the money for our captives would not be furnished till the end of the year 1790. Orders from the board of treasury have now settled this question. The interest of the next month is to be first paid, and after that the money for the captives and foreign officers is to be furnished before any other paiment of interest. This ensures it when the next February interest becomes paiable. My representations to them on account of the contracts I had entered into for making the medals have produced from them the money for that object, which is lodged in the hands of Mr. Grand.

Mr. Neckar, in his discourse, proposed among his bonifications of revenue, the suppression of our two free ports of Bayonne and Lorient, which he says occasion a loss of 600,000 livres annually to the crown, by contraband. (The speech being not yet printed I state this only as it struck my ear when he delivered it. If I have mistaken it I beg you to receive this as my apology, and to consider what follows as written on that idea only). I have never been able to see that these freeports were worth one copper to us. To Bayonne our trade never went, and it is leaving Lorient. Besides the right of entrepot is a perfect substitute for the right of free port. The latter is a little less troublesome only to the merchants and captains. I should think therefore that a thing so useless to us and prejudicial to them might be relinquished by us on the common principles of friendship. I know the merchants of these ports will make a clamour, because the franchise covers their contraband with all the world. Has Monsr. de Moustier said any thing to you on this subject? It has never been mentioned to me. If not mentioned in either way, it is rather an indecent proceeding, considering that this right of freeport is founded in treaty. I shall ask of M. de Monmorin, on the first occasion whether he has communicated this to you through his minister, and if he has not I will endeavor to notice the infraction to him in such manner as neither to reclaim nor abandon the right of freeport, but leave our government free to do either.—The gazettes of France and Leyden as usual will accompany this. I am in hourly expectation of receiving from you my leave of absence, and keeping my affairs so arranged that I can leave Paris within eight days after receiving the permission.—I have the honor to be with sentiments of the most perfect esteem and respect Sir Your most obedient & most humble servt.,

                                                        —TH: JEFFERSON

&

[Portions of this letter that do not concern the events in France have been omitted.]

To John Jay
Sir   Paris June 17. 1789

I had the honor of addressing you on the 9th. and 12th. of May by the way of London. This goes through the same channel to the care of Mr. Trumbul. Having received no letter from you of later date than the 25th. of November I am apprehensive there may have been miscarriages, and the more so as I learn, thro another channel, that you have particularly answered mine of Nov. 19.

... You will have seen by my former letters that the question whether the States general should vote by Persons, or by Orders, had stopped their proceedings in the very first instance in which it could occur, that is, as to the verification of their powers, and that they had appointed committees to try if there were any means of accomodation. These could do nothing. The king then proposed that they should appoint others, to meet persons whom he should name, on the same subject. These conferences also proved ineffectual. He then proposed a specific mode of verifying. The Clergy accepted it unconditionally: the Noblesse with such conditions and modifications as did away their acceptance altogether. The commons, considering this as a refusal came to the resolution of the 10th. inst. (which I have the honor to send you) inviting the two other orders to come and take their places in the common room, and notifying that they should proceed to the verification of powers, and to the affairs of the nation either with or without them. The clergy have as yet given no answer. A few of their members have accepted the invitation of the Commons, and have presented themselves in their room to have their powers verified, but how many it will detach in the whole from that body, cannot be known till an answer be decided on. The Noblesse adhered to their former resolutions, and even the minority, well disposed to the commons, thought they could do more good in their own chamber by endeavoring to increase their numbers, and bettering the measures of the majority, than by joining the Commons. An intrigue was set on foot between the leaders of the Majority in that house, the queen and princes. They persuaded the king to go for some time to Marly. He went on the same day. The leaders moved in the chamber of Nobles that they should address the king to declare his own sentiments on the great question between the orders. It was intended that this address should be delivered to him at Marly, where separated from his ministers, and surrounded by the queen and princes, he might be surprized into a declaration for the nobles. The motion was lost however by a very great majority, that chamber being not yet quite ripe for throwing themselves into the arms of despotism. Necker and Montmorin who had discovered this intrigue, had warned some of the minority to defeat it, or they could not answer for what would happen. These two and St. Priest are the only members of the Council in favor of the commons. Luzerne, Puy-Segur and the others are high aristocrats. The commons having verified their powers, a motion was made the day before yesterday to declare themselves constituted and to proceed to business. I left them at two oclock yesterday, the debates not then finished. They differed only about forms of expression, but agreed in the substance, and probably decided yesterday or will decide to-day. Their next move I fancy will be to suppress all taxes, and instantly reestablish them till the end of their session in order to prevent a premature dissolution: and then they will go to work on a Declaration of rights and a constitution. The Noblesse I suppose will be employed altogether in counter operations; the Clergy, that is to say the higher clergy, and such of the Curés as they can bring over to their side will be waiting and watching merely to keep themselves in their saddles. Their department hitherto is that of meekness and cunning. The fate of the nation depends on the conduct of the king and his ministers. Were they to side openly with the Commons the revolution would be completed without a convulsion, by the establishment of a constitution, tolerably free, and in which the distinction of Noble and Commoner would be suppressed. But this is scarcely possible. *The king is honest and wishes the good of his people, but the expediency of an hereditary aristocracy is too difficult a question for him.*—On the contrary his prejudices, his habits and his connections decide him in his heart to support it. Should they decide openly for the Noblesse, the Commons, after suppressing taxes, and finishing their Declaration of rights, would probably go home, a bankruptcy takes place in the instant, Mr. Necker must go out, a resistance to the tax gatherers follows, and probably a civil war. These consequences are too evident and violent to render this issue likely. *Tho' the queen and princes are infatuated enough to hazard it, their party in the ministry would not.* Something therefore like what I hinted in my letter of May 12. is still the most likely to take place. While the Commons, either with or without their friends of the two houses, shall be employed in framing a constitution, perhaps the government may set the other two houses to work on the same subject: and when the three schemes shall be ready, joint committees may be negociated to compare them together, to see in what parts they agree, and probably they will agree in all except the organisation of the future states general. As to this, it may be endeavored, by the aid of wheedling and intimidation, to induce the two privileged chambers to melt themselves into one, and the commons, instead of one, to agree to two houses of legislation. I see no other middle ground to which they can be brought. It is a tremendous cloud indeed which hovers over this nation, and he at the helm has neither the courage nor the skill necessary to weather it. Eloquence in a high degree, knolege on matters of account, and order, are distinguishing traits in his character. Ambition is his first passion, Virtue his second. He has not discovered that sublime truth that a bold, unequivocal virtue is the best handmaid, even to Ambition, and would carry him further in the end than the temporizing wavering policy he pursues. His judgment is not of the first order, scarcely even of the second, his resolution frail, and upon the whole it is rare to meet an instance of a person so much below the reputation he has obtained. As this character, by the post and times in which providence has placed it, is important to be known, I send it to you as drawn by a person of my acquaintance who knows him well. He is not indeed his friend, and allowance must therefore be made for the high colouring. But this being abated, the faces and ground work of the drawing are just. If the Tiers separates, he goes at the same time: if they stay together and succeed in establishing a constitution to their mind, as soon as that is placed in safety, they will abandon him to the mercy of the court, unless he can recover the confidence which he has lost at present, and which indeed seems to be irrecoverable.

The inhabitants of St. Domingo, without the permission of the government, have chosen and sent deputies to the States general. The question of their admission is to be discussed by the states. In the mean time the government had promised them an assembly in their own island in the course of the present year. The death of the Dauphin, so long expected, has at length happened. The gazettes of France and Leyden accompany this: and I have the honour to be with the most perfect esteem and respect, Sir, Your most obedient & most humble servant,

—TH: JEFFERSON

P.S. June 18. The motion under debate with the commons for constituting their assembly passed yesterday by a majority of 400 and odd against 88. odd. The latter were for it in substance, but wished some particular amendment. They proceeded instantly to the subject of taxation. A member who called on me this moment gave me a state of the proceedings of yesterday from memory, which I inclose you. He left the house a little before the question was put, because he saw there was no doubt of it's passing, and his brother, who remained till the decision, informed him of it. So that we may expect, perhaps in the course of tomorrow, to see whether the government will interpose with a bold hand, or will begin a negotiation. But in the mean time this letter must go off. I will find some other opportunity however of informing you of the issue.

To John Jay
SIR   Paris June 24. 1789

My letter of the 17th. and 18th. inst. gave you the progress of the States general
to the 17th. when the Tiers had declared the illegality of all the existing taxes, and
their discontinuance from the end of their present session. The next day being
a jour de fete could furnish no indication of the impression that vote was likely to
make on the government. On the 19th. a council was held at Marly in the
afternoon. It was there proposed that the king should interpose by a declaration
of his sentiments in a seance royale. The declaration prepared by Mr. Necker, while
it censured in general the proceedings both of the Nobles and commons,
announced the king's view such as substantially to coincide with the
commons. It was agreed to in council, as also that the seance royale should be held
on the 22d. and the meetings till then be suspended. While the council was
engaged in this deliberation at Marly, the chamber of the clergy was in debate
whether they should accept the invitation of the tiers to unite with them in common chamber. On the first question to unite simply and unconditionally, it was
decided in the negative by a very small majority. As it was known however that some
members who had voted in the negative, would be for the affirmative with some
modifications, the question was put with these modifications, and it was determined by a majority of 11. members that their body should join the Tiers. These
proceedings of the clergy were unknown to the council at Marly, and those of the
council were kept secret from every body. The next morning, (the 20th.) the
members repaired to the House as usual, found the doors shut and guarded, and
a proclamation posted up for holding a seance royale on the 22d. and a
suspension of their meetings till then. They presumed in the first moment that
their dissolution was decided, and repaired to another place where they proceeded
to business. They there bound themselves to each other by an oath never to
separate of their own accord till they had settled a constitution for the nation on
a solid basis, and if separated by force, that they would reassemble in some other
place. [This was the Tennis Court oath.] It was intimated to them however that day,
privately, that the proceedings of the seance royale would be favorable to them.—
The next day they met in a church, and were joined by the majority of the clergy.
The heads of the Aristocracy, that is to say the queen, Count d'Artois and Prince de
Conde saw that all was lost without some violent exertion. The king was still at Marly.

No body was permitted to approach him but their friends. He was assailed by lies in all shapes. He was made to believe that the commons were going to absolve the army from their oath of fidelity to him and to raise their pay. *The queen abandoned herself* to rage and despair. They procured a committee to be held consisting of the king and his ministers, to which Monsieur and the Count d'Artois should be admitted. At this committee the latter attacked Mr. Necker personally, arraigned his plan, and proposed one which some of his engines had put into this hands; *for his own talents, go no further than a little poor wit.* Mr. Necker, whose characteristic is the want of firmness was brow-beaten and intimidated, and the king shaken. He determined that the two plans should be deliberated on the next day, and the seance royale put off a day longer. This encouraged a fiercer attack on Mr. Necker the next day; his plan was totally dislocated and that of the Count d'Artois inserted into it. Himself and Monsieur de Monmorin offered their resignation, which was refused, the Count d'Artois saying to Mr. Necker 'No, sir, you must be kept as the hostage; we hold you responsible for all the ill which shall happen.' This change of plan was immediately whispered without doors. The Nobility were in triumph, the people in consternation. When the King passed the next day thro the lane they formed from the Chateau to the hotel des etats (about half a mile) there was a dead silence. He was about an hour in the house, delivering his speech and declaration, copies of which I inclose you. On his coming out, a feeble cry of 'vive le roy' was raised by some children, but the people remained silent and sullen. When the Duc d'Orleans followed however their applauses were excessive. This must have been sensible to the king. He had ordered in the close of his speech that the members should follow him, and resume their deliberations the next day. The Noblesse followed him, and so did the clergy, except about 30. who, with the Tiers, remained in the room and entered into deliberation. They protested against what the king had done, adhered to all their former proceedings, and resolved the inviolability of their own persons. An officer came twice to order them out of the room in the king's name, but they refused to obey. In the afternoon the people, uneasy, began to assemble in great numbers in the courts and vicinities of the palace. The Queen was alarmed and sent for Mr. Necker. He was conducted amidst the shouts and acclamations of the multitude who filled all the apartments of the palace. He was a few minutes only with the queen and about three quarters of an hour with the king. Not a word has transpired of what passed at these two interviews. The king was just going to ride out. He passed thro the crowd to his carriage and into it without being in the least noticed. As Mr. Necker followed him universal acclamations were raised of 'vive Monsieur Necker, vive le sauveur de la France opprimée.' He was conducted back to his house with the same demonstrations of affection and anxiety. About 200. deputies of the Tiers, catching the enthusiasm of the moment, went to his house and extorted from him a promise that he would not resign. These circumstances must wound the heart of the king, desirous as he is to possess the affections of his subjects. As soon as the proceedings at Versailles were known at Paris, a run began on the caisse d'escompte, which is the first symptom always of the public diffidence and alarm. It is the less in condition to meet the run, as Mr. Necker has been forced to make free with it's funds for the daily support of the government.—This is the state of things as late as I am able to give them with certainty at this moment. My letter not being to go off till tomorrow evening, I shall go to Versailles tomorrow, and be able to add the transactions of this day and tomorrow.

June 25. Just returned from Versailles, I am enabled to continue my narration. On the 24th. nothing remarkeable past except an attack by the mob of Versailles on the archbishop of Paris, who had been one of the instigators of the court to the proceedings of the seance royale. They threw mud and stones at his carriage, broke the windows of it, and he in a fright promised to join the tiers.— This day (the 25th.) forty eight of the Nobles have joined the Tiers. Among these is the Duke d'Orleans. The M. de la Fayette could not be of the number, being restrained by his instructions. He is writing to his constituents to change his instructions or to accept his resignation. There are with the Tiers now 164. members of clergy, so that the common chamber consists of upwards of 800 members. The minority of the clergy however call themselves the chamber of the clergy and pretend to go on with business. I found the streets of Versailles much embarrassed with souldiers. There was a body of about 100. horse drawn up in front of the hotel of the states, and all the avenues and doors guarded by souldiers. No body was permitted to enter but the members, and this was by order of the king; for till now the doors of the common room have been open, and at least 2000 spectators attending their debates constantly. They have named a deputation to wait on the king and desire a removal of the souldiery from their doors, and seem determined, if this is not complied with, to remove themselves elsewhere. Instead of being dismayed with what has passed they seem to rise in their demands, and some of them to consider the erasing every vestige of a difference of order as indispensible to the establishment and preservation of a good constitution. I apprehend there is more courage than calculation in this project. I did imagine that seeing that Mr. Necker and themselves were involved, as common enemies, in the hatred of the aristocrats, they would have been willing to make common cause with him, and to wish his continuance in office: and that Mr. Necker, seeing that all the trimming he has used towards the court and nobles has availed him nothing, would engage himself heartily and solely on the popular side, and view his own salvation in that alone. The confidence which the people place in him seems to merit some attention. However the mass of the Common chamber are absolutely indifferent to his remaining in office. They consider his head as unequal to the planning a good constitution, and his fortitude to a cooperation in the effecting it. His dismission is more credited today than it was yesterday. If it takes place he will retain his popularity with the nation, as the members of the states will not think it important to set themselves against it, but on the contrary will be willing that he should continue on their side, on his retirement. The run on the caisse d'escompte continues. The members of the states admit that Mr. Necker's departure out of office will occasion a stoppage of public paiments. But they expect to prevent any very ill effect by assuring the public against any loss, and by taking immediate measures for continuing paiment. They may perhaps connect these measures with their own existence so as to interest the public in whatever catastrophe may be aimed at them. The gazettes of France and Leyden accompany this. During the continuance of this crisis, and my own stay, I shall avail myself of every private conveiance to keep you informed of what passes. I have the honour to be with the most perfect esteem & respect, Sir your most obedient & most humble servt.,

—TH: JEFFERSON

❧

To John Jay

Sir   Paris June 29. 1789

My letter of the 25th. gave you the transactions of the States general to the afternoon of that day. On the next the Archbishop of Paris joined the Tiers, as did some others of the clergy and noblesse. On the 27th. the question of the St. Domingo deputation came on, and it was decided that it should be received. I have before mentioned to you the ferment into which the proceedings at the seance royale of the 23d. had thrown the people. The souldiery also were affected by it. It began in the French guards, extended to those of every other denomination (except the Swiss) and even to the body guards of the king. They began to quit their barracks, to assemble in squads, to declare they would defend the life of the king, but would not cut the throats of their fellow citizens. They were treated and caressed by the people, carried in triumph thro' the streets, called themselves the souldiers of the nation, and left no doubt on which side they would be in case of a rupture. Similar accounts came in from the troops in other parts of the kingdom, as well those which had not heard of the seance royale as those which had, and gave good reason to apprehend that the souldiery in general would side with their fathers and brothers rather than with their officers. The operation of this medicine at Versailles was as sudden as it was powerful. The alarm there was so complete that in the after-noon of the 27th. the king wrote a letter to the President of the clergy, the Cardinal de la Rochefoucault, in these words 'Mon cousin, Uniquement occupé de faire le bien general de mon royaume, desirant, par dessus tout que l'assemblée des etats generaux s'occupe des objets qui interessent la nation, d'aprés l'acceptaion volon-taire que votre ordre a faite de ma declaration du 23. de ce mois; j'engage mon fidele clergé à se reunir, sans delai, avec les deux autres ordres, pour hater l'accomplisse-ment de mes vues paternelles. Ceux qui sont liès par leurs pouvoirs peuvent y aller sans donner de voix, jusqu'à ce qu'ils en aient de nouveaux; ce sera une nouvelle marque d'attachment que le clergé me donnera. Sur ce je prie dieu, mon cousin, qu'il vous ait en sa sainte garde. Louis.' A like letter was written to the Duke de Luxemburgh, president of the noblesse. The two chambers entered into debate on the question whether they should obey the letter of the king. There was a consid-erable opposition; when notes written by the count d'Artois to sundry members, and handed about among the rest, decided the matter, and they went in a body and took their seats with the tiers, and thus rendered the union of the orders in one chamber complete. As soon as this was known to the people of Versailles, they assembled about the palace demanded the king and queen, who came and shewed themselves in a balcony. They rended the skies with cries of 'Vive le roy' 'Vive la reine.' They called for the Dauphin who was also produced, and was the subject of new acclamations. After feasting themselves and the royal family with this tumultuary reconciliation, they went to the houses of M. Necker and M. de Montmorin with shouts of thankfulness and affection. Similar emotions of joy took place in Paris, and at this moment the triumph of the Tiers is considered as complete. Tomorrow they will recommence business, voting by persons on all questions: and whatever difficulties may be opposed in debate by the malcontents of the clergy and nobility, every thing must be finally settled at the will of the Tiers. It remains to see whether they will leave to the nobility any thing but their titulary appellations. I suppose they will not. Mr. Necker will probably remain in office. It would seem natural that he should endeavor to have the hostile part of the council removed, but I question if he finds himself firm enough for that. A perfect cooperation with the Tiers will be his wisest game.—This great crisis now over, I shall not have matter interesting enough to trouble you with as often as I have done lately. There has nothing remarkeable taken place in any other part of Europe. I have the honour to be with the most perfect esteem & respect Sir Your most obedient & most humble servt.,

—Th: Jefferson.

༄

A Fourth of July Tribute to Jefferson
SIR   Paris July 4th 1789

Your intention of withdrawing awhile from this court on a visit to our happy country offers an occasion which we cannot resist, of testifying those sentiments of gratitude and attachment which your conduct has taught us to realize, as the emotions of ingenuous minds towards an illustrious Benefactor.

As citizens of the United States we feel a laudable pride in joining the general voice of our country and of that of the age in which we live in rendering the sincerest tribute of respect to a compatriot so distinguished for his exertions in favour of that country and for the general happiness of mankind; but as temporary residents in a foreign kingdom, a situation in which the grateful heart becomes more susceptible and good actions recieve an additional merit, you will pardon our zeal if it assumes a language which in other circum-stances it might be unbecoming the dignity of a Republican Patriot to recieve. Praise is honorable only in proportion to the freedom and information of the persons from whom it arises; from a depressed subject it is a proof of power and of meanness; from an enlightened freeman, of merit and of gratitude. It is the application of this principle which alone can render public testimonials of this kind acceptable to such good minds as have the goodness to deserve them.

During your residence in this kingdom your particular kindness and attention to every American who has fallen in your way have endeared you to their hearts; and we are sure, as we speak the language which they have often uttered on this subject, that were they all present they would join in this our most cordial acknowledgement. But your conduct in this respect, though in the highest degree noble and generous, makes but a part of the motives of our love and admiration. The benefits resulting to the United States from your various negotiations in Europe excite in us a gratitude of a more extensive and patriotic nature. In these negotiations, your comprehensive views and minute attentions to every interest of every part of the country you represent, at the same time that your policy is directed to the general harmony and happiness of all nations, render you the proper minister of that enlightened people whose cause is the cause of humanity, and whose example we trust will greatly benefit mankind.

As this is the anniversary of our Independence our sensations of pleasure are much increased from the idea that we are addressing ourselves to a man who sustained so conspicuous a part in the immortal transactions of that day—whose dignity energy and elegance of thought and expression added a peculiar lustre to that declaratory act which announced to the world the existence of an empire. Be pleased, Sir, to accept our congratulations on the return of this day: a day which we hope arises with peculiar glory on our hemisphere, as it finds an extensive people happily united under the organization of a new government which promises the most lasting advantages.

May your visit to that country afford you a noble and endearing satisfaction, both as to the prosperity of your particular connections and affairs, and as it may give you an opportunity of rendering new services by your information and advice to that illustrious band of your fellow patriots who must welcome you with every token of respect.

While those of us who remain longer in France shall have reason to regret your absence, yet we cannot but rejoice with you on its occasion, and sincerely wish you a prosperous and happy voyage.

With every sentiment of gratitude and respect we have the honor to be, Sir, your most obedient and very humble servants,

                          —John Paradise   —Philip Mazzei
                          —Samuel Blackden   —E: Haskell
                          —Joel Barlow   —Th. Appleton
                          —Jam. Swan   —Benjn. Jarvis

৩৯

To Thomas Paine
DEAR SIR   Paris July 11. 1789

Since my last, which was of May 19. I have received yours of June 17. and 18. I am struck with the idea of the geometrical wheelbarrow, and will beg of you a further account if it can be obtained. I have no news yet of my Congé.

Tho you have doubtless heard most of the proceedings of the States general since my last, I will take up the narration where that left it, that you may be able to separate the true from the false accounts you have heard. A good part of what was conjecture in that letter is now become true history. A conciliatory propo-sition from the king having been accepted by the Nobles with such modifications as amounted to a refusal, the Commons voted it to be a refusal, and proceeded to give a last invitation to the clergy and nobles to join them, and to examine the returns of elections. This done they declared themselves the National assembly, resolved that all the subsisting taxes were illegally imposed, but that they might continue to be paid to the end of their present session and no longer. A majority of the clergy determined to accept their invitation and came and joined them. The king, by the advice of Mr. Necker, determined to hold a seance royale, and to take upon himself to decide what should be done. That decision as prepared by Necker was favorable to the Commons. The Aristocratical party made a furious effort, prevailed on the king to change the decision totally in favor of the other orders, and at the seance royale he delivered it accordingly. The Common chamber (that is the Tiers and majority of the clergy who had joined them) bound themselves together by a solemn oath never to separate till they had accomplished the work for which they had met. Paris and Versailles were thrown into tumult and riot. The souldiers in and about them, including even the king's life guard, declared themselves openly for the Commons, the accounts from the souldiery in the provinces was not more favorable, 48. of the Nobles left their body and joined the common chamber, the mob attacked the Archbishop of Paris (a high aristocrat) under the Chateau of Versailles, a panick seised the inhabitants of the Chateau, the next day the king wrote a letter with his own hand to the Chamber of Nobles and minority of the Clergy, desiring them to join immediately the common chamber. They did so, and thus the victory of the Tiers became complete. Several days were then employed about examining returns &c. It was discovered at length that great bodies of troops and principally of the foreign corps were approaching Paris from different quarters. They arrived in the number of 25, or 30,000 men. Great inquietude took place, and two days ago the Assembly voted an address to the king for an explanation of this phaenomenon and removal of the troops. His answer has not been given formally, but he verbally authorised their president to declare that these troops had nothing in view but the quiet of the Capital; and that that being once established they should be removed. The fact is that the king never saw any thing else in this measure; [but those who advised him to it, assuredly meant by the presence of the troops to give him confidence, and to take advantage of some favorable moment to surprize some act of authority from him. For this purpose they had got the military command within the isle of France transferred to the Marshall de Broglio, a high flying aristocrat, cool and capable of every mischief.] But it turns out that these troops shew strong symptoms of being entirely with the people, so that nothing is apprehended from them. The National assembly then (for that is the name they take) having shewn thro' every stage of these transactions a coolness, wisdom, and resolution to set fire to the four corners of the kingdom and to perish with it themselves rather than to relinquish an iota from their plan of a total change of government, are now in complete and undisputed possession of the sovereignty. The executive and the aristocracy are now at their feet: the mass of the nation, the mass of the clergy, and the army are with them. They have prostrated the old government, and are now beginning to build one from the foundation. A committee charged with the arrangement of their business, gave in, two days ago, the following order of proceedings.

1. Every government should have for it's only end the preservation of the rights of man: whence it follows that to recall constantly the government to the end proposed, the constitution should begin by a Declaration of the natural and imprescriptible rights of man.

2. Monarchical government being proper to maintain these rights, it has been chosen by the French nation. It suits especially a great society; it is necessary for the happiness of France. The Declaration of the principles of this government then should follow immediately the declaration of the rights of man.

3. It results from the principles of monarchy that the nation, to assure it's own rights, has yeilded particular rights to the monarch: the constitution then should declare in a precise manner the rights of both. It should begin by declaring the rights of the French nation, and then it should declare the rights of the king.

4. The rights of the king and nation not existing but for the happiness of the individuals who compose it, they lead to an examination of the rights of citizens.

5. The French nation not being capable of assembling individually to exercise all it's rights, it ought to be represented. It is necessary then to declare the form of it's representation, and the rights of it's representatives.

6. From the union of the powers of the nation and king should result the enacting and execution of the laws: thus then it should first be determined how the laws shall be established, afterwards should be considered how they shall be executed.

7. Laws have for their object the general administration of the kingdom, the property and the actions of the citizens. The execution of the laws which concern the general administration requires provincial and municipal assemblies. It is necessary to examine then, what should be the organisation of the provincial assemblies, and what of the municipal.

8. The execution of the laws which concern the property and actions of the citizens call for a Judiciary power. It should be determined how that should be confided, and then it's duties and limits.

9. For the execution of the laws and the defence of the kingdom, there exists a public force. It is necessary then to determine the principles which should direct it and how it should be employed.

Recapitulation.

Declaration of the rights of man.

Principles of the monarchy.

Rights of the nation.

Rights of the king
Rights of the citizens.
Organisation and rights of the national assembly.
Forms necessary for the enaction of laws.
Organisation and functions of the provincial and municipal assemblies
Duties and limits of the judiciary power.
Functions and duties of the military power.

You see that these are the materials of a superb edifice, and the hands which have prepared them, are perfectly capable of putting them together, and of filling up the work of which these are only the outlines. While there are some men among them of very superior abilities, the mass possesses such a degree of good sense as enables them to decide well. I have always been afraid their numbers might lead to confusion. 1200 men in one room are too many. I have still that fear. Another apprehension is that a majority cannot be induced to adopt the trial by jury; and I consider that as the only anchor, ever yet imagined by man, by which government can be held to the principles of it's constitution.—Mr. Paradise is the bearer of this letter. He can supply those details which would be too lengthy to write.—If my Congé comes within a few days, I shall depart in the instant: if it does not I shall put off my voiage till the Equinox is over. I am with great esteem Dear Sir Your friend & servant,

—TH JEFFERSON

❧

To John Jay
DEAR SIR   Paris July 19. 1789

... My letter of the 29th. of June brought down the proceedings of the States and Government to the reunion of the orders, which took place on the 27th. Within the Assembly matters went on well. But it was soon observed that troops, and particularly foreign troops, were on their march towards Paris from various quarters and that this was against the opinion of Mr. Necker. The king was probably advised to this under pretext of preserving peace in Paris and Versailles, and saw nothing else in the measure. But his advisers are supposed to have had in view, when he should be secured and inspirited by the presence of the troops, to take advantage of some favorable moment and surprize him into an act of authority for establishing the Declaration of the 23d of June, and perhaps dispersing the States general. The Marshal de Broglio was appointed to command all the troops within the Isle of France, a high flying Aristocrat, cool and capable of every thing. Some of the French guards were soon arrested under other pretexts, but in reality on account of their dispositions in favor of the national cause. The people of Paris forced the prison, released them, and sent a deputation to the States general to sollicit a pardon. The States by a most moderate and prudent Arreté recommended these prisoners to the king, and peace to the people of Paris. Addresses came in to them from several of the great cities expressing sincere allegiance to the king, but a determined resolution to support the States general. On the 8th. of July they vote an address to the king to remove the troops. This peice of masculine eloquence, written by Monsieur de Mirabeau, is worth attention, on account of the bold matter it expresses or covers, thro the whole. The king refuses to remove the troops and says they may remove themselves if they please to Noyons or Soissons. They proceed to fix the order in which they will take up the several branches of their future constitution, from which it appears they mean to build it from the bottom, confining themselves to nothing in their antient form, but a king. A Declaration of rights, which forms the first chapter of their work was then proposed by the Marquis de la Fayette. This was on the 11th.—In the mean time troops to the number of about 25. or 30,000 had arrived and were posted in and between Paris and Versailles. The bridges and passes were guarded. At 3. oclock in the afternoon the Count de la Luzerne was sent to notify Mr. Necker of his dismission, and to enjoin him to retire instantly without saying a word of it to any body. He went home, dined, proposed to his wife a visit to a friend, but went in fact to his country house at St. Ouen, and at midnight set out from thence for Brussels. This was not known till the next day, when the whole ministry was changed except Villedeuil of the domestic department and Barentin Garde des sceaux. These changes were as follows. The Baron de Breteuil President of the council of finance, and de la Galaisiere Comptroller General in the room of Mr. Necker; the Mareshal de Broglio minister of war, and Foulon under him, in the room of Puy-segur;

Monsieur de Montmorin; de la Porte, minister of marine, in place of the Count de la Luzerne; St. Priest was also removed from the council. It is to be observed that Luzerne and Puy-segur had been strongly of the aristocratical party in council; but they were not considered as equal to bear their shares in the work now to be done. For this change, however sudden it may have been in the mind of the king, was, in that of his advisers, only the second chapter of a great plan, of which the bringing together the foreign troops had been the first. He was now completely in the hands of men, the principal among whom had been noted thro' their lives for the Turkish despotism of their characters, and who were associated about the king as proper instruments for what was to be executed.—The news of this change began to be known in Paris about 1. or 2. oclock. In the afternoon a body of about 100. German cavalry were advanced and drawn up in the Place Louis XV. and about 300 Swiss posted at a little distance in their rear. This drew people to that spot, who naturally formed themselves in front of the troops, at first merely to look at them. But as their numbers increased their indig-nation arose: they retired a few steps, posted themselves on and behind large piles of loose stone collected in that Place for a bridge adjacent to it, and attacked the horse with stones. The horse charged, but the advantageous position of the people, and the showers of stones obliged them to retire, and even to quit the field altogether, leaving one of their number on the ground. The Swiss in their rear were observed never to stir. This was the signal for universal insurrection, and this body of cavalry, to avoid being massacred, retired towards Versailles. The people now armed themselves with such weapons as they could find in Armourer's shops and private houses, and with bludgeons, and were roaming all night through all parts of the city without any decided and practicable object. The next day the States press on the king to send away the troops, to permit the Bourgeoisie of Paris to arm for the preservation of order in the city, and offer to send a deputation from their body to tranquillize them. He refuses all their propositions. A Committee of magistrates and electors of the city are appointed, by their bodies, to take upon them it's government. The mob, now openly joined by the French guards, force the prisons of St. Lazare, release all the prisoners, and take a great store of corn, which they carry to the corn market. Here they get some arms, and the French guards begin to form and train them. The city committee determine to raise 48,000 Bourgeois, or rather to restrain their numbers to 48,000. On the 14th. they send one of their members (Monsieur de Corny,

whom we knew in America) to the Hotel des Invalides to ask arms for their Garde
Bourgeoise. He was followed by, or he found there, a great mob. The Governor
of the Invalids came out and represented the impossibility of his delivering
arms without the orders of those from whom he received them. De Corney
advised the people then to retire, retired himself, and the people took possession
of the arms. It was remarkeable that not only the Invalids themselves made no
opposition, but that a body of 5000 foreign troops, encamped within 400. yards
never stirred. Monsieur de Corny and five others were then sent to ask arms
of Monsieur de Launai, Governor of the Bastille. They found a great collection of people already before the place, and they immediately planted a flag of
truce, which was answered by a like flag hoisted on the parapet. The deputation prevailed on the people to fall back a little, advanced themselves to make
their demand of the Governor, and in that instant a discharge from the Bastille
killed 4. people of those nearest to the deputies. The deputies retired, the people rushed against the place, and almost in an instant were in possession of a
fortification, defended by 100 men, of infinite strength, which in other times
had stood several regular sieges and had never been taken. How they got in,
has as yet been impossible to discover. Those, who pretend to have been of the
party tell so many different stories as to destroy the credit of them all. They
took all the arms, discharged the prisoners and such of the garrison as were
not killed in the first moment of fury, carried the Governor and Lieutenant governor to the Greve (the place of public execution) cut off their heads, and set
them through the city in triumph to the Palais royal. About the same instant, a
treacherous correspon-dence having been discovered in Monsieur de Flesselles
prevot des marchands, they seize him in the hotel de ville, where he was in the
exercise of his office, and cut off his head. These events carried imperfectly to
Versailles were the subject of two successive deputations from the States to the
King, to both of which he gave dry and hard answers, for it has transpired that
it had been proposed and agitated in Council to seize on the principal members of the States general, to march the whole army down upon Paris and to
suppress it's tumults by the sword. But at night the Duke de Liancourt forced
his way into the king's bedchamber, and obliged him to hear a full and animated
detail of the disasters of the day in Paris. He went to bed deeply impressed. The
decapitation of de Launai worked powerfully thro' the night on the whole
Aristocratical party, insomuch that in the morning those of the greatest influ-

ence on the Count d'Artois represented to him the absolute necessity that the king should give up every thing to the states. This according well enough with the dispositions of the king, he went about 11. oclock, accompanied only by his brothers, to the States general, and there read to them a speech, in which he asked their interposition to re-establish order. Tho this be couched in terms of some caution, yet the manner in which it was delivered made it evident that it was meant as a surrender at discretion. He returned to the chateau afoot, accompanied by the States. They sent off a deputation, the Marquis de la Fayette at their head, to quiet Paris. He had the same morning been named Commandant en chef of the milice Bourgeoise, and Monsieur Bailly, former President of the States general, was called for as Prevost des marchands. The demolition of the Bastille was now ordered, and begun. A body of the Swiss guards, of the regi-ment of Ventimille, and the city horse guards join the people. The alarm at Versailles increases instead of abating. They believed that the Aristocrats of Paris were under pillage and carnage, that 150,000 men were in arms coming to Versailles to massacre the Royal family, the court, the ministers and all connected with them, their practices and principles. The Aristocrats of the Nobles and Clergy in the States general vied with each other in declaring how sincerely they were converted to the justice of voting by persons, and how determined to go with the nation all it's lengths. The foreign troops were ordered off instantly. Every minister resigned. The king confirmed Bailly as Prevost des marchands, wrote to Mr. Necker to recall him, sent his letter open to the States general to be forwarded by them, and invited them to go with him to Paris the next day to satisfy the city of his dispositions: and that night and the next morning the Count d'Artois and a Monsieur de Montesson (a deputy) connected with him, Madame de Polignac, Madame de Guiche and the Count de Vaudreuil favorites of the queen, the Abbé de Vermont her confessor, the Prince of Condé and Duke de Bourbon, all fled, we know not whither. The king came to Paris, leaving the queen in consternation for his return. Omitting the less important figures of the procession, I will only observe that the king's carriage was in the center, on each side of it the States general, in two ranks, afoot, at their head the Marquis de la Fayette as commander in chief, on horseback, and Bourgeois guards before and behind. About 60,000 citizens of all forms and colours, armed with the muskets of the Bastille and Invalids as far as they would go, the rest with pistols, swords, pikes, pruning hooks, scythes &c. lined all the streets thro' which the procession passed, and, with the crowds of people in the streets, doors and windows, saluted them every where with cries of 'vive la nation.' But not a single 'vive le roy' was heard. The king landed at the Hotel de ville. There Monsieur Bailly presented and put into his hat the popular cockade, and addressed him. The king being unprepared and unable to answer, Bailly went to him, gathered from him some scraps of sentences, and made out an answer, which he delivered to the Audience as from the king. On their return the popular cries were 'vive le roy et la nation.' He was conducted by a garde Bourgeoise to his palace at Versailles, and thus concluded such an Amende honorable as no sovereign ever made, and no people ever received. Letters written with his own hand to the Marquis de la Fayette remove the scruples of his position. Tranquility is now restored to the Capital: the shops are again opened; the people resuming their labours, and, if the want of bread does not disturb our peace, we may hope a continuance of it. The demolition of the Bastille is going on, and the milice Bourgeoise organising and training. The antient police of the city is abolished by the authority of the people, the introduction of king's troops will probably be proscribed, and a watch or city guards substituted, which shall depend on the city alone. But we cannot suppose this paroxysm confined to Paris alone. The whole country must pass successively thro' it, and happy if they get thro' it as soon and as well as Paris has done. I went yesterday to Versailles to satisfy myself what had passed there; for nothing can be believed but what one sees, or has from an eye witness. They believe there still that 3000 people have fallen victims to the tumults of Paris. Mr. Short and myself have been every day among them in order to be sure of what was passing. We cannot find with certainty that any body has been killed but the three beforementioned, and those who fell in the assault or defence of the Bastille. How many of the garrison were killed no body pretends to have ever heard. Of the assailants accounts vary from 6. to 600. The most general belief is that there fell about 30. There have been many reports of instantaneous executions by the mob, on such of their body as they caught in acts of theft or robbery. Some of these may perhaps be true. There was a severity of honesty observed of which no example has been known. Bags of money offered on various occasions, thro fear or guilt, have been uniformly refused by the mobs. The churches are now occupied in singing 'De profundis' and 'Requiems for the repose of the souls of the brave and valiant citizens who have sealed with their blood the liberty of the nation.'—Monsieur de Montmorin is this day replaced in the department of foreign affairs, and Monsieur de St. Priest is named to the Home department. The gazettes of France and Leyden accompany this. I send also a paper (called the Point du jour) which will give you some idea of the proceedings of the National assembly. It is but an indifferent thing; however it is the best.—I have the honor to be with great esteem and respect, Sir, your most obedient and most humble servt.,

—TH: JEFFERSON

P.S. July 21. Mr. Necker had left Brussels for Francfort before the Courier got there. We expect however to hear of him in a day or two. Monsieur le Comte de la Luzerne has resumed the department of the marine this day. Either this is an office of friendship effected by Monsr. de Montmorin (for tho they had taken different sides, their friendship continued) or he comes in as a stop-gap till somebody else can be found. Tho' very unequal to his office, all agree that he is an honest man. The Count d'Artois was at Valenciennes. The Prince of Condé and Duke de Bourbon had passed that place.

∽

To John Jay

SIR   Paris Aug. 5. 1789

I wrote you on the 19th. of the last month with a postscript of the 21st. and again on the 23d. and the 29th. Those letters went by private conveiances: this goes by the London post. —Since my last some small and momentary tumults have taken place in this city, in one of which a few of the rioters were killed by the city militia. No more popular executions have taken place. The capture of the Baron de Besenval, Commandant of the Swiss troops as he was flying to Switzerland, and of the Duke de la Vauguyon endeavoring to escape by sea would endanger new interpositions of the popular arm were they to be brought to Paris. They are therefore confined where they were taken. The former of these being unpopular with the troops under this command on account of oppressions, occasioned a deputation from their body to demand justice to be done on him, and to avow the devotion of the Swiss troops to the cause of the nation. They had before taken side in part only. Mr. Necker's return contributed much to reestablish tranquility, tho' not quite as much as was expected. His just intercessions for the Baron de Besenval and other fugitives damped very sensibly the popular ardor towards him. Their hatred is stronger than their love. Yesterday the other ministers were named. The Archbishop of Bordeaux is Garde des sceaux; Monsr. de la Tour de pin minister of war; the Prince of Beauvau is taken into the council and the feuille des benefices given to the Archbishop of Bordeaux. These are all of the popular party: so that the ministry (M. de la Luzerne excepted) and the Council, being all in Reformation principles, no further opposition may be expected from that quarter. The National assembly now seriously set their hands to the work of the constitution. They decided a day or two ago the question Whether they should begin by a Declaration or rights, by a great majority in the affirmative. The Negatives were of the clergy who fear to trust the people with the whole truth. The Declaration itself is now on the carpet. By way of Corollary to it they last night mowed down a whole legion of abuses, as you will see by the heads of the arreté which I have the honor to inclose you. This will stop the burning of chateaux, and tranquilize the country more than all the addresses they could send them. I expressed to you my fears of the impracticability of debate and decision in a room of 1200 persons as soon as Mr. Necker's determination to call that number was known. The inconveniencies of their number have been distressing to the last degree, tho' as yet they have been employed in work which could be done in the lump. They are now proceeding to instruments every word of which must be weighed with precision. Heretofore too they were hooped together by a common enemy. This is no longer the case. Yet a thorough view of the wisdom and rectitude of this assembly disposes me more to hope they will find some means of surmounting the difficulty of their numbers, than to fear that yeilding to the unmanageableness of debate in such a crowd, and to the fatigue of the experiment they may be driven to adopt in the gross some one of the many projects which will be proposed.—There is a germ of schism in the pretensions of Paris to form it's municipal establishment independently of the authority of the nation. It is not yet proceeded so far as to threaten danger.—The occasion does not permit me to send the public papers; but nothing remarkeable has taken place in the other parts of Europe.—I have the honor to be with the most perfect respect and esteem Sir Your most obedient & most humble servant,

—TH: JEFFERSON

To James Madison
DEAR SIR   Paris Aug. 28. 1789

My last to you was of July 29. Since that I have received yours of May 27. June 13. and 30. The tranquility of the city has not been disturbed since my last. Dissensions between the French and Swiss guards occasioned some private combats in which five or six were killed. These dissensions are made up. The want of bread for some days past has greatly endangered the peace of the city. Some get a little bread, some none at all. The poor are the best served because they besiege perpetually the doors of the bakers. Notwithstanding this distress, and the palpable impotence of the city administration to furnish bread to the city, it was not till yesterday that general leave was given to the bakers to go into the country and buy flour for themselves as they can. This will soon relieve us, because the wheat harvest is well advanced. Never was there a country where the practice of governing too much had taken deeper root and done more mischeif. Their declaration of rights is finished. If printed in time I will inclose a copy with this. It is doubtful whether they will now take up the finance or the constitution first. The distress for money endangers every thing. No taxes are paid, and no money can be borrowed. Mr. Necker was yesterday to give in a memoir to the Assembly on this subject. I think they will give him leave to put into execution any plan he pleases, so as to debarrass themselves of this and take up that of the constitution. No plan is yet reported; but the leading members (with some small differences of opinion) have in contemplation the following. The Executive power in a hereditary king, with a negative on laws and power to dissolve the legislature, to be considerably restrained in the making of treaties, and limited in his expences. The legislative in a house of representatives. They propose a senate also, chosen on the plan of our federal senate by the provincial assemblies, but to be for life, of a certain age (they talk of 40. years) and certain wealth (4 or 500 guineas a year) but to have no other power as to laws but to remonstrate against them to the representatives, who will then determine their fate by a simple majority. This you will readily perceive is a mere council of revision like that of New York, which, in order to be something, must form an alliance with the king, to avail themselves of his veto. The alliance will be useful to both and to the nation. The representatives to be chosen every two or three years. The judiciary system is less prepared than any other part of their plan. However they will abolish the parliaments, and establish an order of judges and justices, general and provincial, a good deal like ours, with trial by jury in criminal cases certainly, perhaps also in civil. The provinces will have assemblies for their provincial government, and the cities a municipal body for municipal government, all founded on the basis of popular election. These subordinate governments, tho completely dependant on the general one, will be entrusted with almost the whole of the details which our state governments exercise. They will have their own judiciary, final in all but great cases, the Executive business will principally pass through their hands, and a certain local legislation will be allowed them. In short ours has been professedly their model, in which such changes are made as a difference of circumstance rendered necessary and some other neither necessary nor advantageous, but into which men will ever run when versed in theory and new in the practice of government, when acquainted with man only as they see him in their books and not in the world. This plan will undoubtedly undergo changes in the assembly, and the longer it is delayed the greater will be the changes: for that assembly, or rather the patriotic part of it, hooped together heretofore by a common enemy, are less compact since their victory. That enemy (the civil and ecclesiastical aristocracy) begins to raise it's head. The lees too of the patriotic party, of wicked principles and desperate fortunes, hoping to pillage something in the wreck of their country, are attaching themselves to the faction of the Duke of Orleans, that faction is caballing with the populace, and intriguing at London, the Hague and Berlin and have evidently in view the transfer of the crown to the D. of Orleans. He is a man of moderate understanding, of no principle, absorbed in low vice, and incapable of abstracting himself from the filth of that to direct any thing else. His name and his money therefore are mere tools in the hand of those who are duping him. *Mirabeau is their chief.* They may produce a temporary confusion, and even a temporary civil war, supported as they will be by the money of England; but they cannot have success ultimately. The king, the mass of the substantial people of the whole country, the army, and the influential part of the clergy, form a firm phalanx which must prevail. Should those delays which necessarily attend the deliberations of a body of 1200 men give time to this plot to ripen and burst so as to break up the assembly before any thing definitive is done, a constitution, the principles of which are pretty well settled in the minds of the assembly, will be proposed by the national militia (*that is by their commander*) urged by the individual members of the assembly, signed by the king, and supported by the nation, to prevail till circumstances shall permit it's revision and more regular sanction. This I suppose the pis-aller of their affairs, while their probable event is a peaceable settlement of them. They fear a war from England Holland and Prussia. I think England will give money, but not make war. Holland would soon be afire internally were she to be embroiled in external difficulties. Prussia must know this and act accordingly.

It is impossible to desire better dispositions towards us, than prevail in this assembly. Our proceedings have been viewed as a model for them on every occasion; and tho in the heat of debate men are generally disposed to contradict every authority urged by their opponents, ours has been treated like that of the bible, open to explanation but not to question. I am sorry that in the moment of such a disposition any thing should come from us to check it. The placing them on a mere footing with the English will have this effect. When of two nations, the one has engaged herself in a ruinous war for us, has spent her blood and money to save us, has opened her bosom to us in peace, and receive us almost on the footing of her own citizens, while the other has moved heaven and earth and hell to exterminate us in war, has insulted us in all her councils in peace, shut her doors to us in every part where her interests would admit, libelled us in foreign nations, endeavored to poison them against the reception of our most precious commodities, to place these two nations on a footing, is to give a great deal more to one than to the other if the maxim be true that to make unequal quantities equal you must add more to the one than the other. To say in excuse that gratitude is never to enter into the motives of national conduct, is to revive a principle which has been buried for centuries with it's kindred principles of the lawfulness of assassination, poison, perjury &c. All of these were legitimate principles in the dark ages which intervened between antient and modern civilisation, but exploded and held in just horror in the 18th century. I know but one code of morality for man whether acting singly or collectively. He who says I will be a rogue when I act in company with a hundred others but an honest man when I act alone, will be believed in the former assertion, but not in the latter. I would say with the poet 'hic niger est, hunc tu Romane caveto.' If the morality of one man produces a just line of conduct in him, acting individually, why should not the morality of 100 men produce a just line of conduct in them acting together?

But I indulge myself in these reflections because my own feelings run me into them: with you they were always acknoleged. Let us hope that our new government will take some other occasion to shew that they mean to proscribe no virtue from the canons of their conduct with other nations. In every other instance the new government has ushered itself to the world as honest, masculine and dignified. It has shewn genuine dignity in my opinion in exploding adulatory titles; they are the offerings of abject baseness, and nourish that degrading vice in the people.

I must now say a word on the declaration of rights you have been so good as to send me. I like it as far as it goes; but I should have been for going further. For instance the following alterations and additions would have pleased me. Art. 4. 'The people shall not be deprived or abridged of their right to speak to write or otherwise to publish any thing but false facts affecting injuriously the life, liberty, property, or reputation of others or affecting the peace of the confederacy with foreign nations. Art. 7. All facts put in issue before any judicature shall be tried by jury except 1. in cases of admiralty jurisdiction wherein a foreigner shall be interested, 2. in cases cognisable before a court martial concerning only the regular officers and souldiers of the U.S. or members of the militia in actual service in time of war or insurrection, and 3. in impeachments allowed by the constitution.—Art. 8. No person shall be held in confinement more than —— days after they shall have demanded and been refused a writ of Hab. corp. by the judge appointed by law nor more than —— days after such writ shall have been served on the person holding him in confinement and no order given on due examination for his remandment or discharge, nor more than —— hours in any place at a greater distance than — — miles from the usual residence of some judge authorised to issue the writ of Hab. corp. nor shall that writ be suspended for any term exceeding one year nor in any place more than —— miles distant from the station or encampment of enemies or of insurgents.—Art. 9. Monopolies may be allowed to persons for their own productions in literature and their own inventions in the arts for a term not exceeding —— years but for no longer term and no other purpose.—Art. 10. All troops of the U.S. shall stand ipso facto disbanded at the expiration of the term for which their pay and subsistence shall have been last voted by Congress, and all officers and souldiers not natives of the U.S. shall be incapable of serving in their armies by land except during a foreign war.'

There restrictions I think are so guarded as to hinder evil only. However if we do not have them now, I have so much confidence in my countrymen as to be satisfied that we shall have them as soon as the degeneracy of our government shall render them necessary.—I have no certain news of P. Jones. I understand only in a general way that some persecution on the part of his officers occasioned his being called to Petersburgh, and that tho protected against them by the empress, he is not yet restored to his station. Silas Deane is coming over to finish his days in America, not having one sou to subsist on elsewhere. He is a wretched monument of the consequences of a departure from right.—I will before my departure write Colo. Lee fully the measures I pursued to procure success in his business, and which as yet offer little hope, and I shall leave it in the hands of Mr. Short to be pursued if any prospect opens on him.—I propose to sail from Havre as soon after the 1st. of October as I can get a vessel: and shall consequently leave this place a week earlier than that. As my daughters will be with me, and their baggage somewhat more than that of mere voyageures, I shall endeavor if possible to obtain a passage for Virginia directly. Probably I shall be there by the last of November. If my immediate attendance at New York should be requisite for any purpose, I will leave them with a relation near Richmond and proceed immediately to New York. But as I do not foresee any pressing purpose for that journey imme-diately on my arrival, and as it will be a great saving of time to finish at once in Virginia so as to have no occasion to return there after having once gone on to the Northward, I expect to proceed to my own house directly. Staying there two months (which I believe will be necessary) and allowing for the time I am on the road, I may expect to be at New York in February, and to embark from thence, or some eastern port.—You ask me if I would accept any appointment on that side of the water? You know the circumstances which led me from retirement, step by step and from one nomination to another, up to the present. My object is a return to the same retirement. Whenever therefore I quit the present, it will not be to engage in any other office, and most especially any one which would require a constant residence from home.—The books I have collected for you will go off to Havre in three or four days with my baggage. From that port I shall try to send them by a direct occasion to New York. I am with great & sincere esteem Dr. Sir your affectionate friend and servant,

—TH: JEFFERSON

P.S. I just now learn that Mr. Necker proposed yesterday to the National assembly a loan of 80. millions, on terms more tempting to the lender than the former, and that they approve it, leaving him to arrange the details in order that they might occupy themselves at once about the constitution.

To James Madison

DEAR SIR   Paris September 6. 1789

I sit down to write to you without knowing by what occasion I shall send my letter. I do it because a subject comes into my head which I would wish to develope a little more than is practicable in the hurry of the moment of making up general dispatches.

The question Whether one generation of men has a right to bind another, seems never to have been started either on this or our side of the water. Yet it is a question of such consequences as not only to merit decision, but place also, among the fundamental principles of every government. The course of reflection in which we are immersed here on the elementary principles of society has presented this question to my mind; and that no such obligation can be so transmitted I think very capable of proof.—I set out on this ground, which I suppose to be self evident, 'that the earth belongs in usufruct to the living': that the dead have neither powers nor rights over it. The portion occupied by any individual ceases to be his when himself ceases to be, and reverts to the society. If the society has formed no rules for the appropriation of it's lands in severalty, it will be taken by the first occupants. These will generally be the wife and children of the decedent. If they have formed rules of appropriation, those rules may give it to the wife and children, or to some one of them, or to the legatee of the deceased. So they may give it to his creditor. But the child, the legatee, or creditor takes it, not by any natural right, but by a law of the society of which they are members, and to which they are subject. Then no man can, by natural right, oblige the lands he occupied, or the persons who succeed him in that occupation, to the paiment of debts contracted by him. For if he could, he might, during his own life, eat up the usufruct of the lands for several generations to come, and then the lands would belong to the dead, and not to the living, which would be the reverse of our principle.

What is true of every member of the society individually, is true of them all collectively, since the rights of the whole can be no more than the sum of the rights of the individuals.—To keep our ideas clear when applying them to a multitude, let us suppose a whole generation of men to be born on the same day, to attain mature age on the same day, and to die on the same day, leaving a succeeding generation in the moment of attaining their mature age all together. Let the ripe age be supposed of 21. years, and their period of life 34. years more, that being the average term given by the bills of mortality to persons who have already attained 21. years of age. Each successive generation would, in this way, come on, and go off the stage at a fixed moment, as individuals do now. Then I say the earth belongs to each of these generations, during it's course, fully, and in their own right. The 2d. generation receives it clear of the debts and incumberances of the 1st. the 3d of the 2d. and so on. For if the 1st. could charge it with a debt, then the earth would belong to the dead and not the living generation. Then no generation can contract debts greater than may be paid during the course of it's own existence. At 21. years of age they may bind themselves and their lands for 34. years to come: at 22. for 33: at 23. for 32. and at 54. for one year only; because these are the terms of life which remain to them at those respective epochs.—But a material difference must be noted between the succession of an individual, and that of a whole generation. Individuals are parts only of a society, subject to the laws of the whole. These laws may appropriate the portion of land occupied by a decedent to his creditor rather than to any other, or to his child on condition he satisfies the creditor. But when a whole generation, that is, the whole society dies, as in the case we have supposed, and another generation or society succeeds, this forms a whole, and there is no superior who can give their territory to a third society, who may have lent money to their predecessors beyond their faculties of paying.

What is true of a generation all arriving to self-government on the same day, and dying all on the same day, is true of those in a constant course of decay and renewal, with this only difference. A generation coming in and going out entire, as in the first case, would have a right in the 1st. year of their self-dominion to contract a debt for 33. years, in the 10th. for 24. in the 20th. for 14. in the 30th. for 4. whereas generations, changing daily by daily deaths and births, have one constant term, beginning at the date of their contract, and ending when a majority of those of full age at that date shall be dead. The length of that term may be estimated from the tables of mortality, corrected by the circumstance of climate, occupation &c. peculiar to the country of the contractors. Take, for instance, the table of M. de Buffon wherein he states 23,994 deaths, and the ages at which they happened. Suppose a society in which 23,994 persons are born every year, and live to the ages stated in this table. The conditions of that society will be as follows. 1st. It will consist constantly of 617,703. persons of all ages. 2ly. Of those living at any one instant of time, one half will be dead in 24. years 8. months. 3dly. 10,675 will arrive every year at the age of 21. years complete. 4ly. It will constantly have 348,417 persons of all ages above 21. years. 5ly. And the half of those of 21. years and upwards living at any one instant of time will be dead in 18. years 8. months, or say 19. years as the nearest integral number. Then 19. years is the term beyond which neither the representatives of a nation, nor even the whole nation itself assembled, can validly extend a debt.

To render this conclusion palpable by example, suppose that Louis XIV. and XV. had contracted debts in the name of the French nation to the amount of 10,000 milliards of livres, and that the whole had been contracted in Genoa. The interest of this sum would be 500. milliards, which is said to be the whole rent roll or nett proceeds of the territory of France. Must the present generation of men have retired from the territory in which nature produced them, and ceded it to the Genoese creditors? No. They have the same rights over the soil on which they were produced, as the preceding generations had. They derive these rights not from their predecessors, but from nature. They then and their soil are by nature clear of the debts of their predecessors.

Again suppose Louis XV. and his cotemporary generation had said to the money-lenders of Genoa, give us money that we may eat, drink, and be merry in our day; and on condition you will demand no interest till the end of 19. years you shall then for ever after receive an annual interest of 12 $5/8$ per cent. The money is lent on these conditions, is divided among the living, eaten, drank, and squandered. Would the present generation be obliged to apply the produce of the earth and of their labour to replace their dissipations? Not at all.

I suppose that the received opinion, that the public debts of one generation devolve on the next, has been suggested by our seeing habitually in private life that he who succeeds to lands is required to pay the debts of his ancestor or testator: without considering that this requisition is municipal only, not moral; flowing from the will of the society, which has found it convenient to appropriate lands, become vacant by the death of their occupant, on the condition of a paiment of his debts: but that between society and society, or generation and generation, there is no municipal obligation, no umpire but the law of nature, one generation is to another as one independant nation to another.

The interest of the national debt of France being in fact but a two thousandth part of it's rent roll, the paiment of it is practicable enough: and so becomes a question merely of honor, or of expediency. But with respect to future debts, would it not be wise and just for that nation to declare, in the constitution they are forming, that neither the legislature, nor the nation itself, can validly contract more debt than they may pay within their own age, or within the term of 19. years? And that all future contracts will be deemed void as to what shall remain unpaid at the end of 19. years from their date? This would put the lenders, and the borrowers also, on their guard. By reducing too the faculty of borrowing within it's natural limits, it would bridle the spirit of war, to which too free a course has been procured by the inattention of money-lenders to this law of nature, that succeeding generations are not responsible for the preceding.

On similar ground it may be proved that no society can make a perpetual constitution, or even a perpetual law. The earth belongs always to the living generation. They may manage it then, and what proceeds from it, as they please, during their usufruct. They are masters too of their own persons, and consequently may govern them as they please. But persons and property make the sum of the objects of government. The constitution and the laws of the predecessors extinguished then in their natural course with those who gave them being. This could preserve that being till it ceased to be itself, and no longer. Every constitution then, and every law, naturally expires at the end of 19 years. If it be enforced longer, it is an act of force, and not of right.— It may be said that the succeeding generation exercising in fact the power of repeal, this leaves them as free as if the constitution or law had been expressly limited to 19 years only. In the first place, this objection admits the right, in proposing an equivalent. But the power of repeal is not an equivalent. It might be indeed if every form of government were so perfectly contrived that the will of the majority could always be obtained fairly and without impediment. But this is true of no form. The people cannot assemble themselves. Their representation is unequal and vicious. Various checks are opposed to every legislative proposition. Factions get possession of the public councils. Bribery corrupts them. Personal interests lead them astray from the general interests of their constituents: and other impediments arise so as to prove to every practical man that a law of limited duration is much more manageable than one which needs a repeal.

This principle that the earth belongs to the living, and not to the dead, is of very extensive application and consequences, in every country, and most especially in France. It enters into the resolution of the questions Whether the nation may change the descent of lands holden in tail? Whether they may change the appropriation of lands given antiently to the church, to hospitals, colleges, orders of chivalry, and otherwise in perpetuity? Whether they may abolish the charges and privileges attached on lands, including the whole catalogue ecclesiastical and feudal? It goes to hereditary offices, authorities and jurisdictions; to hereditary orders, distinctions and appellations; to perpetual monopolies in commerce, the arts and sciences; with a long train of et ceteras: and it renders the question of reimbursement a question of generosity and not of right. In all these cases, the legislature of the day could authorize such appropriations and establishments for their own time, but no longer; and the present holders, even where they, or their ancestors, have purchased, are in the case of bonâ fide purchasers of what the seller had no right to convey.

Turn this subject in your mind, my dear Sir, and particularly as to the power of contracting debts; and develope it with that perspicuity and cogent logic so peculiarly yours. Your station in the councils of our country gives you an opportunity of producing it to public consideration, of forcing it into discussion. At first blush it may be rallied, as a theoretical speculation: but examination will prove it to be solid and salutary. It would furnish matter for a fine preamble to our first law for appropriating the public revenue; and it will exclude at the threshold of our new government the contagious and ruinous errors of this quarter of the globe, which have armed despots with means, not sanctioned by nature, for binding in chains their fellow men. We have already given in example one effectual check to the Dog of war by transferring the power of letting him loose from the Executive to the Legislative body, from those who are to spend to those who are to pay. I should be pleased to see this second obstacle held out by us also in the first instance. No nation can make a declaration against the validity of long-contracted debts so disinterestedly as we, since we do not owe a shilling which may not be paid with ease, principal and interest, within the time of our own lives.—Establish the principle also in the new law to be passed for protecting copyrights and new inventions, by securing the exclusive right for 19. instead of 14. years. Besides familiarising us to this term, it will be an instance the more of our taking reason for our guide, instead of English precedent, the habit of which fetters us with all the political heresies of a nation equally remarkeable for it's early excitement from some errors, and long slumbering under others.

I write you no news, because, when an occasion occurs, I shall write a separate letter for that. I am always with great & sincere esteem, dear Sir Your affectionate friend & servt,

—TH: JEFFERSON

Epilogue

J EFFERSON HAD ASKED FOR LEAVE TO GO HOME IN NOVEMBER 1788 AND RECEIVED no reply. The old Congress no longer existed, the new had yet to meet, no one had the authority to order him home. John Jay finally answered his letter in March; late in August, Jefferson at last got his leave. He was already packed. He had been packed since April, at the ready to take ship. The packing list is an amazing document. He sent ahead to Le Havre to be shipped home 38 boxes, hampers, and trunks, his "phaeton," his "chariot," a long list of plants. He took with him to the port in his carriage more boxes, more trunks. One box contained paintings, another a guitar, a third held a clock. A box for Benjamin Franklin held ten cubic feet of books—to put it mildly, it must have been heavy. Another held six cubic feet of books for Madison. He sent busts of various persons home to various friends. None of his baggage included furniture. He thought he was returning in a few months, so he considered this an official leave, not a good-bye. For the same reason he made little effort to say good-bye to his friends. Shortly before he left, he invited Lafayette, Condorcet, and La Rochefoucauld for dinner. When he found on returning to America that he was not coming back, he had to send for his furniture.

He had obtained an appointment for William Short as chargé d'affaires in Paris (a post he filled until he was appointed American minister to Holland). On September 26 Jefferson, his two daughters, and Sally and James Hemings left Paris for Le Havre, where bad weather kept them stranded for ten days. They sailed then for Cowes, on the Isle of Wight, where the ship they had engaged, the Clermont, was to pick them up. They were forced to wait there almost another two weeks. Jefferson passed the time by writing letters, touring the island, and taking tea and meals with Nathaniel Cutting, an American ship's captain and brother to John Brown Cutting, one of Jefferson's friends.

Cutting kept a diary that gives us glimpses of Jefferson en famille. On one occasion he came downstairs to breakfast at the inn where they were both staying to find Jefferson "instructing his youngest Daughter, Maria (who is about 11 years of age) in the Spanish Language. She was reading part of a Chapter in the Spanish History of the Conquest of Mexico. I was prodigiously pleased with his method of instilling into her tender mind an accurate knowledge of Geography at the same time that he inculcated the purest principles of the Language." When Cutting left for England, he remarked, "I never remember to have experienced so much regret at parting from a Family with whom I had so short an acquaintance. I have found Mr. Jefferson a man of infinite information and sound Judgement, becoming gravity, and engaging affa-bility mark his deportment. His general abilities would do honor to any age or Country." Cutting was equally enchanted with Jefferson's daughters. Nathaniel, like his brother, became Jefferson's lifelong friend.

The weather remained bad while they were stuck in Cowes. On October 7, Jefferson reported in a letter to Short, he went out to buy "shepherd dogs" to take back to America; he finally bought a pregnant "chienne bergere." He also came upon "the body of a man who had that moment shot himself. His pistol had dropped at his feet, and himself fallen backward without ever moving." It was raining at the time; it was in fact, he said, "the most furious tempest of wind and rain I was ever in." Jefferson was not the sort of man, of course, who would regard this accumulation of violence as any kind of omen. In fact his fate, at almost that precise moment, was being decided. Madison's letter to Jefferson on the subject is dated just a day later, October 8. Looking forward to Jefferson's arrival in America, Madison hopes "on a public account to see you as soon as possible after you become informed of the new destination provided for you. It is of infinite importance that you should not disappoint the public wish on this subject…. The President is anxious for your acceptance of the trust. The Southern and Western Country have it particularly at heart. To every other part of the Union it will be sincerely acceptable." George Washington wrote his own letter to Jefferson five days later. He was asking him to become his secretary of state.

When he wrote his incomplete autobiography, which closes with the end of his service in France, Jefferson spent a disproportionate amount of space on his years there. It was obvious that they meant a great deal to him. He had expected to go back, to live out of the public eye, serving his country in Paris, at a distance from home, without fanfare. He was never entirely comfortable as a public man. All of his active political life he kept repeating that what he really hoped to be able to do was to retire to Monticello and live among a circle of close friends, reading and farming. His many enemies always believed he was insincere, but it was a wish he repeated again and again, and readers can make up their own minds about the extent of his ambitions.

But there is no ambiguity about his feelings for France. His five years there may have been, in his own retrospect, the best years of his life. In the last pages of the auto-biography, he wrote this tribute to France and the French people:

"Their kindness and accommodation to strangers is unparalleled, and the hos-pitality of Paris is beyond anything I had conceived to be practicable in a large city. Their eminence, too, in science, the communicative dispositions of their scientific men, the politeness of the general manners, the ease and vivacity of their conversation, give a charm to their society, to be found nowhere else. In a comparison of this, with other countries, we have the proof of primacy, which was given to Themistocles, after the battle of Salamis. Every general voted to himself the first reward of valor, and the second to Themistocles. So, ask the travelled inhabitant of any nation, in what country on earth would you rather live?—Certainly, in my own, where are all my friends, my relations, and the earliest and sweetest affections and recollections of my life. Which would be your second choice? France."

Note on the Text

Thomas Jefferson's complete works are available in several editions, namely the Paul Leicester Ford edition in ten volumes of 1892-99, the Lipscomb and Bergh edition of 1903-04 in twenty volumes, and the still ongoing edition, *The Papers of Thomas Jefferson*, which has been underway since 1950 at Princeton University Press. It is also possible to access Jefferson's correspondence in photocopy of the original manuscripts at the Library of Congress web site.

Of all these the best without any question is the Princeton edition, begun under the general editorship of the late Julian P. Boyd, and that is the source we used for this selection of Jefferson's writings from Paris. The scholarship in this edition is impeccable, and thorough without becoming oppressive. It supercedes all other sources of Jefferson's writings. All students of American history owe the Press a huge debt of gratitude.

SUGGESTED READINGS

The literature on Thomas Jefferson is unlikely ever to stop growing. Biography follows biography on a regular basis. Books on aspects of Jefferson's life or his role in early American history appear constantly. No one is counting, but I would guess that he is the most studied of the Founding Fathers, perhaps because he is the most important—or at least the most enigmatic. I have made a small selection here of what I think are probably the best books to introduce someone to this amazing man.

For Jefferson's life as a whole, the gold standard remains Dumas Malone's six very readable volumes published under the general title of *Jefferson and His Times* and available either as a set or as individual volumes in paperback. The second volume, *Jefferson and the Rights of Man*, covers his years in Paris. The main fault of the book, well-known among Jefferson scholars, is Malone's sometimes excessive admiration for Jefferson.

A recent one-volume biography is Joseph Ellis's *American Sphinx*, which covers selected periods in Jefferson's life, including the Paris years. Another is Willard Sterne Randall's *Thomas Jefferson*, which trails off rather abruptly after Jefferson becomes President but is good on his earlier career. For his years in Paris the best book is *The Paris Years of Thomas Jefferson*, written by William Howard Adams, a Jefferson scholar of the first rank. For the trips Jefferson took while in Europe, George Green Shackelford's *Thomas Jefferson's Travels in Europe, 1784-1789*, is beautifully illustrated with contemporary prints and it fills in many of the details Jefferson left out of his own notes.

Simon Schama's *Citizens*, although it hardly mentions Jefferson, is the account I prefer for the early days of the French Revolution, which Jefferson watched so closely from his catbird seat as Lafayette's friend and adviser. The relationship between Jefferson and Madison is best approached through their correspondence, recently published in James Morton Smith's handsome three-volume edition known as *The Republic of Letters*. The *Adams-Jefferson Letters*, in the edition by Lester J. Cappon, are better known, but Cappon's edition is less generously endowed with footnotes than Smith's and therefore not as informative.

The situation with the Barbary pirates that so preoccupied Jefferson during his Paris years has received some attention lately. To understand that situation a good new source is Frank Lambert's *The Barbary Wars*. To understand the rise and fall of Jefferson's reputation, the best source is definitely Merrill D. Peterson's fascinating book, *The Jefferson Image in the American Mind*.

But nothing quite captures Jefferson so well as Jefferson himself. If you have access to a large library that has the volumes, take advantage of your good luck and browse for a while in the Princeton edition of the *Papers of Thomas Jefferson*. He is a liberal education in his own right.

INDEX